Grover Park George
on Access

Grover Park George on Access

Copyright © 2003 by George Hepworth

Written by:
George Hepworth a/k/a "Grover Park George"

Edited by:
Linda H. DeLonais

Cover Design:
IRubin Consulting

Published by:
Holy Macro! Books
13386 Judy Avenue Northwest
Uniontown, Ohio, USA 44685

Distributed by:
Holy Macro! Books

First printing:
April 2004
Printed in Hong Kong

Library of Congress Data:
Hepworth, George
Grover Park George on Access / George Hepworth
LCCN: 2004101505

ISBN:
0-9724258-9-6

About the Author

George first discovered relational databases in 1994 when he received a copy of Access 2.0 as a reward for participating in a Microsoft usability test. A teacher and instructional designer by training and experience, at first he was hopelessly confused by the strange new way the accompanying Access 2.0 Users' Manual threw around terms like "form", "record", "query" and "table". Figuring it all out required a combination of persistence, patience, trial and error, dumb luck and, as a last resort, formal classes and books. Eventually, Mr. Hepworth felt comfortable enough with his hard-won knowledge of databases in general, and Access in particular, to try making a living at it. He still does, offering his services at www.gpcdata.com. He also takes advantage of every opportunity to learn something new, which is pretty much a daily occurrence.

Mr. Hepworth and his wife, Yolanda, live in Mountlake Terrace, Washington with their daughter, Lyndsey.

Acknowledgements

I would like to thank the following persons for their contributions to this book.

First, thanks to all the regulars at Utter Access, the best Access help forum on the Internet. Your professional influence has made me a better developer in many ways. I couldn't possibly name you all, but I have to mention Gord, who keeps it all running, Jerry who finally *made* me understand normalization, Dana, whose early encouragement and humor helped keep me going, and Anthony, whose enthusiasm and energy are a constant inspiration to me to get better at what I do.

UA rocks!

Very special thanks to a couple of long-time friends and mentors from early on in my career, Rex Moyer and Traci Dysart. Their patience and willingness to share their knowledge and experience paved the way for me in many ways. Thanks guys.

Free tech support sites I frequent regularly:

Utter Access at http://www.utteraccess.com/forums

The Office Experts at http://www.theofficeexperts.com/forum

Experts Exchange at http://www.experts-exchange.com

Table of Contents

This page intentionally left blank.

Foreword

Make databases simple and easy to use? You gotta be kidding me. Ain't no way, no how.

My friends have been deluded into thinking I am something of a computer expert. The truth of the matter is that I made so many computer related mistakes over the years that eventually I was bound to get something right! The trick is that if something does go right then make sure someone is there to see it happen. Combine the two events, finally get it right with someone being there to see it and voila, "Computer Expert."

Being recognized as an "Expert" is easy until someone comes along asking you for help. You have a couple of choices at this point: 1. You can tell the person that you would love to help but you have such a back load of other projects that it will be sometime before you will be able to help. If you are lucky, the person will go to someone else or forget about it, leaving your reputation intact. 2. Try to understand the nature of the problem and call someone who knows. I use this one all of the time. or 3. Well there probably is a three but I've been so successful with one and two that I have not needed a three.

The secret of my success, "Say, wouldn't that be a great title for a book or movie?" is the author of this book, Mr. George Hepworth. George and I have been friends for more years than I can remember. It has only been the last few years when I discovered the untapped treasure of knowledge; he has about designing, developing, and improving databases.

For years, I had struggled with DBase III and IV (I told you it had been a lot of years), Borland's Paradox (now Corel), Lotus' Approach and the industry giant, MS Access. Each of the databases has many nifty templates and Wizards but when it came right down to it there were none that met my specific needs. Attempts to edit the database resulted in some rather creative applications that simply did not work. I would move from one software program to another looking for "The One" that was "User Friendly", translated -- a program I could use without reading the instructions. Form view in Access allows one to re-arrange form fields to create wonderful looking reports. I have some of the best looking reports around, now if they would only work.

From reading, I knew that databases offered much more flexibility than spreadsheets. Trying a variety of databases convinced me that it must be possible to create a database that would do all that I wanted. The problem lay in trying to create a working database, in this millennium.

After many failed attempts and a newfound expertise in adapting spreadsheets, George mentioned that he designed and developed databases. I was determined to see into which of the "Expert" categories above he fit. George is the person from whom one asks for help.

Over the years, I've abused our friendship by asking for help on a number of projects. I'm constantly amazed at how quickly he grasps the intent of my quest despite the imprecision in which it is stated. Not only is the concept readily grasped but it is quickly converted to an actual working database, with enhancements! Oh, joy! Oh, rapture!

George also has the ability to quickly and concisely explain what needs to be done and most importantly, why it needs to be done. Not only do you get a solution to your database problem but you get an education as well - An education that helps you to develop new skills and understanding. The best part, for me, is that I have yet to receive a bill for the many hours of labor he has performed on my behalf. Thanks Amigo.

Note: George has a family and needs to pay his bills. Please do not expect to get his undivided attention for free. You can benefit from his advice by visiting http://www.utteraccess.com/forums where he is an active participant and a genuine expert. You can also visit his website http://www.gpcdata.com for free sample databases or to request a custom database solution.

You've taken the first step in becoming a database expert by selecting this book.

Nope, I was not paid to write this foreword it is my distinct pleasure. Well, maybe it is a little payback for the countless hours spent on my behalf.

Bottom-line, if I can understand how to develop databases from reading this book, anyone can.

~ Bruce Garrett
Jacksonville, Oregon
August 2003

1. What This Book Will Do for You

On more than one occasion, I've worked with programmers and database developers who dismissed Access as a "toy database". I don't hold it against them and I certainly can't argue against the advantages of Oracle or SQL Server for managing corporate Data Warehouses and Customer Relationship Management systems. The truth is many, many Fortune 100 corporations, small mom-and-pop businesses, schools and other non-profit groups, and ordinary individuals use Access to store and report on a huge variety of data in an amazing number of environments. Not one of them considers Access a toy because it does the job they need it to do.

That's basically what this book is all about; through a combination of examples, explanations and do-it-yourself exercises, I will help you learn how to use Access to control and manage the information that matters to you.

Why You Need this Book

I assume most people who have bought this book or are reading it for the first time have a specific project in front of them. Therefore, I wrote the book with that in mind. It follows the steps I would follow in evaluating a new database project, designing, building, implementing, and evaluating the database for a client or myself. If you're looking for specific tips on creating queries, for example, you won't find a query chapter; instead you'll find discussions of queries in several places: creating interfaces for entering new data, providing for lookup of existing data, and creating reports. Use the Index at the back of this book to pursue specific topics.

A Professional Approach

In leading you through the development process, I will share with you my insights into the most productive and professional ways to accomplish those tasks. In other words, if you just want to hack out a quick database and you don't really care much about how you go about it, this book is not for you.

I tried to select examples for the book that would be familiar to you, maybe even useful if you complete them yourself. I also tried to select examples simple enough to complete in a reasonably short period of time. This doesn't mean, however, that what you will learn is simplistic in any way. On the contrary, keeping the subject matter simple allows us to concentrate on the underlying principles so that you can really understand both what you need to do to create an Access database and why you need to do it.

What's in this Book

This book concentrates on Access versions 2000, 2002/XP, and 2003; the examples in it were created in Access 2002. I have seen estimates that Access '97 still makes up somewhere between one-fourth and one-third of existing installations. I also suspect it probably accounts for an even larger percentage of working Access databases. Still, after some deliberation, I elected to focus on the newer versions of Access in this book. For one thing, this book is primarily intended for Access users just starting out, so I assume most of you will be using one of the newer versions (2000/2002/2003). For another, this book is mostly about using Access to create reliable, flexible, and scalable relational databases; the concepts underlying that goal generally do not depend on which version of Access you use. As you incorporate more advanced features into your databases, of course, the differences between versions become more important. Therefore, as we get further into the book, we'll make clear any differences between versions where appropriate.

Finally, I've been working with Access 2003 for some months. Although there are some interesting new features, I haven't found anything compelling enough to suggest you run out and upgrade if you haven't already. Smart Tags, for example, which have been available in other members of the MS Office family for some time, are an interesting addition to Access. Still, they tend to fall into the "so what" category in my opinion. On the other hand, there are some enhancements of interest to more advanced developers, but frankly, most of them are beyond the scope of this book anyway. So if you have Access '97, 2000, or 2002, you'll do just fine with this book.

Get Normal

Officially, this is a book on using Access. Much of the book is devoted to defining, building, and using the objects in an Access database. However, I feel quite strongly that it would be entirely unprofessional for me not to make a concerted effort to help you understand some fundamental concepts about relational databases to prepare you for that effort. The first and most important, concept is that the tables in your database must be *normalized*. You may not know what that means yet, but you will after you finish reading this book!

I can't make this point strongly enough.

To be useful, your database has to be properly normalized.

No combination of clever interface design, sophisticated SQL queries or complex VBA code can ever compensate for an un-normalized database. If you learn nothing else from this book, learn what it means to normalize your databases and implement that knowledge in your databases.

How to Use this Book

If you wish, you can use this book like a self-study course, working your way through the sections and chapters, one at a time, building your skills as you go. If you prefer to skip around, looking for tips on dealing with issues such as naming conventions, table design, sub-queries, VBA code or whatever, please feel free to do so. In any case, the purpose of this book is to help you accomplish one thing: building Access tools that work for you.

You are welcome, even encouraged, to email me your comments or suggestions about this book. I will do my best to answer each and every email. And if I really like your suggestion, I'll see that it gets "recycled" into the next edition.

ghepworth@gpcdata.com

This page intentionally left blank.

2. Why Do You Want to Use Access Anyway?

You may be saying to yourself, "That's a very strange question to ask at the beginning of a book on Access." I assure you, though; it's a very important question to ask before you launch into a database project, especially if you have never built one. Actually, there are two parts to the question. Let's address them one at a time.

Do I Really Need a Database?

Building an Access database is not a trivial task; before you invest your time and effort in doing so, you should be quite sure you're solving the right problem with the right tool.

> If the only tool you have is a hammer, you tend to see every problem as a nail.
>
> Abraham Maslow (1908-1970)
> American psychologist

Understanding the Problem

Take your time and answer the following questions thoughtfully about the project you have in mind. We'll discuss the alternative answers in the next section.

True or False: My project requires calculating or updating a few values on a regular basis and I need to use formulas to do that. Neither the formulas I use nor the items on my list change much and, frankly, I'm not worried about keeping track of what happened in the past. Example: I have to calculate and publish a weekly report summarizing sales for my department's salespeople so their manager can decide who has earned their weekly performance bonus and who hasn't.

True or False: It's important to the success of my project that I can easily locate and report data from several weeks, months, or years in the past. Moreover, I need to filter and sort the data in several different ways, depending on who will see the reports. Example: I have to create and publish a monthly report showing Employee Counts for each of the preceding 24 months, by Company, by Operating Division, by Department, and by Team.

True or False: *I need a database of critical company information so our employees can look things up quickly and easily.* Example: Our phone staff continually misdirects incoming calls to Customer Service Reps in the wrong Department or Team. I need a database of call types and the departments that handle each type so CSR's can look them up and direct calls properly.

What Do My Answers Mean?

Let's review the alternative answers to these three questions and what they might tell you about your project.

Frequent, One-Of Reporting

True or False: *My project is mostly about calculating or updating a few values on a regular basis and I need to use formulas to do that. Neither the formulas I use nor the items on my list change much and, frankly, I'm not worried about keeping track of what happened in the past.*

If you said "True"

The most appropriate tool for this task might be a spreadsheet—or possibly even a table in a Word document—rather than a database. As you probably know, in a spreadsheet, you embed formulas—sometimes very complicated formulas—into the cells on the worksheet right next to the cells containing the values used in those formulas. You can quickly scroll down a column or across a row, changing values in cells as appropriate. When you enter or change the value in a cell or alter a formula, the calculated results display immediately.

Moreover, an advanced Word user could use a table with formulas in the appropriate cells to accomplish a lot of the same functions. The Word document also has the advantage of being easier to format for print.

There's really no hard and fast rule about when you need to create a database versus a spreadsheet or other type of file, but one useful way to look at it is to balance the time and effort required to set it up and maintain it against the results it provides. If you don't need functions specific to a database, it doesn't make much sense to incur the extra effort and expense of creating one when a spreadsheet or Word table will do the job just fine.

If you said "False"

A database probably is the right tool for your job. While you can keep historical data, even very large amounts of historical data, by saving generations of a Word table or spreadsheet, keeping track of that ever expanding directory full of files quickly becomes complicated and, more importantly, risky.

Historical and Multi-Level Reporting

True or False: It's important to the success of my project that I can easily locate and report data from several weeks, months, or years in the past. Moreover, I need to filter and sort the data in several different ways, depending on who will see the reports.

If you said "True"

You're definitely going to be building a database. One key characteristic of all databases is the ability to keep large amounts of data over extended periods of time. The only real limit is the amount of storage space available. A second key characteristic of a database is the ability to filter and sort data into many different combinations. One source of data can feed an almost infinite variety of reports.

If you said "False"

You probably can use a spreadsheet or even a Word document to create a one time only snapshot of data. Again, the key is that the data is needed one time, in one format, and you don't need to re-use that same data over time in other formats.

Job Support Tools

True or False: I need a database of critical company information so our employees can look things up quickly and easily.

If you said "True" or "False"

I'm sorry; this one is sort of a trick question. I threw it in to make an important point about one of the occupational hazards of database development. On more than one occasion, I've been approached by a manager with a request like this one. And on more than one occasion, we've decided that they really didn't need a new database at all.

In this example, the *business* problem is that employees are misdirecting calls. That wastes everyone's time and causes frustration for customers and for employees who get the misdirected calls. However, the problem doesn't necessarily arise out of lack of access to the appropriate information. There are at least three other possible causes that should be evaluated and, if possible, eliminated before starting a database development project.

First, it may simply be a result of *incomplete or inappropriate training* provided to the call screeners. Perhaps those employees answering phones are simply directing calls to the first available Customer Service Representative. In fact, to them, getting calls to a CSR as quickly as possible makes sense in the event that they don't realize that it also makes a difference *to whom* they direct the calls.

Second, it may be a result of *inappropriate or ineffective management.* If managers have failed to communicate that the current behavior is not appropriate, or if they have failed to offer direction and provide rewards for appropriate behavior or impose consequences for inappropriate behavior, the employees answering phones have no incentive to change the way they do it.

Third, *inappropriate or poorly thought-out workflows or limitations in tools* often prevent people from doing their jobs the way they know they should. In this case, for example, it may be a limitation of the phone system that it automatically assigns all transferred calls to the next available CSR by default. Call screeners have no choice about who will get that call. They know there is a problem, but can't do anything about it.

What does all of this have to do with building a database? Well, to repeat a point I made a little earlier, creating a database is not a trivial task, even with Access. If you want to be a competent, professional database developer, the last thing you want to do is invest your time, effort and other resources solving the wrong problem!

At best, the database will go unused because it doesn't meet a real business need. At worst, the managers who paid you for that time and effort are going to ask you some very unpleasant questions when they don't see any return on that investment.

The Right Tool for the Job

Okay, then. At this point you're sure a database is the right tool for the job ahead of you and you're ready dive in and start building Access tables.

Stop, take a deep breath, step away from your PC, and read the next section first.

Why do you want to use Access?

If you're a new Access user, you probably bought this book for a reason not too different from one of the following:

> The person for whom you work has asked you to "do something about _____".

   Fill in the blank with the appropriate crisis in your organization: misplaced phone messages and letters from customers, hassles getting timely attendance reports from classroom teachers, keeping track of scheduled vacation days for everybody in our department, and so forth.

> Someone who used to work for your organization built the Access database you all use every day, but that person left months ago. Now it doesn't work anymore, your predecessor didn't bother with documentation of any kind, and it's up to you to fix it—now!

> You're tired of using an Excel spreadsheet (or a series of spreadsheets) to track dozens (or hundreds) of pieces of equipment used by your department. It's confusing and time-consuming to keep them all updated. You've been told an Access database would be a better choice, but you've never used Access before.

> The organization you work for has a formal (and seemingly un-ending) process for evaluating all proposed IT projects. Your friends in IT have told you Access is just a toy database and what you really need is SQL Server with a web-based front end, but, frankly, you can't wait six months just to get your project on the Resource Allocation Committee's agenda for discussion. With Access, you can build yourself something that works right now, even if it isn't perfect.

> You just upgraded your old PC, including a copy of MS Office. Now, to keep peace in your family, you need to justify that expensive software by building a database to track your spouse's collection of _____.

Fill in the blank with the appropriate hobby: exotic coffee mugs, vacations photos from the south of France, bird sightings in all fifty states, race walking results for their Race Walking club, etc.

Did you see anything familiar on that list? If not, please send me an email at ghepworth@gpcdata.com describing your problem. Who knows, your project might end up as a case study in the next edition of this book.

These projects share four common characteristics. First, according to the criteria we discussed in the preceding section, they all appear to call for a database, even if it's only by management fiat! In addition, you started them because you

- need to solve a specific, more or less well-defined problem,
- have little or no experience or training with relational databases in general and Microsoft Access in particular and
- have little or no time or money to invest in training or professional solutions.

You can take some comfort from the fact you are by no means the first person in this position, you won't be the last, and, above all, you are not alone. You'll get a lot of help from this book, and from some of the other resources described in it. As my mentor, Red Green, likes to say, "We're all in this together."[1]

Let's start by deciding whether or not Access is really the right tool for the job at hand. It takes considerable time, thought and effort to build even a simple Access database correctly and it's a good idea to be prepared before you take on the task. The fact you're reading this book suggests you've already made the decision to do it.

Nonetheless, it's always a good idea to be sure you're on the right path before setting out on a long journey. So let's examine the components of that question next.[2]

---

[1] http://www.redgreen.com/ and on many PBS stations.

[2] This discussion is intended to help new users get a general feeling for the role Access can play in a typical installation. It is not a detailed, technical discussion. If you are still unsure about whether Access is appropriate for your needs after reading this section, you can get additional assistance from several sources, including the discussion forums at www.UtterAccess.com, www.theofficeexperts.com, and, of course, Microsoft's own website, where you can start at http://support.microsoft.com/.

Who Will Use the Database

One of the first questions every database developer should ask is, "Who will use the database?" or more precisely, "How many people will use it?" Or more precisely still, "How many people will use the database *at the same time?*" Theoretically, MS Access 2000/2002 will accommodate up to 255 concurrent users—that's 255 people adding, changing, deleting or looking up records all at the same time. Yeah, right, 255 concurrent users!

The *practical* limit to the number of concurrent users (people at individual workstations simultaneously adding, changing, deleting or looking up records in your database) is quite a bit smaller. Developers will argue over what that limit really is because it is impacted by a number of factors including the quality of the network where the database is located, the amount of memory available on the users' workstations, and the design and installation of your database.

In my experience, a well-designed Access database can support up to 20 concurrent users quite easily. I've heard of a database that supports upwards of 50 concurrent users in a production environment. That seems to be close to the practical limit though. Beyond that number, you are better advised to consider other alternatives like SQL Server or Oracle.

How Much Data Will the Database Hold

This is another important question, though probably not as important as the number of concurrent users. The maximum file size of an MS Access 2000/2002 database is two gigabytes. In addition to the data, that includes system objects as well as all of the objects you create in the database, but it's still a lot of data.

To put that maximum size into perspective, the biggest database on my hard drive at this moment is about 35 megabytes in two separate files, one holding only the records and the other holding the rest of the objects that make the database work.

Access developers refer to this as a "split database". The file holding data is called the "Back End" and the file holding the remaining objects is called the "Front End".

I've heard of production Access databases up to 150 megabytes in a networked environment. Although I don't know for sure, I believe that is only the data portion of that database.

The *practical* limit to the size of an Access database, like the limit on the number of concurrent users, is another matter. If your database sits on a single PC, the only limit on size is the 2-gigabyte limit mentioned above, subject, of course, to the available space on your hard drive.

However, if your database is installed on a network—which means you'll be moving records back and forth between the server and client PCs—network performance becomes a de facto limiting factor on the size of your database. The larger the number of records moving over the network, the slower it will be. Because there are ways to minimize performance problems, it's still possible to run a fairly large database (50 or 60 Megabytes of records) in a network environment.

Again, to try to put that limit in perspective, the Back End database on my hard drive has name, address and phone number records on more than 9,500 potential customers in one table. It has name, SSN, and other details on 2,300 employees in another table. There are an additional 45 tables holding other details on thousands of transactions with those customers. It is a little over 17 Megabytes in size.

The Front End has over 60 reports, more than 120 queries, more than 70 forms and a substantial amount of Visual Basic for Applications (VBA) code. Don't worry if you don't know the meaning of terms like query and form or VBA yet. The important point here is that, although this is a relatively large and fairly complex database, it is still less than 40 megabytes in total size.

What Hardware and Software is Available

The following discussion attempts to answer the question of whether you have adequate resources (hardware and software) to use Access to develop a database.

According to Microsoft's website, Access requires a computer with a Pentium 133 megahertz (MHz) or higher processor; a Pentium III is recommended. Access 2002 requires 170 MB of available hard disk space. You'll also need a CD-ROM drive, a Super VGA monitor, and, of course, a mouse.[3]

Depending on the operating system on your PC, the amount of memory required for Access 2002 varies. Table 2-1 lists the published memory requirements from Microsoft's website.

---

[3] See details at http://www.microsoft.com/office/access/evaluation/sysreq.asp

Operating System	Minimum RAM	Additional RAM for Access 2002
Windows 98, or Windows 98 Second Edition	24 MB	8 MB
Windows Me, or Microsoft Windows NT®	32 MB	8 MB
Windows 2000 Professional	64 MB	8 MB
Windows XP Professional or Windows XP Home Edition	128 MB	8 MB

Table 2-1 Memory Requirements for Access 2002

Again, to give you some perspective, I have an old 233-MHz PC with 96 MB of RAM. It has Windows XP Professional installed. My family occasionally uses it for email and minor word processing tasks, while I use it mostly for testing. It does run my Access 2002 tests, but I don't have the patience to use it for anything else.

I also have a 1.33-MHz PC with 512 MB of RAM and Windows XP Professional that handles all of my Access 2002 development tasks comfortably.

My personal opinion is that, while the great majority of PCs in use today are capable of running Access 2002, you may find performance unacceptable on machines with less than approximately 400 MHz CPU speed and less than 128 MB of RAM. This is true both for the machine on which you will be creating your Access database and for the machines your users will be using.

Networked Environments

I'm going to go out on a limb and say that, if you are working in a networked environment, you probably have adequate resources to use Access to develop your database, subject to the file size and memory limitations previously described for individual client PCs on the network. The server itself is almost certainly adequate.

When it comes time to deploy your application, of course, you'll face some issues you wouldn't have to deal with on a stand-alone workstation. But I think it's safe to assume you can proceed with Access as your database tool. There is a chapter in this book dealing with the issues you'll have to resolve when you prepare your database for deployment into a network.

Access It Is, Then!

Okay, you've stuck with me this far, laying the foundation for the next step, and you are still convinced you want to use Access to build a database. Starting in the next chapter, then, we'll tackle the job, beginning with creating a data model for your project.

3. Data Modeling 101

I have an old cardboard box under my desk[4]. When it was delivered a few years ago, it held 10 reams of copy paper. These days it's full of old pay stubs, paid bills, insurance policies, letters from my bank, and other important financial documents waiting to be transferred to their permanent home in my filing cabinet.

For some purposes, tossing the unsorted papers into my box is sufficient. It's a convenient place to temporarily gather everything into a single container. The difficulty comes when I need to find a document from a few weeks ago. I don't know if it's still in the old cardboard box, or if I've already filed it somewhere in my neatly organized filing cabinet. If I'm lucky, it's in the filing cabinet and I can locate it quickly using the filing system I came up with when I first started using it a few years ago. If it's not, I have no choice but to dig through everything in the box, one piece of paper at a time until I find it. That, I can tell you, isn't much fun.

The Cardboard Box Metaphor

By now you've figured out I'm not really talking about a cardboard box and a four-drawer filing cabinet (although they are real enough features of my office). They are metaphors for some of the things we need to understand in order to build a robust, efficient, and above all, useful database.

In its most fundamental sense, my box is a *database*. That is to say, *it is a collection of data about a particular subject or purpose*. In its current state of (non) organization, my "box database" isn't very useful except, of course, as short-term storage.

My four-drawer filing cabinet comes closer to being a real database. It, too, is a collection. However, it is a collection of information on a particular subject or purpose, organized according to a pre-defined structure, or model.

---

[4] I won't hold it against you if you skip this chapter and run ahead to start building your Access tables. If you are confident you know what a Data Model is and how to build one, and if you can recite the first three Rules of Normalization without peeking, you don't need this chapter anyway. On the other hand, you don't really have anything to lose by learning this stuff now, before you get everything all muddled up, do you?

I say that it holds *information* rather than *data*, because the documents in it are organized, sorted, and stored according to a model I came up with before I started putting documents in its drawers.

It's All About the Data Model

Data becomes information when it is organized. Data by itself, like the hodge-podge of papers in my cardboard box, is not terribly useful. Moreover, it's not terribly important what type of container you keep the data in.

If I simply open a drawer of the cabinet and empty the box into it once or twice a month, I am no further ahead than if I just keep bringing in more boxes to shove under my desk. In fact, I don't really need the filing cabinet at all. I could organize a set of cardboard boxes the same way the drawers in the cabinet are organized because I have a method of organization, or a *Data Model,* independent of the container in which the information is stored.

A data model is a logical description of things we are interested in within a specific situation. It consists of statements defining objects and events, identifying pertinent facts about those objects, and explaining how they relate to one another. Unlike a plastic model of an airplane, a data model is not a physical representation of those things. For that reason we will avoid talking about tables in an Access database, which are the "physical" objects with which a database works, until we have a more-or-less complete data model in place.

That's an important point to keep in mind while building your database. Your data model, *or the way you organize the information in which you are interested*, is independent of the container in which you will store your information. If it's properly designed, the same data model can be incorporated into an Access database, a SQL Server database, or any other relational database application.

Okay, Cardboard Box Guy, Model This

We're ready to look at the process by which you create a Data Model and I think my filing cabinet can work as a very simple example to get us started.

What Do I Want to Keep Track of—the Entities

My filing cabinet contains all kinds of documents: canceled checks, credit card statements, bank statements, bills from our doctor and dentist, renewal notices from our insurance company along with Declarations Pages for our policies, and mortgage papers from when we bought the house. We keep some of them for legal reasons (tax returns, for example) and others for historical reasons (insurance documents, for example). All of these documents are important enough for our family to want to keep them in a safe place where we can refer to them when necessary. These documents are the *entities* around which our filing system is built.

In database terms, an entity is an object in which an organization is interested and about which the organization wants to collect and maintain information. To be an entity, a thing must exist and be distinguishable from other objects. It can be *concrete*—like the pay stubs in my filing. You can feel and see them. It can be *abstract*—a fact or concept like a "forty hour work week". You can't see a "forty hour work week", but we all know what it is, at least in theory.

We define entities by stating what kind thing they are and how they are different from similar things of that kind.

Example: A DOCUMENT is a PAPER or GROUP OF PAPERS that contains information retained for legal or historical reference.

In this case, it was fairly easy to figure out what kind of thing a DOCUMENT is; it's a piece of paper or a group of papers that contains information. It was only a bit harder to describe how a DOCUMENT is different from other pieces of paper that contain information—a newspaper, for example. For this data model, DOCUMENTS are retained for legal or historical reference; other pieces of paper with information on them are not. In another context, my data model might need to define DOCUMENT differently.

Tech Talk—Formal Entity Definition

A formal Entity Definition consists of three parts:

> *Term* to be defined

> *Class* of things in which it belongs

> *Differences* it has with other members of the class.

We can recursively define Entities and Classes to the level of generality or specificity required by the data model we're creating. In other words, a Class is defined using the same formal definition; an Entity defined in one definition can be the Class by which another Entity is defined in a more specific definition. See Table 3-1.

Formal Entity Definitions		
Entity	Class	Difference(s)
PAPER	MATERIAL	Made of cellulose pulp
PRINTED PAPER	PAPER	On which information is printed using mechanical or manual means
DOCUMENT	PRINTED PAPER or GROUP OF PAPERS	Retained for legal or historical reference

Table 3-1 Formal Entity Definitions for
PAPER, PRINTED PAPER and DOCUMENT

Enough Entities Already

Obviously, you don't need to go on defining entities indefinitely. It is only necessary to create enough definitions to fully account for all of the entities of importance in your data model. And, of course, at some point you will reach a level of sufficient generality that it makes no sense to include the definition in your data model.

For example, while DOCUMENT is an entity of interest in my cardboard box database, PAPER and PRINTED PAPER are not. MATERIAL is obviously too general to be of any interest in this data model. However, we will definitely need to continue defining additional types of documents (i.e., members of the Class, DOCUMENT), such as BANK DOCUMENT, INSURANCE DOCUMENT, TAX DOCUMENT, etc.

Hierarchies and Entity Groups

When I start pulling papers out of my cardboard box in preparation for filing them in my filing cabinet, I don't immediately transfer them. First, I sort them by groups: utility bills in one pile, bank records in another, and insurance papers in still another pile. These piles represent an intermediate classification or category of interest to me. Later, when I need to find a DOCUMENT in my Filing Cabinet, those DOCUMENT GROUPS help me focus my search.

For example, if I'm looking for cancelled checks, I start in the section of the drawer that holds BANK DOCUMENTS.

It really isn't necessary to group DOCUMENTS this way to file them in the filing cabinet, but I do it because *it helps me find them a little quicker later on.* That's an important point and we'll come back to it later.

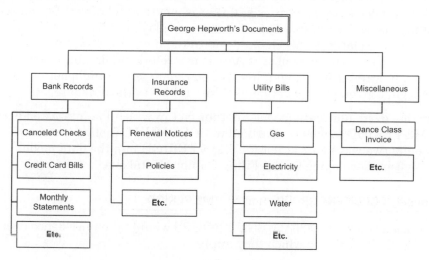

Figure 3-1 Three-level Hierarchy of Document

Figure 3-1 illustrates the three-level hierarchy used in my filing cabinet database (with a lot of detail left out to save space).

As this model of the data in my Filing Cabinet Database shows, George Hepworth's Documents includes DOCUMENT GROUPS—Bank Records, Insurance Records, Utility Bills, and Miscellaneous. Within each DOCUMENT GROUP, there are one or more DOCUMENT TYPES.

For example, the DOCUMENT GROUP called BANK RECORDS includes DOCUMENT TYPES called CANCELED CHECKS, CREDIT CARD BILLS, MONTHLY STATEMENTS, and so forth. The DOCUMENT GROUP called UTILITY BILLS includes GAS, ELECTRICAL, WATER, and others.

In database terms, a collection of similar entities, such as UTILITY BILLS, is an entity GROUP—a group of entities of the same type. The Dance Class Invoices in my filing cabinet comprise another entity GROUP called DANCE CLASS INVOICES; INSURANCE RENEWAL NOTICES are another.

Not All Relationships are Hierarchical

So far, the relationships we've seen between DOCUMENTS in my Filing Cabinet Database are the hierarchical ones in Figure 3-1. As you can see, these relationships group related entities into more specific sub-groups, branching out like the roots of a tree. But there are other kinds of relationships between entities and that is where a Relational Database Management System like Access comes into play. You'll learn more about relationships later in this chapter and in the next. For now, the important thing to remember is Access is a relational database, rather than a hierarchical one, and this gives us some important benefits when we begin converting our data model into tables in the database.

For this particular data model, another fact in which I'm interested is the TIME PERIOD to which a particular DOCUMENT applies. There are actually two ways to incorporate TIME PERIOD into the data model we've been developing for my Filing Cabinet Database.

Group by DOCUMENT GROUP, then by TIME PERIOD

In this data model, DOCUMENT GROUPS would take precedence over the TIME PERIOD to which they apply.

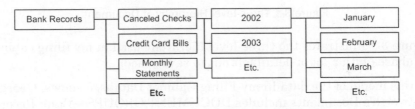

Figure 3-2 Sort by **DOCUMENT GROUP** By **TIME PERIOD**

To find a canceled check for March 2002, I would first go to the section of the filing cabinet where I keep BANK RECORDS, then find CANCELED CHECKS, then CANCELED CHECKS for 2002, and then CANCELED CHECKS FOR MARCH.

Sort by TIME PERIOD, then by DOCUMENT GROUP

In this data model, TIME PERIOD would take precedence over DOCUMENT GROUPS.

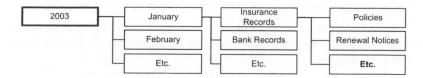

Figure 3-3 Sort by TIME PERIOD by DOCUMENT GROUP

To find a RENEWAL NOTICE for my auto insurance, I would start by looking in the drawer with records for the year, 2003, then the month, JANUARY. In the JANUARY section I'd find INSURANCE RECORDS for JANUARY and, finally, RENEWAL NOTICES.

Choosing a Model—Workflow and Business Rules

Even though this is a very simple database, there are two possible ways to define the relationships between DOCUMENTS, DOCUMENT GROUPS, and TIME PERIODS. Therefore, we have to choose between two data models. Which is the right one?

I've had to address this question in the process of designing every database I've ever built. It is almost always possible to express relationships between certain entities in more than one way. Often, different approaches can be equally valid on the surface.

Therefore, I believe the answer to that question is, "Use the model that best serves the purpose of the database." This choice is only partly dependent on the data itself. Selecting the right data model means carefully evaluating the purpose for which the database will be used and the workflow it will support. Who will use it and how will they use it? What rules apply to using it? And that, in turn, requires you to spend enough time interviewing your customers to fully understand the purpose of the database and the workflow it will support.

The Customer is Always Right

Your customers include the managers or executives who requested the project, the subject matter experts who understand the business processes and workflow which it will support, the end users who will use it as part of their regular workload, and the external customers for whom your organization provides goods or services. Each of these customers is important to the success of the project and each has something valuable to contribute to that success.

Your organization may use the term *Stakeholders* instead of *Customers*. I prefer *Customer* because it helps me remember that I am providing a product for which someone is paying me.

> Managers, of course, hold the decision-making power over your project, so their support is essential. However, that's not the only thing they bring to the table. Their position usually provides them with a broad view of your organization's long-term goals and plans. Their insight can help you make good decisions about the role your database will play in those over all plans.

> Subject Matter Experts (SMEs) are the people with technical expertise and knowledge about the business itself and the workflow your database will support. Working closely with them to share their knowledge is another crucial element in your success.

> End Users are the folks who have to use your database. If they aren't happy with it, they will do their very best to avoid using it, up to and including active sabotage. Make sure they are happy. Make every effort to find out how they do their jobs, what words they use to describe what they do, who provides them with input, and who gets the output they produce. The more you know, the more likely you are to produce a database they will actually use.

> External customers may be directly or indirectly affected by the database you produce. Therefore, the degree to which you account for their needs will vary. When there is some direct interaction, you need to do your best to make it as smooth and flexible as you can. For example, if your database will be used by a Customer Service Rep to look up external customer records, a key factor in providing good service to customers will be making it as easy as possible for your CSRs to find their records.

Choosing My Filing Cabinet Data Model

I don't have to spend a lot of time interviewing myself to find out how I want to use my Filing Cabinet. It was fairly easy for me to pick the data model I want to use, DOCUMENT GROUP-DOCUMENT-TIME PERIOD, the one in Figure 3-2. Here's how I decided.

The way I *retrieve* information is more important, in this case, than the way I *enter* it.

Most of the time, I need to look for a particular DOCUMENT in a particular DOCUMENT GROUP: I want to compare my current electric bill to last year's bill for the current month, or I have a question about the current coverage limit on my homeowners insurance. In the case of bills I receive on a regular cycle, like the electric bill, I could easily get to the right information under either data model because I should find the appropriate DOCUMENT in any TIME PERIOD in which I choose to look— July, 2002 and July, 2003, for example.

However, in the case of my insurance coverage, the DOCUMENT GROUP-DOCUMENT-TIME PERIOD approach is clearly more efficient. For one thing, the policy renews once each year, but I don't remember the renewal date off the top of my head. If I used the TIME PERIOD-DOCUMENT GROUP-DOCUMENT data model, I would have to search through each TIME PERIOD until I found the one with that DOCUMENT in it. Even with a good starting guess, the chances are that I'll have to look in more than one month to find it.

For another, there is only one month associated with each insurance renewal. Once I get to the section of the Filing cabinet where my insurance records are, I'll probably find only one TIME PERIOD there, the one in which the renewal resides. I only have to store a TIME PERIOD if there is something to put in it.

Granted, my little Filing Cabinet is nowhere near as complicated as the Access databases you'll be building in the days and weeks ahead. You will, however, be making decisions about your own data models using processes and principles like these.

Now, let's learn a little bit more about the entities we'll be tracking.

Entities Have Attributes

When we talk about an entity, we are referring to the thing itself. The tables in your Access database will be based on entities. We are also interested in facts about entities. For example, one thing we want to know about a DOCUMENT is the kind of information it contains. We called these DOCUMENT GROUPS. Another thing we need to know is the TIME PERIOD to which it applies.

In database terms, attributes are facts about an entity in which we are interested. To put it another way, one purpose of the database is to capture attributes about the entities in the database.

For the entity DOCUMENT, for example, we have identified two attributes: what *kind of information* it contains and the *time period* to which it applies. In the data model, we called these the DOCUMENT GROUP and TIME PERIOD.

For any given attribute, an entity has only one value. If I have a bill from the gas company, for example, it can only be for gas I consumed during one specific period, such as May 15 to June 15, 2003.The gas company is not free to send me bills for arbitrary, overlapping, or duplicate time periods, or for completely unrelated services such as phone lines to my house. It may seem like I'm only stating the obvious, but when it comes time to create your Access tables, you'll need to be able to count on this one-to-one relationship between attributes and the values they can have.

When we create physical tables in our database, the attributes will become fields in the tables representing the entities.

Enough Attributes

Obviously, we are not interested in capturing every possible fact about an entity, just as we weren't interested in including every possible entity. I don't care, for example, if my bank statements come on blue paper or pink paper, or that my bills from the phone company list international calls separately from other long distance calls. Those are attributes that I don't need or want to keep track of for the purposes of this particular database. However, it is important to the success of your database that you do identify all of the attributes that will be of interest to you before you start creating tables, or as many as possible. I've seldom had the intelligence (or good luck) to identify all of the relevant entities and attributes on the first try. However, the point is always to be as thorough as possible as early as possible in the development process.

Tech Talk—Entities, Attributes and Relationships

So far, I've kept my discussion of entities, attributes, and data models informal because I wanted to help any novices among us grasp the basic concepts before tackling the jargon that goes with them. In the process, I have over-simplified some concepts and omitted others.

So, here's a more formal discussion of what we've covered so far. To do so, though, we'll need to use examples that are somewhat more complex than my cardboard box filing system. It's served its purpose in getting us started, but it will now be left behind.

Entity

An entity is an object or event that exists. It can be differentiated from other objects. For instance, the PC sitting on the floor under my desk, Serial Number 07130-2M2-0120, is an entity. It can be uniquely identified as one particular PC in the universe, although it was part of a production run of hundreds of identical PC's.

An entity can be concrete—a canceled check, for example—or abstract; a concept such as contract, or an event such as transaction. For example, the transaction in which I purchased the PC was an event that occurred on October 21, 2001. The transaction included a salesperson at a local computer store, my credit card, and me. The purchase event itself is an entity. The date, the PC, the salesperson and myself are part of the purchase event.

Entity Sets

An entity set is a group, or set, of entities of the same type, such as all of the canceled checks from my personal checking account. They are all one kind of thing, but are unique and distinguishable from each other in several ways.

Common Members

Two or more entity sets can have members in common. For example, the entity set *school employee*, referring to everyone who works at my daughter's school, and the entity set *school parent*, referring to parents of students in the school, can and do have members in common. Some school employees have children who attend their school. The database term for this principle is that entity sets *need not be disjoint.*

When you are deciding which Access tables you'll need to represent entities, you'll learn more about the importance of this principle.

Attributes

Each entity has a set of one or more attributes. For most entities, such as school parent, there is a fairly well defined set of attributes: for example, name, street, city, state and zip, home phone, and work phone.

As I noted in the informal discussion earlier, it is usually possible to identify more attributes than are of interest within a data model. For example, while school parents are either *male* or *female*, that attribute may or may not be of interest in a database of school parents.

You don't know that, of course, until you've interviewed the customers who will use it. If there is a business reason for keeping that information, you'll need to include it.

However, in my experience, the larger problem in most development projects is failing to include all of the relevant attributes in the initial data model. In other words, it's better to start with a list of all possible attributes and whittle it down, rather than to have to incorporate an overlooked attribute at a point where doing so causes major and, therefore, expensive changes in an existing database.

Domain

Domain refers to the set of permitted values for an attribute. For example, there are only two permitted values in the Domain of Gender, male and female. For ZIP CODE, the Domain is either five or nine positive integers.

Attribute/Data Value Pairs

For each entity in an entity set, there is a set of one or more pairs of attributes and data values; for each attribute, there is one attribute/data value pair. (Nope, that isn't a foreign language, although it might seem like it at first.)

This is a formal way of saying what we've already talked about: an entity has one or more attributes—facts about the entity of interest to our organization. We're simply expanding on this by adding the requirement that, to fully and accurately describe an entity, the attribute must be with an appropriate data value.

For example, consider a shirt. It has several attributes, including size, whether it has buttons, whether it has long or short sleeves, what material it is made of, and what color it is. COLOR, therefore, is an attribute of shirt. However, it would make no sense to refer to the shirt's color without specifying what that color is: red, blue, pink, etc. Red, blue, and pink are the data values for COLOR for this particular entity, SHIRT.

Later, when you learn about the rules of normalization, we'll reinforce the importance of this point. For now, just remember each attribute consists of an attribute and its corresponding data value.

Here's another example. A particular individual in a mailing list database is described by the set of attribute/data value pairs illustrated in Table 3-2:

Attribute	Data Value
FirstName	William
MiddleName	Henry
LastName	Carterfield
NickName	Bill
Birthdate	08/10/1980
Anniversary	6/30/2001
RelationshipType	Friend

Table 3-2 Attribute-Data Value Pairs

As Table 3-2 shows, each attribute specified for one *individual* has one, and only one, corresponding data value.

Relationships

Up to now, I've used the terms relationship and relational in an informal way. I briefly talked about the hierarchy of DOCUMENTS in the course of discussing how we came to group documents for filing. That is one type of relationship, but not the most important type of relationship in a Relational Database such as the ones you will build with Access.

Relationship

A relationship is an association between entities in different entity sets. For example, consider HOUSEHOLD and INDIVIDUAL, which are entity sets in a database of school families. In other words, this database keeps track of households associated with the school and individuals associated with those households.

In that database, an INDIVIDUAL is any person in whom the school has an interest: a school employee, a parent or another relative of a student in the school, or a student in the school. A HOUSEHOLD is defined as one or more persons who share a single address.[5]

---

[5]Although it's not critical to this discussion, it is interesting to recognize that this definition is broad enough to include households consisting of a married couple, a single person, two (cont.)

The relationship between HOUSEHOLDS and INDIVIDUALS is that each HOUSEHOLD consists of, or is made up of, one or more INDIVIDUALS who live at the same location.

For the moment, let's assume that, in this database, an INDIVIDUAL can only reside in a single HOUSEHOLD. We'll consider the opposite situation later in this section.)

Role-based Relationships

We can define the *relationship* between HOUSEHOLD and INDIVIDUAL by specifying the *role* each plays in the relationship between them. Again, for the purpose of this relationship, the role of the INDIVIDUAL is *resides in*. The role of HOUSEHOLD is *residence for*.

> An INDIVIDUAL is a person who *resides in* a Household.
>
> A HOUSEHOLD is a *residence* for one or more INDIVIDUALS.

In a binary relationship, like the one between HOUSEHOLD and INDIVIDUAL, it is possible to state the relationship in terms of either member.

Here are a few other examples of entities involved in this kind of role-based binary relationship.

> A CUSTOMER purchases a PRODUCT.
>
> A PRODUCT *is purchased by* a CUSTOMER.
>
> A STUDENT *is enrolled in* a CLASS.
>
> A CLASS *consists of* one or more STUDENTS.

Descriptive Relationships

Some relationships are descriptive, rather than role-based. For example, in the attendance portion of our school database, a STUDENT can be absent or tardy on one or more occasions. The two entities are STUDENT and ATTENDANCE RECORD. The relationship between them is that a STUDENT *is absent or tardy* on a particular date. ATTENDANCE RECORD captures that information by describing or specifying the date(s) and attendance status of each STUDENT.

---

unmarried partners, a parent and grandparent, and other permutations involving at least one person.

Relationship Set

A relationship set is a set of relationships of the same type that connects entities in one entity set with entities in another. Perhaps the best way to explain this is with an example.

The RELATIONSHIP between CUSTOMER and PRODUCT, as stated above, is:

A CUSTOMER *purchases* a PRODUCT.

Therefore, if we have a group of CUSTOMERS—John, June, and Jerry—and a group of PRODUCTS—a red bicycle, a blue bicycle, and 2 green bicycles—the RELATIONSHIP set between them could be:

John purchases the red bicycle.

June purchases the blue bicycle.

Jerry purchases a green bicycle.

Although the other green bicycle is in the PRODUCT group, it won't participate in a relationship with a CUSTOMER until the customer purchases it. It is not a member of that relationship set until that happens.

Relationship Types

We are primarily interested in three types of relationships. These are:

> One-to-One

> One-to-Many

> Many-to-Many

One-to-One Relationships

In a one-to-one relationship, each entity in one entity set is related to one, and only one, entity in a second entity set. For example, many corporations provide company cars for their employees. There are two ways for the company to do this, depending on which business rule they've adopted.

Business Rules

The business rules of the company determine how cars are allocated and the appropriate relationship is determined by those business rules. First, company XYZ maintains a fleet of cars that employees check out as needed. (This leads to a many-to-many relationship, which we'll come back to a bit later.)

Second, a company can assign one car to one employee for his exclusive use. For example, the ABC Company provides each of its sales managers with a car. This is a one-to-one relationship, assuming, of course, no sales manager is allowed to have two company cars at the same time (another business rule).

> A SALES MANAGER *is assigned* a COMPANY CAR.

> A COMPANY CAR is assigned to a SALES MANAGER.

If you were creating the data model to manage this company's company car fleet, you would need to create a one-to-one relationship between SALES MANAGERS and COMPANY CARS.

One-to-one relationships are the least common. Moreover, when it is time to create Access tables from your data model, most one-to-one relationships can be put into one table. So, pay close to these relationships in your data model to be sure you set up your tables correctly.

One-to-Many Relationships

In a one-to-many relationship, each entity in one entity set is related to one or more entities in a second entity set. For example, a potato grower can cultivate one or more fields of potatoes. This is a one-to-many relationship. If you were building the data model for a government agency tracking pest control for local potato farmers, your data model would need to accommodate this relationship.

> A POTATO GROWER *cultivates* one or more POTATO FIELDS.

> A POTATO FIELD is cultivated by one POTATO GROWER.

One-to-many relationships are the most common and usually the easiest to define and set up in a database. Here are some other examples of one-to-many relationships in some of the databases I've built for customers over the years.

> An INSURANCE AGENCY *employs* one or more INSURANCE SALESPERSONS.

> An INSURANCE SALESPERSON *is employed by* one INSURANCE AGENCY.

> A CLASS *enrolls* one or more STUDENTS.

> A STUDENT *is enrolled* in one CLASS.

In the last one-to-many example above—a STUDENT in a CLASS— the business rule for this elementary school requires a STUDENT to be enrolled in one and only one CLASS during each enrollment period, which is the SCHOOL YEAR. For example, Josefina Carillo is enrolled in the seventh grade at this school. The seventh grade includes Josefina and 22 other students: one class, many students.

A community college, with different enrollment and curriculum requirements, has a different rule about enrolling in classes. The community college allows students to enroll in several classes during the enrollment period, which is the SEMESTER or QUARTER. Each class is independent of the other classes the college offers, so each student has his own unique schedule of classes.

For example, John O'Hara has classes in Math, English, and Biology, while Keiko Yamasaki has classes in Math, Botany, and Electrical Engineering. This is an example of the last type of relationship we'll discuss, Many-to-Many.

Many-to-Many Relationships

In a many-to-many relationship, each of the entities in one entity set is related to one or more entities in a second entity set. Each of the entities in the second entity set is related to one or more entities in the first entity set.

For example, as we saw earlier, Company XYZ's business rule about company cars says any car in the car pool can be checked out by any employee, which creates a many-to-many relationship.

An EMPLOYEE *checks out* one or more COMPANY CARS.

A COMPANY CAR *is checked out by* one or more EMPLOYEES.

Of course, there is another business rule that says an employee can only check out one car at a time, but on any given day, any car in the company car pool can be checked out by any employee: Many cars, many employees.

In the case of the community college classes, any student can enroll in one or more classes during each semester. A class can enroll one or more students.

A CLASS *enrolls* one or more STUDENTS.

A STUDENT *enrolls in* one or more CLASSES.

Here is another many-to-many relationship I encountered while building a database for an elementary school database.

A STUDENT *belongs to* one or more HOUSEHOLDS.

A HOUSEHOLD *includes* one or more STUDENTS.

This one may surprise you at first, but if you think about it for a moment, you'll see how this can, and frequently does, happen. Not that many years ago, the traditional HOUSEHOLD was presumed to be two parents and one or more children. Today, a HOUSEHOLD can be a single parent and one or more children, an unmarried couple and one or more children, or a parent, one or more children, and a grandparent.

Many students don't live exclusively in one HOUSEHOLD. They spend some time in Mom's house and some time in Dad's house. The attendance database I built for this school, therefore, needed to accommodate a many-to-many relationship between STUDENTS and HOUSEHOLDS, based on the real world circumstances our data model revealed.

Business Rules and Data Models

Each organization has its own business rules about how it conducts its operations. With company cars and sales managers, schools and classes, potato growers and potato fields, and each of the other relationships you'll encounter, you'll need to know not just what entities are involved, but how your organization applies its rules to those entities.

In almost every situation where you are defining relationships between the entities in your model of data that your database will track, you'll have to consult your subject matter experts, end users, and managers to learn the business rules that apply. This is the only way you'll be able to create an accurate, usable database.

Business-Specific Entity Definitions

In the example of the community college, it is obvious that it needs to accommodate multiple students in multiple classes, but it can't, or shouldn't, allow students to sign up for more than one class during the same time on the same day. To achieve this result, the college must have a different definition of CLASS than the elementary school, one that includes week days and times as well as enrollment period.

Key Attributes

So far, you've learned that the business of creating a relational database depends on three things.

> Identifying the entities of concern to us

> Identifying and listing their relevant attributes

> Identifying the relationships that link our entities with one another.

To complete the process, we need one additional piece of information, which is the *key attribute* that uniquely identifies each entity in each entity set.

Normally, a key attribute is one of many attributes of an entity. For example, the serial number on the back of my PC, 07130-2M2-0120, is unique; no other PC has that identical serial number. The PC has other attributes of potential interest, such as the CPU speed, amount of RAM it holds and the storage capacity of its hard drive. However, it is that serial number that uniquely differentiates it from all other PCs with similar attributes.

As an individual, I can be uniquely identified only by referring to a combination of attributes. My names, George, Russell, and Hepworth are not individually unique, and probably not even unique in that combination, although I've not met anyone with the same name yet. My social security number is very close to being useful as a unique identifier, especially when combined with my name. In a logical data model, then, we can consider the *combination* of first name, middle name, last name and SSN enough to uniquely define a person.

With these two key attributes, we can uniquely identify the relationship between any two entities, PERSON and COMPUTER EQUIPMENT.

PERSON ID	owns	PC Equipment ID
George Russell Hepworth SSN 555-55-5555	owns	07130-2M2-0120

Table 3-3 Relationship Example

As you might expect, when you convert your logical data model into physical tables in an Access database, one of the most important steps will be setting up key attributes for entities so you can uniquely identify the entities in each table. In a logical model, key attributes are usually fairly easy to identify, but that task can be a bit more challenging when it comes time to create the physical tables.

What is not obvious at this point is you will seldom, if ever, use one of these real world or natural key attributes as the primary key in a physical table. Consider, for example, the problem we've identified with names and social security numbers. In our logical data model, it is the combination of these four attributes that uniquely identifies a person. Access would allow you to set them up as a compound key in a physical table, but that would quickly lead to a lot of problems, problems you'll want to avoid as much as possible.

SSN by itself is more attractive as a key attribute and, in some contexts, it is adequate as a key attribute in a *logical* model. Still, for reasons you'll learn in Chapter Four, it doesn't quite work as the primary key in a physical table.

Further Study

The foregoing discussion of entities' attributes and relationships is really no more than an introduction to a fascinating area of study. My intent is not to prepare you to take on a serious data analysis project. Rather, I want you to be comfortable with the concepts of entity, attribute, and relationship, so you'll be ready to start building well-designed Access tables. If, like me, you're fascinated by the topic, you'll find a list of references for further study in Appendix A.

Creating an Informal Data Model

By now, you should be ready to create your first, informal, data model. Let's start with one that is useful, but fairly easy to set up: a phone number, email, and address database for family and friends. To make it more interesting, I also want it to keep track of birthdays and anniversaries.

Your Data Model

Start by listing all of the things you think you'll need to know to set up the database, things like names, email addresses, mailing addresses, and phone numbers. Don't look at my list on page 3-26 until you've written as many as you can think of yourself. On the following page, list your entities and attributes, and key attributes (the ones that uniquely identify each entity.

Now, on page 3-23 (or on a notepad if your prefer), sketch out the relationships between your entities. Here are some simple conventions to get you started.

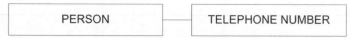

Enclose your entities in rectangles.

Draw lines between related entities. There is a relationship between persons and telephone numbers, for example.

Relationships can be one-to-one, one-to-many, or many-to-many. To indicate these relationships between your entities, use a "1" for the one side and the symbol "∞" for the many side.

Because each person can have one or more phone numbers, we place the ∞ next to phone number. Because one or more persons can use each phone number, we place the ∞ next to person as well.

This, as you know, is a many-to-many relationship.

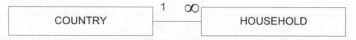

Here is an example of a one-to-many relationship.

Some of my family lives in the United States and some of them live in another country, Venezuela to be precise. That may or may not be an important feature of *your* database. For *my* purposes, it is important, because there are different formatting requirements for telephone numbers and postal codes—in fact there are no postal codes in Venezuela. By definition, a household consists of a group of people living at a single location, so a household can only be in one country. Many households, on the other hand, exist in both countries.

If there isn't enough room on the following pages for your sketch, or if someone else has already used then, take out a yellow pad and start drawing boxes and lines.

Sketch out your Entities and Relationships here.

My Data Model

Let's look at my model for a mailing address, email and phone number database. While I'm explaining what I did and why, you can compare it to your model and the choices you made in creating it. The following discussion will be fairly detailed at some points, probably more detailed than would otherwise be justified for a database as simple as a mailing, phone and email list database. At the same time, I'm going to skip over some of the more technical aspects of data modeling.

To repeat a point I made earlier, this book *is not* intended to make you a fully qualified data modeler or database developer. It *is* intended to illustrate principles I feel are important to grasp before you begin creating the physical tables in the database. One simple example alone won't achieve that goal, although I have tried to pack as much into it as it will bear.

Entities, Definitions, and Attributes

You may have included more or fewer entities than I did and more or fewer attributes for each. Based on the purposes for which this database is intended, I think you should include at least the things I've identified.

As you recall, I defined the purpose of the database to be mailing, email, and phone numbers *along with birthdays and anniversaries*. If I had defined the purpose of the database to be just the mailing, email and phone numbers, I would have included less information, although most of the data model would have been the same.

Since this is quite likely your first attempt at creating a data model, don't worry if you didn't get it quite right on the first try. You'll get better with practice.

In my mailing and phone list data model for family and friends, I am interested in the following entities and attributes. The table on the following page also includes definitions for the entities listed along with an example of each.

Entity	Definition	Example	Key Attribute(s)
Household	Group of people who reside at a single location	Tom & Cindy Hepworth household	Household Name, Head of Household Location, Country
Person	Individual for whom I record a phone number, email or mailing address	Tom Hepworth	First Name, Last Name
Address	Location at which a particular organization or person may be found or reached	2121 E. Haverford St. San Francisco, CA 94107 USA	Street, city, state, postal code
Phone Number	Number assigned to a telephone	415 111-1010	Country code, area code, prefix, extension
Email Address	Electronic address to which electronic messages are delivered	tomh@myco.com	email address

Table 3-4 Entities and Key Attributes

In addition to the key attributes listed above, I am interested in nicknames of friends and family members, any suffixes (e.g., jr.) birth dates, anniversaries and deceased dates of people, what the relationship between each person and myself is (friend or family member), what type of address I have for each person (work or home, PO Box or street address), what type of phone number I have for each person (home, work, cell phone, fax, pager) and what type of email address I have for each person (work, personal, etc.).

Here's my sketch of the entities and relationships.

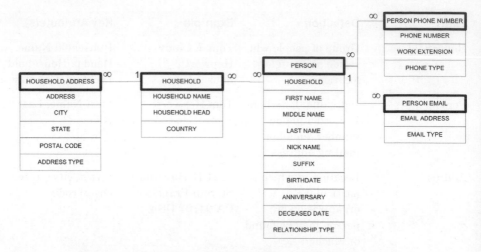

Figure 3-4 Logical Data Model—Phone, Email and Mailing List

I decided that, in addition to the country where a Household is located, I want to have a household name and head of household for each household. The household name is useful when I want to send a Christmas card to all members of a household, for example.

Hedging my Bets

I've included a couple of things in my data model, even though I'm not yet sure I'll later use them in the database. I often do that during the data-modeling phase. In my experience, it is usually a lot easier to go back and delete something if I decide I don't need it, than it is to try to insert an overlooked entity or attribute into a half-finished database.

For example, being able to identify a head of household strikes me as something I want to be able to do, even though I can't think of a way to use it at the moment. I'll keep it in until I make up my mind about its importance.

Managing Data—Delete vs. Inactive

I also decided to include the date when a family member is deceased, partly because it is somewhat relevant to the purpose of this database and partly to make a larger point about managing data and table design. On one level, this may be somewhat trivial in a phone number, email, and mailing list. However, it is worth discussing as it helps illuminate an important principle in database design.

I decided this database would include birthdays and anniversaries. I figured that would allow me to display a list of August birthdays, for example, and quickly look up the appropriate address or addresses at the same time[6]. While I was writing down all of the things about my family and friends it occurred to me that life events, such as births, marriages, divorces, and deaths occur in every family. We celebrate the positive events, like birthdays and anniversaries, and I want them in the list so I can acknowledge them at the proper time. This is, in fact, one of the reasons for making this a database.

On the other hand, I'm not at all sure I'm interested in divorce dates, so I didn't include that information in my model.

Death, however, is a bit more complicated. If someone in my list were to die, I could just remove that person from the list. I don't want to do that, and not just for sentimental reasons. The principles of good database design tell me that I don't want to get into the habit of removing records from a database.

Remember back to Chapter two, when I was discussing the reason to choose Access over Excel for a particular purpose? One of the key factors I mentioned was that a database is good at keeping historical, as well as current, information. On principle, therefore, I don't want to remove data that has some sort of historical significance. I figure information about family members who have passed on falls very definitely in that category. Instead of deleting them, then, I want to include a piece of information that will identify their status. In the database, deceased date will prevent me from accidentally including them on active lists for birthday and Christmas cards.

Status

Deceased date is a specific example of a generally useful piece of information found in nearly all databases: *active and inactive status*. Anytime you have an entity whose status can change over time, you can best handle it by recording the date(s) that status changes rather than deleting or adding new records.

---

[6] I know, Outlook does the same things, maybe even better than my database can do. You probably don't need this database any more than I do. That said, it's still worthwhile designing it as an exercise in learning how to design and built a database.

Who's Related to Whom

Although this is not the only way to do it—and you may have decided otherwise—I decided *addresses* are related to households while *phone numbers* and *email addresses* are related to individuals. Here's how I arrived at that conclusion.

If I ask one of my friends or family members for their address so I can send someone in their household a birthday card, they will all give me the same address, the street address where they live or the P.O. Box where they get their mail. My brother, his wife, and each of their kids will all give me the same address in California, for example.

However, that isn't true if I ask for their phone number. They'll usually respond with their own question, "Do you want my work phone or home phone?" And increasingly, they'll mention a cell phone as well.

The same is even truer for email addresses. Nearly everyone I know has their own email address; most of them have more than one. It is rare, however, to find two or more people sharing an email address.

So, when I set up this database, I decided I would relate mailing addresses to households and email addresses and phone numbers to people.

Gray Areas, Trade-Offs, and Lessons Learned

I could also make a case for treating addresses the same way as I did phone numbers; that is, they are related to individuals rather than households.

Some people in my database are actually business associates rather than friends. The only address I have for them is a work location; I don't know their home address. Moreover, I don't know any of the other household members at that address. In that sense, their addresses can be seen as being related to the person rather than the household.

The opposite is true for most of my family members; I have their home address but not a work address, and I am interested in all of the household members at that address.

In both cases, the applicable business rule is, "When adding new persons to the database, record the address to which you are most likely to send mail: home addresses for family and friends, work addresses for business associates." That's because my mailing list is set up to help me send birthday cards, Christmas cards, or other, similar letters and cards to family and friends. I only need one address per household to do that.

The opposite is true of phone and email lists. When I want to get in touch with someone by phone or email, the choice of numbers or email addresses does matter. During the workday, I want to call the person's work number or use their work email, but during the evening or on the weekend, I want to use their home number, cell number or personal email address.

Relationship Types

The relationship between persons and phone numbers is many-to-many and, for some phone numbers, that's true most of the time. For example, most home phones are shared by all members of the family (although those of you who have teen-agers may feel otherwise) and each of those family members uses more than one phone.

Other phones are used exclusively, or almost exclusively by one person. For example, most cell phones are personal phones. There is clearly only one person in that relationship. Phones, like addresses, are a bit more of a gray area than might first appear.

Lessons Learned

I am spending a good amount of time on this subject, not because I'm particularly obsessed with phones, email and mailing addresses, but because deciding how to handle them in your data model is a special case of a more general issue that frequently comes up when it is time to convert your logical data model into physical tables in Access. Sometimes, you just have to make a choice between two valid approaches.

The decision is based, as much as anything, on the way the data will be used and the business rules that apply to that use. And, as I've stated before, this requires you spend considerable time with your customers, gaining an understanding of their workflow and requirements.

The important thing is that by creating, evaluating, and revising your data model in light of the definitions and business rules you discover, you will better understand how all of the relationships work, or should work. You will be able to make informed decisions about the potential advantages and disadvantages of each approach. Doing so will help you head off problems down the road.

Trade-Offs

The trade-off in my decision to create the relationship between persons and phone numbers instead of between households and people is that I have a many-to-many relationship between them. In a database, many-to-many relationships are almost always more complicated to handle than one-to-many relationships. However, by going that route, I gained something else: an easier way to relate people with the phone numbers I am likely to use to contact them.

Summary

In this chapter, I've given you an overview of the initial phase of creating a new Access database, starting with the cardboard box-to-filing cabinet metaphor. You learned that data becomes information when it is organized according a logical (as opposed to physical) model.

You saw that before you can transfer your raw data from a cardboard box into a filing cabinet, you need to spend time analyzing the bits and pieces of data that make up the information in which you are interested. You need to figure out how you and your users want to use that information, the business rules that will apply, and how to resolve the inevitable ambiguities that arise.

You learned the importance of interviewing your customers to understand the purpose of your database and the workflow it supports.

You learned the definition of common database terms: entity, attribute, key attribute, and relationships. You learned about one-to-one, one-to-many, and many-to-many relationships.

You tried your hand at creating a data model for a mail, email, and phone list database. With that preparation behind you, you're ready to begin creating physical tables for the entities in your data model.

4. Let's Get Physical

By now, you must be really eager to open your copy of Access and start creating tables based on the logical data model of a personal mailing, email and phone list you have created. I think we're ready to do that, so let's get started. In the next few pages, I'll walk you through the set up of the tables in a new database file. I'm assuming that you haven't used Access at all yet, so if you have used Access before, you may prefer to skim through this section and pick up the discussion when we begin creating tables for our new database on page 4-9.

Naming Conventions

In this chapter, you'll also get your first introduction to standard naming conventions. Most professional Access developers, including my students and myself, use some variation of these conventions. These conventional ways of naming Access objects, such as tables and fields, have an interesting history. It is often referred to as *Hungarian notation* in honor of the man credited with originating it, a Hungarian named Charles Simonyi. Beyond the scope of this book, it is worth your time to learn more about its history and development[7].

It's Finally Time to Open Access

Open your copy of MS Access. I'm using Access 2002 (sometimes referred to as Access XP) and the screen shots and examples in this book are all from Access 2002. (And you'll also see that I prefer the "Classic Windows" look to the Windows XP appearance.) If this is the first time you've opened Access, you may see a screen like the one in Figure 4-1. If this is your first database, you shouldn't see any existing files to open. Access offers you several choices for opening an existing database or creating a new one.

---

[7] If you are interested in learning more about this topic, which I personally find fascinating, you can easily find a number of web sites devoted to the subject. Do a search on keywords "Hungarian notation".

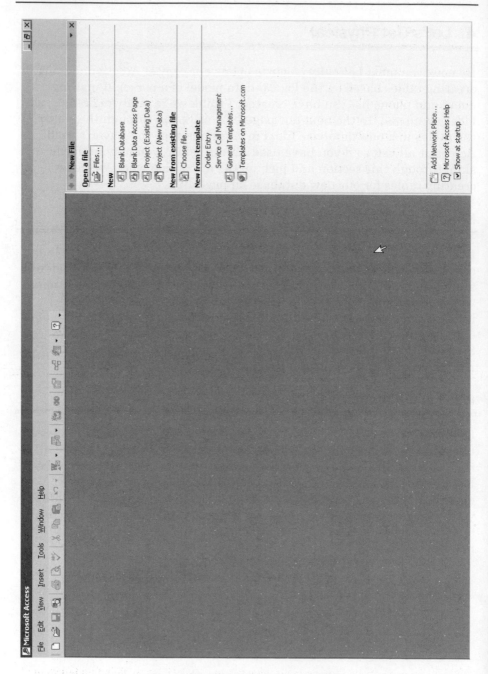

Figure 4-1 Access Opening Screen

New

You can choose to create a new blank Database, new blank Data Access Page, or a Project using new or existing data. This is the option we'll select for our new database.

> Data Access Pages are web pages, published from Access, that have connections to a database. Projects are created to connect to SQL Server databases. Both are beyond the scope of this book.

New from Existing File

Another choice is to use an existing database as a template for your new database. You might choose this option, for example, if you want to create a new database based on one you've already created. You would do so, perhaps, if you had an existing database that wasn't quite what you need. Rather than start completely over, you could create a new version using this option and make your changes in it. Your old database would not be changed, thus preserving it as a backup.

New from Template

Access comes with several templates and you can download others from the Microsoft web site. Frankly, I'm not a big fan of the templates Microsoft provides. For one thing, they can, and often do, create tables that aren't properly normalized. For another, they do not observe good naming conventions. As my friends know, there are few things as irritating to me as a database with non-standard names and un-normalized tables.

Once you become a competent data modeler, you can use the templates for rapid prototyping of new databases. However, you'll find yourself making significant changes to the resulting databases to bring them to a usable condition.

Create a New Database

Click on New Blank Database (Figure 4-2).

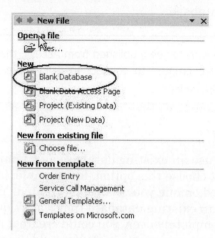

Figure 4-2 New Blank Database

The dialog box will ask you to name your new database (Figure 4-3).

One way to pick a name is to select one that describes the objects in the database. Select a meaningful name; don't use acronyms or unconventional abbreviations. PhoneAddressList.mdb is good; PAL.mdb is not good. PAL might sound like a clever name (the database holds information on my pals), but a year from now you will have forgotten what PAL.mdb stands for. More importantly, other users who see it won't have any idea what it is.

Another possible way to pick a name is to identify the purpose of the database, which in this case is to capture and track personal contacts; PersonalContact.mdb might be good.

Either one would be okay, but to make it easier to refer to it in this book, I finally settled on PersonalContact.mdb and I'll refer to that as your personal contact database.

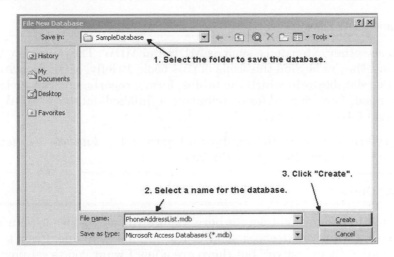

Figure 4-3 Save the New Database

Figure 4-4 shows the *database container*, which is Microsoft's name for the master Access file that contains all of the pieces that actually make up a complete database. In a way, it's the electronic equivalent of my filing cabinet, I suppose. Everything of importance to the database starts out in that container: tables, queries, forms, reports pages, macros and modules. Built into the database container are the rules about how all of those parts work together and the code that makes it all work.

Access appends the extension MDB to these files.

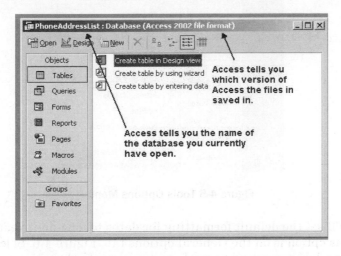

Figure 4-4 Database Window Open to New Database

MDE and MDW Files

You'll see other extensions, such as MDE and MDW. They are also Access files, but they're beyond the scope of this book. Briefly, MDE files are compiled databases in which the tables, forms, reports, etc. can no longer be changed. They're good for distributing a finished database. MDW files are part of Access security.

The preferred name for the window in Figure 4-4 is *database window*. I'll refer to it that way throughout the book.

Setting Options

I'm going to take a slight detour here. Before you add tables to your new database, I want you to check some of the options available. I won't review all of them just yet, but there are a few I want you to set now. Click on Tools-->Options (Figure 4-5) on the menu bar.

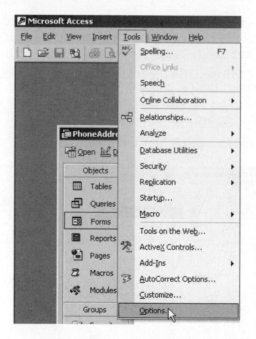

Figure 4-5 Tools-Options Menu

First, you'll set the default formatting for dates to four-digit years (e.g. 2003). This option is on the General options tab, Figure 4-6. Selecting one of these check boxes only changes how dates are displayed — it does not change the data itself. Access stores all dates internally the same way.

We'll be adding date fields to our tables; checking this option ensures they will display the way you want them to display.

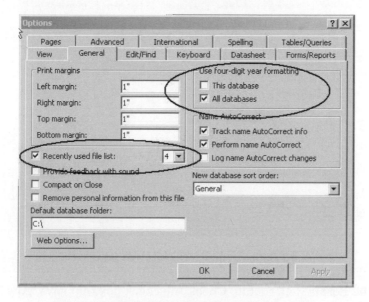

Figure 4-6 Four Digit Years, Recently Used Files

In this same tab, you can set other options, such as the number of files in the recently used file list, the default folder for all of your databases, and default margins for reports. Leave them at their defaults for now. If you want to change any option, you can do so at any time.

I also recommend that you un-check the options to display Hidden Objects and System Objects (Figure 4-7). Advanced developers occasionally do want to see these objects, but they would only be confusing at this point. Just hide them by un-checking them. Leave the other options on this tab at their current defaults.

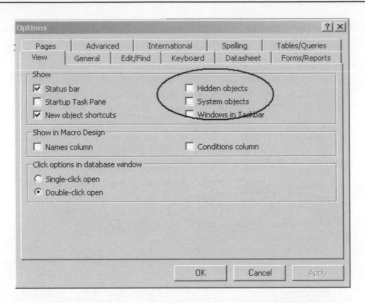

Figure 4-7 Options: Hidden Objects and System Objects

Select the Forms/Reports tab. Check the check box that says "Always use event procedures" as shown in Figure 4-8.

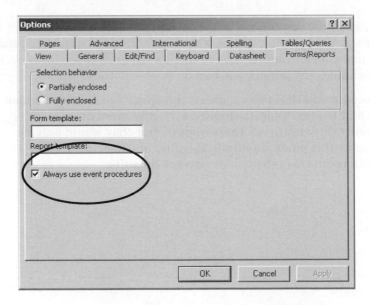

Figure 4-8 Options: Always Use Event Procedures

In Chapter 10, when you're learning how to create more complex forms, you'll need to use event procedures. I'll explain what they are in that chapter.

For now, let's leave the other options set to their defaults. Click on OK to close the Options dialog; you're ready to create your first table.

Create a New Table

Access offers you several different ways to create tables, as illustrated in Figure 4-9.

You can select one of the three options in the Database Window, or select New from the Database Design toolbar, which opens a dialog box with still more choices.

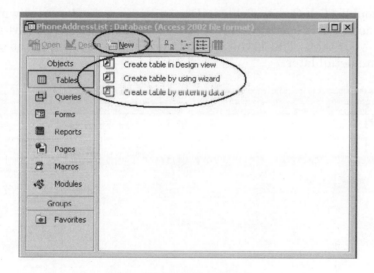

Figure 4-9 Create a New Table

The Database Window options are:

> Create Table in Design View

> Create Table by Using Wizard

> Create Table by Entering Data

Choices and More Choices

One of the mixed blessings of Access is that it usually offers more than one way to accomplish a task. If you find one method more comfortable than another, that is a good thing. On the other hand, multiple choices can be a bit confusing at times. In the rest of this book, I'll mostly show you how to do things using the methods I prefer, but I will also describe other options.

Creating a new table is a case in point. To start a new table, you can double-click on one of the choices in the database window, or click New on the tool bar.

Double-Click on Create Table in Design View

If you double-click Create Table in Design View in the database window, a table design grid opens (Figure 4-10). You can immediately start adding fields to your table. This is the method I prefer. I'll come back and discuss it in more detail later.

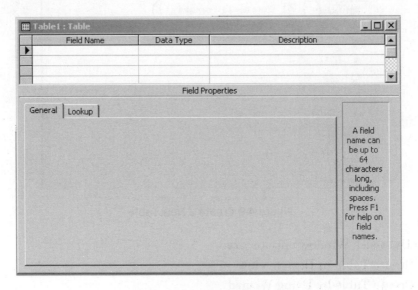

Figure 4-10 New Table Grid

Double-Click on Create Table by Using Wizard

As I said, I prefer to create new tables in design view. While the Table Wizard can give you a head start by offering pre-defined tables and fields, its offerings include non-standard names and un-normalized tables. In my opinion that's not very helpful for beginning developers. So, until you are more comfortable with normalization and naming conventions, I recommend that you avoid the table wizards. They'll only get you started with some bad habits.

Double-Click on Create Table by Entering Data

The third option, Create table by entering data, opens a default table with ten generic fields and a number of blank rows. I seldom, if ever, use this option, for two reasons.

First, it uses default names for fields: Field1, Field2, etc. You have to switch to design view to give them meaningful names anyway. In my opinion, it makes more sense to just start with the names in the first place.

Second, in this approach, fields are defined by entering data into the table, which can limit your flexibility in making changes during the design process. Speaking from personal experience over the last nine years, I have yet to settle on a table design on the first attempt. I suppose it is possible I'm just not that bright, but I don't think that is the case.

Further, although sample data is useful at some point, it seems premature to me to be designing table structures with data already in them. Over time, as you become more adept at creating tables, you may come to the opposite conclusion and prefer to create new tables from sample data. But for now, we'll avoid this approach.

In addition to the three options in the database window, you can select New from the Database Design toolbar.

Click on New

Clicking on New opens a dialog box offering you several options, including both creating tables and importing or linking to other, existing tables.

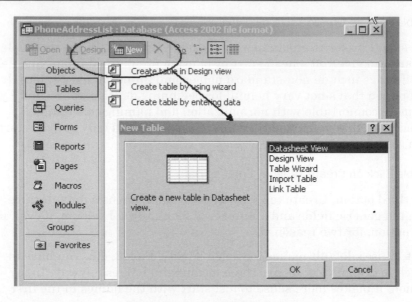

Figure 4-11 New Table Dialog

Selecting Datasheet View from this list opens a default table with ten columns, the same one we discussed earlier as "Create a Table by Entering Data". Same function, different name.

Selecting Design View from this list opens the same New Table Grid as the one shown in Figure 4-10. Same function, same name.

Selecting Table Wizard opens the Wizard dialog. Same function, same name—same reasons not to use it.

Import and Link Tables

At this point, you're not ready to import or link tables. But it is useful to know you do have these options.

Importing tables means you can copy tables from one database to another, somewhat like the way I can move documents from my cardboard box into my filing cabinet (except it moves a copy of the table, not the table itself). You will probably do that often as you build up an inventory of databases with some basic kinds of tables that can be used in a variety of applications. Instead of recreating similar tables over and over, you can just import copies when you need them.

Linking a table means you can create a reference to a table in a different database without physically making a copy of it. This is a very important thing to be able to do. I won't take time here to go into all of the useful things you can do with linked tables because we're concentrating on creating our first new tables. However, do keep in mind that linked tables are very valuable tools that Access provides to you. You'll be happy to have them as an option in the very near future.

First Choice: Design View

As you can see, Access offers a variety of ways to create a new table. As you gain experience and expertise, you'll probably find yourself using one method in preference to the others. Or you may find yourself using different methods in different circumstances. For now, though, let's do it my preferred way: Design View.

Your First Table

For your first table, let's create the Household table from our data model. As you recall, I defined a Household as a group of individuals who reside at a single location. I decided the attributes of a household that are of interest to me include the Household Name, Country, and Household Head.

Either double-click Create Table in Design View in the database window or select New from the Database Design toolbar and then select Design View from the dialog box.

The first field we'll add to the new table is the Household Name (Figure 4-12). It is a text field. The name of the field, as you can see in Figure 4-12 is HouseholdName.

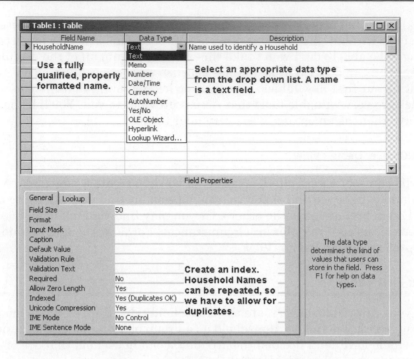

Figure 4-12 Adding Fields to a Table

Field Size

Field size determines the number of characters the field will accept. The default for text is 50 characters, which we'll accept for now.

Naming Conventions

HouseholdName illustrates three important points about standard naming conventions.

> ➢ The name of the field is written out in full and unabbreviated.
> ➢ It is written with *no spaces* between words in the field name.
> ➢ All *words* in the name are capitalized.

Full Names

This is an important point and one new developers frequently overlook.

I can think of several excellent reasons for avoiding contractions and acronyms in names. First, even though acronyms, such as HHN for household name, might make sense to the person creating the table, the chances are very, very good, that someone else is going to be looking at the table sooner or later. At the very least, the full name will help the other person figure out what the field is supposed to be. In addition, it presents a more professional image of you to other developers who see your tables. And finally, you won't find yourself trying to remember what acronym you used, or how you abbreviated a word ("Did I call it HHN, HsHldNm, or HseHldNam?") elsewhere in your database.

No Spaces in Words

In Access, spaces count. To Access, Household Name is not the same as HouseholdName. You and I might not even notice the difference between the two, especially in a long block of code, or in a query.

I hate to tell you how many hours I have wasted tracking down bugs in queries and code, only to discover I had spelled a field name with spaces in one place and without spaces in another: Agency Name vs. AgencyName, for example. If I had learned and used standard naming conventions from the beginning, I would have saved myself an enormous amount of stress in those early years.

In database terms, a space is a delimiter between items; it cannot, therefore, be part of an item's name. Although Access will allow you to put spaces in names, you will have to add special formatting to make sure they are handled consistently. This is, by the way, one of my main criticisms of the table wizard, which generates table and field names with spaces, thereby creating unnecessary complications for you.

Capitalized Words

Some people might object to omitting spaces in field names on the basis that it makes them harder to read: HouseholdName, for example. To make field names more readable, we capitalize the first letter of each word in a name (with some exceptions, such as prepositions). HouseholdName illustrates this point.

Some developers prefer to use an underscore between words, as in Household_name, or Household_Name. That is also an acceptable convention, but one which I prefer not to use. It works well in normal writing, but I find it is almost as easy to overlook an underscore (_) as it is to miss a space in a line of code or in a query. Therefore, I will stick with the conventions described.

You'll learn more about naming conventions as we progress through building this and other tables.

Data Type

Our first field, HouseholdName, is a *text* field. Data type tells you what kind of data a field contains. *Text*, for example, includes letters and numbers used in names of persons, places or things, or telephone numbers and ZIP Codes. *Numbers*, on the other hand, consist of numeric data that can be used in mathematical calculations.

Names normally consist of letters A to Z, but in some cases, like street addresses, they include numbers. Obviously, you don't want to do any kind of math calculation on an address. It may not be as obvious, however, with some kinds of data, such as ZIP Codes, which are entirely made up of numbers. Defining them as text means Access won't try to add two ZIP Codes together.

By the way, this is another reason I do not use the option to create a new table by adding data. Access is smart enough to recognize that my ZIP Code, 98043, consists of numbers not letters. However, it mistakenly defines the data type for that field as Number because it is not smart enough to recognize that specific five-digit format as a ZIP Code. I would have to switch to design view to correct that mistake. Again, it is easier to just do it right the first time, in my opinion.

Other data types you'll frequently use are *Date/Time*, *Currency*, and *Yes/No*. These are fairly self-explanatory. I'll tell you more about them when we need to use them in a table.

You can also define fields as *Memo*, *OLE Object*, and *Hyperlink*. A memo field, as the name suggests, allows for lengthy combinations of letters and numbers, up to 65,535 characters. That is a big advantage for the right type of data, but it also has disadvantages, which you'll learn about in the next section.

An OLE Object is on object created by another application, such as a spreadsheet, document, graphic image, or sound file. Because such files can be very large, it is usually *not a good idea* to include them in your database.

A hyperlink field, on the other hand, is a combination of letters and numbers that make up a hyperlink address, or path to an external file or the URL of a web page. Storing only the address of the external file, not the file itself, is a much more efficient use of database storage.

The last data type I'll discuss here is the *AutoNumber*. I love these things; they are powerful and very useful. An AutoNumber, according MS Access Help, is "a unique, sequential (incremented by 1) number or random number assigned by Microsoft Access whenever a new record is added to a table. AutoNumber fields can't be updated."

The reason for having autonumbers in your database is to create *primary keys* for your tables. You haven't learned about primary keys yet, so I won't delve into them right now. However, I'm sure you'll find them just as exciting as I do when you learn how to use them.

The drop down list of *Data Types* in the field grid includes the option to run the Lookup Wizard. We aren't far enough along in creating our tables to be able to take advantage of the wizard and, frankly, I'm not a big fan of this one anyway. Recently, I've seen too many bad table structures generated by new users as a result of using the Lookup Wizard without understanding good table structure. As is the case with the Table Wizard, I recommend you wait until you really understand how to create good tables and relationships before you use the Wizards.

That is a bit ironic, isn't it? Wizards were created as an aide in creating database objects quickly, but in the hands of an inexperienced person, they cause more problems than they resolve.

Advantages of Defining Data Types

Defining data types makes for more efficient processing in a several ways, including the following:

> Formatting data for display
> Sorting data appropriately
> Allocating storage space efficiently
> Controlling valid input to a field

Formatting Data for Display

Defining a field as Data/Time, for example, tells Access to format data entered into that field in one of the standard date formats. In the U. S., we use the format mm/dd/yyyy (08/01/2003) for dates. In South America, on the other hand, the standard format is dd/mm/yyyy (01/08/2003). The Regional Settings you have selected in the Windows Control Panel determine which format Access will use.

The internal format Access uses to store dates, of course, doesn't change; only the display format indicated by your Windows settings.

Other data types, such a currency, are also formatted according your Windows settings, displaying the appropriate currency symbol for your region.

Sorting Data Appropriately

The data type in a field helps determine how Access sorts data in that field. For example, in a text field, numbers sort as if they were characters, not digits: 1, 10, 100, 2, 20, 200. In a number field they sort as digits: 1, 2, 20, 20, 200. Many dates also sort properly when they are in a date/time field, but not in a text field.

An index, according to Access Help, is an Access feature that speeds up searching and sorting in a table. You'll make your database faster by using indexes on appropriate fields in tables. Memo, Hyperlink, and OLE Object data types can't be indexed. I'll explain more about indexes shortly.

Allocating Storage Efficiently

Some data types take up more storage space than others in your database. As the number of records in the database grows, that becomes more and more of an issue. Number fields can be one-, two-, four-, or eight-bytes long, depending on which subtype you choose. Storage is cheap these days, so this is not as significant an issue as it once was, but it is worth keeping in mind.

Controlling Valid Input to a Field

You can't enter letters into a number field. Defining the data type to be a number, therefore, prevents your users from entering letters in the field. A date/time field, on the other hand, restricts entries to those values that conform to a valid date format: 11/11/1111 is acceptable, 11111111 is not, nor is 13/41/2003.

That should be enough background to move forward with your first field in your first table. As I said earlier, HouseholdName is a text field. The default value is 50 characters. HouseholdName will accept any combination of letters and numbers, up to that maximum of 50.

There are other things to consider when selecting data types. We'll discuss some of them at the appropriate time later in the chapter.

Primary Key Field

Now, let's add our second field to our new Household table. It will be the *Primary Key* for the table. To understand what it is and why it is needed, we'll need to take another short side excursion. This time we'll delve into the subject of Primary and Foreign Keys. I'll keep this discussion as short as possible, but there is a lot to say on this subject, much more than I have space for here. I'll try to tell you enough to understand primary and foreign keys without boring you.

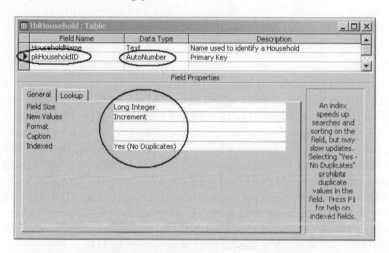

Figure 4-13 New Table Primary Key Field

Primary and Foreign Keys

Choosing a primary key is one of the most important steps in good database design. The Primary Key field uniquely identifies each record in a relational table. You can refer to any record in the table by specifying its primary key. Unfortunately, there is some disagreement on the best way to go about creating primary keys. I'm going to share my views on the subject in the next view pages.

You will find highly qualified developers who disagree with some of the arguments I make here. Ultimately, the choices I've made in this book reflect a combination of my personal experience in designing working databases and input from other Access developers for whose judgment I have great respect.

Key Attributes and Natural Keys

When I was building my logical data model for this database, I identified certain attributes, such as household name, as key attributes. When we are building a physical database from the logical data model, these are usually referred to as natural keys because they occur naturally and they are the key to differentiating between one object, person, or thing and others in the same category. In my case, for example, the unique natural key for household name would be something like the George and Yolanda Hepworth household. That is probably enough information to uniquely identify us here in our hometown, though there is no guarantee another couple with the same names won't move into town sometime in the near future.

A key attribute, or natural key, can be a name, like Ichiro Suzuki. Every baseball fan in Seattle knows who that is. More often, however, it is an identifier like Social Security Number or Employee ID. In a company, for example, the Human Resources manager could refer to an employee as, "John Smith—I mean the one who works in Operations, not the John Smith who works in Finance, nor the one over in Marketing." Or, the HR Manager could just refer to employee 986123 instead. The employee ID uniquely identifies the employee without having to list all of the other attributes distinguishing him from other employees with the same name. In a sense, then, the employee ID *points* to the combination of attributes that makes up the unique individual of interest to HR.

Primary Keys

When it comes time to convert the logical data model into a physical Access table, you'll need keys to uniquely identify entities, but those keys are not the same as their real-world corollaries and natural keys should *not* be used as keys in a physical table.

Let me repeat that. *Natural keys should not be used as primary keys in Access tables.* Primary keys should have no meaning in the natural world outside of the database. Natural keys identify individuals, objects or events *before* they are entered into the database, because they are attributes people use to make such logical distinctions. Primary keys, on the other hand, identify records *after* they are entered into the database. They are different things and should not be used interchangeably.

Primary keys have a special function in relational tables. That function is to uniquely identify each record in order to facilitate relationships between records in two or more tables. As I said before, I strongly believe you should not use a natural key as a primary key in an Access table. In the following paragraphs, you'll find some of the reasons why.

Requirements for Primary Keys

One of the most common mistakes new Access users make is to select Social Security Number or Employee ID as a primary key. I will list only three of the strongest reasons for avoiding natural keys like SSN or Employee ID.

➢ First, *a primary key value can never be null*[8]. It would be impossible to distinguish between records if null values were permitted.

➢ Second, *a primary key must be unique.* No two records in a table can ever have the same primary key.

➢ Third, *a primary key can never be changed.* Once a primary key has been assigned to a record, it can't be changed, just as it cannot be re-used for any other record.

Problems with Natural Keys

The most obvious problem with Social Security Numbers is that not all people have one. Clearly, people in countries other than the U. S. don't. Increasingly, people are reluctant to give theirs out without adequate assurance of security; in a practical sense, this amounts to the same thing as not having one. For example, one District Court in Oregon sent notices to prospective jurors requesting Name, address, birthrate and SSN, plus a signature. (What else would you need to steal an identity?) Needless to say, the response rate from prospective jurors was far less than hoped for.

It is also true that some people in the U.S. don't have a social security number—my two-month-old niece, for example. And even among my friends and family, I can't imagine asking for an SSN in order to enter them into my mailing list!

Moreover, bogus SSNs are all too common. An acquaintance of mine used to work for a small regional health care company. It was not at all uncommon for them to find, in the course of handling a claim for benefits, a person was enrolled under two or more different SSNs. Fortunately, it was not the primary key in their membership tables or they would never have been able to keep things straight.

---

[8] Null is an unknown condition; it is not the same as nothing or zero. Null can mean that you don't know what the value is, or it can mean that the value is not yet determined.

For all of those reasons, a database, such as my personal contact database, cannot rely on SSN. If I decided to ignore these problems and use it anyway, I would have to create fake SSNs in order to avoid violating the first principle listed above. *No primary key can have a null value.* The Oregon District Court cited above, for example, would be forced to create fake SSNs for prospective jurors who refused to divulge their real SSN. And that could create a whole additional set of problems.

Another problem with using natural keys, such as bank account numbers or employee IDs, is that, while they are normally unique within a particular environment, they are not inherently unique in and of themselves. The government can reissue Social Security Numbers, although it is rare for contemporaries to share the same SSN legitimately.

It is true other natural identifiers, such as employee IDs and bank account numbers are unlikely to be re-used within a given organization, especially if there is a reliable mechanism in place for assigning them. However, I believe it is better to completely avoid the possibility of that happening by employing an internal key instead. It is consistent with good database design to do so and there are no compelling reasons not to.

The third major problem that can arise from using a naturally occurring key is the fact that once you start entering records into the database, you are committed to maintaining that key for all future records. For example, let's say an organization chooses its 4 digit Employee ID as the primary key for its Human Resources database. After a few years of growth, the company decides to convert its Employee IDS to a new, more flexible format consisting of two letters followed by 5 digits. The only way to accommodate this change is to revise *all* of the tables in the Human Resources database containing that field or a reference to it.

That conversion is expensive and time-consuming and, ultimately, it would have been unnecessary if the primary key had been a non-meaningful, internally generated value instead. In that case, the change would have been restricted to one field in one table that could be updated with one simple update.

Summary—What are Primary Keys

The primary key of a relational table uniquely identifies each record in the table so relationships between that table and other tables in the database can be defined. With rare exceptions, Access tables should have primary keys. The database developer is responsible for selecting or creating the primary key from among the possible keys identified for that table.

Natural keys, or keys based on naturally occurring attributes such as name or Social Security Number should not be used as primary keys. Primary keys should be meaningless outside of the database in which they are used. As a general rule, users of the database should not see or even be aware of its primary keys.

So, the next question that arises is, "What makes a good primary key?" The best answer, as far as Access is concerned, is usually the autonumber, as illustrated in Figure 4-13.

AutoNumbers for Primary Keys

As previously stated, an autonumber is a unique number, sequential or random, assigned by Access each time a new record is added to the table. Once used in a table, an autonumber is not re-used. An autonumber can't be changed. For those reasons, they are an excellent choice for primary keys.

AutoNumber Data Type

Autonumbers are numbers, more specifically *long integers*. For those of you who may have forgotten some basic math, integers are the whole numbers—1; 3; 600; 9,500—as opposed to numbers with decimals or fractions in them.

In Access, the largest value a long integer can have is 2,147,483,647. That should be large enough for nearly any Access database you or I might design.

Sequential vs. Random

The default method of incrementing autonumbers is sequential. Each number is one larger than the previously assigned number. It's the method you'll use most of the time.

The other method, random incrementing, is mostly relevant to a case where the database is *replicated*, which means two or more copies of the same database are located on different computers. Random incrementing helps to ensure duplicate primary keys won't be assigned to records in the different databases so records in the different databases can be combined at some point.

Re-Use of AutoNumbers not Permitted

Access doesn't re-use an autonumber in normal operation. There are ways around this restriction, but you normally won't want to do that.

Primary Key Notation

The name of the primary key in our first table is pkHouseholdID. This name consists of three parts: a prefix, a root, and a suffix. It follows the naming convention we previously learned except for the prefix, "pk", which means primary key.

This is a relatively recent innovation in Access naming, although I believe it is more widely used in other environments. In all the tables you will see in this book, the primary key will be prefixed this way. We will identify all key fields by affixing "ID" to the end of their name.

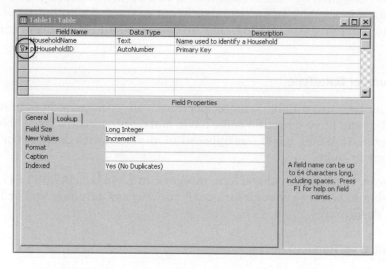

Figure 4-14 New Table Primary Key Designated

Let's take another look at the field grid in Figure 4-13. I've repeated it in Figure 4-14, which also shows that I've now designated this field as the primary key for the table.

As you know, pkHouseholdID is an autonumber and a long integer. It is set to increment new values (as opposed to assigning random numbers). If you look closely at the row selector (the small box at the left end of each row in the field grid), you'll see a small key symbol next to pkHouseholdID. That means I've designated this field to be the primary key for this table.

As is always the case in Access, there is more than one way to designate a primary key. I'll briefly describe each of them.

Access has a rich set of built-in menu and tool bars. Collectively, they are called *command bars* and can appear as *standard menus, toolbars,* and *shortcut menus.* I'm assuming that you are familiar with Office menus and toolbars and that you do not need to pause for a more detailed explanation. If that is not the case, you'll find a quick overview in Chapter 13.

In addition to the built-in command bars, Access allows you to create your own custom menus and tool bars. I'll show you how to create a simple menu bar in Chapter 13.

Right Mouse Click on Field Name—Primary Key

Place the cursor in Field Name and click the right mouse button. In the dialog box that opens, click on Primary Key. This toggles the primary key designation on and off for that field.

Database Design Toolbar—Primary Key

Place the cursor in Field Name in the field grid, find the Primary Key button on the Database Design toolbar (it looks like a little key) and click it to toggle the primary key designation on and off.

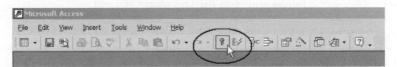

Figure 4-15 Database Design Toolbar, Primary Key

Database Design Toolbar—Index—Primary Key

You can also create the primary key while defining indexes for the table. Place the cursor in Field Name in the field grid, find the Index button on the Database Design toolbar and click it.

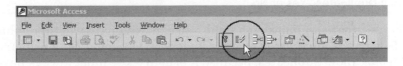

Figure 4-16 Database Design Toolbar, Index

A dialog box opens. In it, you can define indexes for the table. You can also create indexes on any of the existing fields in this table. Most fields can be indexed, but some data types (memo fields, hyperlink, and OLE Object fields) cannot. Note the circled primary key designation.

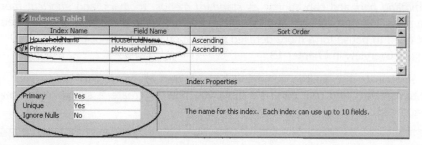

Figure 4-17 Index Dialog

Indexes, With and Without Duplicates

Indexes are another important and useful tool in Access. Briefly, Indexes are a feature that speeds up searches and sorts on tables. You create indexes on fields because you expect to search or sort on the data in them.

For example, the HouseholdName field is indexed because I anticipate sorting lists on that field in my database.

Primary keys are always indexed for the same reason.

Index Names

The Index dialog box allows you to select a field in your database and create an index for it. It also allows you to designate that field as the primary key for the table.

You can rename an index, but I recommend that you not rename the indexes in our tables until you have a little more experience and can anticipate and handle any consequences that might arise out of renaming indexes. Accept the defaults for now.

Allowing Duplicates—Yes or No

When you create an index on a field, you can designate whether values in that field can be duplicated or not. Obviously, you must set a primary key field to *not* allow duplicates, because a primary key must always have unique values in each record.

Other situations may call for setting this option to not allow duplicates. We've already discussed reasons for not using natural keys, such as social security numbers or employee IDs, as the primary key in a table. However, when you do include these values in your table, you want to ensure they are not duplicated.

Setting the Unique option to yes will handle this restriction at the table level. Only one instance of each Employee ID will be permitted in the table if the index for that field is set to prevent duplicates. Access will warn you about the duplication and prevent you from saving the duplicate record.

In other cases you will want to allow duplicate values in a field. So far in our table the only fields we have added are the primary key, pkHouseholdID, and HouseholdName. The pkHouseholdID primary key is set not to allow duplicates. However, because I have brothers, cousins, and nephews who share my last name, I must allow duplicates in HouseholdName in order to add them to the database.

Ignore or Allow Nulls

You can tell Access whether you want to permit null values in a field. You learned earlier that a null value occurs when you don't know what the value is yet. It does not mean the field has no value or that it isn't applicable. It just means you don't know what it is yet.

Again, you already know there can be no nulls in our primary key field, pkHouseholdID. In other cases, though, you might want to permit null values in order to facilitate data entry.

For example, my niece recently had a baby. I know the baby was born a few weeks ago because my brother, her grandfather, called me. However, I don't yet know the baby's name because my niece hasn't had a chance yet to let me know what it is. Therefore, to add the new baby to my family and friends database, I either have to allow null values for first names, or make up a fake first name for her. I don't know what her name is, but I do know she has one! That's a null value. In this case, the right approach is to allow null values for that field in that table.

So far we have one table with a primary key field and one other field in our table, so we'll revisit the null first name decision again later, when I tell you how I decided to handle it in the Person table.

Foreign Keys

Now that you know what a primary key is, what its purpose is, and how to create one, it should be much easier to understand *foreign* keys and to learn how to create them in your tables.

A foreign key is a field in one table that refers to the primary key field in another, related table. It indicates the two tables are related and helps us to define that relationship. As you might expect, we often refer to these as the primary and foreign tables.

Therefore, as we add additional tables to our database, we will need to include a HouseholdID field in those tables that are related to our household table.

Before we can add additional tables, we need to name and save our household table. Find the Save icon on the Database Design toolbar and click it.

Figure 4-18 Save the Table

This will open a dialog box, asking you for a name for your table. The default is Table1. Type in the name for the table, following this naming convention: prefix the name with "tbl" (all lower case) to indicate that it is a table and then add the full name of this table. Use a descriptive name that will immediately tell other users what the contents of the table are. Do not use abbreviations or acronyms for table names.

In our logical model, this is the entity called HOUSEHOLD, which is also a good choice for the physical table. Its name, then, is tblHousehold, with no spaces, upper and lower case for readability. Any database developer, seeing that name, will immediately know what kind of thing it is and something about its contents.

There it is, in Figure 4-19, your first Access table saved and ready for new data to be added. You can open it now to see what it looks like. Go ahead and click on the table to select it and then click Open. It will open to look like Figure 4-20.

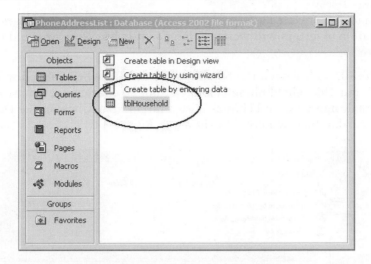

Figure 4-19 First Access Table Saved

Views

The view of the table shown in Figure 4-20 is called *datasheet view*. In datasheet view, you can see the table has a *column* for each *field* in the table (I have only pkHouseholdID and HouseholdName in this table so far.) It also has a *row* for each *record* in the table.

The little arrowhead icon at the left edge of the row, called a *record selector,* indicates which record currently *has the focus,* which is another way of saying this record is the one with which you are currently working.

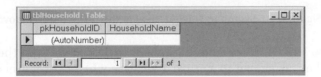

Figure 4-20 First Access Table Open

There are no records in the table yet, so there are no values in the primary key field or the HouseholdName field. The primary key field, pkHouseholdID, is set to AutoNumber, which is indicated by the default value for that field *(AutoNumber).*

Go ahead and enter your household name in your table. It will be the first record. Enter your own last name if you want, or you can use a compound name made up of your name and your spouse or partner's last name. Any combination of letters will work, as long as it is less than or equal to the field size.

If you recall, we accepted the 50-character default when we defined the field. If your Household name is longer than 50 characters, you can switch to design view and change it to a larger size. Click on the Design icon in the database window, as shown in Figure 4-21.

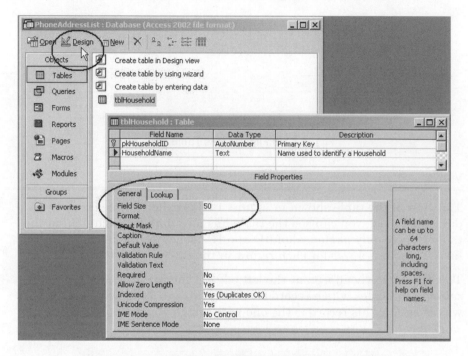

Figure 4-21 Switch to Design View in the Database Window

You can also switch views from datasheet to design view on the Database Design toolbar, as shown in Figure 4-22. Use whichever method you are more comfortable with. I have no preference and do it both ways.

By the way, Figure 4-22 tells you there are two other ways to view a table: PivotTable View and PivotChart View. These allow you to create views of your data similar to Pivot Tables and Pivot Charts in Excel. In this book, though, we'll be sticking mostly with design and datasheet views.

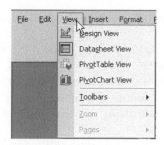

Figure 4-22 Design View—Database Design Menu

Okay, if you need to adjust the field size of HouseholdName to accommodate your own household, find the Field Size property (circled on the property sheet shown in Figure 4-21). Change it to a larger size, save the changes, and switch back to datasheet view.

The maximum size for a text field is 255 characters, more than enough for all but the most unusual of household names, I would think.

I decided to go with a compound name for my household, based on my last name and my wife's last name, Hepworth-Navarro. Typing in the name creates the first autonumber for the Household table.

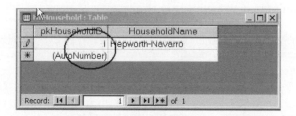

Figure 4-23 First Household Record with AutoNumber 1

We'll come back and make some changes and additions to this table, but for now, that will do. Close it as you would any other Window, by clicking on the Close button in the upper right hand corner. Let's move on and add our second table, the one that will hold address information for each of our households.

Add a Related Table

We have a choice of other tables to add next: persons, phone numbers, mail addresses, or email addresses. It doesn't really matter all that much. I decided I want to add the household address table next because it is the only one with a one-to-many relationship with tblHousehold.

> In the Database Window, click New or double-click on Create Table in Design View.

> Enter names for the fields based on the data model in Figure 3-4, following the naming conventions I described earlier.

> Select the proper data type and field sizes for your fields. Make sure the field size is large enough to accommodate the largest likely entry it will hold, but no larger than it needs to be. (Hint: Address and State fields).

> Click on the Save icon and give the table a name following the naming conventions you learned earlier.

Try your hand at creating your table first, before you look at my address table in Figure 4-24. Remember, you will need to include the attribute fields (address, city, etc.) as well as a foreign key field to relate this table to the main table.

I must warn you. The table in Figure 4-24 includes a field of a type I haven't yet told you about. See if you can figure out which one it is. I'll give you a hint. It is a foreign key field, but it doesn't link this table to the main table, tblHousehold. In fact, it will link the address table to a table we haven't even created yet.

I'm hoping you've learned enough already to understand what that field is, even if it isn't clear yet why it is there.

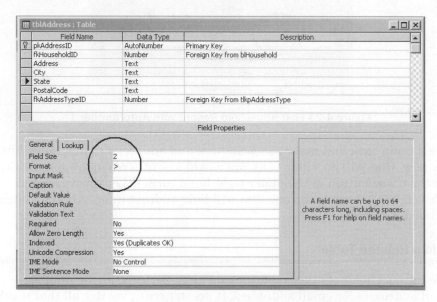

Figure 4-24 tblAddress

Figure 4-24 shows you the fields, in design view, I included in tblAddress. Did you use the same name, or a similar one, for your table? At the very least, did you remember to prefix "tbl" to it, omit spaces, and capitalize each word in the name?

Fields in tblAddress

These are the fields I included in my address table. Yours should include these fields as well.

Primary Key Field

The primary key field for this table, tblAddress, is pkAddressID. Did you remember to prefix "pk", which designates it as the primary key and to append ID, which shows it is a key field? Again, with no spaces and each word capitalized? It is an autonumber, indexed with no duplicates allowed. It is required (no nulls are allowed).

Foreign Key Field

The next field in this table, the one called fkHouseholdID, is the foreign key from tblHousehold. There is one subtle difference, which you may already have spotted, between its name in this table and its name in tblHousehold. Here I used the prefix "fk", meaning foreign key, instead of "pk".

Any developer seeing this field will realize it is a foreign key field from another table and that there is a relationship between this table and the other table, based on this table.

Foreign Keys like fkHousehold, which relate to autonumber primary keys, must also be long integers, but their data type is number, not AutoNumber.

Allow Duplicates in Foreign Key

The foreign key to tblHousehold is also indexed, but it is set to allow duplicates. It must allow duplicates because we have a one-to-many relationship between tblHousehold and tblAddress.

Each household can have *one or more* addresses. A household, for example, can have a street address and a P.O. Box. The household ID for that household must appear twice in tblAddress, once in the record for the street address and again with the record for the P.O. Box. Therefore, the index for fkHouseholdID must be set to permit duplicates.

Other Fields

The other fields in this table are named to reflect to their contents, following the naming conventions previously stated: Address, City, State, and PostalCode (one word, both names capitalized, no spaces). They are all text fields. In my personal contacts database, I changed the field size for Address to 150 characters from the 50-character default. I changed city to 75 characters, State to two characters and PostalCode to nine characters.

I changed these field sizes based on my estimate of what information each will hold. Addresses can be quite long; I wanted to be sure the field would be large enough to hold any likely address. State, on the other hand, will be the two-letter abbreviations used by the U.S. Postal Service.

Business Rules

Some of you may be wondering whether having a two-character field for state is going to be a problem. Remember, some of my family lives in another country. Forcing all State entries to conform to the U.S. Postal Service format means I may have to create abbreviations for states in that country. I made the decision based on my experience, which is that it will work for the country in which I'm interested. The business rule that applies to my situation means it will work. You may have to choose a different field size, depending on the business rule that applies in *your* situation.

Formatting

Figure 4-24 also illustrates how you can format a field. If you look closely at the Format property, circled in the illustration, you'll see the greater than symbol (>). To Access, this symbol means, "always display the contents of this field as capital letters." No matter how you type in the field (wa, Wa, WA, or wA), Access will always display in capitals letters (WA).

There are many other built-in formats in Access and you can create custom formats of your own. You'll see other formats as we create other fields in other tables.

Input Masks

In addition to formatting, you can also specify input masks for many fields. An input mask controls the values a user can enter into a field. For example, we've defined Postal Code as a text field, but we really only want the user to be able to enter digits (zero through nine) and the period

---

(-) character. The input mask allows us to specify the permissible characters for this field. See Figure 4-25.

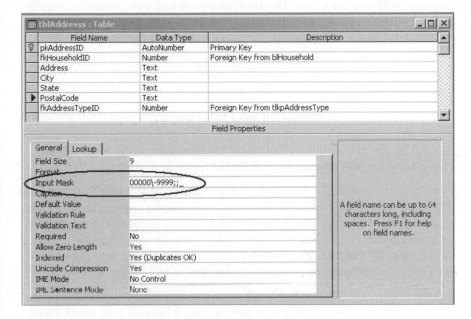

Figure 4-25 Input Mask for PostalCode

The input mask for U.S. Postal Service ZIP Codes is 00000\-9999;;_

This is what that input mask tells Access to do.

> The five zeros mean that five digits are *required*.
> The backslash (\ ) tells Access to *display* the next character "-" exactly as it appears in the input mask.
> The four nines in this mask mean that up to four digits can *optionally* be entered.

The semicolons separate two additional sections of the input mask. This input mask could be written as 00000\-9999;0;_, with a zero after the first semicolon and before the second. That would indicate to Access that it should store the literal character "-" as part of the data in the field. Leaving out that zero, as I did in my address table, tells Access to store the data *without* the literal character. We only display the dash to present the user the familiar "5 – 4" format. It is really redundant information. Therefore, to store it is a waste of space and not good database design, so I chose that option.

The final section of the input mask, after the second semicolon, tells Access to display the underscore for the space where you should type a character in the input mask. In other words, when you place the cursor in this field with the table is in datasheet view, it will display as in Figure 4-26. Your typing will replace the underscores with digits.

Figure 4-26 Input Mask Display

Table 4-1 summarizes the meanings of the three sections of this input mask with examples of data stored by each mask.

As you can see in Table 4-1, incorporating nines for the last four positions in the input mask will allow the user to enter partial extensions, which isn't desirable. However, the alternative is to use zeros and require the user either to enter the full nine-digit ZIP Code for everyone, or nothing for everyone. Of the two alternatives, the second is even less desirable. That's why the default input mask is the way it is.

Access provides you with other built-in input masks for phone numbers, social security numbers, dates and times, and a special password input mask. You can also construct your own input masks using the characters you just learned about, along with several others.

I'll show you how to use some of them in other fields and you can learn how to use others on your own. Input masks are very useful in controlling entries made by users both by giving them a guide to follow and by preventing inappropriate values from being entered.

Input Mask	Meaning	Display	Example(s) of Data Stored
00000\-9999;;_	Require 5 digits (no letters or other characters). Display a dash (-). Accept up to 4 additional digits. Do not save the dash with the record. Display the underscore (_) to indicate entry spaces.	_____-____	980436154 90843615 9804361 980435 98043

Input Mask	Meaning	Display	Example(s) of Data Stored
00000\- 0000;0;_	Require 5 digits. Display a dash. Require 4 digits. Save the dash with the record. Display the underscore.	_____-____	9804-6154
99999\- 9999;;*	Accept up to 5 digits. Display a dash. Accept up to four digits. Do not save the dash with the record. Display the asterisk to indicate entry spaces.	*****-****	980436154 90843615 9804361 980435 98043 9804 980 98 9

Table 4-1 Input Mask Samples

Foreign Key Field to a Lookup Table

The last field I added to tblAddress, fkAddressTypeID, is also a foreign key and is similar to the one that relates tblAddress to tblHousehold. This is the one I warned you about, the one you haven't seen before. It has the same format as the other foreign key I added. The prefix "fk" indicates it is a foreign key. The base name consists of two words that indicate what the field is. The ID suffix is found on all key fields. The table to which this foreign key refers is a *lookup table* called tlkpAddressType as in Figure 4-27.

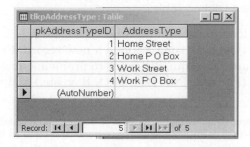

Figure 4-27 Address Type Lookup Table

I haven't created tlkpAddressType yet, but I'll do so now. I'll also explain how it differs from other types of tables and tell you why it is a very valuable little table. Figure 4-27 shows tlkpAddressType with four address types.

Lookup Tables

As you can see in Figure 4-27, a lookup table is essentially a list of values to which you want to refer, or look up, from time to time. You will recall in Chapter Three we referred to a group of acceptable values for an attribute as a *Domain*. In this case, our Address Type look up table lists the domain of acceptable address types—the types we are likely to encounter in the real world. It's much more limited than the domain of U.S. ZIP Codes, for example. There are more than 44,000 five-digit ZIP Codes, without counting all of the nine-digit codes[9].

At the moment, I can only think of four address types: home street, home P.O. Box, work street, and work P.O. Box. I don't know if I'll encounter or think up other types of addresses, so I'll start with these. If I need to add to the list, I can easily open the look up table and add a new type to the list.

Look again at tblAddress. The field in that table called fkAddressTypeID records the type of address for each record. Instead of the full text name, such as Home Street, it contains a foreign key that tells me what value in the look up table applies. If I enter a "1", for example, that record is identified as a Home Street address.

This gives me two big advantages. First, I don't have to type in the whole value each time I add a new address. That can cut down on typing errors. Second, I don't have to decide what to call it each time I add a new address. I simply refer to the values listed in the lookup table and select the foreign key for the one I want.

What if I Don't Have a Lookup Table?

If I didn't have a lookup table of address types, I would have to manually enter an address type each time I added a new record. From experience, I can tell you that approach quickly leads to problems, mostly because of variant spellings (PO Box, P.O. Box, P. O. Box, etc.) and random

---

[9] I actually have a sample database on my hard drive that has a lookup table of U.S. ZIP Codes and the cities to which they correspond. It isn't exactly what most of us think of when we talk about lookup tables, but it could certainly be useful in an application that was recording customer orders from all over the U.S., for example.

decisions about what to enter (home street address, home address, home st. addr., etc.). I would quickly lose control over the values allowed in the address type field.

It is not hard to imagine how much worse that problem would become in a database used by a travel agency, for example. Several different travel agents in an office, each making up their own values to enter into a free form text field for, say, names of airlines, would very quickly come up with a host of variations on airline names.

Validation Rules

There is an alternative method of validating entries built-in to Access. I'll quickly tell you about it and show you how to use it, but I'm sure you'll find lookup tables are much more flexible and easier to use in nearly every case. I occasionally use validation rules, but only in special circumstances.

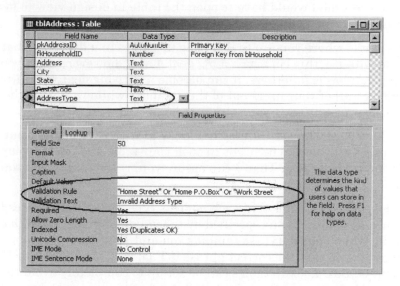

Figure 4-28 Validation Rule

Access allows you to specify *validation rules* for values for most fields. Figure 4-28 shows how you enter a validation rule for a field. Enter the acceptable values, surrounded by quotes, with the word OR between each value, no commas. After the validation rule is added to a field, the table will only accept values on that list for that field. If the user tries to enter any other value, the text you entered in the *Validation Text* property displays and the entry is prohibited.

Lookup Tables vs. Validation Rules

When do you want to use a lookup table, instead of the validation rule built into the table? The answer depends in part on whether you can be certain the list of items in the attribute's Domain is complete and unchanging. For example, in a field that stores a person's gender, there are two and only two values: *male* and *female*. These values are unlikely to change over time and it is very unlikely you'll ever want to add new values. A validation rule on this field would, therefore, work over the long haul.

Moreover, both male and female are familiar, short, and easy to spell words. You and I are unlikely to forget how to spell them or to forget what the acceptable values are.

On the other hand, my list of address types is only preliminary. I'm not sure I won't come across additional address types as I collect new addresses. If I do, I would have to open the table in design view to modify the validation rule and validation text.

At this stage, where you are first setting up tables in a database that only you will use, this isn't such a big deal. Later, however, when you are creating databases for others, it can become a very big deal. You either have to kick all of your users out of the database while you make the change, or wait until everyone else goes home and do it after hours.

Or worse, a user who may or may not know as much as you do about table design may decide he needs to open your table and modify your validation rules for you. That, I can assure you, is something you want to avoid.

A second consideration is that each address type consists of phrases that must be entered exactly as specified by the validation rule. It will become irritating when your database reminds you and your users for the umpteenth time that the correct phrase is P.O. Box, not PO Box or P O Box or P. O. Box. Lookup tables can be set up to completely avoid that problem. I'll show you how to do that with a list box or combo box when we start designing forms for data entry.

A third problem with validation rules can arise when a business rule changes. For example, right now the approved phrase is Home Street. Suppose, for the sake of argument, that after a couple of years you decide that you would prefer Household Street, reflecting the fact that your database tracks households, not homes.

How would you do that? You might think you'd just open the table and change the validation rule for all future entries. But what about all of the existing records that have Home Street in that field? You'd have to change them to conform to the new rule, but Access won't let you change them because of the existing validation rule.

First, you would have to remove the existing validation rule completely, then you would have to run an update query to change all of the values, and then you'd have to apply the new validation rule. As my mother likes to say, that's too much sugar for a cent.

With a lookup table, you only need to open it and change the value of that one field. That's it. You're done. A lot simpler, no?

Summary, Lookup Tables vs. Validation Rules

In short, while you do have the option of using the validation rule property to control input, a small lookup table is usually more flexible and effective in all but a few special cases.

Go ahead and add the tlkpAddressType table to your database. It will have two fields: a primary key called pkAddressTypeID and a name field. I set the index for the name field to Yes (No Duplicates).

Prefix the table name of the lookup table with "tlkp" rather than "tbl" to show it is a lookup table, rather than a data table. Name it for its content, AddressType and save the table in your database.

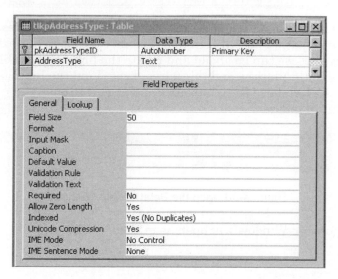

Figure 4-29 Design for Lookup Table

Now you can open it in datasheet view and add the four address types we've identified.

Lookup Fields

Some of you may be looking at Figure 4-29 and thinking, "Hey, what's that Lookup tab and why isn't he telling us about it?" The answer is that lookup fields in tables is one of those ideas that sounds good, but ends up being more trouble than it's worth. Lookup fields make it really easy to create bad table designs. Don't use them until you have mastered the principles of normalization and table relationships. There, you've been warned.

Can You Relate to This?

At this point, our personal contact database has three tables: tblHousehold, tblAddress, and tblAddressType. We know from our data model there is a one-to-many relationship between tblHousehold and tblAddress. We also know the fields that relate these two tables are pkHouseholdID in tblHousehold and fkHouseholdID in tblAddress. It's time to share that relationship information with Access.

Creating Relationships in the Relationship Window

Keeping in mind, though, that we are not through adding tables to this database and that we may still need to add more fields to our existing tables; however, we can go ahead and create the first relationships for tblHousehold, tblAddress, and tblAddressType. Find the Relationship button on the Database Design toolbar and click it to open the Relationship Window.

Figure 4-30 Open the Relationship Window

The Relationship Window will open as in Figure 4-31.

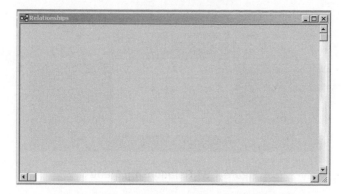

Figure 4-31 Blank Relationship Window

It should be blank at the moment. If you see tables with names like *MSysAccessStorage*, it means you didn't un-check the Hidden and System Objects options as I suggested. Please go back and do so now. These tables are system tables. You should *not* attempt to open or change them. It's better just not to see them at all.

You're ready now to add tables to the Relationship window so you can set up the relationships between them.

As usual, Access gives you at least three different to ways to do this.

1. Click on the Add Table button in the Relationship Toolbar (Figure 4-32).

2. Right-mouse click anywhere on the relationship window to open the relationship dialog box (Figure 4-33).

3. Click Relationships--> Add Table on the Relationship Menu. (Figure 4-34)

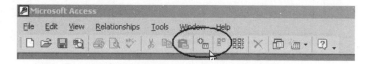

Figure 4-32 Add Relationship Button on the Toolbar

Figure 4-33 Relationship Dialog Box

Figure 4-34 Relationship Menu

Using the method you find most comfortable, open the dialog box to add the three tables in the database to the relationship window.

You can add tables to the Relationship window either by selecting them from the list and clicking Add, or by double-clicking on their names in the list. In the relationship window, they'll look like Figure 4-35

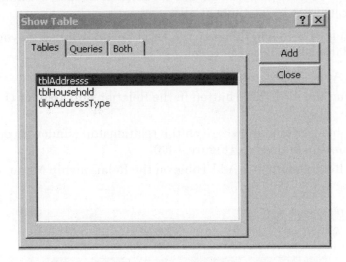

Figure 4-35 Add Tables to Relationship Window Dialog

You're ready to create the first relationship between two Access tables. As Figure 4-36 shows, the primary key in each table appears in bold, while the other fields are normal. The naming convention we choose, in which we attach the "fk" prefix to foreign keys, helps you to spot the foreign keys in each table.

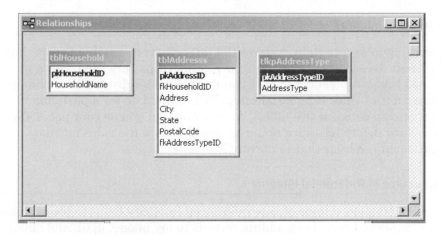

Figure 4-36 Unrelated Tables in the Relationship Window

Let's start with the primary key in tblHousehold and its corresponding foreign key in tblAddress. To tell Access we want to create a relationship between those tables using those keys, we simply drag-and-drop. Click on pkHouseholdID in tblHousehold. Hold down the mouse button and drag that field name over to fkHouseholdID in tblAddress. When you release the mouse button, a dialog box opens, asking you to further define the relationship. See Figure 4-37

Access recognizes that the relationship between the two selected fields is one-to-many, based on the data types and indexes on the fields. Access also offers to let you Enforce Referential Integrity.

Referential Integrity is another powerful tool in Access, so let's take a closer look at how it works.

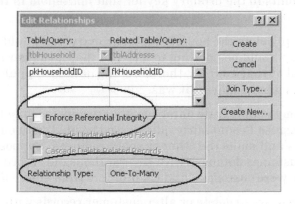

Figure 4-37 Define the Relationship

Referential Integrity

According to Access Help, "referential integrity is a system of rules that Microsoft Access uses to ensure that relationships between records in related tables are valid and that you don't accidentally delete or change related data." Once referential integrity is turned on for a particular relationship between two tables, Access won't let you or your users add, change, or delete records if doing so would violate the rules for that relationship. Why is that important?

Importance of Referential Integrity

Here's a simple example of how referential integrity helps to protect your data. Suppose I have been adding records to my phone, mail, and email database. So far I've added my own household, some of my friends, and my mother. I've also added one address for each of these households. Then, I realize I've added one couple twice—once under the husband's last name and once under the wife's last name because that's the way it was in the old paper-based address book.

In other words, I now have two households in the household table, each linked to an address in the household address table, when I should have only one household linked to both addresses. I need to delete the second household and change the household name for the other to reflect the correct household. I also need to re-link that second address to the correct household.

If I have enforced referential integrity on the relationship between these tables, however, Access won't let me delete the superfluous household name because I have already attached an address to it. The foreign key in that record points to the primary key for that household in the household table.

If I were able to delete the household, its primary key would be gone and the foreign key would be pointing to a record that no longer existed. When I looked at that address, therefore, the database would no longer be able tell me whose address it was.

Of course, in my simple little database, that wouldn't really be so much of a problem, because I could fairly quickly and easily figure out which address it was and make the other changes required. Suppose, however, this were a customer database with several thousand records and the related tables were customers and their orders from your company.

Allowing your users to delete or alter customer records without enforcing referential integrity could have some really disastrous consequences by "orphaning" sales orders, leaving you with no way to identify the customers who had placed them.

Referential Integrity Rules

The following rules apply when you use referential integrity for a relationship between a primary table and its related foreign table[10]:

1. Access will not allow you to enter a value in the foreign key field of the related table if that value doesn't already exist in the primary key field of the primary table.
   In other words, you must always enter the record on the one side of a relationship before you can enter a related record on the many side. (A household before a household address.)

2. Access will accept a Null value in the foreign key field, specifying that the record is unrelated to any record in the primary table.
   In other words, while you can't assign an order to a customer who doesn't exist, you can enter an order that is not assigned to anyone by entering a Null value in the fkCustomerID field.

3. Access won't allow you to delete a record from a primary table if related record(s) exist in a related table.
   In other words, you can't delete an employee record from the Employees table if there are orders assigned to the employee in the Orders table. (This rule can be over-ridden. See page 4-49.)

4. Access won't allow you to change a primary key value in the primary table if that record has related records in any other table.
   In other words, you can't change an employee's ID in the Employees table if there are orders assigned to that employee in the Orders table. (This rule can be over-ridden. See page 4-49.)

In order to enforce referential integrity between two tables, they must meet all of the following conditions:

> The matching field from the primary table must be a *primary key* or have a *unique index*. You can enforce referential integrity on a non-primary key field if it has an index that does not allow for duplicate values.

> The related fields must have the same data type. AutoNumber, an exception, can be related to a number field with a field size property setting of Long Integer.

---

[10] The following discussion is based on the Help file in Access.

> Both tables belong to the same Microsoft Access database. We haven't talked yet about *linked tables* and it is premature to discuss them now. Just remember that although Access lets you link, or connect, to data in Access databases, SQL Server databases, Excel spreadsheets, etc., you can't enforce referential integrity for linked tables.

Summary, Referential Integrity

Referential Integrity is one of a number of powerful tools Access provides to help you manage your data behind the scenes, so to speak. I recommend that you enforce referential integrity on every relationship you create. Doing so transfers responsibility for maintaining those relationships from you to Access, leaving you free to concentrate on other details.

Enforcing Referential Integrity

Go ahead and click on the check box to enforce referential integrity on this relationship (Figure 4-38). You have two other options when referential integrity is enforced: *Cascade Update Related Fields* and *Cascade Delete Related Records*. I've checked only Cascade Update Related Fields. First, let me explain what these options do, then I'll tell you why I selected one but not the other.

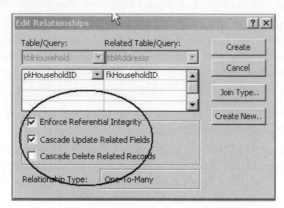

Figure 4-38 Referential Integrity Enforced

Cascade Update Related Fields

If this option is checked, the fourth rule of referential integrity (see page 4-47) is overridden. You *can* change a value in the primary key because cascading updates causes all corresponding records in the related table to be updated to the same value. Changes are cascaded from the primary table to the related table. Access handles the cascading changes for you, again behind the scenes.

Some database design purists argue that permitting cascading changes violates the principle that primary keys can't be changed. Technically, that is true; it does allow you to change an existing primary key. However, because the reason for not permitting changes in a primary key is to prevent records in related tables from being "orphaned" or linked to the wrong records in the primary table, cascading the change from the primary table through all related tables seems to me to be a permissible exception and one whose advantages make it worth employing.

Cascade Delete Related Records

If this option is checked, the third rule of referential integrity (see page 4-47) is overridden. You *can* delete a record from the primary table, the table on the one side of the one-to-many relationships. In addition, all corresponding records in the related table are also deleted. Deletions are cascaded from the primary table to the related table. Access handles the cascading deletes for you, again behind the scenes.

Access does show you a standard warning prior to deleting records, but I seldom, if ever, check this option. Since you don't see any of the related records prior to the deletion—only the primary table record—you don't have a chance to review those records before they are deleted. Once the records are deleted, they are gone. Maybe it's a case of being overly cautious, but I don't want to give Access *that* much control over my records.

Other Options

As you can see in Figure 4-38, there are other options you can set, primarily *Join Type.* Let's save a full discussion of join types for later, when you learn how to create queries to retrieve records from your tables. The default join type, which is called an *inner join,* is the only one you should use in creating table relationships anyway.

An inner join means Microsoft Access selects records from both tables only when the values in the joined fields are equal.

Click OK to save this relationship. Your relationship window should now look a lot like Figure 4-39

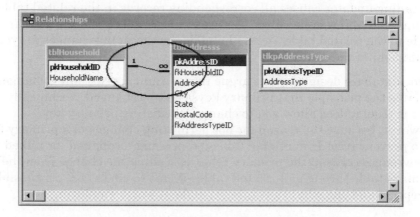

Figure 4-39 First One-to-Many Relationship in Place

Access places the "1" and the "∞" symbols on the line linking the two tables to indicate this is a one-to-many relationship.

Go ahead and create the relationship between tlkpAddressType and tblAddress, using the same drag-and-drop technique. Enforce referential integrity on the relationship and check the option to cascade updates.

Your relationships should now look like the ones in Figure 4-40

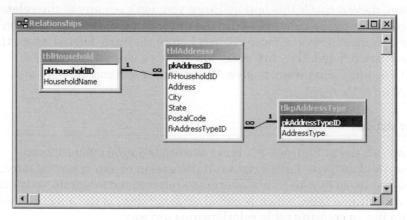

Figure 4-40 Relationships So Far

Taking Stock

You've accomplished a great deal so far in this chapter. Let's stop and take stock of what you have learned so far.

> ➤ How to create a new Access database and give it an appropriate name. You learned Access files have the extension *.mdb.

> ➤ How to set options in Access by setting dates to four-digit years and hiding system and hidden objects.

> ➤ Access usually offers more than one method for accomplishing most tasks, such as creating a new table. You created three new tables using the method I recommend, which is to create the table in design view.

> ➤ How to name tables and fields according to the standard naming convention used by most professional Access Developers. You used those conventions to create and name fields in your tables.

> ➤ About primary and foreign keys; you created them, using autonumbers for primary keys and long integers for foreign keys, for three tables. You gave your keys appropriate names, such as pkHouseholdID and fkHouseholdID, following the standard naming conventions for field names.

> ➤ About indexes, duplicating values, and permitting or prohibiting null values in fields. You learned when you should permit duplicates (foreign key fields, for example) and when you should not (primary keys fields, or natural keys, such as SSN or employee IDs, for example).

> ➤ About data types; you applied different data types to different fields in your tables.

> ➤ About formatting and input masks for fields; you applied them to fields in your tables.

> ➤ About lookup tables and validation rules and created a lookup table for your database. You learned when you might use a validation rule (a small, limited domain of values, such as male/female) and when you should use a lookup table (most cases).

> ➤ How to tell Access about the relationships between tables in your database by opening the relationship window and adding tables.

> ➤ How to create relationships between primary and foreign keys in your tables by using the drag-and-drop method.

> ➤ What referential integrity is and how to enforce it on your tables.

> ➤ What cascading updates and cascading deletes between tables means and how to apply cascading updates to your tables.

Take a quick break, then come back to review everything you've learned about data modeling and creating tables. Then try your hand at creating some additional tables to complete your personal contact database. In the next chapter, I'll show you my versions of those additional tables. And I'll also show you how to handle the third and final type of relationship you'll learn about in this book: many-to-many.

5. Try it Yourself—Create Tables

You've covered a lot of ground and learned a lot about Access even though you only have three tables in your first database so far. Creating those tables, tblHousehold, tblAddress, and tblAddressType, should have prepared you to create most of the remaining tables we need. Go ahead; try your hand at creating three more data tables:

> ➢ person
> ➢ phone number
> ➢ email

And three more lookup tables:

> ➢ one for relationship types
> ➢ one for email types
> ➢ one for phone number types

You'll also need one additional table of a type you haven't seen yet. It's called a *junction table* and it will help us handle the many-to-many relationship between households and persons. I'll show you how to create it.

I'll show you my versions of the additional data and lookup tables. However, I'd like you to try it yourself first. Create the tables, making sure you follow the naming conventions you've learned. Then, open the relationship window, add the new tables to it, and create the relationships between them. Don't forget to enforce referential integrity where it is required.

After you have tried your hand at creating these tables, come back to this chapter and compare your work to mine.

Figure 5-1 repeats the data model, to remind you what should be in each table.

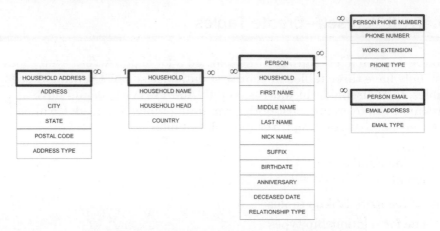

Figure 5-1 Phone Number, Mail and Email Data Model

Data and Look Up Tables

Here are the tables I added to my personal contact database. Yours should be very similar. I'll briefly explain what is in each table and show you the full relationship window with all of the tables in it. I'll start with the lookup tables, then show you the email and phone number tables, and save the person table for last.

Additional Look Up Tables

Figure 5-2 shows the Email Type lookup table in design view.

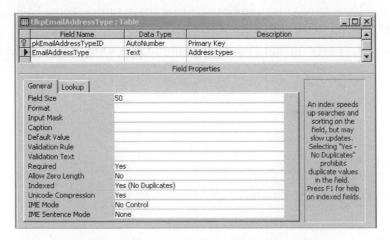

Figure 5-2 Email Type Lookup Table Design View

Figure 5-3 is the table with values in it. Those are my choices for email descriptions; they're the ones I think I will need. Because it is a lookup table, however, I can quickly and easily add new values if and when I need them. Your values may be different and you may have additional email types I didn't think of yet. The important point, of course, is that you can easily change any of the entries in it as you refine your descriptions, because they are in a lookup table.

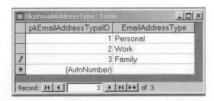

Figure 5-3 Email Type Lookup Table Datasheet View

The second table is the Phone Type lookup table.

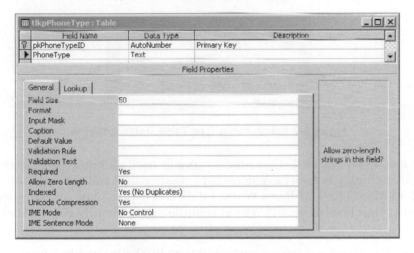

Figure 5-4 Phone Type Lookup Table Design View

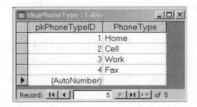

Figure 5-5 Phone Type Lookup Table Datasheet View

The third table is the Relationship Type table.

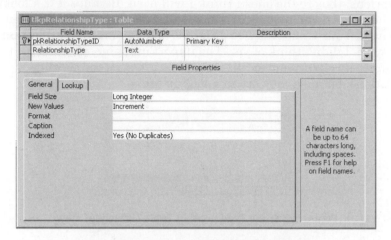

Figure 5-6 Relationship Type Table Design View

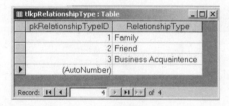

Figure 5-7 Relationship Type Table Datasheet View

You may have included other phone types or used different types than I did. One thing you may have done is to create email and phone types such as Mom's Cell, or Dad's Work. I didn't. Why don't you need to specify them at that level of detail? Why it is sufficient to identify Hone, Work, etc.

Remember, there is a one-to-many relationship between a person and the email addresses and phone numbers. If a cell phone, for example, is linked to Yolanda Hepworth, that tells me all I need to know about who will—or should— answer when I call that number.

If, on the other hand, I had chosen to create the relationship between *households* and email addresses and phone numbers, the additional phone types for Mom, Dad, and Kids would have been necessary because the link would have been to the Hepworth-Navarro household, not to any one person in that household. In order to call my brother's cell phone, for example, I would need to know which number in his household is his.

You may have thought of different types of relationships from the ones I used; I'm concerned only about friends, family and business acquaintances. This is a personal contact database. If you wanted to expand it for other purposes, you'd end up adding additional types of relationships to support it.

Additional Data Tables

You need data tables for phone numbers and email addresses. They are very similar to the address table you created in the previous chapter.

Phone Table

Figure 5-8 shows the phone table, tblPhone, in design view. It includes four fields:

> pkPhoneID — the primary key

> Phone — the actual phone number

> fkPhoneTypeID — foreign key from the phone type lookup table

> fkPersonID — foreign key from the person table

You can see the input mask for phone numbers. It restricts entry of new phone numbers to the pattern specified. Input masks consist of three sections, separated by the semicolon (;).

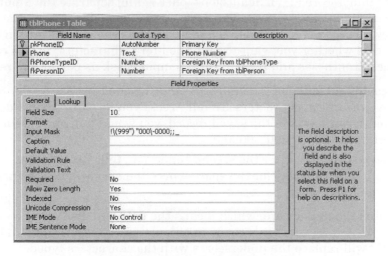

Figure 5-8 Phone Table Design View

Here's what the first section of this input mask says.

> The exclamation mark (!) tells Access to display the field from right to left, rather than from left to right. This is important in a phone number because the area code is optional. If you don't include an area code, the other characters will still format correctly from right-to-left.

> The backslash (\ ) tells Access to display the following character literally. It precedes the opening parenthesis (\( ) in the area code to tell Access to display it exactly as it appears.

> The three nines tell Access to allow either digits or nothing. Blanks entered into the field in those positions are removed when the record is saved. This allows you to omit the area code, if you don't want to enter it.

> The next characters are enclosed in quotes (") "), which tells Access to include them just as they appear (similar to the backslash for a single character).

> The three zeros (000) tell Access that three digits are required in this position.

> The backslash-hyphen combination (\–) tells Access to display the hyphen before the final four digits, which are also required (0000).

With this input mask in place, Access will only permit you to enter values that conform to these rules.

> The final three characters in the input mask are two semicolons and the underscore (;;_). Semicolons, once again, separate the input mask into three sections. The first one, which you just saw, describes how the field is to be entered and displayed. The second section tells Access whether you want to save the literal characters (in this case, the parentheses and hyphen) in the input mask as part of the record.

Leaving it blank, as I did here, or entering one tells Access *not* to save the literal characters. To tell Access you *do* want to include the literal characters in the saved record, you would put zero in that section: !\(999") "000\-0000;*0*;_

> The last section, after the second semicolon, tells Access what character to display for the space where the user will type a character in the input mask.

I used the underscore, which means the field will display (___) ___-____ when it is ready to accept new entries. Typing in this field will replace the underscores with the characters typed.

Figure 5-9 Phone Table Datasheet View

Figure 5-9 shows the phone table, ready to accept new entries for phone numbers.

Email Table

Figure 5-10 shows the email table in design view. It includes four fields.

> ➢ pkEmailAddressID — the primary key
> ➢ EmailAddress — the actual email address
> ➢ fkEmailAddressTypeID — foreign key from the email address type lookup table
> ➢ fkPersonID — foreign key from the person table

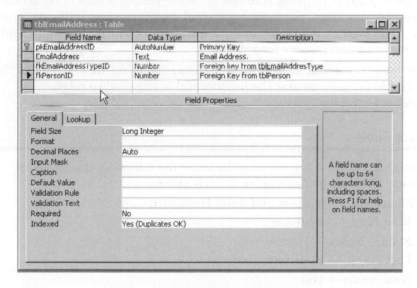

Figure 5-10 Email Table Design View

There isn't much new about this table. Do note, though, that field names follow the standard naming conventions as the other tables do.

Here's the email table in datasheet view, Figure 5-11.

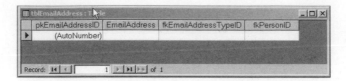

Figure 5-11 Email Table Datasheet View

Data Model and Table Design Trade-offs

The choices I just described about relationships between people, households, and email addresses and phone numbers illustrate and reinforce an important point I made earlier in this book.

Quite often there is more than one way to model the data required for a database; sometimes it is hard to choose between models because each model has advantages and disadvantages. However, all such choices result in trade-offs in the tables required to support the data, the fields required in those tables, and in the type of records in them.

Give yourself plenty of time during the analysis and design phase of your database projects to think through all of the consequences of each choice you make. Any time spent getting a solid design in place will save much more time later on when you are designing and creating the input and output forms and reports for your data.

Now, let's take a look at the two remaining tables for this database: the data table for persons and the junction table required to relate households and addresses.

Person Table

According to Figure 5-1, we need to know the following things about persons. I've included examples of each attribute.

- Household — William and June Hepworth
- First Name — William
- Middle Name — Henry
- Last Name — Hepworth
- Nick Name — Bill
- Suffix — Jr.
- Birth Date — 8/27/2001
- Anniversary — none
- Deceased Date — none
- Relationship Type — Family Member

To create the person table, you'll need a field for all of these attributes *except* Household (I'll explain why in a moment). You'll also need to add the primary key field, which, as you now know, will be an autonumber. In the person table, Relationship Type is a foreign key field.

Figure 5-12 shows the design view of the person table in my database. Yours should be the same, or very similar.

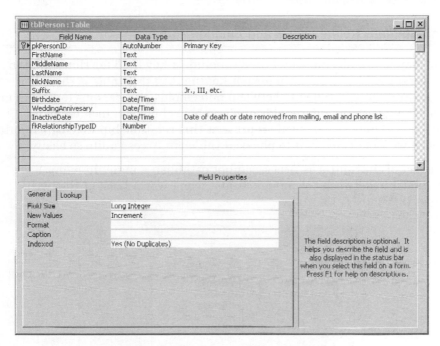

Figure 5-12 tblPerson in Design View

The primary key for tblPerson, pkPersonID, follows the naming conventions you've learned—"pk" prefix to identify it as the primary key and the ID suffix. Yours should also. Other field names, such as FirstName, also reflect the naming conventions you learned about.

Also, note that there is a foreign key field in the table for the relationship type, fkRelationshipTypeID. This foreign key is from one of the three new lookup tables you just created. It will contain the primary key field and the relationship type field.

Tweaking the Tables

In addition, you'll see I changed the name of the Deceased field in the data table to InactiveDate, which better reflects its purpose and meaning.

Although the idea for the field was prompted by consideration of what to do in the event of a death a family member, further consideration suggested a better, more widely applicable name for this field. You, too, will probably find yourself making refinements, or tweaks, like this to many of your databases. It just isn't possible to think of everything up front and a good database analyst is always asking himself if there is a better way to do something.

Many-to-Many Relationships and Junction Tables

You may be wondering why I didn't include a key field for Household in the person table. The reason for not having it in this table is there is a many-to-many relationship between households and persons (one person can belong to many households and one household can include many persons). While we can easily represent this relationship in a *logical* data model, we can't convert it to physical tables in Access quite so easily.

The fact of the matter is Access cannot establish a many-to-many relationship between two tables. It just won't work. Look at the two tables in Figure 5-13.

Figure 5-13 Many-to-Many Tables

You can't create a relationship between the primary key fields in these tables. Moreover, adding an *fkHouseholdID* to tblPerson would result in a one-to-many relationship; one household would have many persons, but each person would belong to only one household.

The opposite relationship would be established if you were to add the *fkPersonID* to tblHousehold. That would result in a one-to-many relationship with one person in many households, but each household would have only one person in it.

Many-to-many relationships require us to create the special type of table I mentioned earlier in this chapter. It is called a *junction* or *bridge table*.

A junction table resolves the many-to-many relationship between households and persons by replacing it with two separate one-to-many relationships. I'll show you how to create one now.

Junction tables consist of three fields, as shown in Figure 5-14:

> Primary key for the junction table

> Foreign key from table one (i.e. tblHousehold)

> Foreign key from table two (i.e. tblPerson)

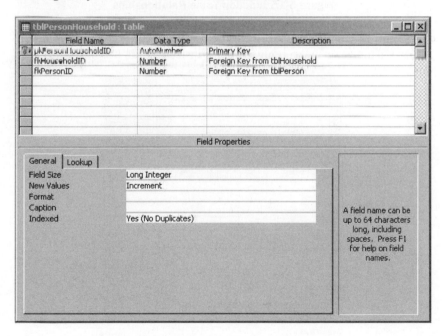

Figure 5-14 Junction Table: tblPersonHousehold

Figure 5-15 shows the relationship window, where I've set up the two relationships between the three tables involved. The junction table, tblPersonHousehold, sits between the other two tables and participates in one-to-many relationships with each.

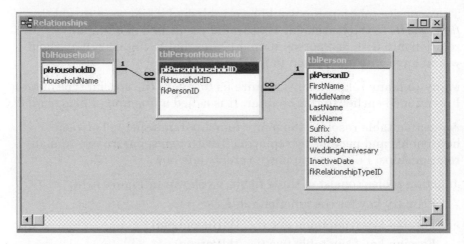

Figure 5-15 Junction Table Relationships

Each person in the person table can be added to the junction table together with one or more households. Figure 5-16 is an example.

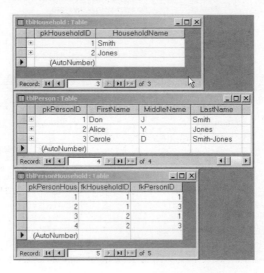

Figure 5-16 Many-to-Many Example

I added two sample households to my database for the purposes of this example: Smith and Jones. I also added three persons: Don J. Smith, Alice Y. Jones, and their daughter, Carole D. Smith-Jones. This is a typical divorced household with parents living in different households and a child or children belonging to both.

In the Household table, the primary key for the Smith household is "1" and for the Jones household, it is "2".

In the Person table, for Don Smith, the primary key is "1", for Alice Jones, it is "2" and for Carole Smith-Jones it is "3".

In tblPersonHousehold, the junction table that joins persons to households, the foreign key for the Smith household—1—appears twice, once for Don Smith (foreign key 1) and once for Carole Smith-Jones (foreign key 3). The foreign key for the Jones household—2—also appears twice, once for Alice Jones (foreign key 2) and once for Carole Smith-Jones (foreign key 3).

By the way, counting the number of times a foreign key appears in a junction table tells you how many related records there are in the other tables. Because Carole Smith-Jones is in two households, the foreign key for her appears twice in tblPersonHousehold. Because there are two members of the Smith household, the foreign key for it also appears twice. Because Don Smith and Alice Jones are members of only one household each, their foreign keys only appear once in tblPersonHousehold, and so on. You can take advantage of that fact for certain kinds of reporting.

While the actual design of a junction table is extremely simple—it consists of only three fields including its own primary key and two foreign keys—the concept is one that many new database developers can find a bit hard to grasp at first. If you are in that category, don't worry too much about it right now. We'll be revisiting the concept several more times throughout this book as we create forms, queries, and reports. You'll have plenty of opportunities to understand.

Household Head

With the person table in place and the many-to-many relationship between households and persons set up with the appropriate junction table, it's time to handle one last detail: designating a household head for each household. You may already have taken a stab at this based on the data model shown in Figure 5-1. I saved it for last because I wanted to get the household-person tables in place first.

One-to-One or One-to-Many Relationship

By definition, of course, a household can have only one head, but the relationship between persons and household heads can be set up either as a one-to-one or as a one-to-many relationship, depending on the business rule you choose.

First, you could say that each household can have one head and that each person can be the head of only one household. Or, you could say that each household can have one head, but that each person can be the head of more than one household.

It seems more appropriate to me to choose the former rather than the latter rule for head of household and that is what I will do here, but you should carefully consider this decision, just as you do for all such considerations in setting up your tables and relationships. If you think that a person can be the head of more than one household, you'll set up your table with a one-to-many relationship, instead of the one-to-one relationship I chose.

Figure 5-17 shows the household key field set up as a one-to-one relationship with tblPerson. It's named following the standard naming convention for field names, prefix (fk), root (HouseholdHead) and suffix (ID). It is also indexed and doesn't permit duplicates values, which is necessary to enforce the one-to-one relationship. In other words, each value for this field must be unique in this table, which means, in turn, that each person in the person table can be the head of only one household in the household table.

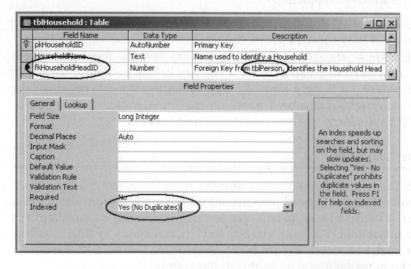

Figure 5-17 Household Head — One-to-One Relationship

Take a close look at the relationships in Figure 5-18.

**Figure 5-18 tblPerson with One-to-One and One-to-Many
Relationships**

Figure 5-18 shows that the primary key in tblPerson participates in two
relationships, one-to-one with tblHousehold and one-to-many with
tblPersonHousehold. The one-to-one relationship allows each person to be
the head of only one household. The one-to-many relationship allows each
person to be part of more than one household. This is one of the
infrequent cases where you'll find a one-to-one relationship between
tables.

The next step is to establish all of the remaining relationships between
tables.

Relationships

Now that you've created all of the tables for your database, it's time to
consider the relationships between them. You should already have taken
a stab at creating the relationships, but we also have discussed some of
the tables in more detail, particularly tblPerson and tblPersonHousehold.

Now is a good time to take another look at your relationships and make
any changes you think you need. Than come back and take a look at the
relationships in Figure 5-19 on the next page.

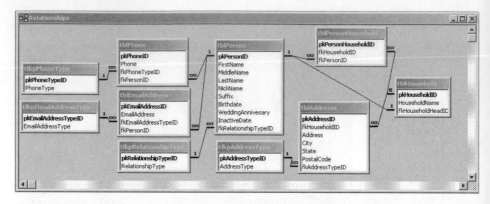

Figure 5-19 Personal Contact Database Relationships

Laid out like this, it is clear that tblPerson is really the main table in the database. That seems appropriate, because the purpose of the database is to handle contact information, mailing addresses, phone numbers, and email addresses for persons who are my friends and family.

TblPerson participates in one-to-many relationships with tblPhone, tblMailingAddress, and tblPersonHousehold. The primary key from tblPerson (pkPersonID) appears as the foreign key (fkPersonID) in each of those other tables.

It also participates in a one-to-one relationship with tblHousehold, where it is linked to fkHouseholdHeadID.

In addition, tblHousehold participates in one-to-many relationships with tblAddress and tblPersonHousehold. The primary key from tblHousehold (pkHouseholdID) appears as a foreign key in those related tables.

Finally, there are four lookup tables, tlkpPhoneType, tlkpAddressType, tlkpEmailAddresstype, and tlkpRelationshipType. Their respective primary keys are foreign keys in the related tables.

Figure 5-19 doesn't show it, but referential integrity is enforced for all of those relationships, as in Figure 5-20.

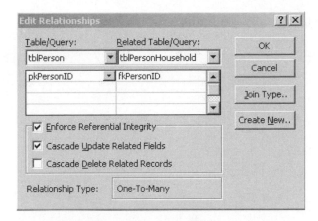

Figure 5-20 Referential Integrity Example

Wrapping Up The Table Design

That does it for the basic table design in your database. It now contains ten tables:

Five data tables

> tblPerson
> tblHousehold
> tblPhone
> tblAddress
> tblEmailAddress

Four lookup tables

> tlkpAddressType
> tlkpPhoneType
> tlkpEmailAddressType
> tlkpRelationshipType

And one junction table

> tblPersonHousehold

You have established the proper relationships between each of the tables in your database.

In the next chapter, we'll use these tables as the basis for a brief discussion of the rules of normalization. If you've created your tables as I've shown you, they will already be normalized, which makes them a good example from which to begin that discussion.

This page intentionally left blank.

6. Normalize Your Data

If you're new to database development, the term normalization is probably also new to you. By the end of this chapter, though, you'll be an expert on the subject (well, almost an expert). You *will* know what database normalization is and why it is important to you. And you will be able to apply the first three rules of normalization to your own databases.

> Because this is probably an initial introduction to normalization for most readers, I'm going to keep the discussion as informal as possible. In doing so, I realize that I may oversimplify things here and there, though I am confident that the discussion as a whole accurately conveys the important points made about normalization. In particular, I want you to understand the importance of eliminating redundancy from your databases, avoiding fields that do not contain the smallest meaningful values, and ensuring that each table in your database contains only related data.
>
> If you want to learn more, or study the formal theory of normalization, you'll find a list of references in Appendix A.

Why Normalization Matters

One rule of business is constant: Change happens. Building an Access database is, in that sense, an act of faith. You can be quite sure you will be called back to work on it when a change in business rules requires a change in your database to accommodate it. I'm sure of that happening because it's happened with virtually every database I've ever built or supported.

While normalization can't prevent the need to change your database, it can go a long ways toward making changes as straightforward, painless, and, from your customers' point of view, as inexpensive as possible.

Moreover, a properly normalized database works smoothly and efficiently with a minimum of maintenance. A non-normalized database is inefficient, inflexible, requires constant maintenance, and is hard to update. The small amount of time you spend normalizing your database will be returned many times over as you create forms, reports, and queries for data entry and reporting. Conversely, skipping over normalization will cost you many, many additional hours of time as you struggle to create or modify entry forms for new data and queries and reports to present information to your users.

Beyond that, non-normalized databases are typically so rigid that even a small change in your business rules can result in hours and hours of work to change tables, forms, reports, and queries. In one case, I was asked to create a new report for an existing database. It turned out that my predecessor, who had created the application, had not normalized the database (specifically, it violated the *first rule of normalization*, which you'll learn shortly) before launching it. After two years of service, one of the key business rules had changed, but users were unable to enter the new data for some records in some situations because of flaws in the table design. The company was unwilling to allocate the resources it would have taken to upgrade the database, so that data was simply not captured.

On the other hand, I was able to create the requested report, but only by creating a series of complex queries to sort and combine records for the report. I estimated that what took me eight to ten hours to do could have been accomplished in a couple of hours, at most, if the original database had been properly normalized to begin with. Multiply those extra six or eight hours by your hourly wage and you can see what the additional cost to your organization could be to create just one report from a poorly designed database.

The Goals of Normalization

Essentially, there are three goals of normalization. The first is to *eliminate redundant data*. The second is to ensure each field in each record contains the *smallest meaningful, or atomic, value*. The third is to ensure each table stores *only related data*.

Eliminating Redundant Data

Look back at the database you just built for address, phone numbers and email addresses for your personal contacts. We set up the address table so each address appears only once, even though several members of a household share that same address.

Rather than repeat, for example, 21922 48th Ave W for each member of the Hepworth family that lives at that address, we enter that address only once, in its own table. We then use the primary key for that record to link it to its household. Not only does that reduce storage requirements for the database, it also reduces the chance of error because you, or your users, don't have to retype the same address over and over again.

Selecting the Smallest Meaningful Values

Sorting and selecting records in your database requires selecting a value or values in which you are interested. For example, suppose you are preparing a list of mailing addresses from your database in order to send out your Christmas cards. Let's say you want to sort the list according to the state in which the addressees live. The address table you created in the previous chapter allows you to do that easily because there is a separate field for State.

On the other hand, if you had not followed good design practices and had therefore created a table with a single name field and a single address field containing street address, city, state, and ZIP code, as in Table 6-1, the task of selecting contacts by state would be quite complicated. How would you sort this table on "State" for example? A skilled developer who knows a lot about writing advanced *SQL Statements* could do it, but it wouldn't be pretty, trust me.

Name	Address
George Hepworth	21922 48th Ave W, Mountlake Terrace, WA 98043
Nancy Wilkerson	123 N. 321St S., Manassas, *VA* 20111

Table 6-1 Example of Fields with Non-Atomic Values

Storing Only Related Data

In the personal contact database you are building, there is one table for addresses, one for phone numbers, and one for email addresses. The phone table stores only data related to phones, the address table stores only data related to addresses, and the email table stores only data related to email addresses.

With the goals of eliminating redundancy, storing the smallest meaningful values in all fields, and storing only related values in a table, all good database designers take the task of normalizing their databases seriously.

The Rules of Normalization

First let's get some terminology out of the way. Database developers say a *database* is *normalized* if it meets the requirements of the rules of normalization. Another—perhaps more precise—way to say the same thing is to specify how many of the rules of normalization the database meets.

We may say, for example, a database is in Third Normal Form, which means its tables meet each of the first three rules of normalization. If the database is only in Second Normal Form, its tables only meet the first two rules, but not the third. The rules are cumulative, so if a database is in Third Normal Form, it is also in First and Second Normal Forms.

For a database to be fully normalized, of course, all of the tables in the database must be normalized. As you'll soon see, normalizing data usually calls for creating new tables and moving fields from one table to another, along with establishing the relationships among those tables.

It makes sense, therefore, to speak both of a normalized *database* and of normalized *relations in a database*. Sometimes database developers do refer to a normalized table or tables, but getting a table to third normal form nearly always requires other tables and their relationships to also be in third normal form; so, in practice, normalization is a database-wide process.

Finally, in most discussions of normalization, the terms table and relation are synonymous and interchangeable. In other words, to say a *relation* is in first normal form is the same as saying a *table* is in first normal form. I'll avoid mixing the terms in this discussion in order to keep down confusion, but when you decide to expand your knowledge by studying other sources, you'll run into both usages.

Cutting You Some Slack

Actually, there are five rules of normalization. As a practical matter, though, you only need to be concerned about the first three. It's not that fourth and fifth normal forms aren't important; it's just that for the kind of database you and I are most likely to build, they are a bit of overkill.

So, in the next few pages you'll learn the first three rules of normalization and how to use them to create flexible, powerful Access databases.

First Normal Form

Over the years, I've read a number of different definitions and explanations of First Normal Form, some very complex, some quite simple. Fortunately, the majority does agree on a couple of points; those are the points I'll emphasize here.

Smallest Meaningful Values

First Normal Form requires that the fields in your table should each contain the smallest meaningful (or atomic) value. I've already told you about the need for breaking values down into the smallest meaningful components.

It should be quite obvious why this makes your database more flexible and efficient. This requirement is usually, though not always, cited as part of the first rule of normalization. I consider it to be one of the most important goals of normalization.

No Repeating Groups

First Normal Form also requires that there should be no repeating groups. That immediately raises two questions, "What's a repeating group?" and "Why are repeating groups bad?" For a quick answer to both questions, open your sample database and look at the Phone table. It has four fields, or columns in it.

> pkPhoneID
> Phone
> fkPhoneTypeID
> fkPersonID

With data in it, tblPhone looks something like Table 6-2.

tblPhone			
pkPhoneID	Phone	fkPhoneTypeID	fkPersonID
1	(425) 697-5819	1	1
2	(425) 876-4444	2	1
3	(425) 876-9999	2	2

Table 6-2 tblPhone with Sample Data

In the previous chapters, I showed you how to create that table and determine what the fields in it are. You also know that the two foreign key fields are there to relate the table to another data table (tblPerson) and to a lookup table (tblPhoneType). Table 6-3 is an alternative to that table—one you should *not* emulate—to illustrate some of the problems that arise out of non-normalized tables.

Because you've already created the properly normalized versions of the tables, you should be able to quickly spot the difficulties with Table 6-3. Instead of foreign keys to the persons table relating Stan Walker to his phone number(s), I've repeated his name here, along with Sue Walker and Shirley Ugeste. I've also combined other fields to create *repeating groups*.

Phones		
Name	Phone	Phone Type
Sue Walker	(425) 999-5555, (206) 222-4444, (425) 555-1122	work, fax, mobile
Stan Walker	(425) 333-4343, (425) 999-3434	mobile, fax
Shirley Ugeste	(208) 444-4545	personal

Table 6-3 Repeating Groups Example One

Table 6-3 illustrates a couple of violations of the components of the First Normalization Rule.

First, the Name field does not contain the smallest meaningful values; it contains both first and last names. If you wanted to select from this table a list of phone numbers for everyone in the Walker Family, for example, how would you go about doing that? With both first and last names in the same field, your query would have to include some pretty sophisticated logic. Obviously, a table with first name and last name fields is much more efficient.

Second, both the Phone and Phone Type fields contain more than one value for both Sue and Stan Walker. Sue has three phone numbers, while Stan has two and Shirley has only one. There is no reliable way to determine which number is the work number, mobile number, or fax number for each. You might suggest the sequence within each field (i.e., the first value in the phone field corresponds to the first value in the phone type field), but can you really count on that?

Notice, for example, that the sequences for Stan and Sue Walker are reversed. Was that done on purpose or by accident? How would you decide? Obviously, you couldn't use sequence as a selection criteria in any case. It should also be quite obvious why the phone table you created for your personal contact database in the previous chapter is a much better design than this.

tbPerson				
pkPersonID	FirstName	LastName	Birthdate	fkRelationshipTypeID
1	John	Walker	10/10/1990	2
2	Mark	Hepworth	1/1/1980	1
3	Alice	Jones	1/1/1970	3

Table 6-4 Excerpt from tblPerson

Here's another example. Table 6-5 shows a non-normalized version of the person table in Table 6-4. (Note that Table 6-4 omits several fields to better fit the page.)

One of the fields in the person table is fkRelationshipType. It is the foreign key from the lookup table called tblRelationshipType and identifies the type of relationship I have with each person: family member, friend, or business acquaintance.

An alternative would have been to create a non-normalized table that looks something like Table 6-5. Instead of a single field for relationship type, there are fields for the three types of relationships we originally identified when we set up the table.

tblPersonNonNormal					
pkPersonID	FirstName	LastName	Family	Friend	BusinessAcquaintance
1	John	Walker		X	
2	Mark	Hepworth	X		
3	Alice	Jones			X

Table 6-5 Repeating Groups Example Two

Problems with Repeating Groups

There are several problems with tables like this. You should quickly spot some of them, while others might not be so obvious.

First, looking at Table 6-5, you can quickly identify the last three columns on the right (Family, Friend, and BusinessAcquaintance) as three types of personal relationships. That's partly because these are already familiar to you from the previous chapter and partly because this is a fairly common, and therefore obvious, kind of data.

However, consider what might happen if you were to open a table in an existing database and see the following fields. Fields like CPT1, CPT2, and CPT3 are usually referred to as *repeating groups* or *repeating fields*. And they are not a good design feature in a database.

tblAppeal			
CaseID	CPT1	CPT2	CPT3
1	20202	20203	20220
2	20203	20220	
3	20202	20203	

Table 6-6 Repeating Group Example with Obscure Field Captions

Not much here to tell you what is going on and, unless you are an expert in the subject matter behind the database, not much chance you'll be able to figure it out on your own. The similar names, CPT1, CPT2, and CPT3 do tell you this must be a *repeating group*; therefore, they each probably represent the same kind of data.

However, this table design also implies that each Case has three, and only three, CPT values. Does this mean Cases 2 and 3 are incomplete because they don't have CPT3 values? Or does it mean a case actually can have 1, 2, or 3 CPT codes associated with it? And what if you run across a case with 4 (or 5 or 6) CPT codes? Can that happen? If so, how would you enter the 4th, 5th, and 6th codes? Is this a problem with the table itself or with the business rules for CPTs? And how would you go about creating a report showing the most frequently used CPT Code?

Resolving these questions will involve at the very least a long, and probably uncomfortable, phone call to your subject matter expert. And that's time wasted on an unpleasant task that shouldn't even have come up in the first place.

Second, there are holes in both tables. It isn't clear from Table 6-5 itself whether family, friend, and business acquaintances are mutually exclusive choices. There are entries in only one column in each row, but that could have been a coincidence because the table actually allows for multiple choices for each record. John Walker is a friend, which means he isn't a family member or business acquaintance, but this version of the table would accept entries for a family member and business acquaintance as well. Is that desirable or not?

The lesson to be learned here is that non-normalized tables like this foster ambiguity, and ambiguity is seldom a good thing, especially in a database. To deal with it in your database, for example, you'd end up adding code to your input forms to control entries in this table; code that is unnecessary with a properly normalized table. So, unless you happen to really enjoy coding, normalize your tables first.

If the business rule that applies is that relationship types are mutually exclusive, then two of the three fields in John Walker's record should always be blank. Holes in a table are not just a waste of storage space, although that is a problem. Holes like this are usually a good indication you are looking at a non-normalized table, with all of the attendant problems that brings. If you see them, it is a good idea to take a closer look at the table design.

The third, and most serious, problem with both Table 6-5 and Table 6-6 is that you are stuck with three, and only three columns for the *repeating values*. You can't add a new relationship type to Table 6-5 or Table 6-6 without changing the structure of the table itself.

Suppose for example, you decide you want to add Parishioners, School Teachers, or Medical Providers as additional relationship types in your address, phone, and email database. The result of those changes will be several new fields in your table, additional holes in the data, plus changes to *all* of your forms, reports and queries that are based on the table. This would call for hours and hours of additional work that would not have been necessary in a table in first normal form.

As a general rule, altering a table by adding or changing fields in it is not a good thing because of the cascading changes it requires throughout the database. Like everything else, there are some exceptions, such as when you discover you've left out an important attribute of an entity.

However, if you find yourself thinking about adding a field, that should send up a large red flag that your table might not be normalized. And that means you need to re-analyze the whole structure of your tables.

Other Problems with Non-Normalized tables

Actually, there are additional, serious problems with tables like those in Table 6-5 and Table 6-6. Those problems won't appear until you start creating queries to produce reports, so I won't go into them here. Suffice it say a table that is not in first normal form is a source of endless complications and many hours of extra, unnecessary work.

First Normal Form Defined

You should now have a pretty good idea what first normal form is and why it is important to you. Let's take a closer look at some of the textbook definitions for first normal form. A table is said to satisfy the First Rule of Normalization, or to be in First Normal Form (often abbreviated as 1NF) if and only if each attribute of the table is atomic. In other words, to be in 1NF, each column in the table must contain only a single value and each row must contain the same columns. Another common way of stating the First Rule of Normalization is a *table shall contain no repeating groups.*

Some writers say putting a table into First Normal Form (1NF) requires you to eliminate duplicative columns (a.k.a. repeating groups) from the table. Eliminating repeating groups means you must create separate tables for each group of related data and identify each row in those tables with a unique primary key.

You Can Look It Up

Putting tables in first normal form requires creating new tables for repeated groups and moving them from the original table. As you already know, this also calls for the creation of primary and foreign keys to establish the relationships between tables.

Quite often, though not always, the tables that result from normalization are lookup tables—tables like tlkpPhoneType, tblAddressType, tlkpEmailAddresstype, and tlkpRelationshipType in our address, phone, and email database. You've successfully created these tables and you already learned about the practical advantage they offer. Now you also have a better understanding of the database theory behind them—they eliminate repeating groups.

Second Normal Form

As I've already told you, the rules of normalization are cumulative, so in order to be in Second Normal Form (2NF), a table must also be in First Normal Form. Beyond that, the second rule of normalization states each non-key attribute in the table must be functionally dependent upon the primary key. Before you starting rolling your eyes, take a look at the following examples of tables that *do* (Table 6-7) and *do not* (Table 6-8) meet this requirement. (I've omitted columns from the original address table to make the following examples fit on the page.)

tblAddress					
pkAddressID	fkHouseholdID	Address	City	State	PostalCode
1	1	21922 48th Ave W	Mountlake Terrace	WA	98043-
2	1	PO Box 45	Mountlake Terrace	WA	98043-

Table 6-7 Table in Second Normal Form

There are two key fields (one primary key and one foreign key) in the version of tblAddress shown in Table 6-7. There are also four non-key fields. To be in Second Normal Form, each of the four non-key fields must be functionally dependent on the primary key. The primary key, pkAddressID, is assigned to each unique address in tblAddress. Each of the four attributes in the table—address, city, state and postal code—is part of the address; that is, it is functionally dependent on the table's primary key. Now, look at the version of tblAddress in Table 6-8.

tblAddress						
pkAddress ID	fkHousehold ID	Household Name	Address	City	State	Postal Code
1	1	Hepworth	21922 48th Ave W	Mountlake Terrace	WA	98043
2	1	Hepworth	PO Box 45	Mountlake Terrace	WA	98043

Table 6-8 Table Not in Second Normal Form

Table 6-8 is not in Second Normal Form, because one non-key attribute (HouseholdName) is *not* dependent on the primary key (pkAddressID) for the table. Instead HouseholdName is dependent on fkHouseholdID, the foreign key from tblHousehold. In fact, you can easily see it's also a field from our sample table, tblHousehold.

Although Table 6-8 illustrates quite clearly the idea behind Second Normal Form, it is not a mistake most people would be likely to make because HouseholdName is so closely linked to fkHouseholdID; also, it's fairly obvious that it would duplicate information to have it repeated in this table.

Here's an example (Table 6-9) of a mistake that *is* common among novice Access developers. This table has a couple of different problems, including a non-key field, HouseholdHead, that is not functionally dependent on the primary key for the table.

New Access developers are more likely to create problem tables like Table 6-9 than they are Table 6-8, possibly because it looks and feels a bit more like a typical address book. Also, people who have worked with Excel spreadsheets tend to create Access tables like this because it looks a lot like the spreadsheets with which they are familiar. For this reason, modeling Access tables on Excel spreadsheets is seldom, if ever, a good idea.

tblAddress						
pkAddress ID	Household	Household Head	Address	City	State	Postal Code
1	Hepworth	George	21922 48th Ave W	Mountlake Terrace	WA	98043
2	Hepworth	George	P O Box 45	Mountlake Terrace	WA	98043
3	Johnson	Mark	10111 NE Blake	Wayan	ID	83285
4	Johnson	Mark	P O Box 12A	Wayan	ID	83285

Table 6-9 Table Not in Second Normal Form

The rule is that second normal form requires every non-key field in a table to be functionally dependent on the primary key. In Table 6-9, HouseholdHead is dependent on the Household, not on the address. Adding this field to the table doesn't add any information about the address itself.

Putting tables into second normal form usually requires fields like HouseholdHead to be moved to another table. In this case, it would be moved into our existing table, tblHousehold, as Table 6-10 shows.

tblHousehold		
pkHouseholdID	**HouseholdName**	**HouseholdHead**
1	Hepworth	George
2	Johnson	Mark

Table 6-10 tblHousehold with Household Head

This table is similar to, but not identical with our actual household table in which Household Head is a foreign key, not a text field; but otherwise, it illustrates how you go about putting your tables into second normal form by moving non-key fields that are not dependent on the primary key into another, more appropriate table.

The next step, as you now know, is to replace HouseholdHead with the appropriate foreign key from tblPerson.

Here's another look at the actual tables from our sample database, showing them in second normal form. Pay special attention to tblPerson. Does every non-key field in this table depend on the primary key?

tblPerson								
pkPersonID	**First Name**	**Middle Name**	**Last Name**	**Nick Name**	**Suffix**	**Birthdate**	**Wedding Anniversary**	**Inactive Date**	**fkRelationship ID**
1	George	Russell	Hepworth	Grover Park George		1/1/1901			1
2	Yolanda	Rosa	Hepworth			1/1/1902			1
3	Walter	Ray	Johnson			1/1/1903	1/1/1990		2
4	Annie	Marie	Johnson			1/1/1904	1/1/1990		3

Table 6-11 tblPerson Second Normal Form

tblHousehold		
pkHouseholdID	HouseholdName	fkHouseholdHeadID
1	Hepworth-Navarro	1
2	Johnson	2

Table 6-12 tblHousehold in Second Normal Form

tblAddress						
pkAddressID	fkHouseholdID	Address	City	State	Postal Code	fkAddressTypeID
1	1	21922 48th Ave W	Mountlake Terrace	WA	98043	1
2	1	P O Box 45	Mountlake terrace	WA	98043	2

Table 6-13 tblAddress Second Normal Form

Third Normal Form

Once your tables are in second normal form, it's time to consider the requirements of third normal form.

The third rule of normalization states that all attributes that are not dependent upon the primary key must be eliminated by creating an additional table and moving those attributes to it.

Let's go back and look at the table in Table 6-13 to see what that tells us about this table. Is it in third normal form? Is every attribute in the table (address, city, state, and postal code) dependent only on the primary key? The correct answer is they are not. City and state depend on the postal code. In other words, for a given postal code, you can determine the corresponding city and state by using a lookup table. Granted, that table would be very large indeed.

As you may recall, I have such a table with well over 44,000 entries for US ZIP Codes. Adding postal codes for Canada, the United Kingdom, and other countries would add many thousands more. Placing tblAddress in Third Normal Form, however, would require you to add the table containing the city, state, and Postal Code pairings to the database and to remove the city and state fields from tblAddress.

pkAddressID	fkHouseholdID	Address	fkPostalCodeID	fkAddressTypeID
tblAddress				
1	1	21922 48th Ave W	1	1
2	1	P O Box 45	1	2
3	2	10111 NE Blake	4	1
4	2	P O Box 12A	4	2

Table 6-14 tblAddress Third Normal Form

pkPostalCodeID	City	State	Postal Code
tlkpPostalCodes			
1	Mountlake Terrace	WA	98043
2	Phoenix	AZ	85040
3	Monroe	WA	98272
4	Wayan	ID	83285

Table 6-15 tlkpPostalCodes

Know When to Say When

Together, Table 6-13, Table 6-14, and Table 6-15 form a good example of the old saying that sometimes it's good to know when to break the rules. A database purist might well insist that, because Table 6-13 isn't in third normal form, it should be changed to the design in Table 6-14 and Table 6-15. A more practical person might well argue the added benefits gained by normalizing this particular table in this particular situation are outweighed by the additional complexity required to manage the relationships.

I usually come down in the latter camp when it comes to addresses, especially in a relatively small database like this one. I would not normally go to the trouble of placing an address table in third normal form in a situation like this.

However, that isn't always the case. For example, if this were a customer database for a large on-line retailer, doing tens of thousands of transactions a day for customers throughout the United States, I might well go in the opposite direction on the assumption that recording addresses for tens of thousands of customers justifies a more efficient, properly normalized database in which the names of cities and states are recorded only once in a postal code lookup table like the one in Table 6-15.

Here's another example, one where I would insist on moving the data into third normal form. This example comes from a project-tracking database where different projects were assigned to project managers.

tblProjectManager			
pkProjectID	ProjectTitle	Manager	ManagerPhone
1	EDI Rejects	George	(425) 697-5819
2	Contact Management	Allan	(206) 555-1212
3	School Attendance	George	(425) 697-5819
4	Licenses and Permits	David	(425) 888-1111

Table 6-16 tblProjectManager not in Third Normal Form

The manager's phone number is not dependent on the project; it is dependent on the manager. The solution is to move that field to another table as in Table 6-17 and Table 6-18.

tblProjectManager		
pkProjectID	ProjectTitle	pkManagerID
1	EDI Rejects	1
2	Contact Management	2
3	School Attendance	1
4	Licenses and Permits	3

Table 6-17 tblProject Manager Third Normal Form

Table 6-17 shows the result of applying third normal form to the project manager table. The phone number field is gone. I've also converted the Manager field to the appropriate foreign key field from the manager table. Table 6-18 shows the result of moving the phone number field to the proper table, tblManager.

tblManager			
pkManagerID	FirstName	LastName	ManagerPhone
1	George	Hepworth	(425) 697-5819
2	Allan	Hepworth	(206) 555-1212
3	David	Hepworth	(425) 888-1111

Table 6-18 tblManager Moving to Third Normal Form

Note that tblManager is based on the assumption that each project manager has one and only one phone number. If that is not the appropriate business rule, you would add a separate table for manager phone numbers with a one-to-many relationship, much like the phone table in our sample personal contact database.

Summary—The Normalization Process

You've now studied the first three rules of normalization and seen examples of tables that do and do not conform to those rules. This rather informal discussion is really only a jumping off point for you. For example, I didn't even touch on the fourth and fifth rules of normalization.

As you move from building simple, single-user Access databases to enterprise-level databases, you'll need to learn and apply those rules as well. However, I am sure you are now better prepared to create and normalize your databases. Now, go ahead and try your hand at normalizing the following table as an exercise.

This page intentionally left blank.

7. Try It Yourself—Normalization

Here's a table that might have been created by a database novice to track sales for a small mail order business. It looks like it was originally an Excel spreadsheet. In fact, the business originally did use a spreadsheet for this purpose. The business owner decided the spreadsheet had become too unwieldy and imported it into Access. That's actually a fairly common progression for databases like this.

Your task is to apply the first three rules of normalization to this table and create the appropriate normalized tables and relationships. You'll need to add primary and foreign keys to the tables you create. I've retained only five records to serve as examples for this exercise.

Create a new database. Give it a name that makes sense to you (perhaps CatalogSales or SalesDatabase).

The table, shown in Table 7-1 is called Catalog Sales. Using the fields and records in Table 7-1, create new tables for your database by applying the rules of normalization. When you're done, compare your solution to mine to see how close you came. Be forewarned, though, this is a bit more complex than the address, phone number, and email list database we created for our first example.

> I had to show the records in Table 7-1 as *columns* and the fields as *rows* in order to fit the table to the format of the pages in this book; it may be a bit confusing at first because it is oriented oppositely from previous examples. Otherwise, Table 7-1 contains all of the fields in the database in one large table. Take a few moments to study the table layout to be sure you understand it before starting the normalization exercise.

It should take you an hour or two to work through this exercise; tackle it when you're fresh and have enough time to devote to it.

Start by identifying all of the entities represented (such as customers and salespersons). Don't forget entities can be concrete (as in items sold) or abstract (as in sales transactions).

As you identify the entities and the attributes that belong with them, think about the various tables you'll need to represent them. Follow the rules of normalization you learned in the previous chapter to help you decide which tables you'll need and why.

When you split out fields to create new tables, don't forget to add primary and foreign key fields to link the resulting tables together.

Follow standard naming conventions for creating both table and field names. You may want to choose different names from those in Table 7-1. Pick names that are meaningful to you, but avoid acronyms and abbreviations.

Finally, this exercise is a step up in complexity from the previous sample database you created, so you may find yourself struggling a bit here and there. It's all part of the learning process and shouldn't discourage you at this point.

Check back here for help if you get stuck. I'll give you my solution, along with an explanation of how and why I arrived at that solution later in this chapter.

Catalog Sales					
Order Number	1001	1002	1003	1004	1005
Date	8/1/2003	8/2/2003	8/3/2003	8/4/2003	8/5/2003
Customer	J. B. Bennington	Carlos Reyes	Andy Graham	Carlos Reyes	Ivan Wallace
Customer Address	123 N 321st St, Seattle WA 98111	321 N 123rd Street, Seattle, WA 98133	111 W 22nd Ave, Seattle, WA 98122	321 n 123, Seattle, WA 98133	P O Box 1202, Seattle, WA 98111
Shipping Address	same	321 N 123rd St, Seattle, WA 98133	109 W 22nd Ave, Seattle, WA 98122	Same as street	222 E 11th Ave, Seattle, WA 98112
Order Date	8/1/2003	8/2/2003	8/3/2003	8/4/2003	8/5/2003
Shipping date	8/4/2003	8/5/2003	8/6/2003	8/7/2003	8/8/2003
Salesperson	Danny	June	June	Walt	Danny
Item One	AX1000	AX2000	AX2000	AX1000	DX1000
Item One Price	$29.99	$49.99	$49.99	$29.99	$39.99
Item One Quantity	2	3	1	1	1
Item One Total Cost	$59.98	$149.97	$49.99	$29.99	$39.99
Item Two	AX2000		DX1000	DX1000	
Item Two Price	$49.99		$39.99	$39.99	
Item Two Quantity	1		2	3	
Item Two Total Cost	$49.99		$79.98	$119.97	
Item Three	DX1000				
Item Three Price	$39.99				
Item Three Quantity	1				
Item Three Total Cost	$39.99				
Order Subtotal	$149.96	$149.97	$129.97	$149.96	$39.99
Sales Tax Rate	8.9%	8.9%	8.6%	8.9%	8.9%
Sales Tax	$13.35	$13.35	$11.18	$13.35	$3.56
Order Total	$163.31	$163.32	$141.15	$163.31	$43.55

Table 7-1 Catalog Sales Table

Figure 7-1 is the relationship diagram for the normalized tables I created from Table 7-1. These tables represent the entities involved in a catalog sale along with the supporting lookup tables.

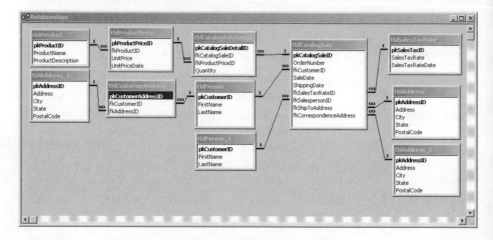

Figure 7-1 Catalog Sales Tables

Steps to Normalization

What follows is, in general, the sequence I followed in creating and normalizing these tables. You may have gone about it from a different direction. That doesn't matter as long as you arrive at a similar solution with similar, if not identical tables and relationships.

Actually, as you'll see in the following discussion, the procedure I followed wasn't as direct as it might have been had I followed a strict path through the rules of normalization. Because I was working from an existing table, with numerous design problems, there were points where it was impractical to move all of the tables to first or second normal form before addressing other issues.

Standard Naming Conventions

First, I renamed the main table to conform to standard naming conventions. I called it, tblCatalogSale. I could also have called it tblSale, or tblOrder, both of which are fairly common names for tables like this. In fact, order tracking is a fairly common database function and one you're likely to find useful.

Before I started the normalization process, I went through each table and converted the existing names according to standard naming conventions.

As you read the rest of this discussion, you'll see standard names applied to all of the tables and fields in the database along the way. I am going to assume, from this point forward in this chapter, you'll always use standard names and that I don't need to point them out to you.

First Normal Form

Next, as I worked my way through the fields in this table, I started looking for the two things First Normal Form requires: (1) All fields must represent the smallest meaningful values and (2) there must be no repeating groups.

Repeating Groups

The first things I spotted were the repeating groups representing items sold and their price. These include Item One, Item One Price, Item One Quantity, Item One Total Cost, Item Two, and so forth. First Normal Form says repeating groups should be moved to their own table, so that was the first change I made.

I created tblCatalogSaleDetail and moved the detail items to it. This left an interim table that looked something like Table 7-2. I called it tblCatalogSaleDetail because it contains the repeating details for each sale while the main table, tblCatalogSale, retains other attributes related to each catalog sale. For example, order 1001 consists of three items, AX1000, AX2000, and DX1000, which are the details for the order.

Once that table was set up, I was able to delete the repeating groups—a total of twelve fields—from the original table, tblCatalogSale.

tblCatalogSaleDetail (interim)				
Order Number	Item	ItemPrice	Item Quantity	ItemTotalCost
1001	AX1000	$29.99	2	$59.98
1001	AX2000	$49.99	1	$49.99
1001	DX1000	$39.99	1	$39.99
1002	AX2000	$49.99	3	$149.97
1003	AX2000	$49.99	1	$49.99
1003	DX1000	$39.99	2	$79.98
1004	AX1000	$29.99	1	$29.99
1004	DX1000	$39.99	3	119.97
1005	DX1000	$39.99	1	$39.99

Table 7-2 Interim Version tblCatalogSaleDetail

Primary and Foreign Keys

Next, I decided I didn't want to use Order Number (a natural key) as a primary key, so I added a new primary key field, pkCatalogSaleID, to the catalog sale table. I used it as a foreign key field, fkCatalogSaleID, in the catalog sale detail table. The primary key, pkCatalogSaleID, is an autonumber whereas fkCatalogSaleID is a long integer number. Access automatically created the primary key values for the existing records in tblCatalogSale; I manually added them to the appropriate foreign key field in tblCatalogSaleDetail.

The result was something like Table 7-3. That's all we'll do with this table for now, but we'll revisit it again in applying second and third normal forms.

tblCatalogSaleDetail (interim)						
pkCatalogSale DetailID	fkCatalog SaleID	Order Number	Item	Item Price	Item Quantity	Item Total Cost
1	1	1001	AX1000	$29.99	2	$59.98
2	1	1001	AX2000	$49.99	1	$49.99
3	1	1001	DX1000	$39.99	1	$39.99
4	2	1002	AX2000	$49.99	3	$149.97
5	3	1003	AX2000	$49.99	1	$49.99
6	3	1003	DX1000	$39.99	2	$79.98
7	4	1004	AX1000	$29.99	1	$29.99
8	4	1004	DX1000	$39.99	3	119.97
9	5	1005	DX1000	$39.99	1	$39.99

Table 7-3 tblCatalogSaleDetail with Primary and Foreign Keys

The next step was to repeat the process with the Customer field, which also didn't have the smallest meaningful data in it. The table again had repeating values (Carlos Reyes appeared twice) that were not foreign keys to another table. The solution, as you know, was to create a new customer table, move the customer field(s) to it, and create the foreign key field for customer ID in tblCatalogSale.

tblCustomer		
pkCustomerID	FirstName	LastName
1	J. B.	Bennington
2	Carlos	Reyes
3	Andy	Graham
4	Ivan	Wallace

Table 7-4 tblCustomer

I then repeated the process with the Salesperson field, creating tblEmployee and moving the salespersons to it. I used a more general name for the table because a catalog company would probably have other, non-sales employees who might need to be included in the employee table at some point. It doesn't hurt to set the database up to anticipate future needs and I didn't lose anything by renaming the table to tblEmployee, since all salespersons are also employees.

tblEmployee			
pkEmployeeID	EmployeeID	FirstName	LastName
1		Danny	
2		June	
3		Walt	

Table 7-5 tblEmployee

At this point it dawned on me that both customer and employee tables have the fields for first and last name. And that meant I'd overlooked an important fact about *people*. Customers and employees are both people. In fact, I can think of other people in whom this retail store would also be interested, suppliers' representatives, for example.

So, it looked as though I should have a person table, just as we had in the personal contacts database. I gave some thought to creating a lookup table to record the status of people in my person table (for example, Customer or SalesPerson), but I decided that wasn't necessary, as you can see in Table 7-7.

This is looking ahead a little bit, but you can see in Table 7-7 that we had two people-related foreign keys, fkCustomerID and fkSalesPersonID. These fields take care of status for each person in a transaction.

Also, notice in Table 7-6 that moving customers and employees into one table meant I had to create different primary keys for customers.

tblPerson			
pkPersonID	PersonID	FirstName	LastName
1		Danny	
2		June	
3		Walt	
4		J.B.	Bennington
5		Carlos	Reyes
6		Andy	Graham
7		Ivan	Wallace

Table 7-6 tblPerson

Also note, I inserted a field in tblPerson for PersonID, which could either be an employee or a customer ID, and also one for last name, even though I don't know the values for those fields for our salespersons right now. I am quite sure I will need those values at some point, even though the original spreadsheet didn't include them. Of course, it may turn out that this is a small company that doesn't use employee IDs or track customers by a customer ID, but I would prefer to come back and remove an unneeded field later, rather than add one I'd overlooked.

Next, I removed the salesperson field from tblCatalogSale and replaced it with the foreign key from tblPerson. I decided to call the field fkSalesPersonID, because it is intended to identify the person who closed the sale, even though it is the foreign key from tblPeson. You may choose to call it fkEmployeeID instead. It's possible to make a case for either choice.

Status Determined by Relationship

You can now also see why we don't really need a separate status table for people. Both fkCustomerID and fkSalesPersonID in tblCatalogSale are linked to pkPersonID in tblPerson.

Because one person can be both a customer and a salesperson, even in the same transaction, we only need to enter that person's primary key in the appropriate foreign key field or fields to indicate their status for that particular transaction.

Status, in other words, is not a *permanent* attribute of a person. Status depends on the person's role in a specific transaction and will change from time to time. The relationship between tables is enough to fully account for it.

Also, because we can manage the relationship between persons and their role in any given transaction by recording their primary key in the transaction, we can do away with separate tables for employees and customers, reducing the complexity of the database by a small, but significant, amount.

Address Table

After I removed the repeating groups and added the primary and foreign keys for customers and salespersons, tblCatalogSale looked like Table 7-7.

tblCatalogSale					
pkCatalogSaleID	1	2	3	4	5
Order Number	1001	1002	1003	1004	1005
Date	8/1/2003	8/2/2003	8/3/2003	8/4/2003	8/5/2003
fkCustomerID	4	5	6	5	7
CustomerAddress	123 N 321st St, Seattle WA 98111	321 N 123rd Street, Seattle, WA 98133	111 W 22nd Ave, Seattle, WA 98122	321 n 123, Seattle, WA 98133	P O Box 1202, Seattle, WA 98111
ShippingAddress	Same	321 N 123rd St, Seattle, WA 98133	109 W 22nd Ave, Seattle, WA 98122	Same as street	222 E 11th Ave, Seattle, WA 98112
SaleDate	8/1/2003	8/2/2003	8/3/2003	8/4/2003	8/5/2003
ShippingDate	8/4/2003	8/5/2003	8/6/2003	8/7/2003	8/8/2003
fkSalesPersonID	1	2	2	3	1
OrderSubtotal	$149.96	$149.97	$129.97	$149.96	$39.99
SalesTaxRate	8.9%	8.9%	8.6%	8.9%	8.9%
SalesTax	$13.35	$13.35	$11.18	$13.35	$3.56
OrderTotal	$163.31	$163.32	$141.15	$163.31	$43.55

Table 7-7 tblCatalogSale After Removing one Repeating Group

Table 7-7 still had a repeating group: Customer Address and Shipping Address. First normal form requires that I move these fields to a new table. Also, these fields are not atomic; that is, they don't have the smallest meaningful values in them.

When I moved them to the new table, which I called tblAddress, I also split the values out into the appropriate attribute fields: address, city, state, and postal code.

Table 7-8 shows the resulting address table in first normal form.

tblAddress				
pkAddressID	Address	City	State	PostalCode
1	123 N. 321st St	Seattle	WA	98111
2	109 W 22nd	Seattle	WA	98133
3	111 W 22nd Ave	Seattle	WA	98122
4	P O Box 1202	Seattle	WA	98111
5	321 N 123rd St	Seattle	WA	98122
6	222 E 11th Ave	Seattle	WA	98112

Table 7-8 tblAddress in First Normal Form

Selecting a Table Design

The addresses in Table 7-8 are a mix of mailing and shipping addresses for customers. One option at this point would have been to create a lookup table for address types and identify each address in tblAddress as one or the other.

However, a customer could change his or her mind about where future orders are to be delivered. In other words, the customer could have one order shipped to address one and the next order shipped to address two. So, rather than designate a particular address *itself* as shipping or mailing, I decided to make that designation part of the order table (that is, the catalog sale).

For each order in tblCatalogSale, therefore, there is one foreign key to indicate the shipping address for that order and another foreign key to designate the mailing address for any paperwork associated with the order. Table 7-9 shows the result of that step. Later, when I show you how I set up relationships for these tables, I'll discuss this step in more detail.

tblCatalogSale					
pkCatalogSaleID	1	2	3	4	5
Order Number	1001	1002	1003	1004	1005
Date	8/1/2003	8/2/2003	8/3/2003	8/4/2003	8/5/2003
fkCustomerID	4	5	6	5	7
fkMailingAddressID	1	5	3	5	4
fkShippingAddressID	1	5	2	5	6
SaleDate	8/1/2003	8/2/2003	8/3/2003	8/4/2003	8/5/2003
ShippingDate	8/4/2003	8/5/2003	8/6/2003	8/7/2003	8/8/2003
fkSalesPersonID	1	2	2	3	1
OrderSubtotal	$149.96	$149.97	$129.97	$149.96	$39.99
SalesTaxRate	8.9%	8.9%	8.6%	8.9%	8.9%
SalesTax	$13.35	$13.35	$11.18	$13.35	$3.56
OrderTotal	$163.31	$163.32	$141.15	$163.31	$43.55

Table 7-9 tblCatalogSale with Foreign Keys for Shipping and Mailing

I made additional changes in tblCatalogSale as I moved through the other rules of normalization. In particular, there were fields in Table 7-9 that I removed because they were not dependent on the primary key for the table.

Second Normal Form

Second Normal Form states a table should not contain any non-key fields are not functionally dependent on the table's primary key. The most recent version of tblCatalogSaleDetail, shown in Table 7-3, has a candidate field—Order Number. Order number is determined not by the primary key for tblCatalogSaleDetail, but by the foreign key from tblCatalogSale. Placing the table in Second Normal form requires eliminating that field, as shown in Table 7-10.

tblCatalogSaleDetail					
pkCatalogSale DetailID	fkCatalog SaleID	Item	Item Price	Item Quantity	Item Total Cost
1	1	AX1000	$29.99	2	$59.98
2	1	AX2000	$49.99	1	$49.99
3	1	DX1000	$39.99	1	$39.99
4	2	AX2000	$49.99	3	$149.97
5	3	AX2000	$49.99	1	$49.99
6	3	DX1000	$39.99	2	$79.98
7	4	AX1000	$29.99	1	$29.99
8	4	DX1000	$39.99	3	119.97
9	5	DX1000	$39.99	1	$39.99

Table 7-10 tblCatalogSaleDetail Partial Second Normal Form

I noticed that the Item is another natural key and that Item Price really depends on the value of that field rather than the primary key. To correct this problem, I needed to add a new table for the items sold. I decided to call it tblProduct, rather than tblItem, and created it to look like Table 7-11. I hope you also saw the need for this table, or one very much like it.

tblProduct			
pkProductID	ProductName	ProductDescription	UnitPrice
1	AX1000	Universal Control Adapter, Single Channel	$29.99
2	AX2000	Universal Control Adapter, Dual Channel	$49.99
3	DX1000	Field Monitor, Hand Held	$39.99

Table 7-11 tblProduct

As you can see in Figure 7-1, I made another change to the product table after this. The second rule of normalization tells us to eliminate fields whose value is not dependent on the primary key. There is a field in Table 7-11 that is only partially depend on the product, although it may not be obvious at first glance. That field is Unit Price. Here's what I did to resolve that problem and why.

Calculated Fields

As we all know, prices do change, usually increasing. Therefore, unit price depends both on the product and *the date of the sale*. Storing the unit price for a product as part of the product detail would create a static price for it, one that doesn't reflect the time dependency. Therefore, the database must allow for price changes and it must do so as easily as possible. One option, which might occur to some novices, would be to add a new record to the table with the new price each time it changes. That would look like Table 7-12.

tblProduct			
pkProductID	ProductName	ProductDescription	UnitPrice
1	AX1000	Universal Control Adapter, Single Channel	$25.99
2	AX2000	Universal Control Adapter, Dual Channel	$49.99
3	DX1000	Field Monitor, Hand Held	$39.99
4	*AX1000*	*Universal Control Adapter, Single Channel*	*$29.99*

Table 7-12 tblProduct—Poor Design with Duplicate Product Data

This solves one problem by creating another. Product AX1000 is duplicated, along with its description in the table. Eliminating redundant data is one of the goals of normalization, so this is obviously heading in the wrong direction.

Another option might be to simply change the price field each time a price changes. That avoids duplicating data, but at the expense of historical data. Once the current price replaces the prior price, there is no reliable way to know what it was previously.

That might not appear to be a problem at first—the product table is used to generate new orders—but the value of the database as a historical tool would be compromised. Moreover, it wouldn't address the fact that prices do depend in part on the date of a sale.

The solution, shown in Table 7-13, is to create a new table: tblProductPrice. The price for each product is listed, along with the date that price became effective. Product 1 for example, was priced at $25.99 from January 1, 2002 until July 1, 2003, at which point the price changed to $29.99. This allows us to remove the price field from tblProduct, removing the partial dependency and placing it in second normal form. It also creates a history of price changes.

tblProductPrice			
pkProductPriceID	fkProductID	UnitPrice	UnitPriceDate
1	1	$25.99	1/1/2002
2	2	$49.99	1/1/2002
3	3	$39.99	1/1/2002
4	1	$29.99	7/1/2003

Table 7-13 tblProductPrice

tblProduct		
pkProductID	ProductName	ProductDescription
1	AX1000	Universal Control Adapter, Single Channel
2	AX2000	Universal Control Adapter, Dual Channel
3	DX1000	Field Monitor, Hand Held

Table 7-14 tblProduct Second Normal Form

Now tblCatalogSaleDetail can refer to the foreign key from tblProductPrice rather than to the natural key, as in Table 7-15.

Why the foreign key from tblProductPrice rather than tblProduct? Remember, the *sale* price is the unit price for a particular product as *of the date of the sale*. That value can only come from tblProductPrice. Because the foreign key in tblProductPrice tells us which product it is, we can trace back to the product itself through this table.

The next field to be removed from tblCatalogSaleDetail is UnitPrice. Why? Because it is functionally dependent on fkProductPriceID, not pkCatalogDetailID. In other words, sale price is determined by the unit price for the product at the time of the sale—information stored in tblProductPrice and not needed again in this table.

tblCatalogSaleDetail				
pkCatalogSale DetailID	fkCatalog SaleID	fkProduct PriceID	Item Quantity	Item Total Cost
1	1	4	2	$59.98
2	1	2	1	$49.99
3	1	3	1	$39.99
4	2	2	3	$149.97
5	3	2	1	$49.99
6	3	3	2	$79.98
7	4	4	1	$29.99
8	4	3	3	119.97
9	5	3	1	$39.99

Table 7-15 tblCatalogSaleDetail with Foreign Product Key

The next new table I created was tblSalesTaxRate, which is based on the same logic as tblProductPrice.

tblSalesTaxRate		
pkSalesTaxRateID	SalesTaxRate	SalesTaxRateDate
1	8.6%	9/1/2000
2	8.9%	10/1/2002

Table 7-16 tblSalesTaxRate

I also replaced the sales tax rate in tblCatalogSale with the appropriate foreign key from tblSalesTaxRate. We only need one sales tax rate because it is the same for all sales. It is related to tblCatalogSale because the same sales tax rate applies to the entire order. Fortunately, in this example, there is only one sales tax rate to account for. If we needed to account for different sales tax rates for different locales, the tables would be correspondingly more complicated.

Taking Stock

You've made a lot of progress already, but there is more work to do on the new tables we've created. Let's pause to take stock of the changes so far. At this point, the tables and the fields in the database include:

- ➢ tblCatalogSale
  - pkCatalogSaleID
  - OrderNumber
  - Date
  - fkCustomerID
  - fkMailingAddressID
  - fkShippingAddressID
  - SaleDate
  - ShippingDate
  - fkSalespersonID
  - OrderSubtotal
  - fkSalesTaxRate
  - SalesTax
  - OrderTotal
- ➢ tblCatalogSaleDetail
  - pkCatalogSaleDetailID
  - fkCatalogSaleID
  - fkProductPriceID
  - ItemQuantity
  - ItemTotalCost
- ➢ tblProduct
  - pkProductID
  - ProductName
  - ProductDescription
- ➢ tblProductPrice
  - pkProductPriceID
  - fkProductID
  - UnitPrice
  - UnitPriceDate

- ➤ tblAddress
  - pkAddressID
  - Address
  - City
  - State
  - PostalCode
- ➤ tblPerson
  - pkPersonID
  - PersonID
  - FirstName
  - LastName
- ➤ tblSalesTaxRate
  - pkSalestaxRateID
  - SalesTaxRate
  - SalesTaxRateDate

These tables are in second normal form and ready for further normalization. Third Normal Form is next.

Third Normal Form

The third rule of normalization tells us to eliminate all attributes that are not dependent on the primary key. I can see both tblCatalogSale and tblCatalogSaleDetail still have fields that violate this rule. I hope you spotted them as well, both because they are not completely obvious and also because they represent another very common kind of error beginning Access developers often make. If you've already identified them, you're well on the way to designing good Access databases.

I'm referring to the *calculated* sales tax, subtotal, and total fields:

- ➤ tblCatalogSale
  - Order Subtotal
  - Sales Tax
  - Order Total
- ➤ tblCatalogSaleDetail
  - Item Total Cost

Calculated Fields

These four fields are all *calculated* by multiplying the value in one field (such as the unit cost for an item) by another (for example, the order quantity, or number of items ordered). They do not depend, therefore, on the primary key for the table itself, but on the value of the other non-key attributes in the table. Not only that, but storing both the calculated field and the fields that are used to calculate it creates redundant data.

The third rule of normalization tells us to eliminate such fields. Previously, you saw that we usually do that by moving the fields to a new table. This time, you will take advantage of the fact that you can have Access perform that basic math calculation (in this case, price * quantity) whenever you need it.

That means you can eliminate *calculated fields* like this one completely from the database. Anytime you need to display the calculated value in a report, for example, you can recalculate it from the other fields. Therefore I removed these fields, but didn't move them to another table at all. Later we will discuss how to put those calculations back into sales reports or forms if necessary.

Then I noticed there that were three date fields: Date, SaleDate, and ShippingDate. It appeared that Date was a redundant field, duplicating SaleDate, so I removed it next, leaving only SaleDate and ShippingDate.

After I removed the calculated and redundant fields, tblCatalogSale looked like Table 7-17.

tblCatalogSale					
pkCatalogSaleID	1	2	3	4	5
OrderNumber	1001	1002	1003	1004	1005
fkCustomerID	4	5	6	5	7
fkMailingAddressID	1	5	3	5	4
fkShippingAddressID	1	5	2	5	6
SaleDate	8/1/2003	8/2/2003	8/3/2003	8/4/2003	8/5/2003
ShippingDate	8/4/2003	8/5/2003	8/6/2003	8/7/2003	8/8/2003
fkSalepersonID	1	2	2	3	1
fkSalesTaxRateID	2	2	2	2	2

Table 7-17 tblCatalogSale Third Normal Form

At this point, tblCatalogSale was in third normal form. There were no repeating fields, all fields had the smallest meaningful value, and there were no redundant values. All of the non-key values were functionally dependent on the primary key and all values were dependent on the primary key.

Table Characteristics—tblCatalogSale

> *pkCatalogSaleID* is the primary key field for the table and is an autonumber. OrderNumber is the natural key, which is assigned to all orders, and is the external, real-world value that users of the database will see and use to lookup catalog sales. We don't know at this point how the order number will be generated, of course. We only know that it is there and that it must be stored in the table.

> *fkCustomerID* is a foreign key from tblPerson and identifies the person who made the purchase. fkSalesPersonID is also a foreign key from tblPerson and identifies the employee who completed the sale. A person can be an employee or a customer or both; therefore, the field in this table (frkCustomerID or fkSalesPersonID) to which his or her primary key is linked determines that person's *status for a given transaction.*

> *fkMailingAddressID* and *fkShippingAddress* key are both foreign keys to tblAddress. SaleDate is the date the sale is recorded in the database and ShippingDate is the date the order is scheduled to ship. Both are date fields.

> *fkSalesTaxRateID* is a foreign key from tblSalesTaxRate and identifies the sales tax rate in effect at the time of the sale.

> All of the foreign keys are long integers, linking to autonumber primary keys in other tables.

> *tblCatalogSaleDetail* is not quite in third normal form. It has one field—ItemTotalCost—that is a calculated field; it depends not on the primary key but on the values of ItemPrice and ItemQuantity. To move this table to third normal form, we remove the calculated field, as shown in Table 7-18.

tblCatalogSaleDetail			
pkCatalogSale DetailID	fkCatalog SaleID	fkProduct PriceID	Item Quantity
1	1	4	2
2	1	2	1
3	1	3	1
4	2	2	3
5	3	2	1
6	3	3	2
7	4	4	1
8	4	3	3
9	5	3	1

Table 7-18 tblCatologSaleDetail Third Normal Form

Of the remaining tables in the database, all were in third normal form at this point, except for tblAddress. The data in the table suggested it could be moved to third normal form by creating a postal code table, as discussed in the previous chapter.

tblAddress				
pkAddressID	Address	City	State	PostalCode
1	123 N. 321st St	Seattle	WA	98111
2	109 W 22nd	Seattle	WA	98133
3	111 W 22nd Ave	Seattle	WA	98122
4	P O Box 1202	Seattle	WA	98111
5	321 N 123rd St	Seattle	WA	98122
6	222 E 11th Ave	Seattle	WA	98112

Table 7-19 tblAddress Not in Third Normal Form

I decided not to do that, but as you can see from the repeated values for city and state, you could just as easily come to the opposite decision.

Throw in a Junction Table

The last table I created for this database came at the end of the normalization process, when I was thinking about how I would use this database.

In creating the shipping and mailing address foreign keys for the catalog sale table, I was focusing on the relationships between each order and the address(es) associated with it. But it also occurred to me I might want to use this same database for another, related, purpose: creating a mailing list for the catalog.

For that reason, I decided to create a junction table, tblCustomerAddress, to make creating the mailing list easier. It's a junction table with foreign keys from tblPerson and tblAddress.

tblPersonAddress		
pkCustomerAddressID	fkPersonID	fkAddressID
1	4	1
2	5	5
3	6	2
4	6	3
5	7	4
6	7	6

Table 7-20 tblCustomerAddress New Junction Table

Because customers and addresses are related through the catalog sale table, I really didn't *have* to have an additional customer address table, but it would definitely make creating mailing lists easier.

I would not have expected most novice Access developers to handle addresses the way I did in this exercise. I would have expected them to include CustomerID as a foreign key in tblAddress, along with an AddressTypeID for shipping and mailing addresses, as in Table 7-21.

That doesn't mean they would be wrong, only that it was a little easier to identify and set it up that way without a lot of experience with Access; moreover, that is what I showed you in the previous chapters.

		Alternate tblAddress				
pkAddress ID	fkCustomer ID	Address	City	State	Postal Code	fkAddress TypeID
1	4	123 N. 321st St	Seattle	WA	98111	1
2	6	109 W 22nd Ave	Seattle	WA	98122	2
3	6	111 W 22nd Ave	Seattle	WA	98122	1
4	7	P O Box 1202	Seattle	WA	98111	1
5	5	321 N 123rd St	Seattle	WA	98133	2
6	7	222 E 11th Ave	Seattle	WA	98112	2

Table 7-21 Alternate tblAddress

The problem in this particular database, as previously described, is that some addresses are actually both shipping and mailing addresses, while others are one or the other. Table 7-21 doesn't accurately reflect that fact, as it designates each address as one or the other. The junction table gives us more flexibility.

Just as we discovered for customers and salespersons, the status (shipping versus mailing) of an address is determined by its role in a particular transaction. It isn't a permanent attribute of the address itself.

Creating the Relationships

After I created and normalized all of the required tables, I opened the relationship window and established the relationships between tables. Figure 7-2 shows the full set of relationships again. Before you study more it closely, revise the tables in your database to match mine, open the relationships window and create the relationships between tables in your database. Make sure you enforce referential integrity wherever possible. Then take a look at Figure 7-2.

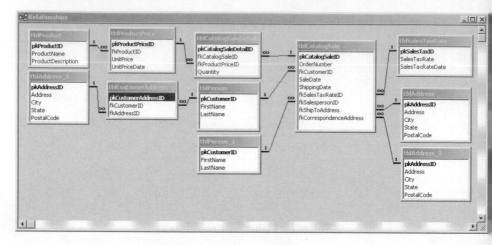

Figure 7-2 Table Relationships

First, let's just run quickly through the relationships and then take a closer look at the address relationships.

> *tblCatalogSale* is the central table. It has a one-to-many relationship with tblCatalogSaleDetail—each sale has one or more product details associated with it. Together, these tables contain the core data for all catalog sales. All of the other tables directly or indirectly link to tblCatalogSale via one or more relationships.

> *tblProduct* has a one-to-many relationship with tblProductPrice— each product has one or more prices associated with it. Product prices are dependent in part on the effective date of the price, which is stored in tblProductPrice. There is a one-to-many relationship between tblProductPrice and tblCatalogSaleDetail; each product/price combination can be included in many sales transactions.

> *tblPerson* has two one-to-many relationships with tblCatalogSale. Each employee (salesperson) can close one or more catalog sales (fkSalespersonID). Each customer can place one or more catalog sale orders (fkCustomerID). We have two copies of the person table in the relationship window, even though is only one table, to make it easier to see the relationships.

> *tblSalesTaxRate* has a one-to-many relationship with tblCatalogSale. Each sales tax rate applies to one or more catalog sales. This sales tax rate table assumes there is only one rate in effect at any point in time. If there were different concurrent sales tax rates, as would be the case for a business with multiple locations in different states, the

---

table would be more complex. Of course, many other aspects of the database would also be more complex.

Address Table Relationships

The address table relationships in this database are a little more advanced than the ones you've seen so far, but once I explain what I did with them, I'm sure you'll quickly get the idea.

I created one table for all addresses, tblAddress. It is only in second normal form, partly because it seemed to me to add an unnecessary level of complexity in an already complex situation. I also didn't want to include foreign keys from other tables in it because it already participates in three one-to-many relationships with other tables. Enough complexity already!

As I already described, the foreign key to tblAddress is found twice in tblCatalogSale, once as the shipping address and once as the mailing address for that order. It wasn't necessary to do so, but I added three copies of tblAddress to the relationship window so I could show these relationships a little more clearly. You'll see that in Figure 7-2.

In addition to the relationships with the catalog sale table, tblAddress is also related to the junction table called tblCustomerAddress. I added this third relationship in order to facilitate a mailing list independent of any existing catalog sales. tblCustomerAddress is a typical junction table with two foreign keys, one from tblCustomer and one from tblAddress. You learned how to create them in the previous chapter.

The Bonus Factor

Note that, because tblCustomerAddress *does not depend on an existing catalog sale* to connect a customer with an address, the direct customer to address relationship also allows us to record *potential* customers and their addresses along with existing customers. While it is admittedly a bit more complex to have three relationships on the address table, the result is a much more powerful, flexible, and useful database.

We're All Normal Here

That's it. You've accomplished a great deal so far and I hope you've learned something along the way. You have created two sets of normalized tables.

Don't worry too much if your first attempt at normalizing a database took a little longer than you thought it would, or if you didn't come up with exactly the same tables and relationships I did. In fact, apart from the time I spent writing about the normalization process, it took me more than an hour to analyze and make the necessary changes, and I changed my mind a couple of times, particularly with regard to the best way to handle addresses. And I came up with the exercise in the first place!

If this was your first attempt at normalization and it took you a couple of hours to do it, that's pretty good. Congratulate yourself, take a short break and get ready to move on. In the next chapter we'll start designing forms so you can enter data into your brand new tables. The example we'll use in Chapter 8 is the personal contact database you created for addresses, phone numbers and email addresses.

Backup, Backup, Backup

This would be an excellent time to make a backup copy of the database. I'm going to assume you know how to use Windows Explorer to make copies of files.

Close your database, find it on your hard drive and make a copy in a safe place. It should be called PersonalContacts.mdb or something similar. Do that now.

Then get ready to add some new records.

8. Getting Data Into Your Database—Simple Forms

In this chapter and the next two, I'm going to show you how to add new records to your database. We'll use the personal contact database you created in Chapter 5. To refresh your memory, the tables in that database look like this in the relationship window.

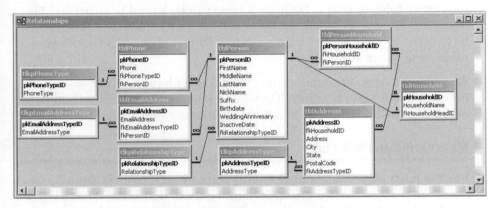

Figure 8-1 Personal Contact Database Relationships

Forms, the Primary Data Input Tool

The Access tool we use to add records to tables is called a *form*. A form is a database object primarily used to enter data into a database, or to format existing data for on-screen display. Forms can also be used to control the way users interact with the database and the data in it. The four different ways to use forms are:

> For *data entry* to add new records or modify existing records

> For *data display* to show the user existing records

> For *custom dialog boxes* to interact with users

> For *menus* or *switchboards* users can use to navigate from place to place within the database

In this chapter, I'll be showing you how to create and use forms for the first two purposes: to add and modify data and to display data. I'll tell you more about menus and switchboards in a later chapter.

Bound and Unbound Forms

Most forms are *bound* to an underlying table (or to a query[11]). What does it mean to say a form is bound? It means the form has a direct connection to its bound table or query, so opening the form automatically retrieves records from that record source. When you create a new form, you usually start by telling Access you want that form to use records from a particular table or query. Because a form can be bound to either a table or a query, Access calls both of them the form's *record source.* Forms can have other types of record sources, but we'll just start with these two— tables and queries— for now.

An unbound form, therefore, is one that doesn't have a record source; it's not bound to a table or query. They are useful for things other than data entry and you'll learn more about them, starting in Chapter 12.

Main Forms and Sub Forms

For the most part, you'll add or modify data in each table in your database through a separate form bound only to that table. That's not a hard and fast rule, but it applies to the majority of your tables.

However, we can also *nest* forms—place one form inside another. That's an especially good way to handle data entry for two tables with a one-to-many relationship between them, such as tblPerson (one side) and tblPersonHousehold (many side) in our personal contact database. In main form-sub form designs, the two forms are bound to two different tables; however, nesting one inside the other allows us to use some powerful tools built into Access for handling one-to-many relationships.

Unbound Forms

Because we are concerned with adding new records to our database— and therefore using bound forms—you may be wondering when you would use an unbound form? There are several different situations in which you'll use unbound forms, but the most common use is for custom dialog boxes (as in Figure 8-2) and switchboards (as in Figure 8-3).

---

[11] A query is another Access tool. Queries allow you to select fields from one or more tables and display them together in a single datasheet view. I'll tell you more about queries later in this chapter.

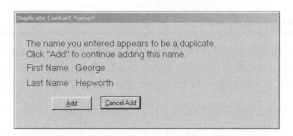

Figure 8-2 Unbound Form—Custom Dialog Box

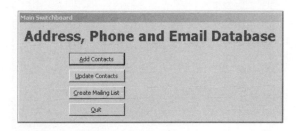

Figure 8-3 Unbound Form—Switchboard

You'll learn more about creating forms like these later, when you begin to refine the user interface for your Access database. For now, let's start creating a bound form to add new records to the tables in your database.

Bound Forms for Data Entry

It can be a bit difficult to decide where to start. Should you go right to the heart of the database and start designing a form to add new people based on tblPerson? Or should you start with a form to add households, based on tblHousehold? Or maybe you should tackle forms for the various lookup tables (tlkpAddressType, tlkpPhoneType, and so forth) first. They have only a few fields in them, which might be a little simpler to create.

Since this is the first form you and I have designed together, let's start with some simple ones, data entry tables for the lookup tables (such as tlkpPhoneType). We'll design forms through which you can manage the contents of your lookup tables. Once you have a handle on creating basic forms, you can move on to more complex forms for more complex table relationships.

Start Access and open your copy of the personal contact database. In the database window, select Forms as shown in Figure 8-4. It should be empty accept for the two menu choices for creating new forms. For your first table, it will be okay to use the wizard. Unlike the table wizard, the form wizard is not likely to lead you astray.

Learning Strategy for Forms

In this chapter, you'll learn how to create simple forms. In the next chapter, you'll create some more advanced forms; in the chapter after that, you'll learn how to put them together in main-form-to-sub-form designs.

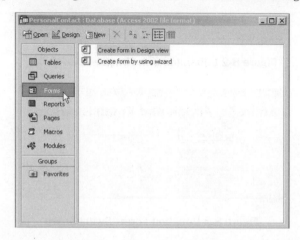

Figure 8-4 Create a New Form in Database Window

Double-click Create form by using wizard. A dialog box like the one in Figure 8-5 opens.

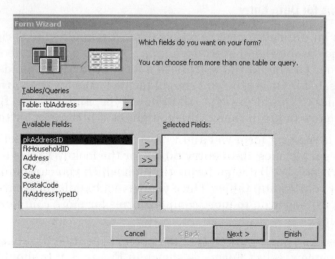

Figure 8-5 New Form Wizard

Figure 8-5 asks which fields you want on your form. Remember, a form's record source can be either a *table* or a *query*. You have a lot of flexibility in selecting fields through the wizard, but you must start by selecting one or more tables or queries.

The form wizard has a drop down list, or combo box (labeled Tables/Queries in Figure 8-5), with all of the tables and queries in the database. You can select any of them for your form. You can also select fields from individual tables and combine them in the form without creating a new query, but we won't do that until you've had a little more practice with basic forms.

Take a look at the combo box, or drop down list, shown in Figure 8-6. As you probably know from using other Windows applications, clicking on the small box at the right end of the drop down—circled in Figure 8-6—opens the list from which you can select an item, in this case a table.

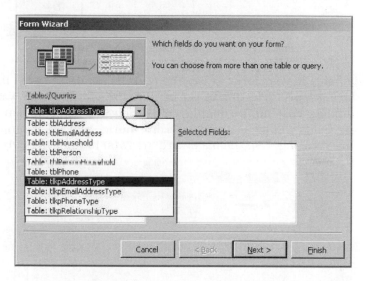

Figure 8-6 Select a Table or Tables for the Form

I want to start with the first lookup table on the list, tlkpAddressType. Click on it to select it. The available fields in that table display in the field below. In this case, there are two fields available in tlkpAddressType, pkAddressTypeID and AddressType.

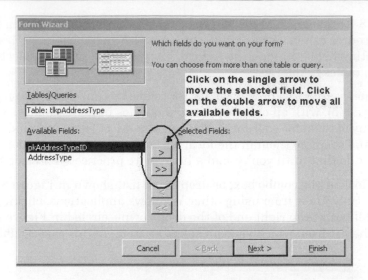

Figure 8-7 Available Fields, Form Wizard

To include fields in your form, select them in the available fields list and click on the appropriate button in the center of the form. If you want to include all fields, click on the double-arrow. Selected fields appear on the right. These fields will be part of the record source, which is bound to the form you are creating. Use the backward arrow(s) to remove fields.

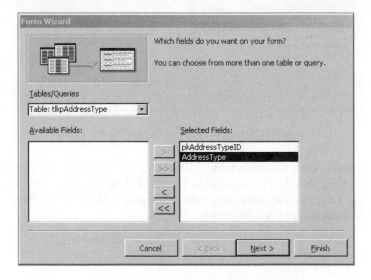

Figure 8-8 Selected Fields, Form Wizard

Click on Next. The wizard offers you a chance to pick from several pre-defined layouts. This selection controls the default placement of the fields on the form. Click each of the options available to see a preview of the approximate layouts for your form.

I selected Tabular for the lookup table we're creating. Tabular layout places the names of fields at the top of the form with values for the fields in columns below their names.

Choose the same layout so we're in synch in the following discussion. You can choose other layouts for future forms. Of course, in the final database, you'll want all of the forms to be similar in appearance, but while you're learning it's okay to experiment a little. See how the different layouts affect placement and size of controls on the form.

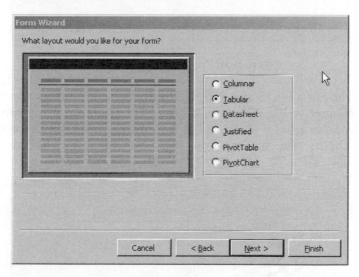

Figure 8-9 Pre-defined Tabular Form Layouts

After you've experimented a little, select the Tabular layout and click on Next. The next step is to select a style.

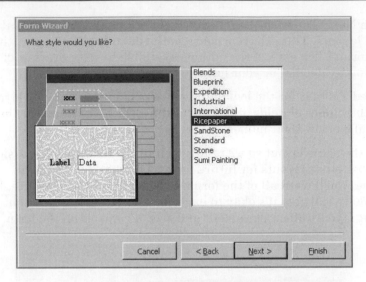

Figure 8-10 Pre-defined Form Styles

Frankly, I'm not a fan of any of the default styles. My tastes run to simpler, cleaner styles. However, because I elected to use the form wizard, I had to select a style, so I picked the Ricepaper style for this example. Do the same in your database so we stay in synch. Then click Next.

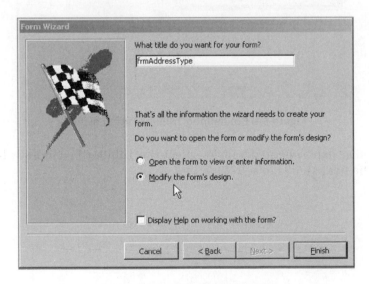

Figure 8-11 Form Wizard Finish

The last step in the wizard is to name your form and decide whether you want to open it to display data or if you want to further modify the default design. Let's give it a name first, following the standard naming convention for forms. Then we can make some additional changes.

Standard Naming Convention for Forms

The form name I selected is based on the standard naming convention for forms. Following the same rules as we did for tables, we attach a three-letter prefix to the name of the form to indicate it is a form. The prefix for forms is "frm". The rest of the form name, AddressType, is two words, both capitalized and with no spaces between, making the full name of this form frmAddressType. You'll follow this same convention for all of the forms in your database.

Modify the Table Produced by the Wizard

I wanted to modify the design, so I selected that option next, but if you are anxious to see your first form, you can go ahead and look at it. Figure 8-12 shows what that looks like after the form wizard creates it.

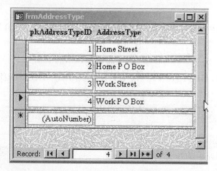

Figure 8-12 First Form based on tlkpAddressType

Access' form wizard created the table with the tabular format I requested. Field names (pkAddressTypeID and AddressType) are displayed at the top of the form. The form wizard added a line below them. Records are displayed in two columns below the names in two fields, one for the primary key and the other for the address type.

Typical Modifications

At this point, the form is completely functional and you could use it just as it is. However, there are a few things I want to change to make it more user friendly. First, the form wizard uses the actual field names (pkAddressTypeID and AddressType) for labels. You will want to change then to more natural names.

Also, the form displays the primary key field, pkAddressTypeID. I make it a hard and fast rule in designing databases that users should *never* see primary keys; in fact, they don't necessarily need to know they even exist. All the user needs to see is the address type field anyway.

Remember, we used an autonumber for our primary key, which means Access takes care of creating and assigning new ones automatically, whether anyone ever sees them or not. Therefore, I'm going to hide the primary key from the user by making that field invisible on the form.

We'll do that next, and also make some other changes to the form design, so find the Form Design icon on the toolbar and click it. It has a small ruler, triangle and pencil on it. Look at Figure 8-13.

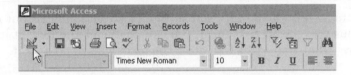

Figure 8-13 Click to Change Form to Design View

The form changes to design view, which looks like Figure 8-14.

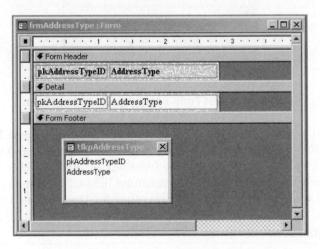

Figure 8-14 Form in Design View

As you can see in Figure 8-14, all forms can have three sections: *header*, *detail section,* and *footer*. The pre-defined layout I selected for this form created the header and footer sections. However, form headers and footers are optional and most of the time I don't use them for forms. This form does have a header and footer, and there is a reason for that.

As you can see in Figure 8-14, the *field names* are in the header and the *fields themselves* are in the detail section. This arrangement allows Access to display the field names once at the top of each column of values, as you saw in Figure 8-12, while repeating each of the fields as many times as necessary in the detail section.

Controls

Control is the name Access gives to objects on a form. For example, frmAddressType has two controls on it: the text fields shown as pkAddressTypeID and AddressType in Figure 8-14. These controls are *bound* to the corresponding fields in the form's underlying record source.

> Actually, labels are also a type of control, although they are different from other types of controls in a couple of significant ways:
>
> 1.   They can't be bound to fields in a record source
> 2.   They are normally attached to other controls on a form.
>
> Otherwise Access itself treats them like other controls. You can use code, for example, to manipulate labels on a form, just as you can other controls.

Most of the time, labels are linked, or attached, to text fields and allow you to display natural names for the text fields to which they are attached. In fact, you can translate labels into other languages without changing the names of the fields to which they are attached. You can go a long way towards customizing your database for use in many countries simply by changing labels.

In Figure 8-14, the labels for the two text fields are in the form header, as previously mentioned. They appear only once on the form because the header is displayed only once.

There are many other types of controls: list boxes, combo boxes, radio buttons, command buttons, and so forth. I'll show you what they are and how to use them as you build more complex forms. For now, we'll only be working with labels and text boxes.

Default View

Compare Figure 8-12 to Figure 8-14. You should have noticed that, in design view, the detail section of the form includes only one instance of the field controls. However, in form view, which displays records to the user, there are multiple instances of those fields, one for each value in the underlying record source. How does the form do that?

For the answer, let's take a look at one of form's properties, Default View. Find the Property Sheet icon on the toolbar (it looks like a hand holding a sheet of paper, Figure 8-15). Click it to display the form's property sheet. The property sheet opens, as shown in Figure 8-16.

Figure 8-15 Form Property Sheet on the Form Design Toolbar

The property sheet allows you to set or change how the form displays on the screen, how it responds to events, how it handles records in its record source, and a number of other properties. For now, I'm only interested in a couple of properties, the ones circled in Figure 8-16, Caption and Default View.

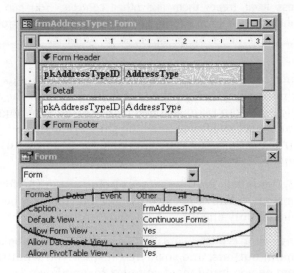

Figure 8-16 Form in Design View with Property Sheet

First, look at the property labeled Default View. It is set to *Continuous Forms* for this form. Continuous forms view means Access will display the form header and footer only once—at the top and bottom of the form. However, it will display the *detail* section of the form over and over, in a continuous sequence, as many times as it takes to display all of the records in the underlying record source.

Add New Records Icon

In this case, where tblAddressType has four records, it results in the view shown in Figure 8-12.In addition to the four existing records, the form also displays a set of empty fields at the bottom of the list where you can add new records to the table. You can tell new record fields in most forms by the fact they have a star, or asterisk (*) in the gray box at the left side of the form. I'll tell you a little more about that later in the chapter.

Form Caption

We also need to change the form's caption. That's the text that displays at the top of the form window. Look at Figure 8-12. Do you see the caption for this form as the wizard created it? By default, the wizard used the form name I gave to the form while I was creating it, frmAddressType. That's not a very user friendly name (although it does follow standard naming convention for forms!), so I want to change the caption in the property sheet.

Find the property called Caption in the form's property sheet (as shown in Figure 8-16) and type over the name there. Let's give this form the caption "Address Types". When you've changed the caption, find the Form View icon on the toolbar (Figure 8-17) and switch back to form view to see the result of your change.

Figure 8-17 Form View Icon, Form Design Toolbar

The form should now look like Figure 8-18. The caption for this form is now a natural language name, Address Types, but the captions and field names for the controls on it are still those taken from the underlying record source, pkAddressTypeID and AddressType. Switch back to design view where you can change their captions. Their names also need to be converted to standard naming conventions.

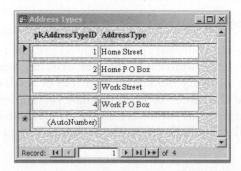

Figure 8-18 Form with Natural Language Caption

Label and Control Names

We're going to do two things at the same time, (1) change the captions for the labels in the form header, which are the names your users will see, and (2) give the labels proper names following the standard naming conventions. Then we'll do the same with the other controls on the form, the two text fields.

First, find the caption in the label for each field and change it. I used Address Type ID and Address Type. Remember, these are the names your users will see. It's important to pick meaningful names, but it's equally important to keep them as concise as possible. (And do make sure you spell them correctly). You don't want long labels taking up all of the space on your forms. You've seen how I changed the name of the form by finding the Caption property on the property sheet. Do the same for both labels.

With the form in design view, click the label. Find the Caption property on the property sheet and type in the new caption. Then, find the Save icon on the toolbar and click it to save your changes. Switch back to form view to see your changes. Once you're happy with the captions for the labels, switch back to design view and give each of the labels and fields on the form their standard names.

One reason I don't like to use the form wizard is that it gives labels and fields names based on the fields in the underlying record source. This results in names that follow standard naming conventions for tables, but not for forms.

Table 8-1 lists the default names assigned by Access and the standard names to which I changed them.

Control Type	Default Name Assigned by Access	Standard Name
Label	pkAddressTypeID_Label	lblAddressTypeID
Label	AddressType_Label	lblAddressType
Text Field	pkAddressTypeID	txtAddressTypeID
Text Field	AddressType	txtAddressType

Table 8-1 Standard Object Names for Form Controls

For labels, prefix the three-letter abbreviation "lbl" to indicate the control is a label and then add the name of the label, capitalized with no spaces.

For text fields, prefix the three-letter abbreviation "txt" to indicate the control is a text field, then add the name of the control, capitalized with no spaces. Go ahead and make these changes to the field and label names on your form.

Making Fields Invisible

The last step we want to take is to hide the primary key field from the user. Switch back to form design view and open the property sheet for the form. Click on the primary key field to select it and then find the Format tab on the property sheet. Look for the Visible property. See Figure 8-19. It defaults to Yes, meaning the field will be displayed on the form. Change it to No, hiding the field.

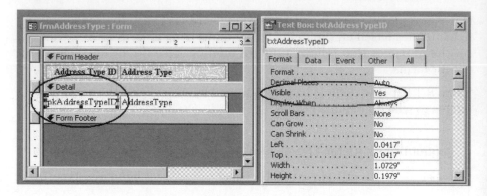

Figure 8-19 Setting the Visible Property

Switch back to form view to see the result. Figure 8-20

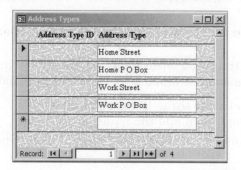

Figure 8-20 Form with Hidden Field

The primary key field, txtAddressTypeID, is not visible anymore. It's still there, in the same place on the form, but you can't see it. The label for the field is still visible, though, and there is a blank space on the form where the field lies. That doesn't look very tidy, so the last step will be to hide the label and re-organize the form to make it look better. Switch back to design view, find the Visible property for lblAddressTypeID and change it to No as well.

Now, we want to push the invisible controls out of the way and move the other field, txtAddressType, and its label into their place on the form. Since the field is invisible anyway, it doesn't matter where it is positioned on the form.

Normally I accomplish that by setting the height and width of a hidden field to zero and moving it to the upper left hand corner of the form. As you can see in Figure 8-21, I set the properties for Left, Top, Width, and

Height for this field to zero, which moved it to the far left edge and the top of the detail section, and also made it zero inches high and zero inches wide. You can just barely see it in Figure 8-21, as a tiny square at the end of the arrow. In form view, you can't see it at all.

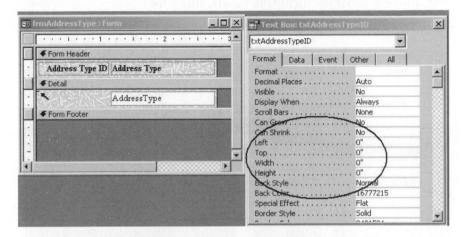

Figure 8-21 Hidden Field Moved Out of the Way

Hiding or Removing Labels

Now that it's out of the way, you can do the same to its label. Usually, I just delete labels entirely; they're not visible and they aren't needed anyway, but sometimes I just hide them and move them out of the way. Pick whichever method feels best to you.

Moving and Aligning Controls

With the primary key field hidden and moved out of the way, you can move the remaining field to the left, filling in the empty space on the form.

Moving the Controls

Click on the control and hold down the left mouse button (right button if your mouse is set up to be left-handed) to drag it. In this case, you are dragging it to the left, into the blank space vacated by the primary key field.

Another way to move a control is to click to select it, then to use the up and down, left and right arrows to nudge the control into position. (In Access 97 you have to hold down the shift key while nudging controls.)

Aligning Controls

To re-align the left edge of the field with its label in the form header, hold down the shift key while clicking on both controls to select them. You can select multiple controls, including labels, this way.

Now, select Format-->Align-->Left from the menu (Figure 8-22).

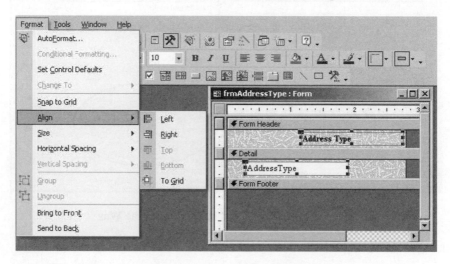

Figure 8-22 Align Fields on a Form

The label for the field will move to the left until the two controls line up along their left edges. Switch back to form view to see the results.

Experiment with other alignment options (align top, align right, etc.) to see how Access handles each option. When you are finished experimenting, realign the label and control on the left, about a quarter of an inch or so from the left margin.

Figure 8-23 Form View

At this point, you can leave this form and go on to create similar forms for the other lookup tables in your personal contact database. If you want, you can use the form wizard to create the basic form and modify it to make it more user friendly and to conform to standard naming conventions.

In my database, I will make some additional modifications to this form, as well. For one thing, I plan to remove the background image. Images not only take up space, bloating your database unnecessarily, they tend to be distracting, from my point of view. I'll leave that decision to you, but the forms I'll show you from now on will be as plain and simple as possible.

Create a Form from Scratch

Next, I'm going to walk through creating a form from scratch, starting in design view, which is the method I usually prefer. As I mentioned earlier, I prefer cleaner, simpler forms than those created by the form wizard and I can create them just as quickly without it, I think.

Create a Form in Design View

For the next form, let's select another of the lookup tables. Either double-click on Create Form in Design View in the database window, or select New from the toolbar.

Figure 8-24 Create Form in Design View

The Form dialog box opens, offering you several choices about how to create the new form. (Are you still surprised at the number of different ways to do nearly everything in Access?) This time, select Design View and then select the next lookup table from the dropdown List. Scroll down the list to tlkpEmailAddressType as shown in Figure 8-25. Then click on OK to continue.

Access displays the blank form, ready to be designed (Figure 8-26), along with a dialog box showing the fields in the form's record source, tlkpEmailAddressType. The default form name applied by Access is form1 and, unlike the pre-defined tabular layout, the default layout doesn't include the form header and footer. Access doesn't know yet what you want the layout to be, so it defaults to the most basic choices.

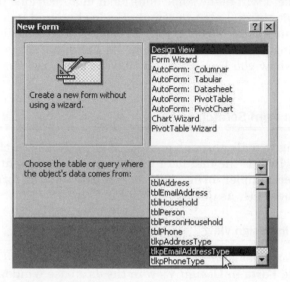

Figure 8-25 Select a Record Source

Access may also open the Field List for this form's record source. You can use it to add fields to the form.

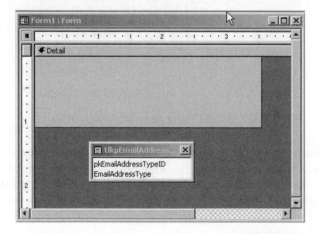

Figure 8-26 Blank Form with Field List Displayed

To make this form look like the one you previously created with the wizard, you should change its default view to continuous forms, add the form header and footer, and give the form a background image. I will convert it to continuous forms view, add the header and footer to carry the labels, but I won't add a background image. I'll leave it up to you to decide whether to include images in your own forms, but for my money, they're a waste of time and storage space.

We want this form to be continuous because it will display the choices from our lookup table. We also want the form header so we can place the labels on it.

To display the header and footer for the form, select View from the menu and scroll down to find Form Header and Footer and click to select it; see Figure 8-27. Access will add the form header and footer with default heights. Since we don't need the footer, you can shrink it down to a zero height. As always, Access provides a couple of different ways to do that. First, you can open the form's property sheet, click on the form footer to select it, find the Height property for that section in the property sheet, and change it to zero.

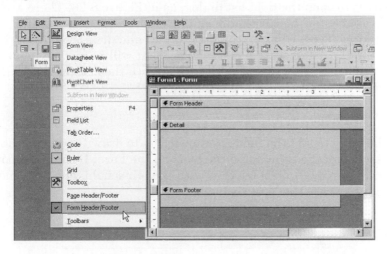

Figure 8-27 Add a Form Header and Footer

The other way to shrink the form footer is to move the cursor over the bottom edge of the footer until it changes to look like Figure 8-28. Click and hold the left mouse button (right button if you are left-handed) and drag the footer up until it is not visible.

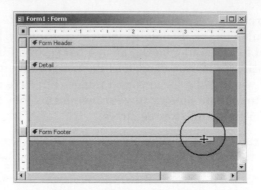

Figure 8-28 Cursor Changed to Resize Form Section

Adding Fields Manually

Guess what! There are two ways to add fields to your form.

Click and Drag

One way is to open the field list dialog, as in Figure 8-26. There are two fields available for the current form, pkEmailAddressTypeID and EmailAddressType. Click on the field names and drag them from the field list to the detail section of the form. That will create the fields, with their attached labels in the default format with the default field names. Try that now with the primary key field.

Draw on the Form

The other way to add the fields to the form is to draw them onto the detail section of the form using the tools on the Form Design Toolbox toolbar, Figure 8-29. We'll try that with the other field, but first I need to explain how to use the Toolbox toolbar.

Figure 8-29 Form Design Toolbox Toolbar

The Form Design Toolbox Toolbar

The Form Design Toolbox toolbar has icons for most of the types of controls you're likely to add to a form, along with a tool to select objects and an icon to toggle the control wizard on and off. Click on one of these buttons to draw a control of that type onto your forms.

Custom Visual Aid Toolbar for this Book

Before I describe the buttons on the toolbar, I need to point out that the top row of buttons in Figure 8-29, the ones in the top rectangle, are the default button styles you'll see in Access. Because you can customize toolbars like this one, you can add other buttons for other types of tools, or remove some of the ones shown in Figure 8-29.

Therefore, for the purposes of this book, I created a new visual aid Toolbox toolbar (outlined in the lower rectangle) with the names of the various buttons next to the icons. I hope you find it helpful as you read through the next few pages. Unfortunately, though, you won't find that particular visual aid toolbar in your copy of Access unless you also take the time to create one like it for yourself.

Left to right in Figure 8-29, the items on the Form Design toolbar include:

> *Control Selector.* After adding a control on a form, click this icon to enable selection of other controls for further modification or deletion.

> *Control Wizard.* When the control wizard button is down, the control wizard is turned on. The wizard will help you create certain controls (such as list and combo boxes). When the control wizard button is up, the control wizard is turned off. The default is On. I keep it on most of the time.

  For the rest of the time you are using this book, please keep the control wizard turned on. A lot of what I will be showing you depends on the wizards being active.

> *Label Control.* Click on this button to add a label to your form. Normally, labels are created when you add any other type of control and are attached to that control. You can also add unattached labels to your forms. You might do that to display instructions about using the form to your users, for example.

> *Text Box.* Click on this button to add a text box to your form. Text boxes are the basic type of control. They are normally bound to a field in the underlying record source and can accept or display the text in that field. For example, Address, City, State, and PostalCode will all be bound to text fields on forms created to add or modify addresses.

> *Option Group.* An option group is a sort of master control that contains a subset of other controls: option buttons, check boxes, or toggle buttons. The option group control itself is bound to the underlying field in the record source. The value of the option group is determined by the value of the option button, check box, or toggle button selected by the user for that option group.

For example, an option group control might be bound to a gender field in the underlying record set. The two possible values for that field (its domain, to use the proper database term) are Male and Female. The option group would contain two radio buttons, one for the male value and the other for the female.

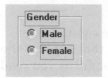 The etched line around the radio buttons indicates the option group itself. It's bound to the field called Gender in the underlying record source. Its only two possible values, mutually exclusive, are the radio buttons in the control, in this case male and female.

I find myself using option groups only rarely.

> *Toggle Button.* A toggle button has only two binary values: on/off, yes/no, true/false, etc. When it is down, one of the two values is stored in the bound field; when it is up, the other value is stored in the bound field. Toggle buttons are very useful for capturing values that are truly binary.

> *Option Button.* Sometimes called *radio buttons*. They are normally used within option groups, as described above. In an option group, option buttons force a user to select one of several mutually exclusive values because selecting one of the buttons in the group automatically deselects the other options.

As stand-alone controls on a form, radio buttons work like toggle buttons, storing one of two binary values in the field to which they are bound.

> *Check Box.* Similar to option buttons, they are used in an option group to select mutually exclusive values for the option group. They can also be made stand-alone so they store one of two binary values. You might use check boxes when you want to indicate a series of yes/no choices on a survey, for example.

In Access 2002, toggle buttons, radio buttons, and check boxes can all be made *triple state*. Triple state means they will cycle through states for yes, no, and null.

As you recall, null means the value for that particular record is not known. Setting the Triple State property for these controls to Yes will allow your form to capture all three states for each field. Setting it to No will force Access to display a null value as No.

> *List Box.* A list box can display a list of possible values for the field to which it is bound. You've probably seen list boxes many times in Windows applications and you should have a pretty good idea of how

they work. I'll show you how to create one a bit later in this chapter and tell you more about its options.

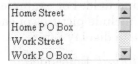 Clicking on one of the values in the list stores that value in the field to which the list box is bound.

➢ *Combo Box.* Combo Boxes are very versatile and powerful controls; one of my favorites and also one I use a lot. They are, as the name suggests, a combination of two other types of controls: text boxes and list boxes. Combo boxes will accept typed-in text, like a text box, but they also have a pre-populated list of values, like list boxes, which you can select by clicking on them.

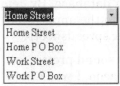 You've seen combo boxes many times already and you've used them to make selections in the form wizard. I'll show you how to create one and tell you more about its options.

➢ *Command Button.* Command buttons are used whenever you want to send instructions to Access to perform some action. Clicking on the button triggers code (or a macro) to perform the required function. Wizards will help you create command buttons for some common functions, like opening or closing a form, or sending a report to your printer. As you gain experience and proficiency with Access, you'll write more of your own code to run from command buttons on your forms.

➢ *Image Frame.* The next tool on the toolbar, which looks like a mountain with the sun in the upper right hand corner, inserts an image into your form. *I advise you to use them sparingly.* Image files can be large and embedding them into forms causes your database to grow very quickly. One place I do like to use them, though, is to insert a company logo into a form or report for my customers who have logos. It helps customize the application and make it look more professional.

➢ *Unbound Object Frame.* An unbound object frame is a lot like an image frame, except it can accommodate other objects, like Excel spreadsheets and Word documents, as well. With the unbound object frame tool, you can add a picture or object to a form. Images and objects in an unbound object frame *don't* change as you move from record to record.

➢ *Bound Object Frame.* The bound object frame works a lot like the image and unbound object frames, except that, as the name suggests, the bound object frame is bound to a field in the underlying record source. As you move from record to record, the picture or object can change, depending on the contents of that bound field. For example, if you were to create an employee database and include pictures of each employee, you would use a bound object frame to display them.

Image and object frames can be *embedded* or *linked*. Embedded images and objects become part of the database file. This quickly adds to the size of a database. Linked objects can also be inserted into the database, causing it to grow. However, because linked images and objects retain their the connection back to the original source—image file, Word doc, Excel spreadsheet, and so on—you can display an icon on the form to represent the linked object without adding it to the file, thus saving a large amount of space in your database. By default, double-clicking the icon opens the linked object in the application originally used to create it, such as MS Excel for spreadsheets.

At this point, image and object frames probably sound pretty complicated. They can be and, partly for that reason, I won't be showing them to you in this book. Of course, the ability to link Excel spreadsheets, pictures, and documents to your database gives you some powerful tools and you'll want to learn how to use them at some point in your career.

Right now, though, we need to finish our review of the tools on the Form Design toolbar.

➤ *Tab Control.* You've seen tab controls in many Windows applications.

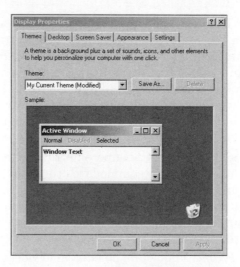

Figure 8-30 Tab Control From Windows Desktop

Figure 8-30 is one you may have used to change your own desktop. It has tabs for Themes, Desktop, Screen Saver, Appearance, and Settings. Clicking on each tab presents a different set of options.

You can add controls like this to your Access Forms. Their major advantages are the ability to group controls like text boxes and command buttons for related functions onto a single tab and to conserve screen space by showing each tab, one at a time.

> *Subform / Subreport.* The next icon helps you to create subforms (and subreports) on your forms. When you click on this icon and draw a shape onto your form, it actually starts a wizard to guide you through the steps in adding a subform. I'll show you subforms in a later chapter.

> *Lines and Rectangles.* The next two icons on the Toolbox toolbar in Figure 8-29 are for creating line and rectangle shapes on your forms. You can often help your users navigate a complicated form by careful grouping and separating of controls this way.

> *More Controls.* The last control on the top row of Figure 8-29, the one that looks like a wrench and hammer, gives you access to an additional set of controls.

I'm not going to spend a lot of time talking about them for a couple of reasons. First, the specific controls available to you are those which are installed and registered on your PC, and that varies from PC to PC. I can't be sure which controls you might or might not have available to you. Second, many of these controls are not very well documented and are not all that easy to use. They're better left for a time when your skills with Access are up to the task. I like to use a few of them, such as the calendar control, which places a dynamic calendar on a form.

Unfortunately, my experience has been that even within a single organization, different PCs have different versions of the same calendar control installed, or different calendars, or none at all. Unless you are building a very sophisticated application and have a lot of say in how your users' PCs are configured, it's just a lot safer to stick to the basics.

Controls You Will Use Most Often

Those are the main controls you'll be using in the near future. The ones you'll use the most are text boxes, combo boxes, list boxes and command buttons. You'll also find radio buttons and check boxes useful, either as part of options groups or by themselves.

Now, let's return to the task of adding controls to the form for our email address types.

We're going to add a second text box to hold the names of the email address types. Find the icon for text boxes on the Toolbox toolbar (it's the one with "**ab|**" on it).

Click it and then draw the shape of the text box onto the detail section of your form. It will look like Figure 8-31.

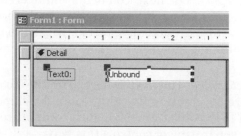

Figure 8-31 Text Box Drawn Onto Form

Access assigns a default name (Text0) to the control and creates a label for it with the default name as the caption. You know how to change those names, so go ahead and do that. This field will hold the primary key, so rename it txtEmailAddressTypeID. Rename the label lblEmailAddressTypeID.

Next, we need to tell Access to which field this text box should be bound. On the property sheet for the form (to open it, click on the icon that looks like a hand holding a piece of paper), find the property called Control Source. Select pkEmailAddressTypeID from the drop down list (combo box), which contains a list of all of the fields in the underlying record source.

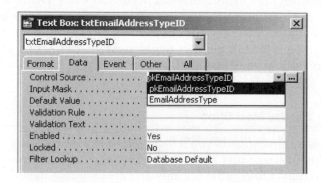

Figure 8-32 Control Source for a Newly Created Control

The text box will now look like Figure 8-33.

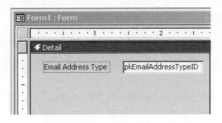

Figure 8-33 New Text Field

Now, because it's the primary key, make it invisible and move it out of the way by setting the Top, Left, Height, and Width properties to zero. You can either delete the label or make it invisible and move it out of the way. (Of course, there is no point in renaming the label and changing the caption if you intend to delete it, but go ahead and do that this time, for practice.)

Add a second text box for the other field in this table, EmailAddressType. Select the text box tool, draw the text box on the form, set its control source, rename it and its associated label, and change the label's caption as you did for the first text box. Then move it to the upper edge of the detail section of the form.

To make this form look more like the first one, we need to add the form header and make a couple of other changes. Select View on the menu bar and then click on Form Header/Footer.

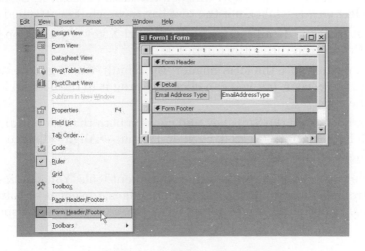

Figure 8-34 View Form Header

You can shrink the footer section as before by moving the mouse over the lower edge until it changes to the horizontal bar with up and down arrows. Click and drag it up as far as it will go.

Next, we need to change the default view to continuous forms. Open the form property sheet, find the Default View property, and change it to continuous forms.

Now, you need to move the label from the detail section to the header. To see why you need to do that, switch to form view and look at the result.

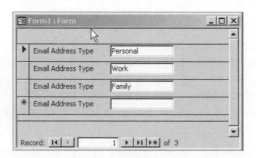

Figure 8-35 Continuous View with Label on Detail Section

The label duplicates down the form along with the field. Of course, you could leave it like that, but it does seem a bit cluttered in comparison to the first form we created and it's also a waste of space. Let's move the label to the form header.

1. Switch back to design view. Click on the label to select it. Be careful to select only the label, not the text box to which it is attached.

2. Cut it from the detail section with the Ctrl-X key combination (or use the Cut icon on the editing menu).

3. Now, paste it into the form header. By default, it will go into the upper left corner, but you can click and drag it to the desired location on the form.

4. Now, hold down the Shift key and click on both the text box and label. With both controls selected, click on Format-->Align-->Left to align them along their left edges.

   While you're there, note the other alignment tools. You can line controls up along their top edges, right edges, top edges or bottom edges. In designing good-looking forms, these are all handy shortcuts.

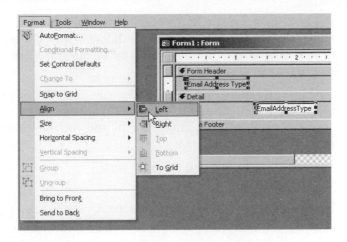

Figure 8-36 Align Controls

Record Selectors

Look at Figure 8-35. Do you see the little arrowhead in the small box on the left end of the top row? That's called a *record selector*; it indicates which record is the one currently selected in the form. In other words, the form displays all of the records in the underlying record set, but only one record at a time can be selected.

Another way of saying this is to say this record *currently has the focus*. Switch your form to form view and move through the records to see how the record selector behaves. As you click on an address type, the record selector moves to that record.

In continuous forms like this, record selectors are quite useful as visual clues. However, in other forms, which are set to single view and show only one record at a time, I find them distracting and usually turn them off.

Look also at the bottom row of the form, the one with no entry in the text box. That's the row where you can add new records to the form and, thereby, into the underlying table. It has an asterisk, or star, next to it. That's the symbol for New Record. When you see it on a form, you can add a new record there.

Font Selection

There is one more change I want to make to this form. Compare the fonts for the labels in Figure 8-31 and Figure 8-35. They are different, partly because they were created differently, but they need to be the same on these forms and throughout the database. Consistency is a key factor in designing good interfaces. I need to make both forms look the same by selecting one font and using it for both of these forms and all of the other forms we will create later.

There are few hard and fast rules here, so you can choose font styles and sizes that look good to you. However, you should always avoid flashy colors (reds, greens, neon shades, and so forth) and you should pick fonts that are easily readable at many sizes.

> Fonts like **Tahoma and** MS Sans Serif are good.

> Fonts like Times New Roman are okay.

> Fonts like `Alcott` and Boulder are not good.

> **Arial** is not particularly good for forms, surprisingly enough. It looks good in print, but I've found it is not so good on forms.

The key is to find a font that looks good and use it consistently across all forms in your database.

Font size depends partly on screen resolution (e.g., 800 x 600, 1024 x 768, etc.) and partly on how many controls your forms have on them. Cluttered forms call for slightly smaller fonts, and vice versa. Again, stick with readable sizes (no smaller than 8 points and no larger than 14 or 15 points), but make them consistent across all of your forms.

I have a rule of thumb that says that your users will not really notice good form design, but they will notice—and object to—bad form design. If your choice of fonts elicits comments, therefore, you are probably on the wrong track.

I prefer MS Sans Serif to Times New Roman, although I've used both. I opened both of the forms I just created in design view to change their fonts to the MS Sans Serif. I decided I liked the fonts on these forms at 10 points and I made the labels bold.

You'll find buttons for these properties on the Format toolbar. I won't go over its functions in detail here, as most of them are standard Windows functions and features, font size and style, text alignment and color.

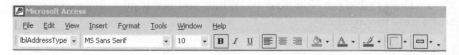

Figure 8-37 Format Toolbar

The toolbar also has drop down lists and buttons to select controls on the form to change fonts, font sizes, fore colors and weights, text alignment (left, center, or right), background colors, fore colors, border colors, and styles and the appearance of controls (flat, sunken, raised, etched, shadowed, or chiseled). You can use all of these formatting features to create a pleasing appearance for the controls on your forms.

For the text fields on our first set of forms, which permit entry or modification of records, I chose black for the fore color (that is, the text), white backgrounds, no border and a sunken appearance. I made the fields on both forms the same width and height (1.75" wide, 0.2083" high).

Actually, Access automatically sets height to fit the font size used in the control, so I usually don't change it manually. I set the left edge of the controls on both forms to 0.2" and the top edge of the labels to 0.05" from the top of the form header. I set the top of the text fields at 0.03" from the top of the detail section.

While I was at it, I also made both forms the same width (2.5"). I set the height of the form headers to 0.25" and the height of the detail sections to 0.3". The results were forms that look like Figure 8-38.

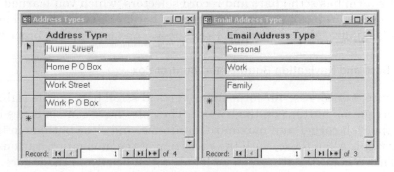

Figure 8-38 Identically Formatted Forms

Experiment with Control Formats on Your Forms

I believe the best way to get comfortable with formatting is to experiment yourself, especially with things like font sizes, colors, etc. So, rather than go into a lot of detail on these features, I'm just going to suggest you make a back up copy of one of your forms and experiment with it for a while. Use the toolbar to change the fonts, colors, and appearances of the controls on it. Add and remove borders from labels and text fields. Move controls around and make them larger and smaller.

When you are finished experimenting with your back up copies, delete them and reopen your real forms. Revise them to match mine. Open the property sheet for the forms and select Form from the control list, as in Figure 8-39. Find the properties for form width and set them to match mine.

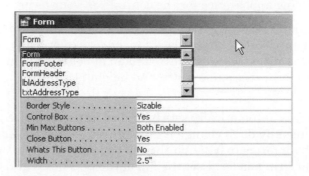

Figure 8-39 Setting Form Width and Other Properties

While you're here, scroll up and down the property sheet to see the other properties you can set for a form. For example, you can control whether or not a form has scroll bars and record selectors, which you learned about earlier. You can control what type of border the form has, whether it has Maximize, Minimize, and Close buttons, and many other properties.

Scroll Bars and Navigation Buttons and Control Box

As Figure 8-38 shows, our forms have vertical scroll bars on the right side and navigation buttons on the bottom. They also have control boxes in the upper left corner and maximize, minimize, and close buttons in the upper right. All of these, with the exception of the navigation buttons, are standard Windows features, so we'll only touch briefly on them here.

Think about the way these forms are designed. The forms are in continuous view, which means each record in the underlying record source is displayed in a vertical list, which you can navigate by using the scroll bar on the right edge of the form. Like other standard Windows scroll bars, it moves you rapidly up and down the list. Once the record you are looking for becomes visible in the form, you can click into it with the mouse to select it (give it the focus).

Navigation Buttons

The navigation buttons also move the focus from record to record in the form. The total number of records in the record set appears at the right side of the navigation buttons and the currently selected record appears in the navigation box in the center. When you click on one of the arrowheads in the navigation box, you can step forward to the next record, step back to the previous record, jump to the last record or jump to the first record. If you type a number in the navigation box and press enter, you jump to the record that is currently in that *relative* position in the current record set.

Redundant Controls

You don't really need both the scroll bar and navigation buttons on this form. They do essentially the same thing and are thus redundant to a large extent.

On continuous forms like these, I prefer to use only the scroll bars. Switch to design view, find the Navigation Buttons property on the forms and turn them off.

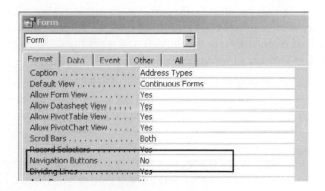

Figure 8-40 Turn Off Navigation Buttons

Now the forms should look like Figure 8-41.

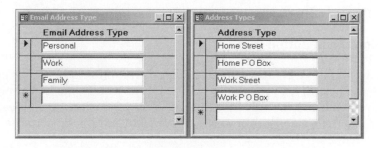

Figure 8-41 Forms without Navigation Buttons

You can also see in Figure 8-41 that the number of records in the record source determines how many rows display on the form in continuous view. With smaller record sets like these, you won't miss having the navigation buttons at all. With record sets numbering in the hundreds or thousands, you might want to have the navigation buttons available. It's nice to have the flexibility to design forms to meet your users' needs, isn't it?

Auto Resize and Auto Center

Other properties you can set for forms include auto resize and auto center. If you set these properties to Yes, the forms will automatically resize themselves to the same size each time they open and place themselves as close to the center of the screen as possible.

That means if you open two forms with Auto Center set to Yes, the second one will land right on top of the first. That may or may not be what you want. It can be an advantage, for example, if you want to open the second form for a temporary reason without closing the first. The second form will hide the first while you are working on it. When you close it, the first form will be visible again.

On the other hand, if you wanted to work on both forms at the same time, having one land on top of the other would be a hindrance. Again, deciding which way to go calls for a careful analysis of your users' needs.

Other Form Properties

There are a number of other form properties under your control, including whether or not the form, once opened, can be moved (not available in Access 97 or 2000), whether it has a picture embedded in it as a background (as in our first form created by the form wizard), how records are displayed and so on. We'll see some of them when we create more complex forms in the next chapter.

Add a Command Button

The forms you have created thus far don't have command buttons on them. And normally, I probably wouldn't put any on forms like these, which are primarily intended for maintenance of the look up tables. You can just use the Close Button in the upper right hand corner of the form to close them.

Still, in order to round out your picture of forms with something fairly simple, we'll go ahead and add command buttons to each of these forms.

(We'll take the buttons off again later.) The function of these buttons is simply to close the form when you click the button.

Open either of the two forms in design view. I started with frmAddressType. Click on the Command Button icon on the Toolbox toolbar, as shown in Figure 8-42. Draw a button on the form. Most good form designs have command buttons on the right, rather than the left, and most often they will be at the bottom rather than the top of the form. In order to place the command button at the bottom of this form, we need to make the form footer larger, as in Figure 8-42.

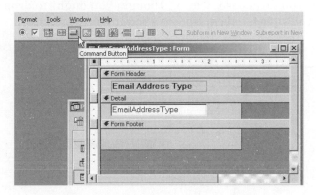

Figure 8-42 Command Button Tool

When you've drawn the command button and released the mouse, a command button wizard will open, asking you what you want this new command button to do. Tell it you want to perform a Form Operation, specifically, Close Form.

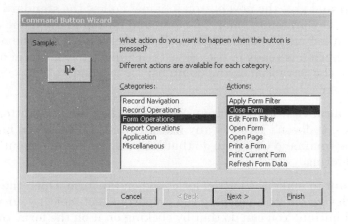

Figure 8-43 Command Button Wizard Step One

Click on Next to go to the next step in the wizard. In this step, you can choose whether the button has a picture or text on it. The standard Windows icons are available. For example the default for the Close action is the closing door with the arrow pointing out of it. I seldom like to have icons on buttons. I prefer text, mostly because I think it is usually clearer what the button does. Also, you can customize text on buttons to give your users better hints as to what buttons do.

I like to call buttons that close forms "Done" rather than "Close", but that's a personal preference. You can use either one, or a different term altogether. If you do choose "Close", though, you ought to drop the word "form" from the suggested caption; it's redundant.

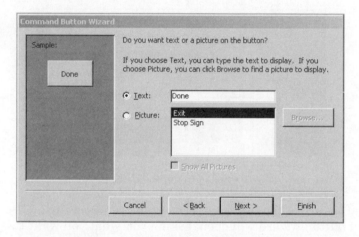

Figure 8-44 Command Button Wizard Step Two

Click Next and give the new button a name. Follow the standard naming conventions by prefixing "cmd" for command button to the name of the button. I called mine cmdCloseForm. Then click Finish and the new command button is ready to use. Save the changes to your form by clicking on the Save icon on the menu bar, or by going to File-->Save on the menu bar.

Switch to form view and try it out. When you click the new button, the form closes. It doesn't give you any warning first. I'll show you how to modify the command button to do that later, when we talk about more advanced forms.

First, I want to make the button look good on the form. Open the form again in design view and display the property sheet. Select your new command button. You can do that by clicking on it on the form, or by selecting it in the combo box on the property sheet. Click on the Format tab of the property sheet and look at the properties there. I am mostly interested in the size and location of the command button and the font used in its caption.

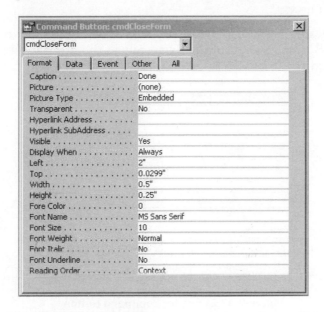

Figure 8-45 Command Button Property Sheet, Format Tab

I set the top of the button to match the top of the label on the form and set its left edge to 2" from the left edge of the form. I also set it to be 0.25" tall and 0.5" wide. That size seems best to me, although you are free to choose any dimensions that seem appropriate to you.

I also selected 10-point MS Sans Serif normal as the font for its caption. The result looks something like Figure 8-46. Click the Done button to close the form.

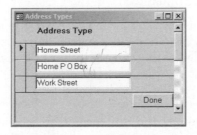

Figure 8-46 Command Button in Place

How the Button Works

Do you want to see how the button works? I knew you would, so I'm going to show you now.

Switch to design view, display the property sheet, and select the Command Button. Now, find the Event tab on the property sheet. It will look like Figure 8-47.

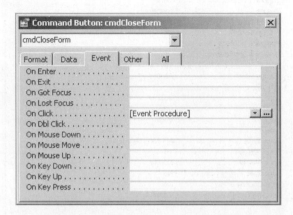

Figure 8-47 Events for Command Button

The events listed here, such as On Enter, On Exit, On Click, and so on, refer to actions the user takes while interacting with the control. As you can see, the wizard we just ran created an *event procedure* that runs when you click on the button.

Event procedures can be a bit more complicated than the one we just created. As you can see, you can create other procedures that run when you first press the mouse button down on the command button, or when you double click on it. Those other event procedures are a bit advanced for us right now, so we'll just focus on the Click event you just created.

Place the cursor in the On Click property. Two things happen when you do that. The property box changes to a drop down list displaying options for that event. (Right now there are no other options available.)

The Builder Button

More importantly, though, the Builder button appears at the right end of the field. It's a small command button with three dots on it. Click on it to open the Visual Basic Editor and look at the contents of the event procedure you just created. It will look like Figure 8-48.

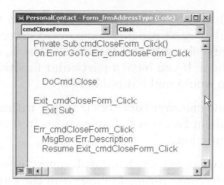

Figure 8-48 Event Procedure for Your First Command Button

This is a standard piece of Visual Basic for Applications (VBA) code, as the wizard created it. I'll quickly run through each line here and explain what they are and what they do. First, however, let me explain a little bit about the code window itself.

Code Module

The title bar for this *code module* tells you it is attached to the form called frmAddressType. Each form in your database can have its own module for code, filled with event procedures specific to that form.

There are two combo boxes at the top of the code window. The *object list* on the left contains a list of the form, sections of the form and the controls on it. Scroll down the list to see the objects in it for yourself. The *event list* on the right contains a list of the events associated with each object selected in the other combo box. Try selecting different controls and observing how the events list updates to match.

Each object in the form has several different events associated with it. At this point it may seem a bit overwhelming to have so many choices, but we'll be sticking to a few basic ones for now so don't worry.

Now, look at the lines of VBA in the code window itself. There are eight lines, each performing a specific function.

Line One

Line one *Declares* the event procedure, sets its *type* and gives it a *name*.

```
Private Sub cmdCloseForm_Click()
```

The key word *"Private"* tells Access this piece of code is only to be used by the form to which the module is attached. In other words, it is private to frmAddressType. Other objects (forms and reports) in the database don't know about it and they can't use it[12]. Some event procedures are *public*, which means that any object in the database—that is, other forms or reports—can call them. If you have a particular function that can be used in many places, you would make it public.

The next word in line one says that this is a *sub*, rather than a *function*. You'll be learning about two types of procedures in this book: subs, like this one, and also functions.

For our purposes, we can say the basic difference between subs and functions is that *subs cause things to happen* in the database (such as closing a form) while *functions return values* of some kind. For example, if we wanted to run a piece of code to count the number of households in the database, we'd use a function instead of a sub. The function would count the records and give us back a number.

The next word in line one is the *name* of this event procedure. *Form events* are a combination of the *name of the control* to which they are attached (i.e., cmdCloseForm) and the *event* that causes it to run (clicking the button). The underscore (_) is a required part of the name. Any time you create an event procedure for a control, it will have a format like this.

The *parentheses* [( )] at the end of the event procedure are required for all subs and functions. Sometimes you'll see other words inside them. I'll explain those at the appropriate time.

Line Two

Line two of the sub sets up *error trapping*. That means, if something goes wrong while Access is trying to process the code here, you want to handle the error by transferring control to a section of the procedure set up specifically to do that. This is referred to error trapping and it allows you to handle errors as gracefully as possible.

You want prevent your users from seeing raw error messages that would only confuse them. You also want to tell Access how to recover from certain kinds of errors. Of course, the only kind of errors for which you can provide *error handling* are those you can anticipate. And that means you'll need to do a lot of testing to find them all.

```
On Error GoTo Err_cmdCloseForm_Click
```

---

[12] That's not 100% true, but the way you would go about accessing functions on other forms is the subject for a much more advanced discussion.

This error trapping code says, "If an error occurs (On Error), go immediately to (GoTo) the label Err_cmdCloseForm_Click". Look down the code to find the label. Like all labels, it is followed by a colon (:). If an error occurs, the line immediately following the label is processed next.

Line Three

Line three is the only line in the event procedure that "does something" to your form. Specifically, it closes the form.

```
DoCmd.Close
```

This line consists of a keyword (DoCmd) and an action (Close).

> An excellent way to learn more about keywords in VBA is to place the cursor over the word in a code module and press "F1" for help. You'll usually get examples as well as explanations and descriptions in help. I think it's save to say that many developers have acquired a significant amount of knowledge just that way.

More accurately, DoCmd is an Access object and Close is one of the methods associated with it. For our purposes right now, just remember that you can use the object, DoCmd, along with one of its many methods to carry out actions like opening and closing forms, adding or deleting records in a table and many other very useful things. Did you notice the dot between the object and its method? That's a very important part of the syntax and the code won't work without it.

Line three is actually sort of a shortcut, because it doesn't tell Access which thing you want to close. When Access comes across a line of code like this, it assumes you are referring to the current form, the one where this code is running. If that's *not* what you meant, you could be in for a surprise.

The full syntax for DoCmd.Close can include the name of another object, too, as in

```
DoCmd.Close acForm, "frmOtherForm"
```

Here, the code tells Access you want to close a different object—not the one where the code is running. It tells Access the other object is another form (acForm) and the name of the other form is fmOtherForm.

Line Four

This line is the label to which Access returns after recovering from an error. It's there because of the error handler below. If your user ends up going through the error handler, it will process the error according to your instructions and send him back to this line. If the code works properly and there are no errors, of course, the code will come to this line from the one just above it.

Line Five

This line is always the last one executed by the procedure. It tells Access to exit the event procedure (sub, in this case) and get ready to handle the next event triggered by the user. If the code executes properly, it won't get past this line to the error handler below. If there is an error, the error handler will send control back to this line after it does its work.

Lines Six through Eight

These lines are the basic error handler. Here's how they work. If an error occurs, Access has already been instructed to GoTo the label in line six. When it gets there, it starts processing again on line seven.

Line seven tells Access to show the user a message box. The contents of that message box are the description of the error. It might look like Figure 8-49.

Figure 8-49 Error Message Box

When the user clicks on the OK button in the error message, the next line in the error handler is processed.

The line,

```
Resume Exit_cmdCloseForm_Click
```

tells Access to resume processing at the label provided, which, as you just learned, leads to the Exit command.

If you want to do things other than just show the user a message when an error occurs, as I'm sure you will, you can place code for that here in the error handler, followed by the Resume command shown above.

Line Nine

All event procedures must have an End statement at the end. Here it is End Sub. If this were a function, it would be End Function.

Your First Code

There you have it. Your first piece of VBA code. While it's true the control wizard helped you to create it, you do know how it works now. You'll soon be learning how to create other, more complex, VBA codes for other purposes.

Rather than drag you through those details now, though, I'm going to have you take a break, then come back and create forms for each of the remaining look up tables in our contacts database. You'll need one for tlkpPhoneType and one for tlkpRelationshipType. You can either use the form wizard or create them from scratch. If you choose to use the form wizard, I strongly urge you to remove the image from the form after you create it. Find the Picture property on the property sheet and delete the image, as shown in Figure 8-50.

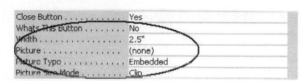

Figure 8-50 Remove the Form Image

Shortcut to Creating New Forms

You're back, rested and ready to go on.

Before you tackle creating new forms from scratch, I'm going to share with you a shortcut for creating a group of similar forms. The first two forms we created ended up being almost identical. Except for their record sources and captions, they were the same. We went to some trouble, in fact, to make them look and display the same. Why not take advantage of the fact that Access, like other Windows applications, has the Save As option for objects to avoid some of that work?

Try this with a form you want to duplicate for a different record source.

1. Open an existing form in design view.
2. Click on File-->Save As from the menu bar.
3. The dialog box shown in Figure 8-51 will open.

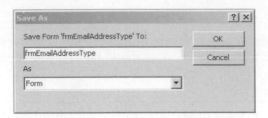

Figure 8-51 Save as Dialog for Forms

4. Replace the name with the name of the new form you want to create, such as frmPhoneType, and click OK.

5. The new form is created and ready to be modified.

Change the Record Source and Control Source

The newly copied form will look like its parent and it will have the same record source, so the first thing to do is open the property sheet and change the record source.

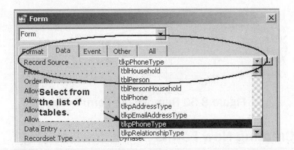

Figure 8-52 Change Record Source for Duplicate Form

Next change the control source for the two text fields on the form. One at a time, select them from the drop down list on the property sheet and change their control sources. Even though the Primary Key field is invisible and has a zero height and width, you can select it in the drop down list and edit its properties. And don't forget to change the captions for the form and the labels. Finally, change the field names to reflect their control sources.

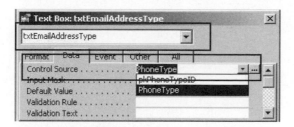

Figure 8-53 Change Control Sources on Duplicate Form

Repeat these steps for the other lookup form, creating frmRelationshipType.

You should now have four forms, identical in size, layout and function. The form names are frmAddressType, frmEmailAddressType, frmPhoneType, and frmRelationshipType. Only the names of the fields on them and the captions for the labels are different. And, of course, they each have different record sources.

You don't have to do anything special to the command buttons on them because, as you recall, the code in them is generic. The close command is the short cut:

```
DoCmd.Close
```

If the close method specified a form by name, you would have to change it for each form.

Navigation on Forms

In this last section of Chapter 8, I want to tell you a little bit about moving around in, or navigating, Access forms. You should be familiar with tab and mouse click behavior, which is common to most Windows applications, so I won't go into a lot of detail there. Instead I want to concentrate on what happens on a form when you navigate through the fields on it.

Open one of four simple forms you just created. When it opens, the cursor should be in one of the fields on the form, as in Figure 8-54. You can't see the flashing cursor on the printed page, but you can see the small arrowhead on the left. That's the record selector that indicates that this record has the focus. When you press the tab key to move from Home Street to Home PO Box, the focus shifts from the first field to the next.

Most controls on a form can have the focus. In Figure 8-54, for example, the Done button gets the focus when you click on it to close the form.

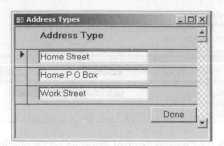

Figure 8-54 Focus on a Field in Form

When you navigate a form, what you are doing is *shifting focus* from one control to another. You can use the Tab key, in most cases, or the mouse to do that.

Triggering Events on a Form

One of the most important consequences of shifting focus from one control on a form to another is *shifting focus triggers events*. For example, when you change or add a value in one of the fields on the form in Figure 8-54, the new or changed value normally is *not* saved to the underlying record set until the control loses focus, triggering the After Update event. (You can write VBA code to change the default event behavior.)

That's an important point to remember. Simply entering values into a text box isn't enough to save the new values to the underlying record source. The After Update must be triggered to save the change. That normally happens within a workflow as users tab or click from field to field, but not always, so be aware of the need to trigger the update event. You'll learn more about how controls behave when they receive or lose focus in the following chapters.

From Simple to Intermediate

The four forms you created in this chapter are bound to the four look up tables in your contacts database. After the first time you use them to add the values for your look up tables, you probably won't use them very much, but they've already served a major purpose by giving you a chance to learn a good deal about creating basic forms in Access. Still like most maintenance-type forms, they'll make your live easier by being there even though you won't use them often.

Much of what you learned from these simple forms applies to the more advanced forms you'll be creating next. In the next chapter, you'll learn how to create forms with a few more features.

Backup, Backup, Backup

This would be another excellent time to make a backup copy of the database. Close your database, find it on your hard drive and make a copy in a safe place. Do that now.

This page intentionally left blank.

9. Getting Data Into Your Database—Intermediate Forms

The next set of forms I'll show you how to create are for regular data entry and modification. We'll need them to add households, people, and their related contact data into the various tables in our database. They'll be more complex than the *maintenance* forms you created in Chapter 8 and less complex than the *nested* forms you'll create in Chapter 10.

Select Forms-->New in the database window. The new form dialog box opens, offering you a choice of ways to create the new form. Select Design View from the list. Then, in the drop down list at the bottom of the form, select tblHousehold. Click OK to move to the next step.

You should see a blank form and the field list with all of the fields contained in the table that is the record source for this form. The property sheet may also open, depending on whether or not you left it open the last time you designed a form.

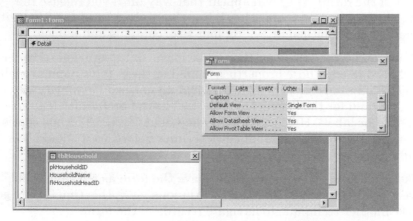

Figure 9-1 New Blank Form for tblHousehold

Drag and Drop Fields

This time, I'm going use a different method of adding fields to the form. I will drag the fields from the field list and drop them onto the form as a group. I'll move them into position later. You can hold down the shift click and select all three fields, or use control click to select them one at a time. Either way, once they are all selected, drag them to the detail section of the form, as in Figure 9-2.

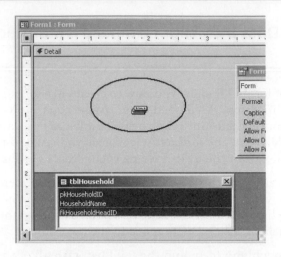

Figure 9-2 Dragging Fields to the Form

Figure 9-2 shows the group of fields as stacked icons (in the circle in the center of the form). They will appear that way until you release the mouse button to drop them. They'll line themselves up of the form with default settings for height, width, font size, captions and names.

Just as you learned to do for the simple forms in the previous chapter, you'll need to edit those properties, changing the default names to follow standard naming conventions and providing natural language captions for labels and for the form itself. Use "txt" as the preface for text fields and "lbl" for labels. Hide the primary key field. Give the form a caption, and so on. You've done all that several times before, so it should be a familiar task.

Make all of those changes now, then save the form as frmHousehold. Save it as single view rather than continuous view, this time. We're going to use another technique to navigate records in the form.

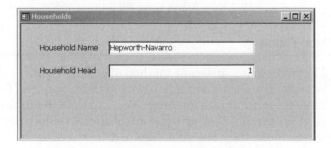

Figure 9-3 frmHousehold, Step One

At this point, the form looks like Figure 9-3. Notice I removed the navigation buttons, record selectors, and scroll bars. The first record in the underlying record set displays in the form. Without the scroll bars, record selectors, and navigation buttons, there is no obvious way to navigate to other records, although a way does exits: Page Down and Page Up keys. Press them to watch the form move through the records in your table.

Navigating with a Searching Combo Box

Now, switch back to design view and we'll add a new control that will allow us to navigate quickly and easily through all of the records in the form.

You may recall I told you combo boxes are one of my favorite controls. Here's a place where I think they are especially useful. On the Toolbox toolbar, click on the Combo Box icon. Look back at Figure 8-29 in the previous chapter if you can't remember which one that is.

With the combo box control selected, draw a rectangle on the form. Put it just above the text field for household name. You may have to push that text box down a little to make room. When the control is drawn, a dialog box opens, asking you what you want this combo box to do.

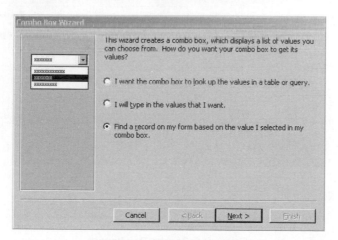

Figure 9-4 Combo Box Dialog

We want the third option: Find a record on my form based on the value I selected in my combo box. That's the technique we'll use to navigate through the records in the form. Click on the radio button for that choice and then click Next.

The next dialog box shows you the available fields from the record source for the form. In this form, there are only three fields: pkHouseholdID, HouseholdName, and fkHouseholdHeadID. We'll use only two of the three: pkHouseholdID and HouseholdName, so select them in the list and click on the button with the single arrow (>>) on it. I'll explain later why you don't want to include the household head field in this searching combo box.

After you've selected the fields for the combo box, click Next.

What Just Happened?

The wizard has taken the values you selected from the underlying table and put them into a list. The combo box will display the records in that list on the form. This is the list half of the combo box I told you about.

Format the Combo Box

The next step is to provide some rules for Access to follow in displaying the items on that list to your users. Figure 9-5 shows the wizard with sample data from the table you just selected.

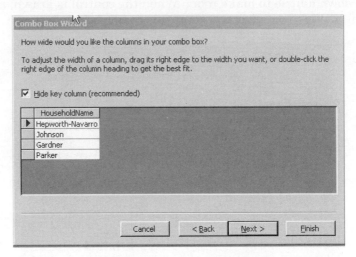

Figure 9-5 Combo Box Layout

Access knows you don't want your users to see primary keys, so it hides them by default. Leave that checkbox checked to keep the key hidden. Access also offers its best guess as to the appropriate width of the columns in the combo box, based on the sample data available in the wizard.

Since the sample data is only a part of the full list, it may not include the widest value, if it is further down the list. You may have to adjust the column later, but for now, let's accept the default. Click Next to move on.

Access wants to know how to label this combo box. The next dialog box is asking for the caption to place in the label attached to the combo box. It offers a default name, but you should change it, as shown in Figure 9-6 to a natural language caption. You'll have a chance to rename the combo box and label later.

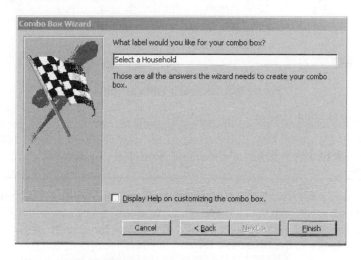

Figure 9-6 Select a Caption for the Label

Click Finish to see your completed combo box. Depending on how tall and wide you drew it on the form, you may have to adjust its location, width and height to get it to fit properly. Make the font size the same as the other controls on the form. Make sure the font is the same as well.

Check through the other options on the Format menu for ways to make the controls on your form look good. Align your controls (hold the shift key while selecting them), make them all the same height or width, or space them evenly vertically and horizontally on the form.

For example, if your controls are too far apart, you can decrease the space between them (and make the spaces equal at the same time), as in Figure 9-7. When you're done, switch back to form view to evaluate the result. Don't spend too much time here because you'll be adding more controls to the form and that will probably mean more layout changes later.

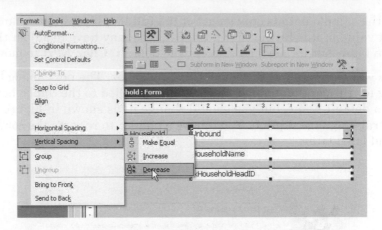

Figure 9-7 Decrease Vertical Spacing

Access has given your new combo box a default name, something like Combo0, or Combo1. Don't change that for now. First, I want to show you how the combo box works on the form. Switch to form view.

> If you haven't already added some Household names for testing, take a few minutes now to do so; it will help you see and understand this combo box better if you have real data to look at. Put your household name and the names of some of your friends and family in the household table.

Click on the combo box and start typing one of the household names you know is already in your household table. The combo box will attempt to match up what you type with the name. This is the *text box* half of the combo box at work. When you have a match, press the Tab key to move to the next field. You can also move by using the mouse to click on one of the other fields.

The form will update itself to display the household name you just selected in the combo box. Try it out a few times, then click on the down arrow at the right end of the combo box. That will display a list of the names in the combo box, its list half. You can scroll down it or click on a name to select it. That's the list half of the combo box.

Okay, now that you've tried it out, let's go back to design view and see how this all works.

Combo Boxes and Visual Basic for Applications Code

To understand how the combo box works, you're going to have to learn a little bit more about Visual Basic for Applications, or VBA. The combo box runs a little piece of VBA code each time you select a value from its list. You saw another event procedure, a very simple one, when you created a command button for your first set of forms.

This one is a bit more complex, but if you're an experienced programmer, this part will be relatively easy. If not, I'll show you everything you need to know for this combo box. You'll be writing your own VBA code in no time.

Switch to design view for the form and open the property sheet to the Event tab. Click on the combo box or select it from the drop down list on the property sheet. You'll see a list of events, including After Update, with the words [Event Procedure] in it. Just as you saw in the previous chapter, that means there is a little piece of VBA code in the code module for this form, code that runs every time your or someone else updates the combo box.

An *update event* occurs when the user selects a name on the list and then shifts the focus to another control by pressing Tab or Enter, or by clicking with the mouse. It's a little more complicated than that behind the scenes, I suppose, but for now, that's enough to figure out what the form and combo box are doing.

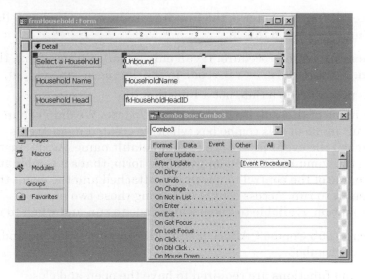

Figure 9-8 Event Procedure for the Combo Box

In the property sheet, select the After Update event property. The builder button will appear. It's that little button with three dots on it. Press that button to open the VBA code window.

You should be looking at the VBA code that runs whenever the combo box runs. It looks like Figure 9-9.

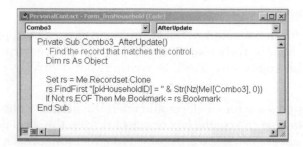

Figure 9-9 VBA Procedure—After Update

VBA Code

There are the two combo boxes at the top of the code window. You should recall that the one on the left contains the names of the form, form sections, and controls on the form for which you want to create code. The one on the right tells Access to which event it should attach the code.

```
Private Sub Combo3_AfterUpdate ()
```

As you recall from Chapter 8, the first line in the code window tells Access (and you) three things:

1. This is a private procedure. It can only be called from within this form. No other form or VBA code in the database can get to it.

2. This procedure is a Sub, not a Function.

3. The name of this sub is Combo3_AfterUpdate. We didn't change the default name of this combo box when we created it, so Access attached the event procedure to that default name. Again, just as with the command button on your first form, that's a combination of the name of the control to which it is attached and the event that causes it to run. Access counts on having those two pieces of information available to know which code to run and when to run it.

In this case, sub Combo3_AfterUpdate will run after someone updates the value of combo3.

All subs and functions are required to have the open and close parentheses after their names [( )]. Sometimes you'll see other things inside the parentheses. I'll explain them later, when we see an event procedure that includes them.

Code Comments

The second line of code in Combo3_AfterUpdate is a remark, or comment.

```
' Find the record that matches the control.
```

The Access wizard placed it there when it created the sub as a description of what the sub does. Self-documented code includes a lot of comments because it helps other developers follow the logic of the code.

Comments are preceded by a single quote, or apostrophe, ('). Access' code processor recognizes that as a signal not to try to process anything on the rest of that line.

Declaring Variables

The third line of code contains a Dim, or *variable declaration statement*[13], declaring a variable, called RS, that it defines as an object.

```
Dim rs As Object
```

In programming terms, a variable is a generic name like RS, which represents a value that can change from time to time. It's like in algebra, where you can write an equation like $A + B = 12$. A and B are variables representing values that change.

In database work, you often need to calculate values like the time spent on a project (Project stop time – Project start time), or count things (the number of households without email addresses). Using the Dim statement or one of its variants, you declare the variables (ProjectStopTime, ProjectStartTime, and HouseholdCount) that will be used in those calculations.

Option Explicit

Actually, you can write code without declaring variables. I will only tell you about that; I won't show you any examples because it is a dangerous thing to do and it is usually considered poor programming practice by

---

[13] I have no idea where the name *Dim* came from. Sorry. It's just the way VBA declares variables. I stopped worrying about where the name came from a long time ago, when I realized I could write code quite well without knowing that particular piece of information.

---

competent developers. In fact, Access provides a way for you to force the declaration of all variables before using them.

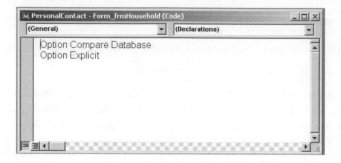

Figure 9-10 Option Explicit

This is the *declarations* section of the *code module* (or container for the VBA code) attached to the form called frmHousehold. Notice that in the combo boxes at the top of the code window, the selections are (General) and (Declarations). These are, obviously enough, the *general declarations*. They apply to all of the code in this module.

The Option Explicit statement is the one we're most interested in. It tells Access you want to *require* all variables to be explicitly declared before they can be used. In other words, with the general declaration Option Explicit you are telling Access it can't use any variable in this module until after you have explicitly given it a name.

All of your code modules should have the Option Explicit declaration in them. It prevents many hard-to-track-down problems later on.

Variable Type

Usually, you'll also tell Access what kind of variable it is. In Combo3_AfterUpdate, the variable RS is declared as an *Object*. Objects, to Access, are things like tables, forms, queries and record sets.

Declare the Object

```
Set rs = Me.Recordset.Clone
```

The fourth line in Combo3_AfterUpdate tells Access what kind of object RS is and uses the *Set* statement to initialize it to a particular value. In this case it is a clone of the form's record set. I'll explain record set clones in a minute.

Me

The key word "Me", as you learned in the previous chapter, refers to the form or report where the code is running. In this case, of course, that's frmHousehold. There are other, more formal, ways to refer to forms, reports, etc. You'll need to use them when you refer to one object (like a form) from another one. For now, we'll stick to a single form.

Clone a Record Set

One of the properties of the form (that is, Me) is its *record set*; that is to say, the set of records from the underlying table or query that are to be displayed on the form. The record set for this form comes from tblHousehold. This may seem a bit circuitous, but in order to find a particular record in the record set, Access needs to create a copy, or *clone*, of it. This line of code tells Access to do create the copy and to call the resulting clone "RS". After this statement is executed, the form has available to it *two* record sets, which are clones of each other.

Search a Record Set

The fifth line of code tells Access to search through the cloned record set until it finds the first matching record; that's the rs.FindFirst part of the code.

```
rs.FindFirst "[pkHouseholdID] = " & Str(Nz(Me![Combo3], 0))
```

Search Criteria

The rest of the line, the part following the FindFirst action and starting at the quote, is the *criteria* Access will use to identify the record. Specifically, that criteria says, "Search through the cloned record set RS looking at each of the values in the field called [pkHouseholdID]. Keep looking until you find the first record where that value is the same as the value in the control called [Combo3] on Me" (the form where this code is running).

For example, if the value in Combo3 is 5, the matching record in the record set clone will also have the value 5 for its primary key.

String Handling Functions

There are two additional functions in that line, "Str" and "Nz". They're used a lot in Access, especially Nz, so let's take a closer look at them.

Str

The first function, Str, converts a number to a string, or text value. For example, if you wanted to compare two ZIP Codes to see if they were the same, you'd want to treat them as text or strings.

In this case, the combo box wizard inserted the string conversion function into the code because the wizard can't know ahead of time what types of values you will search on. It just goes ahead and converts everything to strings to be safe. All numbers can be treated as if they were strings, but the reverse is not true. To be safe, therefore, the wizard treats everything as if it were a string. Since we know the primary key in tblHousehold is an autonumber and is therefore a long integer, the Str function isn't really needed here, but Access didn't know that when it created the combo box.

Nz

The second function, Nz, is a really handy one. It's good to learn about it now, because you'll find yourself using it a lot and its name isn't really all that obvious, unlike many of the other common functions. Nz converts Null values to non-null values.

If, for example, there is no value in the combo box after it is updated, the code to search for matching households would fail with an error message to the user because there would be nothing to search with; it is *null*, or unknown. Converting nulls to zeros ensures there will always be *something* to search with, so the rest of the code will run as it is supposed to run.

Of course, this piece of code can't find any records with the zero value because we're using autonumbers, so there should not be any primary keys with the value zero; but at least it will complete the search without causing an error.

Move to a Record

The sixth line of code tells Access what to do once it has found the matching record, if it exists.

```
If Not rs.EOF Then Me.Bookmark = rs.Bookmark
```

Conditional Instructions in VBA

This is a special case example of the general class of instructions called *conditional statements*. A lot of VBA code depends on this basic kind of logic, so let's pause to take a closer look at conditionals.

Essentially, conditional statements provide branches in your code where you tell Access to do one thing under some circumstances, but to do something else under other circumstances.

Only *one* of the branches in each conditional gets executed.

You have to construct the test carefully to be sure you are getting the results you expect and want, of course, but they give you a lot of control.

Standard Syntax

A fully formed conditional statement has at least five parts. Its basic outline is like this:

```
(1)IF  (2)(criteria to evaluate)  (3)Then
    (4)(Do something here)
(5)  END Tf
```

Conditional statements begin with (1) the keyword IF, (2) followed by some criteria you want to evaluate. Then, (3) depending on the outcome of that evaluation, (4) you want your application to do something. Finally, (5) end the conditional statement.

A great deal of the VBA code you write in the near future will be based on exactly this type of conditional instruction. If one condition exists, you want the database to take one action; if another condition exists, you want the database to do nothing at all.

Other Conditional Statements

In addition to the basic If...Then...Else conditional structure you just saw, there are a couple of other variations.

```
(1)IF  (2)(criteria to evaluate)  (3)Then
    (4)(Do something here)
(5)ELSE
    (6)  (Do something different here)
(7)  END If
```

In this case, the addition of a second set of instructions following the word ELSE tells Access to do one thing if the criteria are met, or to *do something different* if they are not met. That's different from doing nothing if the criteria are not met, as in our first example above.

For example,

```
IF intCountofBooks > 12 then
    MsgBox "Large Order"
ELSE
    MsgBox "Small Order"
END IF
```

This conditional tells Access to display different messages to the user, depending on how many books are in an order.

In this example, Access has calculated the number of books in a book order as intCountofBooks. That value is passed into the conditional to be evaluated. If the count of books in the order is greater than twelve, the conditional statement presents a message box that tells the user this is a large order, otherwise the message box tells the user it is a small order.

Another variation you'll use is:

```
(1) IF (2)(criteria to evaluate) (3)Then
    (4)(Do something here)
(5)ELSEIF (6) (another criteria) (7) Then
    (8) (Do something else here)
(9) END If
```

For Example,

```
IF intCountofBooks > 12 then
    MsgBox "Large Order"
ELSEIF intCountofBooks > 6 Then
    MsgBox "Medium Order"
ELSE
    MsgBox "Small Order"
END IF
```

This time, if the value of intCountofBooks is greater than twelve, the first branch of the conditional is true and the user is shown a message stating that this is a large order. Processing drops to the END IF statement from there. Neither of the other two Else statements is evaluated.

If intCountofBooks is twelve or less, processing drops to the next line starting with ELSEIF. Here, the test is whether intCountofBooks is greater than six. If so, the user is shown a message stating that this is a medium order and processing drops to the END IF statement.

If intCountofBooks is six or less, processing drops to the next line, starting with ELSE. This line doesn't do any further testing. The user is shown the small order message box. Processing stops at END IF.

The other type of conditional structure you'll sometimes see is the one that started us on this diversion.

```
If Not rs.EOF Then Me.Bookmark = rs.Bookmark
```

It's a condensed version that checks the condition in the IF part of the statement and carries out the instruction after the Then keyword when the IF statement is true. It's all on one line and doesn't need the closing keywords END IF. It's restricted to cases like this where there is one simple instruction to be carried out when the condition evaluates to true.

With that background, you're ready to take a look at the line of code.

```
If Not rs.EOF Then Me.Bookmark = rs.Bookmark
```

What this Conditional Statement Does

EOF means End Of the File. It is a yes/no value. Either you are looking at the end of the file (or record set) or you're not. The IF statement tells Access: "If, after completing the FindFirst search, you have not yet reached the end of the file, then set the form's bookmark to the record set clone's bookmark." You well may ask, "What does that mean and how does that work?"

Before the search starts, you are at the beginning, not the end of the file, so EOF will be false. If FindFirst doesn't match a record during its search, it will continue until it reaches the end of the file. At that point EOF will become true. When Access starts to process the If statement following its search, rs.EOF will either be true, meaning it searched through the record set to the end without finding a match or false, meaning it did not reach the end of the file because it found a matching record in the record set clone.

In other words, if EOF is not true, Access found a matching record in the clone of the record set before it reached the end. (It found a record where the value of the primary key, pkHouseholdID, is the same as the value of combo3). The command was to find the first matching record, so as soon as it found that record it stopped the search and moved on to the next line of code.

The Bookmark property is, as its name suggests, a flag, or bookmark, or pointer that designates one particular record out of all of the records in the record set. Because RS is an exact clone of the form's record set, the bookmarks for each record are the same for both record sets.

Once Access finds the bookmark for a record in the record set clone, it can use the value of that bookmark to move the focus *on the form* to the record in its record set with the matching bookmark. That's the Then part of the if-then statement.

The last line in the sub tells Access the fun is over, time to quit processing the code and wait for you, the user, to trigger another event.

When this code has run, the form will either display the record it found in the search, or it will display the same record as when the search started because it didn't find a match to move to.

No Error Trapping

You may have noticed that Access didn't add any error trapping to this sub. As an exercise in code writing, why not go ahead and add it yourself, following the template in the Done buttons on your simple forms. You'll need the GoTo statement, the exit label and exit sub statements, the error-handling label, the error message and resume statements. When you're done, compare your error handling to Figure 9-11.

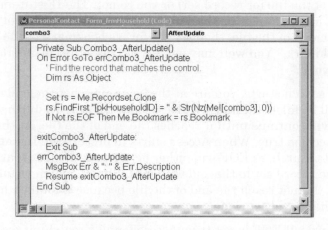

```
Private Sub Combo3_AfterUpdate()
On Error GoTo errCombo3_AfterUpdate
    ' Find the record that matches the control.
    Dim rs As Object

    Set rs = Me.Recordset.Clone
    rs.FindFirst "[pkHouseholdID] = " & Str(Nz(Me![combo3], 0))
    If Not rs.EOF Then Me.Bookmark = rs.Bookmark

exitCombo3_AfterUpdate:
    Exit Sub
errCombo3_AfterUpdate:
    MsgBox Err & ": " & Err.Description
    Resume exitCombo3_AfterUpdate
End Sub
```

Figure 9-11 Error Handling Added to Code

String Concatenation

I added one additional enhancement to the error handler I created for this event procedure.

```
MsgBox Err & ": " & Err.Description
```

I *concatenated,* or *joined,* two separate objects into a single string that the error message box will display.

Concatenation is a very important tool; so let's take a few seconds to look at how it works. We'll also need to learn a little about errors in VBA code.

"Err" is an Access object that returns the *number* of the error that occurred. The error number is quite useful to you, the *developer,* because you can use error numbers to decide how to handle different types of errors. For example, you may want to ignore errors of type 3114, but tell the user about any other error that occurs. You can even write conditional error handlers, using If...Then statements, to take different actions for different kinds of errors based on the error number raised.

On the other hand, most users have no idea what error 3114 is and probably couldn't care less. If you show them a message like Figure 9-12, you'll only make them angry.

Figure 9-12 Error Number Only

Therefore, in addition to the error number itself, you may want to show the user Access' description of the error. (I started to call it a plain language description, but I realized that is only true if you speak computerese as your first language.) That's done with the statement Err.Description.

The ampersand (&) is the *string concatenation* operator. It tells Access to put the elements together into a single string. Here, the result will be the error number followed by a colon and one space, then by the error description. The colon and space are surrounded by quotes (": ") to tell Access this is plain English that needs to be included just as it is. The resulting error message will look something like Figure 9-13.

Figure 9-13 Error Message with Error Number and Description

Of course, if this were a real error handling routine, you'd want to replace the standard Access error description with one that means more to the user, but this will do as an illustration of the technique. You'll find string concatenation to be a very useful technique in many places throughout your Access applications, in queries an on forms and reports as well as in VBA.

Now that you've learned more about writing VBA code and have even tried your hand at writing your own VBA, let's go back and finish up the discussion of the combo box on the form.

Why I Prefer Combo Boxes to Scroll Bars and Navigation Buttons

It may already be clear to you why searching combo boxes are more user friendly than the standard navigation buttons and scroll bars, but I'll take a few moments here to explain my opinion.

First, both scroll bars and navigation buttons are blind searches; you either move forward or backward through a record set, one record at a time, or in small leaps and jumps. You probably have a general idea of where you are in the record set—near the front, near the middle, near the end—but finding a specific record is always a matter of getting close and then moving one record at a time until you find the right one.

If you are using navigation buttons, the record number box in the navigation buttons moves you to the specific record entered into it; but how do you know ahead of time which record number that should be? Same problem; you can get close, but you always have to move one record at a time to find an exact match.

On the other hand, the combo box handles a lot of the searching for you. When it is set to match a typed entry, it moves to the exact record you want to select by matching the letters you type with the values in its list.

Not only that, it shows the identifying keys—the names displayed in the combo box list—as *natural language keys* your users can understand and relate to.

If they prefer to use the list portion of the combo box, users can scroll and scan the list quickly and only move to another record when they find the one they want in the list. They can either select from the list or type to match and get to the exact record much more quickly and easily.

Just remember that searching combo boxes are not, and cannot be, bound to any of the records in the underlying record set.

VBA Behind the Combo Box—Further Study

The VBA code behind the searching combo box is only seven lines long (thirteen with the error handling added), including the comment, but a great deal happens when it runs.

I have bombarded you with a lot of information about VBA code, and in a short space, too. I hope I've given you enough to whet your appetite to learn more VBA without overwhelming you too quickly.

In any event, I wanted to give you a taste of it so you'd not be intimidated. Still, you'll definitely want to spend more time in in-depth study in the near future.

One very useful trick I've used countless times over the years is to let Access do some of the legwork for you. The Help system is quite good (although I think the Access 97 version was better, sigh). It is context sensitive. That means you can put the cursor on a word in the VBA code module and press F1 to get an explanation and discussion of the term; often an example is included. You can cut and paste examples into your database and try them out to see how things work. It's not always easy, but it is well worth the effort.

Make a backup copy of your new form. Then take a short break to play with your new combo box before you tackle the next step, in which we'll make some refinements to the combo box and learn how to create a SQL statement.

Creating SQL Statements

Switch to form view and look at the values in your combo box and in the text box for Household head. It should like something like Figure 9-14.

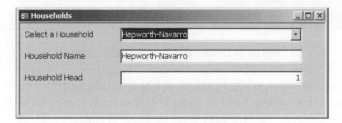

Figure 9-14 Foreign Key Displayed

In the household head field, the value displayed for the household head is the foreign key from tblHousehold. That's accurate, of course, because the, but wouldn't it be better to show the actual name of the household head instead? In fact, didn't we already decide never to show primary keys? Shouldn't we also hide the *foreign* keys? Yes, let's get rid of them.

The field on the form that displays the household head still shows the foreign key. That's accurate, but not too user friendly. Instead of that foreign key, we want to show the name of the person.

Using List Boxes to Provide Choices for a Field

Let's take care of that now. Switch to form design view, open the form's property sheet and select the household head field.

Its control source is fkHouseholdHeadID, the foreign key from tblPerson. We won't change that property. We want this field to *store* the foreign key in the table, so we don't want to change that. We do want the control to *display* names from the related table.

There are, as you might guess, several ways to do that. I'll only show you one way now. We're going to change this control from a *text box* to a *list box*. Then, we'll use tblPerson as the row source for that list box control.

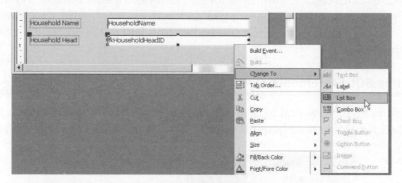

Figure 9-15 Convert Text Box to List Box

With the form in design view, select the household head ID field, then right mouse click on the field to open the shortcut menu, as in Figure 9-15. Select Change To and List Box. txtHouseholdHeadID will change into a list box.

Don't surprised when it grows taller, taking up more space on the form. However, there won't be any other obvious changes until you select other properties from the property sheet.

Open the property sheet for this form, select the new list box, and then select the Data tab for the newly created list box. It will look like Figure 9-16.

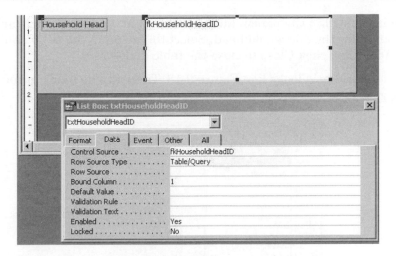

Figure 9-16 List Box Properties

You can see that the control source for this field is still fkHouseholdHeadID. That means the list box is still bound to the underlying foreign key field in the table, but because it is now a list box, it can also *display* whatever you enter into the Row Source property.

To open the query builder for this list box, click on its row source property and then the builder button at the end of the line. This time, we'll build the query for this field from scratch, rather than going through a wizard. When the query grid opens, it will also display the table dialog as in Figure 9-17, because at this point there are no tables in the query window and Access knows you'll need to add at least one table to create a query.

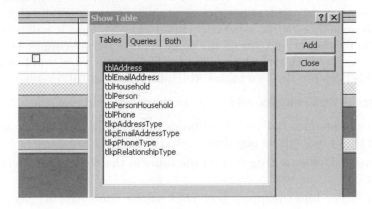

Figure 9-17 Add Table Dialog

We're interested in the person table, the one that will supply first and last names for the household head. Select tblPerson in the dialog and click Add. Then click Close to close the table dialog.

The query grid now looks like Figure 9-18. There are no fields in the query grid yet.

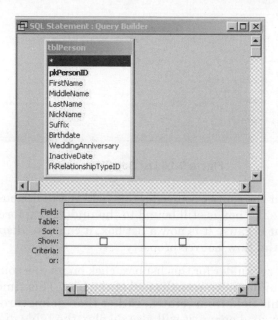

Figure 9-18 Table in Query Window

We'll need three of the fields from tblPerson to fill the list box that will display household heads. First, we need the primary key field (I hope that's obvious by now; we need the primary key because it will provide the value for the foreign key in the related table.) The primary key tells Access which record in tblPerson to use. The primary key and foreign key link fields between the two tables, tblHousehold and tblPerson.

There are several ways to add fields to the query grid (surprised?).

> You can *double-click on a field name* in the table in the table window and that field will be populated into the grid below.

> You can *click and drag* it from the table in the window down to the grid.

> You can go into the query grid, *click on the Table row* to select the table name, and then move up to the Field row and select pkPersonID from the list of available fields in that table.

The primary key should be the first field on the left in the query grid. That's really important. I'll show you why in a few moments. First, though, let's add the name fields that we need to create the display.

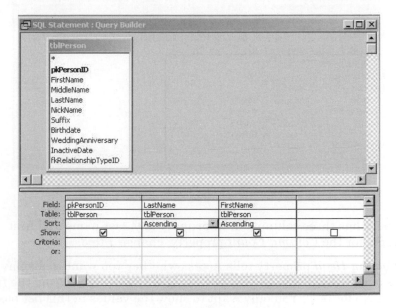

Figure 9-19 Query in Design View

In the second column, add the last name; in the third, add the first name. Set the sort orders for both to Ascending. The result will look like Figure 9-19 in design view and Figure 9-20 in datasheet view.

pkPersonID	LastName	FirstName
1	Hepworth	George
3	Hepworth	Lyndsey
2	Hepworth	Yolanda
4	Johnson	Walter
(AutoNumber)		

Record: 1 of 4

Figure 9-20 Query in Datasheet View

Now, close the query window. Let's save this query as qrySelectHouseholdHead.

Now, we need to tell Access how to display the new columns in this list box. Originally we had only *one* value there, the foreign key, but now there are *three* columns in the query. We need to tell Access to show the other columns and hide the primary key. With the form in design view, find the Format tab on the property sheet and look for the properties outlined in Figure 9-21.

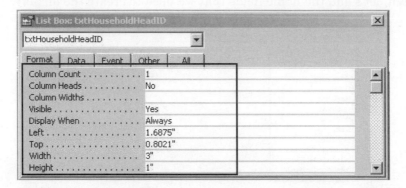

Figure 9-21 List Box Properties

The query has three columns in it: primary key, last name and first name. So, for the *Column Count* property, change *1* to *3*.

The *Column Head* property tells Access whether you want to display the names of the columns in the list box along with the values from the fields. Leave it No for now. You only want to show the values in this list box, not the names of the fields they come from.

The *Column Width* property controls how wide the columns within the list box are. There will be three numbers here, one for each column. As always, we do *not* want to see the key field, so set its width to zero inches. Last Name and First Name are probably similar in length, so let's make the width of those columns one inch each. We can change them if they don't fit the values in the query. The list box itself is three inches wide, more than enough to display the two one-inch columns. It is also one inch high.

Switch your form to form view. Try out the searching combo box and see how this new list box works when you search on households in the searching combo box. Notice that the name selected in the list box changes each time you update the combo box to move to a new record; assuming, of course, that you've designated one person as the head of that household. If you haven't, you won't see the move, although it does occur.

Behavior of List Boxes

The list box displays *all* of the people in the database. As your contacts grow, the number of items in the list will grow. When the number of items extends past the bottom of the list box, the vertical scroll bar will appear on the right side, as in other Windows applications.

Because the list box is bound to the household head field in tblHousehold, the name selected in the list box changes as the form moves through records in the table.

Now, how does that work? Switch back to design view, open the property sheet and select the list box. I'll tell you how it works.

Bound Columns in List Boxes

Select the Data tab on the property sheet. Just below the Row Source property, you'll see the Bound Column property.

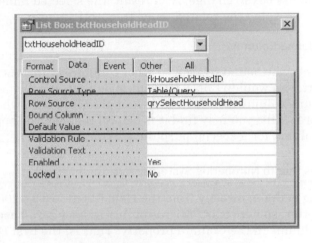

Figure 9-22 Bound Column Property

Remember when I told you it was really important to have the primary key for the query in this row source in the *first column on the left*? This is the reason why. The value in that column, the first one, is the one that is *bound* to this field.

The control source for this list box is fkHouseholdHeadID in tblHousehold. The bound column for the query in its row source is pkHouseholdHeadID from tblPerson. The pkPersonID and fkHouseholdHeadID fields (the primary key from tblPerson and the foreign key from tblHousehold) define the household head relationship between tblHousehold and tblParent.

Creating the Relationship

When you make a selection from the list in the list box, the value in the bound column (the primary key from tblPerson) is saved to the underlying, or bound, field in tblHousehold (that is, the foreign key from tblPerson is saved as fkHouseholdHeadID in tblHousehold). That's how you go about telling Access about the relationship between the two tables with a list box.

Displaying the Related Values

In a case where the searching combo box moves the form's focus to a new record, the value forcing the change *changes*, causing the value of bound column in the list box to change. As a result, the selected name in the list box changes to display the related name from tblPerson.

Using Other Bound Columns

You can change the bound column to other columns in the query, but for the most part, you wouldn't need or want to do that. It's a lot simpler to leave the bound column as it is in this example. Of course, when you've acquired more skills, you may find it is helpful to make the bound column a different column for a special purpose.

Complications Due to Numbering Systems

The following is taken directly from the Help file in Access 2002. I can't say it any better, so here it is. "Microsoft Access uses zero-based numbers to refer to columns in the Column property. That is, the first column is referenced by using the expression Column(0); the second column is referenced by using the expression Column(1); and so on.

However, the Bound Column property uses one-based numbers to refer to the columns. This means if the Bound Column property is set to *1*, you could access the value stored in that column by using the expression Column(0)."

In other words, the bound column is column (1) on the *form*, but within the *query*, it is column (0). That is probably going to be the source of confusion to you at some point, just as it has been for many, many others.

It's not worth worrying about too much at this point, because you'll be putting the primary or foreign key for your query in the first column on the left (column (0)) and making the bound column for the list box column (1), as I've suggested. Sooner or later, as you learn more advanced techniques, you'll have to deal with it again.

For now, the most important thing to remember is the bound column normally means the first one on the left in the query that provides the records for the list box.

Changing Selected Values in the List Box

If you want to select or change the value of the foreign key bound to the list box, all you need to do is click on one of the other items in the list. The value on the bound column on that row will be saved to the underlying fkHouseholdHeadID field in tblHousehold.

In other words, if you want to change the head of the Hepworth-Navarro household from George to Yolanda, simply click on Yolanda in the list box to select that name. That saves the new foreign key—the one referring to Yolanda's primary key in tblPerson— to tblHousehold.

Housekeeping Chores—Control Names

Before we wrap up the discussion of this list box and move on, we have to take care of a couple of housekeeping chores. I'm referring specifically to the names of both the combo box and list box we just created. First, when we created the combo box, Access gave it a default name, combo3 (or whatever it was in your database). Also, when we created the control for fkHouseholdHeadID, it was a text field and we named it txtHouseholdHeadID to reflect that fact. We need to correct both of these names now to conform to standard naming conventions.

The list box is the easiest to deal with, so let's tackle it first. Open the form in design view, open the property sheet, and select the list box. On the Other tab of the property sheet, change the Name property from *txt*HouseholdHeadID to *lst*HouseholdHeadID. The prefix "lst" stands for list box.

Updating the Event Procedure

Because there is no event procedure attached to lstHouseholdHeadID, changing its name has no further effects on the list box. That's not true for the combo box, however.

You can change the name of the combo box just as easily as you did the name of the list box; you can do that in your database next. However, doing so creates a complication we also have to deal with. You may already have made a guess as to what it is.

Go ahead and rename it from combo3 (or whatever its name is in your database) to cboSelectHousehold. The name SelectHousehold tells you what the combo box does on this form and the "cbo" prefix means that it's a combo box.

Disappearing VBA Code

Now, select the Event tab of the property sheet and see what is behind the After Update property for the newly renamed combo box. (Click in the field and then click on the event builder button that opens at the end of the field.) The event procedure is empty! What happened to the code that was there before; where did it go, and why?

Event Procedure Names

You may recall I told you the names of event procedures for controls on a form consist of two components, the *name of the control* and the *event for which it is to be run*. We just changed the name of the combo box. Access can no longer match the event procedure called combo3_AfterUpdate to the combo box, which is now called cboSelectHousehold. It's up to you to manually find the old event procedure and rename it so it works with the combo box under its new name.

It didn't really go away; it only moved. It will be found in the General section of the form's code module as shown in Figure 9-23.

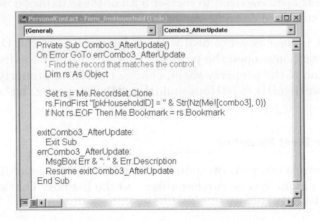

```
Private Sub Combo3_AfterUpdate()
On Error GoTo errCombo3_AfterUpdate
    ' Find the record that matches the control.
    Dim rs As Object

    Set rs = Me.Recordset.Clone
    rs.FindFirst "[pkHouseholdID] = " & Str(Nz(Me![combo3], 0))
    If Not rs.EOF Then Me.Bookmark = rs.Bookmark

exitCombo3_AfterUpdate:
    Exit Sub
errCombo3_AfterUpdate:
    MsgBox Err & ": " & Err.Description
    Resume exitCombo3_AfterUpdate
End Sub
```

Figure 9-23 Orphaned Event Procedure

Rename the Event Procedure

You'll have to make two changes to it. First, change its name to the new name of the combo box, cboSelectHousehold_AfterUpdate. Don't overlook the underscore between the name and event. It's required. Access will immediately recognize it belongs to the combo box and reattach it for you, as in Figure 9-24.

Update Control References

The last step is to update the references to the control in the event procedure itself. I did that, as shown in Figure 9-24. Notice I left the old control name in a line that has been commented out by placing an apostrophe (') at the beginning of the line. Access will ignore that line.

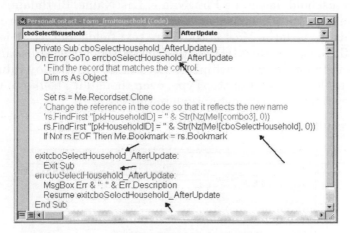

Figure 9-24 Update Control References in Renamed Event Procedure

While you're cleaning up names in the code module and controls, check the labels on the form too; make sure they also conform to proper naming conventions, e.g. lblSelectHousehold, etc. Then save your form and check it out to make sure all of the changes you've made work correctly.

Try it Yourself

Now that you've created the household form, why don't you go ahead and create a similar form for persons. In fact, you may want to try the shortcut method I previously told you about. Open frmHousehold and use the Save As method to create a new form called frmPerson.

This time updating the copied form will require a few additional steps, including updating the query for the searching combo box and changing the names and VBA references to conform to standard naming conventions. You should have enough practice to be able to handle it.

Give it a try and then check back here for a look at my solution. At this point, of course, neither your form nor mine is finished, but you've been patient for quite a while and it's time to stretch your muscles a bit on this form.

My Design for frmParent

I started by copying frmHousehold as frmParent. Then, I changed the record source from tblHousehold to tblParent. tblParent has more fields than tblHousehold, including FirstName, LastName, Birthdate, fkRelationshipTypeID, and so on. You'll need to add controls for all of these fields to the form. Most of them are text fields. But as we learned with the fkHouseholdHeadID field on frmHousehold, we will want to make the field for fkRelationshipID a list box. It will *display* values from a related table, tlkpRelationshipType, even though it's *bound* to the foreign key field for relationship type in tblPerson.

The end result looks like Figure 9-25.

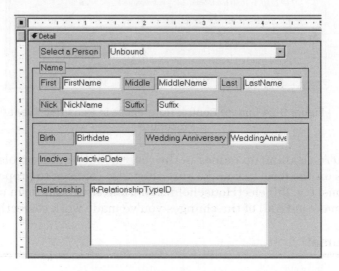

Figure 9-25 FrmParent Layout

I created the text and list box fields on the form and moved them around a bit until I ended up with a layout I felt comfortable with. Yours could be similar or quite a bit different. It's partly a matter of taste and partly a matter of functional design.

Moving from left to right, top to bottom, the fields on the top part of the form are:

> *cboSelectPerson* This field works just like its counterpart on frmHousehold. I modified the code to refer to this combo box by name. It is an unbound searching combo box.

> *txtFirstName* The control source for this field is FirstName.

> *txtMiddleName* The control source for this field is MiddleName.

> *txtLastName* The control source for this field is LastName.

> *txtNickName* The control source for this field is NickName.

> *txtSuffix* The control source for this field is Suffix.

I drew a box around all of the name fields with the rectangle tool and put a label on the box to describe the related fields in the box. That allowed me to remove the word Name from each of the other labels in this section, saving quite a bit of screen space in the process.

In the center of the form, there is another group of related controls.

> *txtBirthdate* The control source for this field is BirthDate.

> *txtWeddingAnniversary* The control source for this field is WeddingAnniversary.

> *txtInactiveDate* The control source for this field is InactiveDate.

I drew a second box around this group of fields to keep the overall layout of the form consistent even though I didn't put a label on them (mostly because I couldn't come up with one I liked).

On the bottom of the form I put the list box to select relationship types for people.

> *lstRelationshipTypeID* The control source for this field is fkRelationshipTypeID. This is a list box. Its bound column is column one.

Here is the query that is its *row source*.

Row Sources for Combo and List Boxes

Here's the row source I created for the searching combo box on frmParent. It has four columns, although only two of them are displayed in the combo box. You can tell that by the un-checked checkboxes in the Show row of the last two columns on the right. It also has a *concatenated* string in the second column.

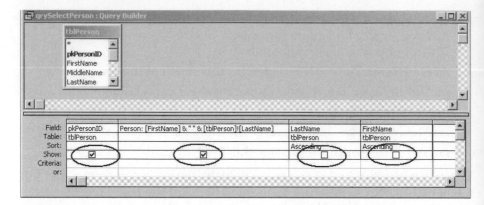

Figure 9-26 Row Source for cboSelectPerson

The query in Figure 9-26 ended up as it did partly because of the way combo boxes display their contents on a form and partly because of the way queries work. Since this is probably not exactly the way you want them to work, let's look at it a little more closely.

Display Characteristics of Combo Boxes

Figure 9-27 is the row source for the combo box in Figure 9-28. It's different from the one we want to use because, when it's closed, it only shows the person's first name, as you can see in Figure 9-28.

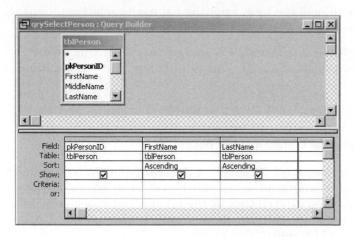

Figure 9-27 Row Source for Simple Combo Box

The query in Figure 9-27 is very simple with three fields. When you look at it here, it would seem to be just the thing for a combo box that selects persons from the person table, but as you can see in Figure 9-28, the display behavior of the combo box thwarts that goal.

Figure 9-28 Combo Box Displaying One Column when Closed

When the list portion of a combo box is opened, as in Figure 9-29, all of the columns appear, enabling you to select the appropriate entry from the list. Unfortunately, however, in its closed state, the combo box only displays the first visible column in it, as in Figure 9-28.

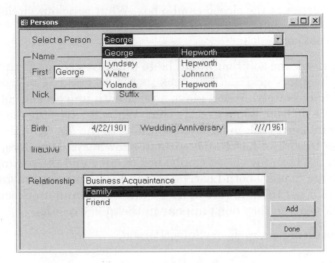

Figure 9-29 Open List in Combo Box

If there were only one George in the table, it might not be such a big problem to see only the first name in a closed combo box, but that's obviously not going to be the case for very long as you continue to add new records to the database.

Part of the solution, as shown Figure 9-26, is to create a *concatenated field,* composed of first name and last name, that displays in the one visible column in the closed combo box. We use an alias with the concatenated fields—in this case the alias is Person—as the name of the column in the query.

Sorting Characteristics of Queries

You can see a series of check boxes under the columns in the query, in the row labeled Show. The first two on the left are checked and the other two are not. Only the two checked columns will be displayed in the query results. Why, then, do we include the other two, un-checked and invisible columns? The answer is, they are included only to *sort* the list.

Sorting, as you previously learned, works from left to right: the leftmost sort occurs first, followed by the next sort in order, moving to the right across the query grid. Therefore, in order to sort first on LastName, and then on FirstName, LastName must be to the *left* of FirstName. Since the concatenated field with the alias Person starts with FirstName, we can't sort on it without placing LastName to its left. That conflicts with the display properties of the closed combo box. What a vicious circle!

Another Access Query Trick

You might think the solution would be to place LastName to the left of Person in the query grid and un-check its Show checkbox so it doesn't display. Unfortunately, Access plays a trick with un-checked columns that prevents us from doing exactly that. When it saves the query, Access automatically moves all un-checked columns to the *far right*, defeating the attempt to sort on LastName without showing it. Therefore, to accomplish the both the closed combo box display and the sorting we want, we have to place both LastName and FirstName at the *far right end of the row*, set them to sort in ascending order, and un-check their Show checkboxes so they don't appear in the query results.

Save the resulting query as qrySelectPerson.

Relationships

Figure 9-30 shows the row source for the Relationship Type list box. It's pretty simple and straightforward, with two columns. Note the primary key is in the first column, the bound column in the list box.

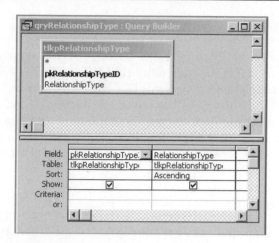

Figure 9-30 Row Source for lstRelationshipType

Here's what the form looks like in form view.

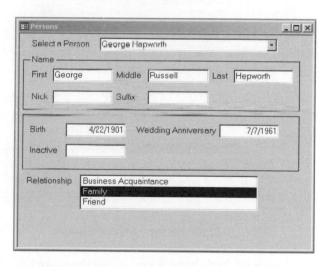

Figure 9-31 frmPerson in Form View

We don't have to worry about sorting and displaying columns with a list box as we did with the combo box. All of the visible columns remain in view.

Command Buttons

The next step is to add Close or Done buttons to both frmHousehold and frmParent. Since you've already done that before, I'm going to leave that step to you to complete on your own. Use the command button wizard to place the command buttons in the lower left portion of each form. Name both buttons cmdCloseForm or cmdDone and save and close the forms. The code in the event procedure for these command buttons should be the same as in the other forms you have already created. Place the buttons and try them out a couple of times.

Add New Records

Switch to form view and take another look at frmPerson. It should be similar to Figure 9-32.

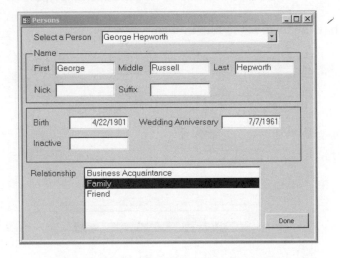

Figure 9-32 frmPerson with Done Button

It's almost complete now, but there is one important function missing. You may already have noticed the problem and wondered when I was going to do something about it. The searching combo box only allows us to select from *existing* records; there is no obvious way to add *new* records. As you learned in the previous chapter, you can use the Page Down and Page Up keys to move through the records, but that is a clumsy way of going about it.

A better alternative is to add another command button.

Switch to design view, click on the Command Button icon on the Toolbox toolbar and draw a new command button just above the Done button. When the command button wizard opens, select Record Operations from the categories list and Add New Records from the actions list. Then click Next to move to the next step in the wizard.

Select the Text radio button and change the text for the label from Add Record to Add. Then click on Next to move to the final step in the wizard.

Give the new command button a name that follows the standard naming convention and reflects its purpose. I chose cmdAddRecord. Click Finish when you're done.

Your new button will look something like Figure 9-33.

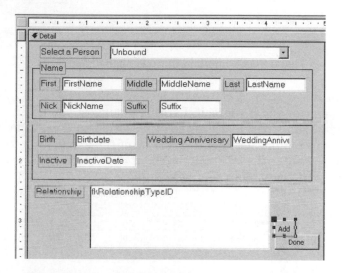

Figure 9-33 Form with Add Button before Formatting

As you can see, new command buttons often don't fit quite right when you first draw them onto the form (unless you're a much better artist than I am). Drag this one up a little so that it doesn't overlap the control below it, if necessary. Then hold down the Shift key while you select both command buttons by clicking them with the mouse. Use the Format menu to align the buttons and size them to the same height and width. When you're finished they should look like Figure 9-39. Now, switch back to design view and take a look at the event procedure for this new command button.

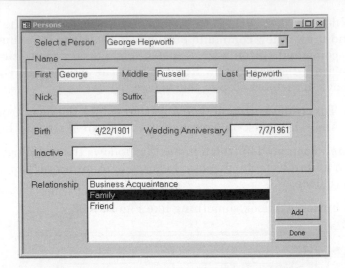

Figure 9-34 Command Buttons Aligned and Sized

The code in this event procedure will look like Figure 9-35. It has no error handling; you can add it yourself. I strongly suggest you try it; practice is always a good thing! Open one of the other forms with error handling in it and use it as a guide, or copy it from one of the examples in the book. Make sure you enter the label names accurately. Access will give you an error message if you make a typing mistake.

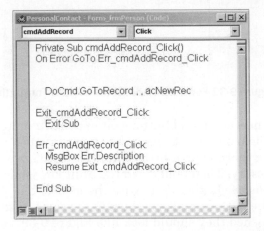

Figure 9-35 Event Procedure for Adding New Records

You've already seen similar event procedures; so I'll only discuss the one new line here, the one that says:

```
DoCmd.GoToRecord , , acNewRec
```

This line of code tells Access, "When the command button that activates this code is clicked, move the form's focus to a different record, specifically, to a new record."

It has the same DoCmd object you saw before, followed by the required (.) or so-called "dot operator", but this time it uses the method GoToRecord. The record to which this line of code sends you is acNewRec, that is, a new record for the record set.

Intrinsic Constants

acNewRec is an *intrinsic constant*. Visual Basic for Applications defines constants to simplify your programming. Constants can be used anywhere in your code in place of the actual values. For example, five is the actual value VBA uses to indicate that new record. Since you and I are not very likely to remember that five means New Record, the Access folks created the constant acNewRec to represent it. There are many other VBA constants. Here's what Microsoft says about constants.

"A constant represents a numeric or string value that doesn't change." You can use constants to improve the readability of your Visual Basic code and to make your code easier to maintain. In addition, the use of intrinsic constants ensures that code will continue to work even if the underlying values that the constants represent are changed in later releases of Microsoft Access.

Intrinsic constants have a two-letter prefix identifying the object library that defines the constant. Constants from the Microsoft Access library are prefaced with "ac"; constants from the ADO library are prefaced with "ad"; and constants from the Visual Basic library are prefaced with "vb".

For example:

- acForm
- adAddNew
- vbCurrency"

Standard Syntax

This line of code also includes a couple of commas in the middle. The standard syntax for the GoToRecord method includes a couple of *optional* sections that are omitted here and represented by the commas.

```
DoCmd.GoToRecord , , acNewRec
```

You can leave an optional argument blank in the middle of the syntax, but you must include the argument's comma. If you leave one or more trailing arguments blank, don't use a comma following the last argument you specify.

Missing Arguments

The missing optional arguments in this line of code are the *object type* (which would be *form,* because this code is running from the form module for frmPerson) and *object name* (which would be *frmPerson*, or the form on which the code is running). Leaving them out of the code means that Access defaults to the form where the code is running.

Put Add buttons on both frmPerson and frmHousehold. Because the code in them is generic, they should be identical except for their labels within the VBA error handling.

Further VBA Study

It should be quite obvious from the limited examples I've shown you that Visual Basic for Applications, or VBA, is a very powerful and useful tool that will make you a much better database developer. Unfortunately, I just don't have room in this book to give you more than a cursory look at some of the more common functions. Therefore, I suggest you take some time, either now or after you finish this book, to study it further.

I've found one of the most effective ways to get started with that study is to do just what I've shown you here. Use the command button wizard to create command buttons and study the resulting event procedures. To find out what each part does, place the cursor on a word like DoCmd and press the F1 key. Access Help is context sensitive, so it will usually open a help window with a description of that keyword and often will provide additional examples of how to use it.

With that, we're ready to make one final change to the form and move on to more complex form designs.

Tab Order and Tab Stop

This new form has a number of controls on it and I've moved them around a little bit while getting them lined up the way I want, so the next step is to check the tab order for fields on the form and reset it if necessary. What do I mean by tab order? Glad you asked.

One way to move from field to field on an Access form is to use the Tab key. Try this yourself. In form view, place the cursor in the first field on your form (upper left on the form) and press Tab. Watch where the cursor moves as you continue to tab from field to field. Does it go where you expect it to go? If so, great, you're more organized than I am. But if not, here's what happened. Switch back to design view and open the property sheet for the form. Select the searching combo box from the drop down list on the property sheet, then select the Other tab. You'll see properties called Tab Stop and Tab Index as shown in Figure 9-36.

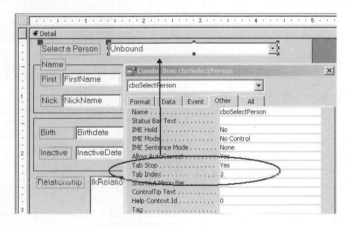

Figure 9-36 Tab Stop and Tab Index Properties

When you press the Tab key in form view, the cursor moves from the control that currently has the focus to the next control in the tab order. The tab *index* that Access sets when you add each new control to a form, tells Access which control to move to next within the tab order.

In other words, each time you add a new control to the form, Access assigns it the next tab index in the sequence. That may or may not be the order in which you want to move in the final version of the form, of course, but Access has no way of knowing that during the design phase. It only knows the order in which you placed controls on the form.

As you add and move controls around while creating and designing a form, the tab order often gets out of sequence with what you want it to be. Fortunately, Access provides a way to reset the tab order when you're finished adding and moving things around.

In Figure 9-36, the tab index for cboSelectPerson is three. Tab order is zero-based, so that means it is the *fourth* control in the tab order. This makes sense, because it was the fourth control we created on the form (after txtPersonID, txtFirstname, and txtLastName); Access placed it fourth in the tab order when it was created. Now, however, we want it to be the *first* control because it is at the top of the form. When we open the form, we want the cursor to start there.

Click on the Tab Index property in the property sheet and then use the builder button to open the tab order dialog. Here's where you'll reset the tab order for your form.

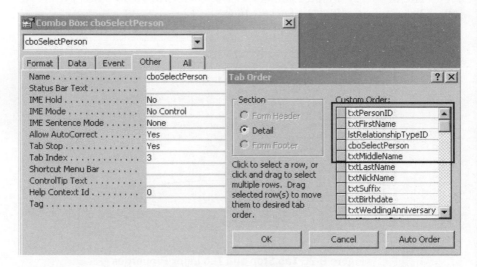

Figure 9-37 Tab Order Dialog

Figure 9-37 shows the current tab order for the form. Notice that the hidden field that holds the primary key is the first field in the tab order; its tab index is zero. We'll leave it that way and come back to talk about it more in a minute, but we do want to rearrange the order of the other controls.

The easiest way to do that is to click Auto Order on the dialog. Access will change the tab order to reflect the controls *current positions* on the form, moving from left to right, top to bottom. Usually, but not always, that is the order in which you want the tabs to appear.

If you want to set the tab order manually, you can also click the small gray box at the left edge of each control to select it, then drag the control up or down until it is in the position you want. When you have controls stacked vertically in columns, for example, you may want to change the tab order so that Access tabs down one column first (instead of left to right across columns) then moves to the top of the next column. You'll have to set that tab order manually.

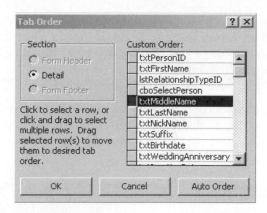

Figure 9-38 Click and Drag Tab Order

In Figure 9-38, I've selected txtMiddleName in order to drag it up the list to a position immediately after txtFirstName. The result of rearranging the tab order shows up in Figure 9-39.

Figure 9-39 Proper tab Order for frmPerson

If you have a number of controls on a form, not all of the controls appear in the dialog box (which annoys me a good deal), but you can scroll through the list to verify that the order is the way you want it to be.

The next step is to decide what to do with the command buttons you added to the form. Do you want the Tab key to move focus to them or should the Tab key only move the cursor through the text fields on the form? Switch to form view again and tab through the controls to see what I mean.

From the relationship type list box, the Tab key moves focus to the Add command button and from there to Done. If that is what you want to have happen, you can leave it that way, but what if you only want to tab from the relationship list box back to the searching combo box, bypassing the two command buttons? How would you do that?

The answer is to change the Tab Stop status of the two command buttons from Yes to No. Switch to design view, find the Tab Stop property on the property sheet and select the first command button. Change its Tab Stop property from Yes to No.

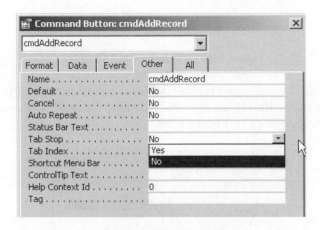

Figure 9-40 Set Tab Stop to No

Access will now ignore this command button when moving through the tabs on the form. You don't need to change its Tab Index property.

And that brings us back to the hidden field, txtPersonID, which holds the primary key field. It won't be in the tab order because it is *invisible*. Therefore, it doesn't matter all that much where it is in the tab index. However, to keep things orderly and help avoid confusion when I go back to look at a form I created some time before, I usually move the hidden fields to the front of the tab index, as shown in Figure 9-38.

Intermediate Form Complete

With that, let's move on to a more complex form design. You've actually learned a great deal about forms, as well as something about queries and VBA while creating your first six Access forms. You should feel good about your ability to transfer that knowledge to other form design tasks. Of course, there's still a lot more you can do with forms, but with the basics you've acquired so far, you can now create usable forms of your own.

You learned how to create both list and combo boxes and to modify the queries that populate tem. You learned how to customize them by concatenating strings to display the proper text. You learned how to sort on hidden columns. And you learned how to make list and combo boxes display some, or all, of the columns they hold

You learned that the control source for a list or combo box can be a foreign key field in one table, while the bound column of the list or combo box is the primary key in a related table, enabling you to assign foreign key values quickly and easily.

You also learned a little bit more about Visual Basic for Applications, or VBA, which you used to create a searching combo box on two forms.

In the next chapter, we'll take forms to the next level by learning how to nest a subform into a main form.

Backup, Backup, Backup

This may sound familiar: This would be an excellent time to make a backup copy of the database. Close your database, find it on your hard drive and make a copy in a safe place. Do that now.

This page intentionally left blank.

10. Getting Data Into Your Database —Complex Forms

You've already accomplished a great deal and learned quite a bit about form design by creating your first six forms. In this chapter, we'll take it one step further and create more complex, nested forms for your database. We'll use a combination of main forms and sub forms. The main form we'll use is one of the two forms you completed in the previous chapter, frmHousehold. We'll add a subform to it so that you can use it to assign persons to households.

Add Sample Data

It will be helpful to have sample data in your database before you begin more detailed study about using forms to manage and add records in the database. So, if you haven't already done so, please take a few moments to add a few household names in the household table and in the persons table in your sample database. Include at least your own immediate family members and one or two friends and business acquaintances.

You may designate household heads for households by entering their primary keys from tblPerson into the fkHouseholdHeadID field in tblHousehold. When you're done, come back here to continue reading about managing records through the forms. I'll show you a more efficient way to do it.

Also, open the junction table between tblHousehold and tblPerson, the one named *tblPersonHousehold,* and enter foreign keys from your sample households and family members. That should look something like Figure 10-1. In Figure 10-1, there are primary keys for two households, household 1, with three family members (fkPersonID 1 to 3), and household 3, with one family member (fkPersonID 4). If you have any questions about what these foreign keys mean, please take a few moments to re-read chapters four and five before you go on.

pkPersonHouseholdID	fkHouseholdID	fkPersonID
1	1	1
2	1	2
3	1	3
4	3	4
(AutoNumber)		

Record: 4 of 4

Figure 10-1 Sample Data in tblPersonHousehold

Main Form—Sub Form Strategy

The basic strategy for using nested, or embedded forms, is that a *main form* is bound to records from a table on the *one* side of a one-to-many relationship. A *subform* is bound to records from the table on the *many* side of that relationship. If the relationships between tables are properly defined in the relationship window (Figure 8-1), Access can use that information to help you create the links between the records in the main and sub forms and take over much of the legwork of associating records between the two tables.

Unrelated Sub Forms

The primary importance of the main-/subform strategy to you as a database developer lies in their ability to manage relationships between the tables that are their record sources. There are, however, other legitimate uses for subforms. It is possible to nest an unrelated subform on a main form. In this chapter I'm going to concentrate on their ability to manage one-to-many table relationships.

Add a Subform

It's time now to add a subform to our main form. There are two reasons we want to do that:

➢ To display related records from two tables in a single view

➢ To make it easier to add and modify related records in the tables

In our example database, we'll add a new subform to frmHousehold. Open frmHousehold in design view. Grab the lower edge of the form and drag it down so there is plenty of open space to add the subform. It should look something like Figure 10-2.

By the way, the two command buttons on the form don't show up in Figure 10-2 because I moved them out of the way so they won't interfere with the subform design. We'll put them back in place after the subform is added.

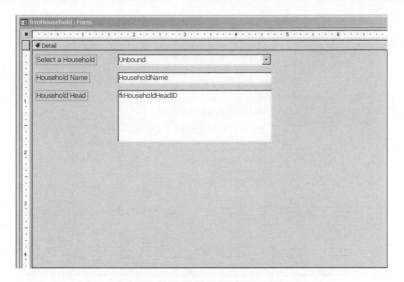

Figure 10-2 frmHousehold Before Adding a Subform

The record source for the main form that you created in Chapter 9 is tblHousehold. The record source for the subform is the related table, tblPersonHousehold. For each record in the record source for the main form, the sub form can display *one or more* related records from its record source.

Open your household form, frmHousehold, in design view. Locate the subform tool on the Toolbox toolbar and click to select it.

Figure 10-3 Subform Tool Selected on the Toolbox Toolbar

Draw the space for your subform on the detail section of your existing main form. Place it below the other controls and above the command buttons. You don't know yet how large it needs to be, but give it plenty of space. You can adjust it later if necessary. The Subform Wizard will open (Figure 10-4). It offers two choices: use an existing form, or build one from a table or query.

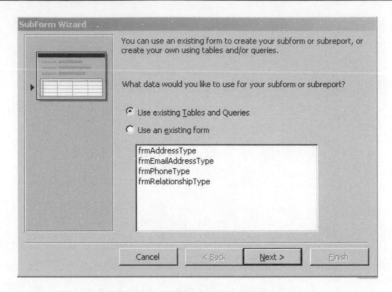

Figure 10-4 Subform Wizard Step One

Since we don't yet have a form to use, click on Next to select a table in the next step, Figure 10-5. The table you want is called tblPersonHousehold. Locate tblPersonHousehold in the combo box listing tables and queries. The fields in that table will populate the list below it, as in Figure 10-5.

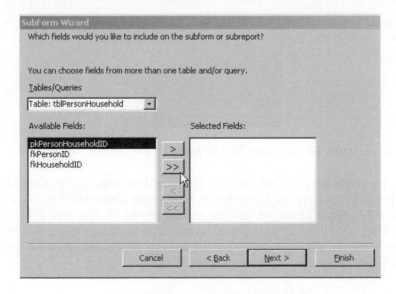

Figure 10-5 Subform Wizard Step Two

We want all three of the fields to be on the subform, so click on the double-arrow button to move them to the right hand list. Then click Next to move to the next step in the wizard.

Pre-defined Relationships

This step is very important in making your main and sub forms work together. You, with help from Access, designate the link between the two forms, which depends on the relationships defined for the tables in the main and sub forms.

Access already knows about the relationship between tblHousehold and tblPersonHousehold because you created that relationship in the relationship window. Further, Access knows that the primary key field for tblHousehold is pkHouseholdID and that the corresponding foreign key in tblPersonHousehold is fkHouseholdID.

Therefore, Access assumes that you want to link your main and sub forms using those fields. That's shown in Figure 10-6. (Unfortunately, the list box that suggests the linking fields is not wide enough to show the full text of the suggested link. You may want to click Define my own to verify the suggested fields yourself.)

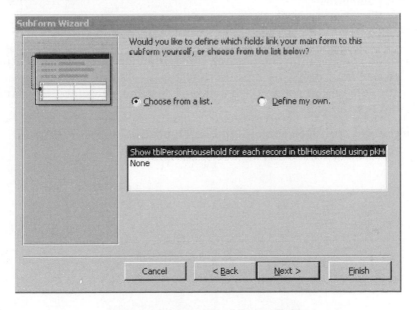

Figure 10-6 Selecting Linking Fields

Normally, you will accept the default selection here; after all, that's why we go to the trouble of establishing primary and foreign keys and relationships. When you get to more advanced kinds of forms, though, you may find it necessary to define your own linking fields. In a few cases, you will not need or want linking fields. For now, just accept the default Access offers and move on.

Master and Child Fields

Access refers to the linking fields as the *master* and *child* fields. The *master link field* is the key field from the main form and the *child link field* is the related key field from the subform. Usually, though not always, the master linking field will be a primary key and the child linking field will be the corresponding foreign key.

Having linking fields between your main and sub forms means that each time you select a new record in the main form (which displays households), the subform will also update to display the corresponding record or records from its record source. Pretty cool, huh? And very important, too.

Names for Subforms

In the next step of the subform wizard you are asked to either accept the default name (which you shouldn't) or give the subform a name of your own (which you should). The naming convention for subforms is to attach an "s" to the "frm" prefix to indicate that it is a subform, but otherwise to follow the convention you've used before. This time, therefore, the name is sfrmPersonHousehold.

The forms will now look something like Figure 10-7.

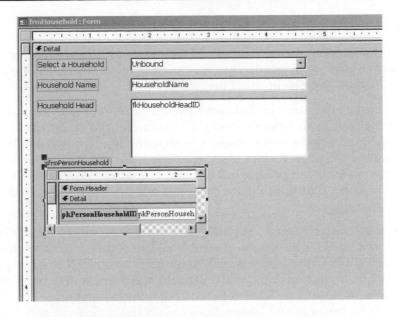

Figure 10-7 Main Form with Sub Form Added

Your new subform is now nested, or embedded, in the main form. In some ways, the subform control that holds the subform is similar to the other controls on the form (combo, list, and text boxes). Access has given it a label with a default caption, just as it does for other controls. It has also given the control itself a name.

The default name Access used for the subform control is the same as the name of the subform in it.

That might be a bit confusing at first. Let's talk.

Subform Control versus Subform

The *subform control* is on the main form. It contains a *subform* within it. The control has its own name and set of properties. By default, Access gives it the name of the subform that it holds.

The *subform* itself exists as a separate form in the database, which you can verify by looking at the forms in the database window. You can open the subform independently of the main form in which it is embedded.

The subform has its own name, the one you just gave it. If you wish, you can give the control that holds the subform a different name to avoid confusion, although I seldom bother to do that.

Changing the Form in a Subform Control

Any of the forms in your database can be inserted into a subform control on another form, with one exception—the form on which the subform control resides can't be inserted into itself.

You can take advantage of that fact to display different subforms at different times, or to different users. For example, you might show managers and supervisors a subform with more detail or less detail than the subform you show to data entry operators. We won't be going that far with this example in this chapter, though. I mention it here mainly to stress the point that the subform control is not the same thing as the form it contains.

Access automatically attaches a label to the subform control. Sometimes I remove the label for a subform control from the main form, depending on whether I think the subform is self-explanatory by itself. Let's just give this one a more natural caption, Household Members, and leave it on the main form. After a little bit of reformatting (making font sizes consistent and aligning controls and labels), here's what the main form now looks like in form view.

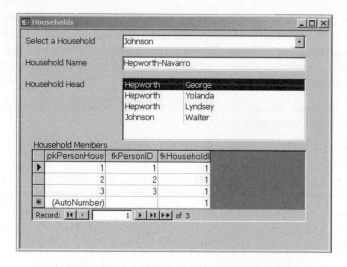

Figure 10-8 Main Form, Sub Form in Form View

Kind of ugly isn't it? Still, it will work as described. If you pre-loaded some sample households and people as I suggested, you can select different households from the searching combo box at the top of the form and watch how the subform updates to show matching records from tblPersonHousehold.

Let's make the subform more presentable. Switch back to design view. Select the subform control and double-click on it to open it for modification. Or use the Toolbox toolbar to open the subform.

Figure 10-9 Edit Subform Icon on the Toolbox Toolbar

When Access creates subforms like this one, the default view is datasheet view, rather than single or continuous forms. Switch the subform to datasheet, both single and continuous views; see what it looks like in each.

For subforms like this one, which holds records from the many side, I prefer the datasheet view, although I have also used the continuous view in some applications. Either one works fine. The main argument in favor of datasheet view is that is more compact and, arguably, more flexible than continuous view. The main advantage of continuous view is that you have more control over formatting and you can add other controls (such as a Delete command button) to a continuous view form; controls that do not work in datasheet view.

Remove the Form Header and Footer

First, remove the header and footer from the form. They don't show up in datasheet view anyway. Locate View-->Form Header/Viewer on the menu and deselect it.

Hiding and Showing Controls in Datasheet View

As you recall, tblHouseholdPerson is a junction table. It has only three fields in it, pkPersonHouseholdID, fkHouseholdID, and fkPersonID. The subform also contains those three key fields: the primary key for tblPersonHousehold, the foreign key from tblHousehold, and the foreign key from tblPerson.

As always, we hide the primary key on the form—your users don't need to see it and it isn't necessary to have it visible for the form to work as a subform.

We'll also hide the foreign key from tblHousehold on the subform. Access is responsible for keeping fkHouseholdID in the sub form synched up with pkHouseholdID on the main form, so you don't have to worry about it and you don't need to see it, either. That's another advantage of subforms. However, hiding the controls on a datasheet is a different matter than it is on one of the other views.

Hiding Controls in Datasheet View

Simply setting a control's Visible property to No doesn't do the trick on a form in datasheet view. Try that out. Set the Visible property for txtPersonHouseholdID to No and switch to datasheet view. The column is still displayed.

There's a different way to hide columns in datasheet view. I'll show you how to do that next.

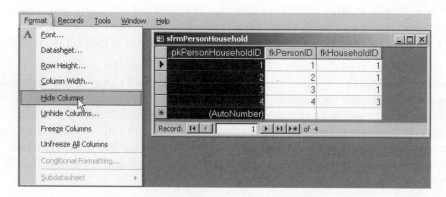

Figure 10-10 Hiding Columns in Datasheet View

With the subform in datasheet view, select the column or columns you want to hide by clicking on the gray box at the head of the column. Then, select Format-->Hide Columns from the menu bar. Do this with both pkPersonHouseholdID and fkHouseholdID. The form will now look like Figure 10-11. The other two columns are still there, you just can't see them.

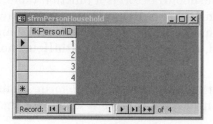

Figure 10-11 Subform with Hidden Columns

We're now ready to make the other modifications to the subform to make it appear the way we want it to show up in the main form.

Convert Text Box Control to Combo Box

The next thing we want to do is to change the text box that holds the foreign key from tblHousehold to a combo box so that we can see the names of the individuals, not their foreign keys. You've done that before. Step through the same procedure you used last time to create the row source for this combo box.

Click on the text box in design view and then right mouse click to display the short cut menu and select Change to -> Combo Box. The control source for this combo box is still fkPersonID, but it will now allow us to choose a row source based on tblPerson to display the names of the persons in the list portion of the combo box.

Open the property sheet, select the Data tab and then select the combo box on the form. Place the cursor in the Row Source property for the combo box and, when the builder box appears at the right end of the property, click it to add tables to the SQL statement for this control.

You could use the same query that you previously created for the searching combo box on frmPerson. It has the primary key from tblPerson and the concatenated names of individuals in it, so it would be quite acceptable to reuse that query here. The ability to reuse them is, in fact, one of the advantages of creating saved queries. If you choose to do that, the next step would be to designate the bound column and make sure that the combo box shows the correct number of columns.

Figure 10-12 Reuse a Query as a Row Source for Another Combo Box

As an exercise, however, I'm going to make the row source for this combo box something else. I clicked on the builder button to open the query builder and right-clicked on the query window. When the Add Table dialog opened, I added tblPerson to the query window. Then, I added three fields to the query grid below. The result looked like Figure 10-13.

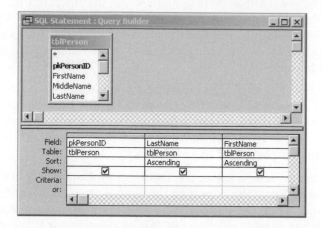

Figure 10-13 Unsaved SQL as Combo Box Row Source

Notice that the Primary key is the first column on the left and that the sort order is set for LastName, then FirstName, in ascending order.

This time, however, instead of saving this as a named query, *I just clicked on the Close button on the query builder.* Access asked if I wanted to save the SQL Statement as it appears in the query builder. By clicking Yes, I saved the raw SQL directly to the row source for the combo box, without giving it a name or saving it as a query.

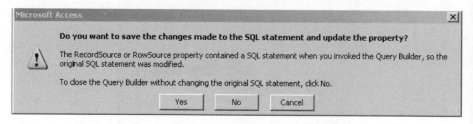

Figure 10-14 Prompt to Save Raw SQL

Now when you look at the row source for this combo box, you see the raw SQL statement instead of a query. To see what the SQL statement looks like, you can open it in a zoom box. You won't be editing the SQL statement yet, as that is a task for when you are a bit more experienced, but it is worth taking a look at it to see what raw SQL actually looks like.

Place the cursor in the Row Source property for the combo box and hold down the Shift key. Press F2 and the zoom box will open to show you the entire SQL statement, which is saved as the row source for this combo box.

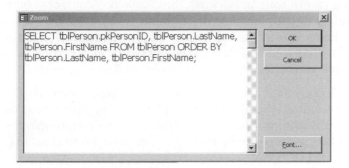

Figure 10-15 SQL in Zoom Box

Here's the SQL as shown in Figure 10-15.

```
SELECT tblPerson.pkPersonID, tblPerson.LastName,
tblPerson.FirstName FROM tblPerson ORDER BY
tblPerson.LastName, tblPerson.FirstName;
```

SQL uses keywords like SELECT to tell the database what to do with the records it retrieves. Here, it is telling Access to select a group, or set, of records for display. Other SQL keywords include APPEND, which adds records to a table, and DELETE, which removes records from a table.

Following the SELECT keyword is a list of fields to be selected. Here we are asking for only three of the ten available fields in the table: pkPersonID, LastName, and FirstName.

Following that, the FROM keyword indicates which table the records should be selected from. In this case, of course, it is tblPerson.

The last section of the SQL statement, indicated by the key words ORDER BY, tells Access how to sort the records, first by last name, then by first name. The default order is ascending. If you wanted the sort order to be from Z to A, you'd add the keyword DESC for descending order at the end of the ORDER BY clause.

All SQL statements must end with the semi-colon (;).

Saved queries generally have some speed advantage over raw SQL in list and combo boxes, but for the sake of learning how to use another option, let's leave this one here just as it is. This database will not get large enough for that speed difference to matter.

Bound Column, Column Count, and Column Width

The next step is to make sure the bound column for this combo box is set to the first column, which is the one that holds the primary key for the underlying record source. Because the combo box control is bound to the corresponding foreign key field in tblPersonHousehold, selecting a primary key from the records in the combo box also saves that value to the foreign key field in tblPersonHousehold. Next, on the property sheet, select the Format tab and look for the properties outlined in Figure 10-16.

When we first created this field, it was a text box. Converting it to a combo box enabled it to display multiple columns, but Access didn't know how many it would need, so it defaulted to a single column. Our SQL statement has three columns to display, so we need to change Column Count from "1" to "3".

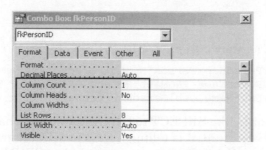

Figure 10-16 Column Count and Column Width

Next, we need to tell Access how wide to make the columns. We never want our users to see primary or foreign keys, so the first column width should be zero inches. Until we've analyzed the form in datasheet view, we don't know for sure how wide the other two columns need to be, so let's just start with one-inch widths and see how that looks.

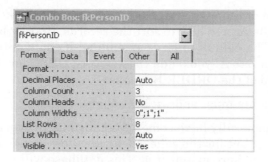

Figure 10-17 Column Widths Set

Now, switch back to datasheet view to see the result. In datasheet view, as you can quickly see for yourself, you can adjust the width of the displayed column; so the column widths in the combo box are really not all that critical as long as they are wide enough to show the entire value in each column.

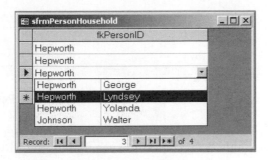

Figure 10-18 Subform in Datasheet View

The subform is starting to look pretty good, but as I reviewed Figure 10-18, I spotted a problem with the way I created the row source for this combo box. You may have noticed it already, too.

When combo boxes are *closed*, as in the first two rows in Figure 10-18, they only *display* one column, regardless of the actual number of columns they contain. You can only see the other columns in a combo box when the list is opened, as in the third row in Figure 10-18; that's the record with the little record selector icon in the left margin. That sort of display would be okay for selecting new records, but it could be quite confusing when you are just looking at the combo box on a form.

Same Problem, Same Solution

In fact, this is the same problem we solved for the searching combo box in the previous chapter and the solution is the same. Just as we did there, we need to revise the SQL statement for the combo box to show the concatenated person name in a single column. Figure 10-19 shows that revised SQL statement with the concatenated alias and sort fields added.

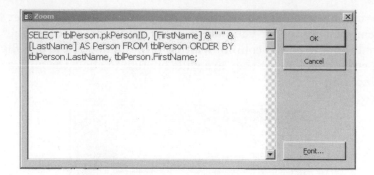

Figure 10-19 Revised SQL with Concatenated Alias Person

The revised SQL statement has the same SELECT clause, which tells Access to retrieve fields from the table specified by the FROM clause, which is tblPerson.

```
SELECT tblPerson.pkPersonID, [FirstName] & " " & [LastName]
AS Person FROM tblPerson ORDER BY tblPerson.LastName,
tblPerson.FirstName;
```

Three fields are selected, just as before, but in this SQL statement, the first and last names are combined into a single alias, *Person*, as indicated by the AS keyword. Aliases are counted as a single column in a combo box, regardless of the number of items concatenated into them.

The ORDER BY clause tells Access to use LastName and FirstName to sort on, even though they are not displayed in the query results except as part of the *Parent* alias.

Since there are now only two columns to display, you'll need to find the Column Count property for the combo box and change it from three to two. Also, make the column widths zero and one inches.

Now, switch back to datasheet view so you can see the result of these changes. Click on the right hand edge of the column and drag it wider and narrower to see how the combo box responds to changes in width in the column.

What the Subform Displays

When opened directly, not as a subform on the main form, this form displays all of the records in tblPerson. When it is opened as a subform within the main form, the master and child linking fields you previously defined for the main and sub forms will cause it to display a filtered set of records matching the main form. Pretty cool, huh?

Form Clean Up

Before we go on, switch back to design view and clean up the fields on this form by giving them all standard names (txtHouseholdID, cboPersonID, etc.)

You don't need to bother making the primary key invisible, because that property is controlled at the datasheet level by using Format-->Hide Columns.

Also, change the name and caption for the label for the remaining field, the one that does show, cboPersonID. An appropriate caption for that column might be Person.

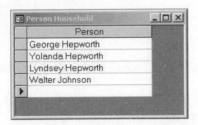

Figure 10-20 Completed Subform

Actually, the form caption won't appear when a form is displayed as a subform inside the main form, so you could get away with not adding a new form caption, as shown in Figure 10-20.

I like to keep things tidy, though, by giving it a proper name anyway. Also, there is always a chance someone will open the form independently of the main form, so it's best to keep it clean and neat.

Now, close the subform and go back to the main form. Switch the main form to form view and select a few household names from the searching combo box to see how the subform follows it. It will look something like Figure 10-21.

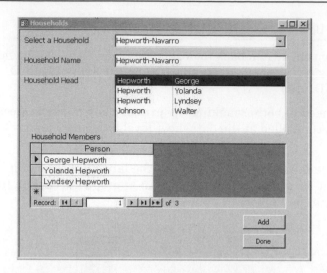

Figure 10-21 frmHousehold with Subform

It works like we want it to and looks very close to what we want, but there are a couple more adjustments left to make.

First, we want to adjust the width of the control holding the subform to better fit its contents—there's a lot of empty space on the right side. Let's make it narrower and maybe a little shorter, to make better use of the space.

Also, the subform has navigation buttons in it, which are not appropriate in this type of form. The records are visible in the rows in the datasheet; it's easy to tab or use the mouse to move from row to row, making the navigation buttons superfluous. However, if the number of rows in the datasheet rows were beyond the height of the subform control, it would be nice to have a scroll bar to scroll up and down the form.

So, we have to open the subform in design view, remove the navigation buttons from it and add a vertical scroll bar.

To do that, switch the main form to design view and open the subform. (Double-click on it in the main form, or select it and then click on Subform in New Window on the Toolbox toolbar.) Make the format changes in the property sheet as shown in Figure 10-22.

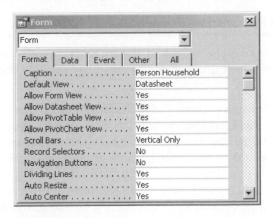

Figure 10-22 Format the Subform

As Figure 10-22.shows, I've changed the Scroll Bar property to vertical only and the Navigation Buttons property to No. Save the changes and close the subform.

Now, grab the right edge of the subform *control* with the mouse and drag it to the left to make it narrower. You may have to make a couple of tries to get it exactly like you want it. You can shorten it a little also, if you want. Oh, and while you're here, go ahead and set the tab order for the controls on the main form to the sequence you want them to be in. Those adjustments appear in Figure 10-23. It can still stand to be adjusted a little more, but it's quite close now.

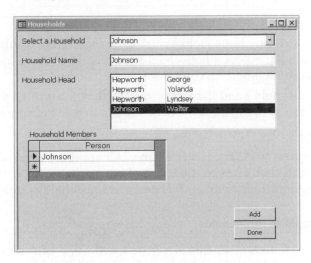

Figure 10-23 Adjusted Form Format

Assigning New Persons to a Household

We're ready to take a closer look at the interaction between the main and sub forms. Let's take a quick step back and review how the tables are related.

tblHousehold contains records for each *household* in our contact database. tblPerson contains records for each *person* in our contact database. While creating the data model for this database, I decided that any one person could be a member of one of more households, as might happen with kids in a divorce situation. So I added the junction table, tblPersonHousehold, to link persons in the person table with households in the household table, rather than create a one-to-many relationship between households and persons.

That junction table requires, however, that you must enter a person into the person table *before* you can add that person to a household. No exceptions. Therefore, in the subform above, which has tblPerson as the row source, you can only assign persons to households if they previously exist in the person table.

We can't get directly to the persons table to add new people through this form, so that's potentially a problem. I'll show you how we deal with it in the next section. First, let's look at the way you assign existing persons to households using the subform you just created.

Assigning Household Heads to Households

This step is actually very straightforward.

> Select an existing household by using the searching combo box on frmHousehold. Select a household for which you have already added one or more members in the person table.

> In the household head list box, scroll down the list until you find the name of the person you want to designate as the household head.

> Click on the name to select it.

That's all there is to it. Try it a few times. Change the head of household for a family and then change it back. As long as the name of the person is in the list designating them as the head of a household is quite easy.

Assigning People to Households

Assigning people to households is a little more work, but not all that much more. Again, start by selecting a household from the searching combo box. If you've already selected the head of household, the list box will reflect that choice.

Now, place the cursor in the subform. You can do that in a couple of ways.

The subform control, like other controls on the main form, has a tab index on the main form. That means you can reach it by using the Tab key, just as you would any other control. If you have set the tab order so that the subform follows the household head list box in the tab index, you can tab straight to it after selecting the household head from the list.

The other way to get to the combo box on the subform is to use the mouse to click on it.

Combo Box Behavior in Datasheet View

Look closely at the subform, circled in Figure 10-34. Even though the field on the subform is a combo box, just like the searching combo box at the top of the man form, the drop down arrow to open its list isn't visible.

The reason it doesn't appear is that, when a form is displayed in *datasheet* view, combo boxes on that form look just like ordinary text boxes until they receive the focus.

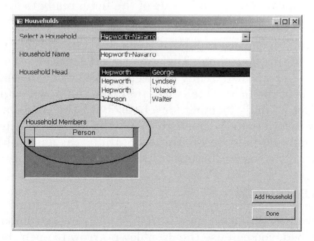

Figure 10-24 Empty Row in a Subform

However, as soon as the cursor enters this combo box, giving it the focus, the drop down arrow will appear, alerting you that it is a combo box, ready to accept new records.

To assign people from the list to the household selected on the main form, you only need to select their names from the list in the combo box. Try that for the members of the household you just selected.

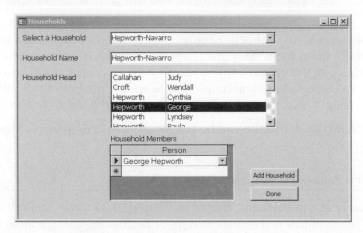

Figure 10-25 Adding Records in a Combo Box on a Subform

With the cursor in the combo box, giving it the focus, the appearance of the combo box changes in a couple of ways. As I just told you, the drop down arrow appears on the right side of the field, ready to open the list of available values.

In addition, as you can see in Figure 10-25, I've already selected myself as a member of this household. The subform presents another field, just below the one I just added, ready to accept another new record. The icon at the left side of the field (*) tells you that this is a new record. Each time you select a family member for a household, the subform offers you another new record field. To move to it, use the Tab key or the mouse. Leaving the current field (in Figure 10-25, that's the one with my name it) automatically saves its current value to the underlying record set.

More Combo Box Behavior

There are two ways to select names from the list in the combo box. First, as I've described, you can use the drop down arrow to open the list and select a value from there.

Combo boxes have an Auto Expand property. Switch to design view. Double-click on the subform control to open it in design view. Select the combo box and display its property sheet. Select the Data tab. It should look like Figure 10-26.

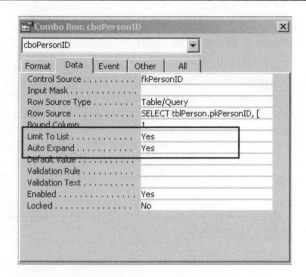

Figure 10-26 Auto Expand and Limit to List Properties

We're interested in the two properties outlined in Figure 10-26. They are Auto Expand and Limit To List.

Auto Expand

With its Auto Expand property set to Yes, the combo box will attempt to match text you type into it against existing values in the list. For example, the value shown in Figure 10-25 is my name, George Hepworth. Instead of opening the drop down list and clicking on that name to select it, I could also start typing the name: G, e, etc. The combo box will offer me the first value matching what I've typed, which is George Hepworth. As long I continue to type matching letters, Access will continue to offer the matching choice.

However, if I type in a name that isn't in the list, Georgina, or mistype the name, such as Georrge, Access will realize that this is a new name (or a mistake) and stop offering the chosen name, which no longer matches. Of course, if there were two Georges in the list, you'd have to continue typing the rest of the name to select the right one.

Advantages and Disadvantages of Auto Expand

The advantage of auto expand to match existing records should be obvious. Instead of having to scroll down a long list of values in the list portion of the combo box, you can start typing in the value you expect to select. If Access finds it, it will automatically offer it as the choice. Just tab on to the next control to select the offered value. That's one reason I prefer searching combo boxes to navigation buttons and scroll bars on forms.

The main disadvantage of the Auto Expand property only becomes apparent when you have a very, very long list of values. Performance takes a hit with auto expand turned on. That's a bit ironic, I guess, because the longer the list of values to choose from, the more valuable it is to *not* have to scroll through the whole list. Fortunately, as PCs get faster and more powerful with more memory and faster hard disks, this is much less of an issue than it was with Access 2.0 back in 1995.

The next question is what happens when Access can't match the value you type to one of the existing values in the list? That's controlled, in part, by the Limit To List property.

Limit To List

The Limit To List property determines whether or not Access will allow you to add a new record to the table that provides its row source by typing that new value into the combo box. When it is set to No, Access will add any new value you type in the combo box to the underlying record source, if you want it to do so. When it is set to Yes, Access will only let you select existing values from the list (choices are limited to the list) and it won't attempt to add any new values.

Occasionally, you might want to let Access add new values through the combo box, but usually not. You'll remember that the bound column of this combo box is the primary key for tblPerson, so Access could automatically assign a new primary key to any value you added through the combo box. However, there are other considerations. The most obvious one is illustrated in Figure 10-25. That combo box displays a concatenated value, FirstName & ' ' & LastName, rather than the two underlying fields FirstName and LastName. You can't let Access try to add a value typed in the combo box, because the appropriate fields in tblPerson aren't available to the combo box.

For that reason, and some other technical issues that I won't go into here, it's almost always best to set Limit To List to Yes and add new records to the underlying record source through another method. And that leads us to the next consideration, handling errors.

Graceful Error Messages

Setting the Limit To List property to Yes brings up another issue—handling "errors" gracefully. I put errors in quotes because there is more than one kind of error.

First, there are *bug-type* errors. You've heard of bugs in software, which means that the developer made some kind of error in logic or syntax that causes code to fail when it runs. Those errors, unfortunately, are almost inevitable. I may be going out on a limb a bit with this statement, but I'd be willing to bet that no programmer who ever lived has produced completely bug-free code in every application. The error trapping and handling codes I showed you in Chapters 8 and 9 are mainly aimed at that type of error.

The second type of error really isn't an error at all, at least not in my opinion. Access can't tell the difference, though, so it handles this type of error the same way.

I'm talking about the type of error caused when a user enters a value into the combo box that isn't in its list. Access considers this an error because the Limit To List property tells it to accept only values on the existing list. If you or your users don't select one of those values, that's an error. Such errors occur all the time because people just don't think the way computers do. I don't think of that as an error, but Access does.

You can now better see, perhaps, how important good error handling can be in maintaining a smooth, cordial relationship between your users and your database. If you let Access tell them that they've committed an error when all they did was try to enter a new name on a list, well, that's just not a good thing.

Try it yourself. Make sure the Limit To List property is set to Yes for the combo box on your subform. Enter a new name in it, one that you haven't pre-loaded. Tab to the next row to change the focus and trigger the After Update event. Observe what happens.

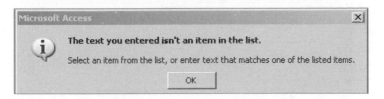

Figure 10-27 Standard, Generic, Access Error Message

As error messages go, this one isn't all that bad. However, you might want to change it so that it includes a suggestion about resolving the problem; you might also want to make it more specific to the combo box that generated it. Let's learn some more VBA so we can do that.

Handling Errors in a Combo Box Not In List Event

Switch again to design view, open the subform and select the combo box. Open the property sheet and select the Event tab. Find the property called "On Not In List". Click the property field as shown in Figure 10-28. We want to add a new event procedure here, one that will run when you or your user enters a value that isn't in the combo box' list. This will be a custom error message that Access will display instead of the generic one it would otherwise use.

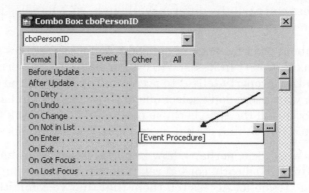

Figure 10-28 Adding a New Event Procedure

Click the builder button on the right side of the property field to open the code module. The empty code module opens, ready for you to add your VBA.

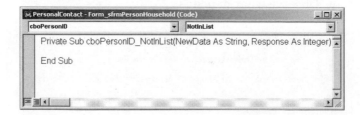

Figure 10-29 Empty Code Module, Ready for New Code

Access assigns the name to this event procedure, which as you already learned, is a combination of the control and the event, cboPersonID_NotInList, joined by the underscore. It is private, which means it can only run from this form.

Arguments in an Event Procedure

Notice that the parentheses after the event procedure's name include a couple of variables. Remember, I told you that would happen and here's an example. The two terms inside the parentheses are referred to as *arguments*. Arguments are values passed into an event procedure, values the procedure needs in order to complete its function.

Here, NewData is the value just typed into the combo box, the value that doesn't already exist in the list. When the Item Not In List event occurs, it calls this procedure and passes the text you typed to the procedure as NewData. NewData is defined as a String (as opposed to a number, a date, etc.).

Response is, as the name suggests, a value your VBA code will set to tell Access how to respond to the error. It is an integer that represents values like one, two, three, etc.

The On Not In List event passes in a *default* value of one for Response, which means that Access should offer to add the new value to the underlying record set.

Now, I'm going to show you the entire code that I want you to enter into your form. Then I'll explain how it all works.

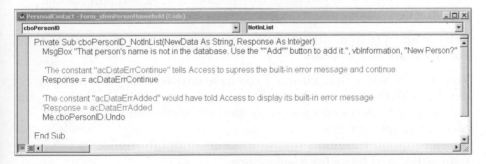

Figure 10-30 Custom Error Message

Here's the code from the event procedure. The line breaks are different from those in the actual event procedure because of the font size I used below. That's important.

When you create your own event procedure, use the line formats in Figure 10-30, not the lines below.

```
Private Sub cboPersonID_NotInList(NewData As String,
Response As Integer)
  MsgBox "That person's name is not in the
  database. Use the ""Add"" button to add it.",
  vbInformation, "New Person?"
   'The constant "acDataErrContinue" tells Access
   to supress the built-in error message and
   continue
  Response = acDataErrContinue
   'The constant "acDataErrAdded" would have told
   Access to display its built-in error message
  'Response = acDataErrAdded
  Me.cboPersonID.Undo
End Sub
```

I've already described the event procedure declaration, which includes the name and arguments, NewData and Response.

The next line creates a message box that shows a custom message to you or your user. You have a lot of flexibility in creating custom messages, but they do have a standard syntax that you must follow.

```
MsgBox prompt[, buttons] [, title] [, helpfile, context]
```

You create the message box by building it up from the building blocks show above. The only *required* element is a prompt, which is the text displayed in the body of the message box.

You can specify one or more command buttons for the message box, Yes, No, OK, Cancel, etc. If you leave this element out, Access will use the default, OK.

You can add a custom title to the message box, one that replaces the standard "Microsoft Access".

You can also add a Help button if you have created a help file for your database. That's beyond what we'll be learning in this book. However, the code module in Access does a pretty good job of offering you help with code in a couple of ways.

Help with Visual Basic for Applications

You can get help for VBA code in at least two fairly accessible ways.

One way I've already mentioned is that you can use the F1 key to request context sensitive help. Place the cursor on the keyword, press F1. Most of the time Access offers a description of the word along with background information on the method, object, or event, plus one or more examples.

A second way Access assists you is by offering syntax help when it recognizes that you have started to enter a particular keyword in the VBA editing window. Look at the code in Figure 10-31. This is what appeared when I was writing the code to create the custom message box. The Access code editor recognized the keyword "MsgBox" and presented an Intellisense control tip with a template for standard message boxes. In fact, as you enter elements of the code, the control tip text converts the current element to bold text. In Figure 10-31, for example, the optional (Title) element is bolded, indication that I'm currently working on the title for the message box.

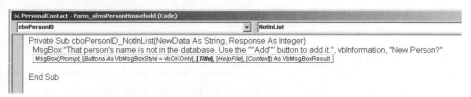

Figure 10-31 Code Control Tip Offering Help

Even better than that, however, is the kind of help illustrated in Figure 10-32.

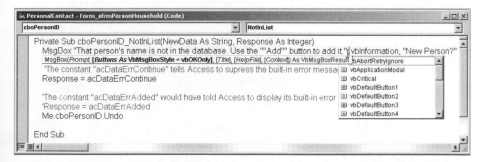

Figure 10-32 Help with Constants in VBA Code

Look at what happens when the code editor recognizes that I'm ready to enter the buttons for the message box. It drops down a list of button constants to choose from. Not only do you not have to remember the values to create a particular type of button or buttons, you don't even have to remember the intrinsic constants for buttons. Access offers you a list of them when it thinks you need them.

By the way, you should remember the term *constant* from our previous discussion of VBA code. A constant is a pre-defined term that represents values used in VBA. Instead of remembering that 64 is the value you need to display the Information style buttons, you can use vbInformation instead. To see a list of all VBA constants and their values, search MS Access help.

Now you know one of the secrets of learning to use VBA to write code for your applications: if you can remember a keyword for something, there is a good chance you'll have access to a lot of built-in help in using it. Moreover, if you're like me, the challenge of figuring out keywords and how to use them is a big part of the fun of using Access.

Unfortunately, this kind of help isn't available for all of the code you'll be writing. We can only dream of the day when Microsoft's developers become that ambitious, I suppose.

What the Custom Message Box Does

My custom message box tells Access to display the text "That person's name is not in the database. Use the "Add" button to add it." in its body. It also tells Access to display the vbInformation style button. And it tells Access to use the phrase "New Person?" as the title of the message box.

Here's the resulting message box as it displays on the screen.

Figure 10-33 Custom Error Message Displayed to User

This message appears when you or a user enters a name into the combo box that isn't already in the list. This message identifies the specific problem encountered and offers a solution to it.

The next line of code is a comment. It's preceded by the apostrophe (') so Access won't try to process it.

The next line changes the value of the variable, Response.

```
Response = acDataErrContinue
```

This line changes the value of the variable, Response, from the default value passed into the procedure, that is, from one to zero. One means to offer to add the new value; zero means to continue without showing any other error messages.

The constant *acDataErrContinue* represents the value zero. The constant *acDataErrAdded* represents the value one. While they're not exactly easy to remember, they are a lot easier to remember than the values they represent.

I added a couple of other commented lines in Figure 10-30. If you add them to your code module, you can see how the two different responses work by commenting out the first line and uncommenting the second.

The last line of code is there to "correct" the error made by the user.

```
Me.cboPersonID.Undo
```

What this line of code does should be self-evident. It undoes whatever the user typed in the combo box that caused the error. It's a small tidying up step. It's not necessary; you could let the user undo it manually. However, since the new name has to be added through a different method (clicking on the Add button), it is a small courtesy to the user to tidy up this field for them.

Try It Out

Once you've added this event procedure to your combo box, save and close the subform, and open frmHousehold in form view. Try out the combo box with the new custom error handling in place by entering a name that you know isn't in the list. When you tab or click away from the combo box, the message box should appear. When you click OK, the name you just typed should be cleared from the combo box and it will be empty, ready for you to either try again or add a new person to the database. I'll show you how we're going to do that later in this chapter.

Keep adding family members to the household you just selected until you've added everyone to the list, then select another household on the main form and add a second household. To do that, you'll need to change the focus from the subform to the searching combo box on the top of the form.

Leaving a Sub Form—Ctrl-Tab

You can tab through the fields in a subform until you reach the end. When you press the Tab key again, the focus will move to the next control in the tab order on the main form. However, if you don't want to tab through all of the fields in the subform to get to the end, you can hold down Ctrl and press the Tab key to leave the subform and move the focus to the next control in the tab order.

Now let's take the next step in making this form meet all of our needs in adding new households and new people to the database.

Adding New Records through the Form

With the form open in form view, click on Add. That will send the form to a new, empty household record, ready to accept a new household, Figure 10-34.

The text field for Household name will be empty, ready to accept a new value. Also, the household head list box and family member combo box will no longer have any persons selected, because this is a new household with no household head and no members.

If the cursor is not already there, move it to the household name text field and type in a name from your contact list. Then click Add to send the form to another new record.

Click on the searching combo box and look for the name you just entered. It isn't there (or it shouldn't be anyway.) But why not—you just added it, didn't you?

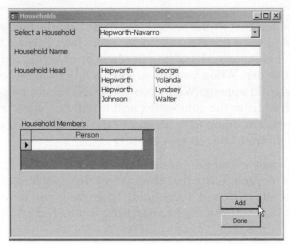

Figure 10-34 Add New Household

Timing Issues with Record Sets

The reason you don't see the new household name in this searching combo box immediately after you add it is because the combo box got its records when the form was first opened, and that happened *before* you added the new name. It still has that original set of records, which didn't include the one you just added.

You have to *force* the combo box to update its record source after you add a new record to tblHousehold. There's more than one way to do that, but one of the simplest is to force the combo box to requery the household table each time you click the Add button. That way, each time you click the button, the most current records will appear in the combo box, ready to be selected for searches.

Why It Works That Way

If you click on Add while an existing record has the focus in the form, requerying the combo box doesn't have any effect—there are no new records to include in the row source for the combo box so it just returns the same set of records that it had before.

However, if you click on Add *after* typing in the name of a new household, that record is immediately saved to the household table. It will then be included in the row source for the combo box when it requeries the table, which is exactly what we want. In the next section I'll show you how to force the searching combo box to requery its record source.

Modify the VBA for the Add Button

I'm going to show you how to write your own VBA code and have you add it to the form's code module. Writing VBA code really isn't all that difficult to do, as you'll soon find out. Besides, you already know a couple of ways to get help from Access.

Open the form in design view and select the Add command button. Open the property sheet and select the Event tab. Find the On Click event and use the builder button to open the form's code module. It will look something like Figure 10-35.

Figure 10-35 Add Record Code

We need to add one line of code that will force the combo box to requery its row source *after* a new record is added. Here is the code:

```
Me.cboSelectHousehold.Requery
```

As you already learned, Me refers to the form on which the code is running. It is followed by the dot operator, then the name of the control on the form (cboSelectHousehold), and then again the dot operator. The last element of the code is the Requery command. It tells Access that you want cboSelectHousehold to rerun the query that provides its row source, updating the list displayed in the combo box.

In this case, you can place the requery code either before or after the new record code. It will work either way for this particular case. However, I would recommend that you place it after the new record command, as in Figure 10-36.

Figure 10-36 Revised Add Command Button Code

Revise the code for your Add button and try it out. Switch back to form view and try adding more household names from your contact list. Check the combo box to be sure it is updating itself properly. This time new household names should appear in the searching combo box as soon as you click the Add button after typing in a new name.

Actually, clicking the Add button in order both to add new records and to update the combo box in a single event procedure is not necessarily the best way to do it. Still, it's a pretty simple approach and it illustrates the process quite well. We can make it more sophisticated and user friendly using more advanced techniques, but that's a subject for another book, I'm afraid.

Next, let's look at the next part of the problem—designating people as heads of households.

Designating Heads of Households

It should be readily apparent that only people who are already in the person's table can be designated as heads of households. So, if the person you want to designate as a household head isn't in that table, you need to add them somehow. We have created a separate form for adding persons, so one obvious approach would be to open that form each time we add a new household, add the people in it, then close the form and requery the household head list box and the subform in the household form. In fact, that's the approach I'll show you first. Later we'll look at an alternate, more sophisticated method with a real user interface.

Open the household form in design view. We're going to add a new command button to it that will open frmPerson. Let's put this button next to the household head list box.

To add this command button, click on the Command Button icon to open the wizard. Use the mouse to draw a button on the form.

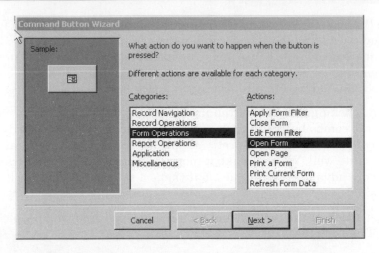

Figure 10-37 Command Button Wizard, Open Form

When the wizard opens, select Form Operations and Open Form and then click Next to move to the next screen. From the list of forms on the next page of the wizard, select frmPerson and then click Next.

On the next page of the wizard, you have two choices. You can have the form open to display *one particular record*, or you can have it open to display *all of the records* in its underlying record set. Because we're interested in adding new records and we don't want to search for any particular existing record, select the second choice.

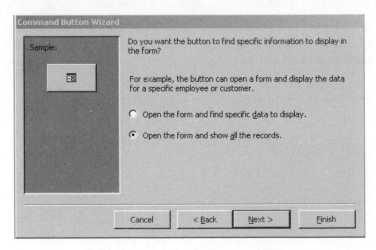

Figure 10-38 Open to Display All Records

Click Next to move to the next page of the wizard, where you'll select the caption for the button.

I chose a caption that tells the user exactly what this button's function is: Add Person. Click Next to go to the next page of the wizard where you'll name the new command button. Call it cmdAddPerson.

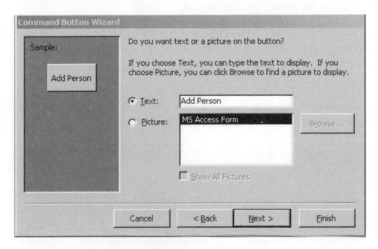

Figure 10-39 Select a Caption

The new command button on my form appears as in Figure 10-40.

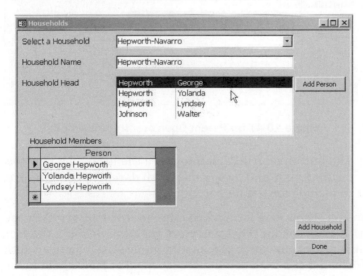

Figure 10-40 New Command Button and Modified Button

Figure 10-40 shows that I made another change to the form as a consequence of having added this new command button. I noticed that the caption on the existing Add button needed to be more specific as well, so I changed it to Add Household.

It's not uncommon to make minor adjustments like this during the design stage. Stay alert to such opportunities.

Now you can click on the New Person button to add people to tblPerson. Try your command button out to see what happens when you click it. It should look something like Figure 10-41.

With the person form open, you can add household members to the person table. Go ahead and do that now, adding family members for one of the households you previously entered in the household table.

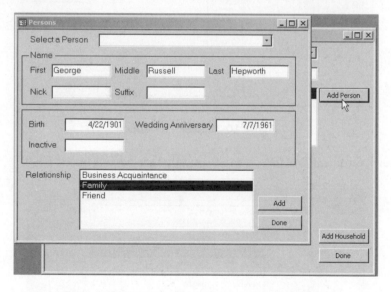

Figure 10-41 frmParent Open over frmHousehold

Click the Add button on frmPerson to move the focus to a new record and enter the person's first and last name, birth date and other information you want to include for the person.

Click Done on the person form when you are finished entering the family members in a household. That will close the form, leaving the Household form visible again. However, you should immediately notice another problem. The list box with candidates for head of Household hasn't changed, even though you just added new people to the table from which its row source is drawn.

Also, when you click on the combo box in the subform, you see the same problem—the people you added aren't available as family members yet.

This time, however, you should know why the record sets for these controls haven't changed. That's right, it's the same problem we dealt with in the searching combo box. We need to requery that household head list box on the main form and the family member combo box on the sub form to force then to update their contents with the newly added people in tblPerson.

User Interaction Strategy

Up to this point we've largely been creating forms without thinking a lot about the overall application in which we'll use them or how the forms relate to one another.

In fact, in the previous example, I deliberately led you down a false path to make a point. Sorry, I'll make it up to you now.

The complications arising out of the need to requery row sources on one form after adding records through the other form should alert us that we need to stop for a moment to consider the interactions between these two forms and the tables that provide their record sources.

Because of the way the household and person tables are related (many-to-many with a junction table between them), we can add records to either tblPerson or tblHousehold at any time without having an effect on the other table.

However, we can only link persons to households —by adding their respective foreign keys to the junction table—if both the household members and households already exist in their respective tables.

Moreover, we can only identify the head of a household by selecting an existing person from the person table. That means that, while we can add a household independently from its members, we can't complete it without those family members.

Independent Data Entry Forms

For the data entry forms, those three considerations about table relationships mean that we can add new households to the household table through that form, with or without adding people who are members of that household, and that we can add new people to the person table through that form, with or without adding their corresponding households.

In that sense, the two forms function independently from one another.

One approach to the workflow could be to add every person in your current contact list to the database in one session without indicating to which household he or she belongs. You'd have, at that point, a list of people, but you'd have no way to group them into families because there are no households to which they could be assigned.

Then you could go back to add all of the households into the other table.

In the final step, you could assign the people in your database to their respective households and designate one of those people as the head of each household. Nothing wrong with that workflow at all.

Interrelated Data Entry Forms

In another sense, though, the data entry forms are closely related. A *complete* household isn't set up until the household name, the household members and the household head are all entered, which requires that you add related records to both tables and, therefore, make entries through both forms as part of the complete workflow for each household.

In that approach to data entry workflow, you would enter households from your contact list into the database as a unit, first the household using the household form, then the people using the person form, and then back to the household form to designate the household head and family members. You could also start by adding the members of a household through the person form and switch from that form to the household form to complete it in a single step.

Designing Forms to Support Workflow

Which approach you take to setting up the workflow in your database depends to a large extent on how you think about the process of setting up a household and on your personal preferences. Moreover, things change over time. When you're setting up the database for the first time, it would be more efficient to load all of the people on your current contact list first and then to set up their households. Later, when you're adding new households one at a time, that is less important, because completing a single household requires switching from one form to the other form in any event.

In my case, for example, I started out thinking about a household as a unit and began leading you through the form design process by making the Household form the starting point, with the family members being adding as the second step. You might say it's a natural world concept of a family and one that other people might start with as well.

However, in the database world, that approach would have created a minor complication when it came time to add family members to the database that represents that natural world: we would have had to force the household form to requery its list and combo boxes to support that workflow. We can avoid that, so let's consider the alternative.

If we make *frmPerson* the base form and start the workflow by adding individual people to the person table, we shouldn't run into the requery problem. We can add any number of people to the table without assigning them to a household and we won't need any of those names as household head until after we've set up a household.

We can move the button that opens the second form to frmPerson from frmHousehold. When frmHousehold opens, it loads with all of the existing records from tblPerson already in the row sources for the household head list box and family member combo box. No need to force a requery. So long as you and your users always start with people and add households afterwards, the forms don't need to be requeried to work.

Generalizing the Lesson

While the two-part workflow in setting up a household and its family members isn't terribly complicated, it is a good example of the kind of analysis you'll need to do in creating the forms and user interface for your database applications. Give it plenty of thought and don't be afraid to reverse directions if you discover that your original design isn't the most effective.

I'll return to the subject of user interface design in Chapter 13.

Where Were We Just Now?

When we paused to take a closer look at interface design and workflow, we had just finished adding a button to the household form that opens the person form. On further consideration, I came to the conclusion that we should have done it the other way around. The base form should be frmPerson and we should have the Add button open frmHousehold after we enter the people. Fortunately, making that change is a lot easier than coming up with VBA code to force frmHousehold to requery its list and combo boxes.

Move a Command Button from One Form to Another

Open both forms—frmHousehold and frmPerson—in design view. We're going to use the standard Windows cut and paste commands to move a command button and its VBA code from one form to the other.

The process involves several steps, but they're all quite simple.

Move the Command Button

First, select the Add Household button on the household form. Cut the button from the form. That will only affect the button itself, not its event procedure. That will require a second step.

Click on the person form to select it. Paste the command button to the form. It will land in the upper left corner of the detail section of the form, so you'll need to click and drag it to a more appropriate place.

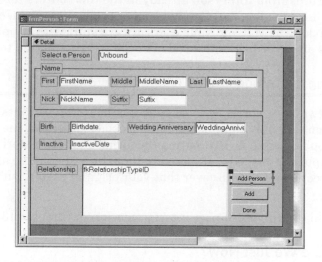

Figure 10-42 Moved Command Button

As Figure 10-42 shows, you'll need to change the captions on some buttons and change their size to create a uniform set of buttons.

Change the caption on the new button from Add Person to Add Household because it will be used to open the household form. Change the caption on the Add button to Add Person, because that is what it does on this form.

Check the names of both buttons. The old Add button should have been called cmdAddPerson or cmdAddRecord. That name doesn't need to change, but the name of the new button you just pasted onto the form needs to be changed to cmdAddHousehold, because its new function is to open the household form to add new households.

Move the Event Procedure

Select frmHousehold again. You're going to move the event procedure for the Add button from this form to the other one. You could avoid this step by re-creating the command button and its event procedure on frmPerson, using the command button wizard as you did to create it before. As an exercise, though, it's worth going the process so you can see how to do it this way.

Find the Code Module

With the command button removed from the form, you can't use the builder button on the Event tab of the property sheet to get to it. Access, as you might guess, does offer an alternative way to get there. On the menu bar, select View-->Code, as in Figure 10-43

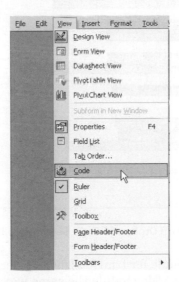

Figure 10-43 Select View->Code from the Menu Bar

This will open the form's code module to the General section. Click to open the drop down list in the right hand combo box, the one that lists events and procedures for this code module.

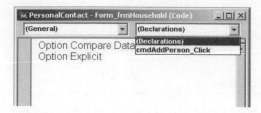

Figure 10-44 Orphaned Event Procedure

You'll find the orphaned event procedure left behind when you removed the command button from the form. Moving that button didn't move or delete the event procedure, but because its control is gone, the code is no longer attached to any of the controls on the form.

You can select cmdAddPerson_Click from the combo box and see the code. Select the entire event procedure and cut it from the code module.

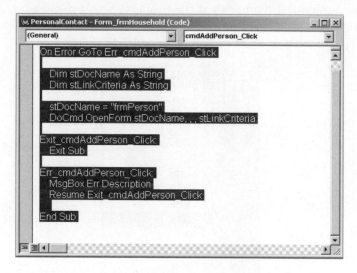

Figure 10-45 Orphaned Code Selected to be Moved

Now, close the code module for frmHousehold, select the other form, frmPerson, and open its code module the same way you opened the code module for frmHousehold.

It should also open to the General section. Paste the code you just cut from frmHousehold here.

Make sure you place the insertion point below the Option Explicit declaration before you paste the code.

The event procedure you just pasted into this code module will also be orphaned, because you renamed the command button when you pasted it onto this form (I am assuming, of course, that you did do that when I asked you to do so).

First, we're going to rename this event procedure so that it is reattached to the proper control. Then I'll explain its contents and edit it so it works correctly in its new home.

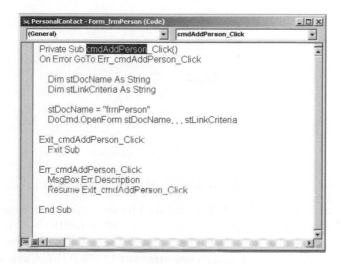

Figure 10-46 New Event Procedure Pasted and Ready to Edit

In Figure 10-46, I've highlighted the name of the control in the event procedure's name. As you recall, event procedure names consist of the name of the control to which they are attached and the event that triggers them.

To reattach this event procedure to its control on the new form, therefore, all you have to do is replace the name of the old control with the name of the new one. Go ahead and do that in your event procedure. Access will immediately reattach it to the control, as indicated by the control combo box. See Figure 10-47.

Figure 10-47 Renamed, Reattached Event Procedure

Now that the event procedure is renamed and reattached, you'll need to edit the rest of the code. Notice for example, that the error trapping line in Figure 10-47 still refers to the old control. Go ahead and replace all of those references with the name of the new control. Be careful when editing the labels; they have to have the colon (:) at the end of label.

Now, let's examine the code, see how it works, and how it needs to be edited to work correctly in its new home.

```
Private Sub cmdAddHousehold_Click()
On Error GoTo Err_cmdAddHousehold_Click
    Dim stDocName As String
    Dim stLinkCriteria As String
    stDocName = "frmPerson"
    DoCmd.OpenForm stDocName, , , stLinkCriteria
Exit_cmdAddHousehold_Click:
    Exit Sub
Err_cmdAddHousehold_Click:
    MsgBox Err.Description
    Resume Exit_cmdAddHousehold_Click
End Sub
```

First, the code declares two variables, stDocName and stLinkCriteria.

This code, which was originally generated by the command button wizard, prefixes the variable names with "st" to indicate that they are strings (as opposed to dates, numbers, objects, etc.). I prefer the three-letter prefix "str", so I'm going to change that in my VBA. I suggest that you do the same.

Make that change and then click on the Compile icon. It resembles a little stack of papers. You'll find it on the Code Module Toolbar.

Figure 10-48 Compile Your Code

There are a couple of reasons for compiling your code, one a bit too technical for a discussion here, the other a bit more practical.

The technical reason is that Access takes the "English-like" code you write in the code module and converts, or compiles, it to a "Machine-like" version that your PC understands. (For the purists out there, I realize that's something of an oversimplification, but it should convey the basic thought.)

The practical reason is that requesting a compilation of the code forces Access to attempt to compile it immediately. If there are *syntax* errors in your code, Access will highlight them. For example, while renaming the variables from "st..." to "str...", you may change one instance and overlook another. Access won't. Assuming you've declared Option Explicit for your code, Access won't let spelling variations or misspellings slip into the code.

When you click the compile button, if nothing seems to happen, your code is syntactically valid. Of course, it can have errors of logic that won't show up until it runs, but at least you know it is syntactically correct.

The next step is to change the name of the form to open from frmPerson to frmHousehold. You'll find that in line five.

```
strDocName = "frmPerson"
```

Change it to

```
strDocName = "frmHousehold"
```

Access creates this code format by default. It isn't the only way to do it, and, in my opinion, it's unnecessarily complicated, but it does have the advantage of giving us a good example of how you can use a variable in your code.

The variable called strDocName can take nearly any value you want to assign to it. In this case, we're assigning it the name of the form we want to open, frmHousehold.

Here, strDocName is a string, or text, variable. It takes the name of a form. String variables must be placed in quotes (" "), as you see above.

The other line I want to explain in this event procedure is this one.

```
DoCmd.OpenForm strDocName, , , strLinkCriteria
```

It uses the DoCmd object—which you've seen before—along with the OpenForm method to open the form. The previous line assigned the value frmHousehold to the variable, strDocName, so the open form command loads that form.

The commas after the form name represent *optional elements* of the open form instructions, options that are not included in this instance. However, because the code includes the final optional element, designated by strLinkCriteria, the commas have to be there as placeholders.

The link criterion, strLinkCriteria, is superfluous for our purposes here, but the wizard creates this code by default. I'm just going to ignore it for now, since it doesn't impact what we need to do. You may wish to take a few moments, though, to use the F1 key to read Access' help file on the OpenForm command to see what it would do if we used it.

After the edits, Figure 10-49 shows what the event procedure in my sample database looks like. I've added some comments to it. Read them carefully.

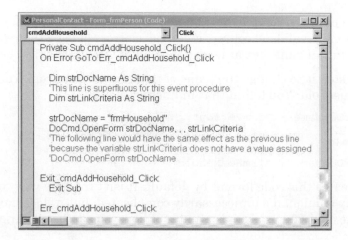

Figure 10-49 Revised Event Procedure with Comments

Switch back to form view and try out the new Add Household button. As long as you open the person form first and add people before opening the household form with this command button, the list and combo boxes on the household form will always contain the complete record set from tblPerson. Of course, for that to work, you and your users must follow this workflow consistently.

Remaining Issues

There are some other things, mostly minor, about the way these two forms work so far that can be improved. Mostly that has to do with the fact that you have to click the Add button both before and after adding a new person or household to the database.

Another issue you might want to look at is the relative positions (and tab order) for the three command buttons on frmPerson. Look at Figure 10-50. That's the way they are stacked on my form. You may prefer to move Add Person above Add Household. Done should stay on the bottom. Thinking about how you and your users will be working, decide what the best sequence is. Set the tab order for the controls on the form to match.

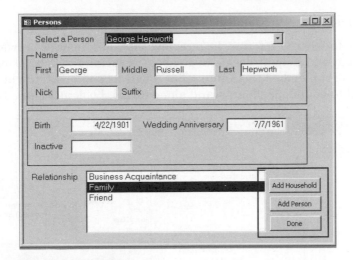

Figure 10-50 Position and Tab Order for Command Buttons

Try it Yourself

Another, more significant, thing I want you to look at is the requery action for the searching combo box on frmPerson. Look back at page 10-34, where we discussed requerying a combo or list box after adding a new record. We didn't make that modification for the combo box on frmParent yet; I left it as an exercise for you. Go ahead, switch to design view, open the event procedure for the add Person button, and add the requery code as described on page 10-34.

Additional Data Entry Forms

At this point, then, you should have two main *data entry* forms, one for adding households and one for adding people, and also four simple *maintenance* forms for addresses types, phone types, email address types and relationship types. In addition to those main forms, we have one subform, embedded in the household form, which allows us to assign people to households in the junction table.

I count a total of seven forms in the forms collection of our contacts database, including the subform. We still need to add three more forms to the collection.

Those forms will allow us to add
➢ addresses,
➢ phone numbers and

> email addresses for households and people.

Before we tackle those forms, let's review the relationships between the tables. That will help us decide to go about creating the new forms whether we can embed them into other forms as subforms or whether they need to be independent, stand alone forms. Look at Figure 10-51.

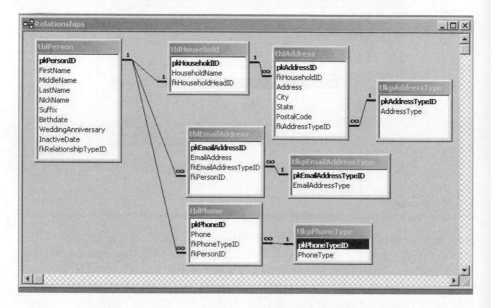

Figure 10-51 Relationships for Addresses, Phones and Email

As Figure 10-51 shows, the three contact tables, *address, phone* and *email,* are all on the many side of a one-to-many relationship.

> For each household, there are one or more addresses.

> For each person, there are one or more phone numbers and one or more email addresses.

That suggests the new forms can, and should, be set up as subforms on the main forms for households and persons, respectively.

We'll accomplish our goals by adding a second subform to frmHousehold to handle the addresses and two subforms to frmPerson to handle phone and email. You already created two main forms and a subform, the one for household members, so you should have a basic idea about how to add the addresses subform to frmHousehold. It's really quite similar to the one you already built, except that its record set has more fields. That means the subform will have more columns in the datasheet. Otherwise, the process of adding it should be familiar.

Go ahead and try it. Then, come back to this chapter and compare my approach to yours.

My Suggested Subforms

Figure 10-52 shows the subform after I added it to the household form.

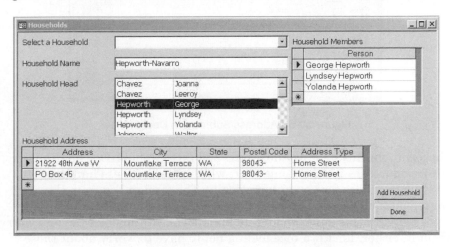

Figure 10-52 Household Address Sub Form

Notice that I ended up moving the Household Member subform to a new location in order to make room for the new address subform. Layout is controlled by two considerations, functionality and appearance. I think that using space on a form effectively is a very important aspect of both.

You may prefer a different arrangement than mine, and that's fine. Just keep in mind that your users will be looking at that form often, and the easier it is for them to navigate from control to control, the better they'll like it and the less likely they will be to complain.

Hiding Primary and Foreign Keys

This subform is designed to display in datasheet view. It looks like this in design view. Take note of the names for the fields and the label captions.

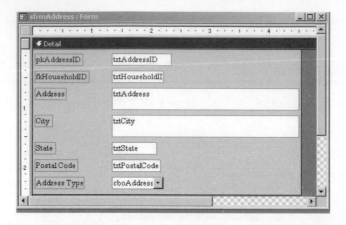

Figure 10-53 Address Subform in Design View

The form contains both pkAddressID and fkHouseholdID. The primary key for addresses is an autonumber, which means Access handles creating new ones for you automatically. The foreign key from the household table is handled by Access via the Master and Child linking fields between this subform and its main form, so you don't have to worry about it, either. Isn't it a nice feeling not to have to worry about those details?

When you switch the form to datasheet view, all of the fields show up as columns, whether their Visible property is set to Yes or No. You can hide columns (i.e. fields) in datasheet view by selecting the column and then selecting Format---->Hide Columns from the menu bar.

You can rearrange the column order from left to right, if you need to do that, by clicking on the head of the column and dragging it to the desired location. You can also change the font of the fields in the datasheet. Select Format-->Font to open the font dialog and select the new font.

Switch back to design view and select the Format tab on the property sheet for the subform. Set the Scroll Bar property to vertical only. Set the Navigation Buttons property to No. Adjust the width and height of the subform to fit the address subform, making sure that it is wide enough to display all of the visible fields.

Adding New Address Records

Adding new address records is a lot easier with a one-to-many table than it was with the many-to-many table for family members or household heads. All you need to do is tab or click into the first field in the subform and start entering the new values. Look for the asterisk (*) at the left end of the record row, which tells you that you're adding a new record.

Enter the values, moving across the row, for address, city, state and zip. Then use the drop down list in the combo box for Address Type to select one of the values there.

Additional Enhancements

There a few additional enhancements you can make to the household form and its address subform, but I'm going to save them for a future discussion. For now, let's turn our attention to the phone and email subforms on the person form.

Phone Number Subform

You may want to go ahead and add the phone and email subforms to the person form on your own. I would like to think that by now you could manage that task pretty well. However, I'll walk through the process for the phone number form here as a refresher.

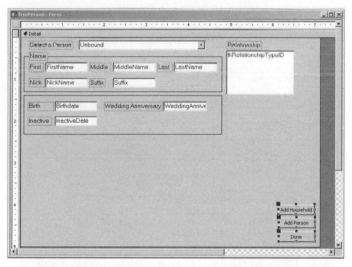

Figure 10-54 Making Space for the Phone Subform

Clear Space on the Form

I moved the relationship list box to the upper right and moved the command buttons down and to the right, opening space on the form for the phone subform.

Draw the Subform Control

The next step was to select the Subform icon from the Toolbox toolbar and draw it onto the form. The wizard opened, asking whether I wanted to create a form from a table or query or use an existing form. Because I didn't have an existing form, I chose the first option.

Create a New Subform

On the next page of the wizard, I selected tblPhone and added all of its fields to the subform. Clicking Next took me to the next page of the wizard, where I accepted the master and child linking fields suggested by Access. These are the primary and foreign keys for the two tables. On the last page of the wizard, I named the new subform sfrmPersonPhone, following the standard naming convention for subforms.

Manage Subform and Subform Control Layout

Access placed the new subform on the form, ready for me to reformat and modify. As you can see in Figure 10-55, the default size is probably not going to be adequate. I think it needs to be wider.

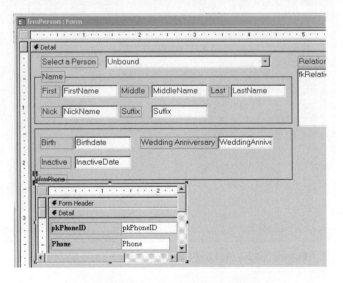

Figure 10-55 Newly added Subform

Before I change the size of the subform *control* on the main form, I'm going to modify the *subform* itself. To do this, open it, either by double-clicking on it in the main form or using the subform button in the menu.

Subforms don't display headers and footers anyway, so I removed the form header and footer (View-->Header/Footer on the menu). Then I changed the names of the fields and labels to conform to the naming conventions, e.g. txtPhone, cboPhoneTypeID, and the captions of the labels to plain English language labels.

Hide Key Fields on the Subform

Next, I switched to datasheet view to hide the primary and foreign key columns for the person and phone tables. To hide the key fields, I clicked on their column heads and selected "Format-->Hide Columns" from the menu bar. I didn't hide the phone type foreign key, though; we'd need it later. At this point the subform looked like Figure 10-56.

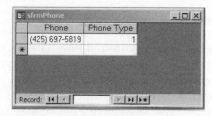

Figure 10-56 Subform With Key Fields Hidden

Subform Cleanup

As you can see there were a few more things to clean up. I needed to change the form's caption and to remove the navigation buttons. Also, I needed to convert the phone type field to a combo box so it can display the text values for the phone types.

I switched to design view and changed the form's caption, set the Navigation Buttons property to No, and set the Scroll Bar property to Vertical Only. The last step was to convert the phone type field to a combo box.

Convert Text Box to Combo Box

To convert the text box to a combo box, I selected it and right mouse-clicked on it to open the short cut menu. From there I selected "Change to --> Combo Box".

To add a new row source to the combo box, I selected the Data tab on the property sheet and clicked on the builder button at the end of the Row Source property. That opened the query builder, where I selected tlkpPhoneType. I dragged its two columns down to the query grid, making sure the primary key was in the leftmost column. I closed and saved the resulting SQL without converting it to a query, but you can make it a query in your database (Call it something like qryPhoneType, if you do.)

I verified that the bound column for this combo box was column one, the column that holds the primary key from tlkpPhoneType, and that the control source for this combo box was fkPhoneTypeID. To finish it off, I moved to the Format tab, where I gave the combo box two columns and set their widths to zero inches and one inch, respectively. That hid the primary key, but left the corresponding text visible.

At that point I closed the subform and changed the caption of the subform control on the main form to Phone, which was enough to identify it.

New Subform and Subform Control Complete

Figure 10-57 shows what it finally looked like. There's plenty of room there to add the other subform for email addresses. I'll leave adding it to you as an exercise. You can duplicate the phone subform as a short cut because it is identical except for its record source and captions on labels. Open the phone subform in design view, then click File-->Save As from the menu bar. Name it sfrmEmail. Change its record source; rename the fields and labels on it. Change the row source for the email type combo box and save it. It's ready to embed next to the phone subform, as in Figure 10-58.

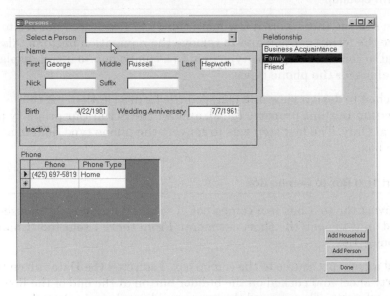

Figure 10-57 Completed Phone Subform

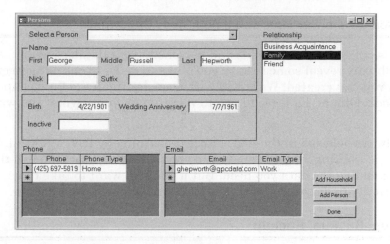

Figure 10-58 Completed Person Form

Forms Wrap Up

That should just about wrap things up for the basic set of forms in your database. With the set of forms you've learned how to create, you can now add all of the pieces of data you need to add to set up a complete household with all of its family members, the household address and phone and email addresses for the people in the database. You also have four maintenance forms to manage phone, email, address and relationship types.

You've taken a brief look at the interface design level by figuring out the best way to coordinate data entry between the household and person forms. There's a good deal more you can do with interface design and the forms we just created certainly can be improved in that area, but we'll save that discussion for the last chapter.

Now, let's turn our attention to using the data in your database effectively by learning how to create reports to get the data back out.

Before we do that, however, I'd like to suggest that you add some more of your contacts to your database. That way you'll both get some first hand experience with using the forms and have some more real data in your database to make the reports look more realistic. I'm going to load my database with bogus names because I'm sure that most of my family and friends don't want to see their names published in this book.

Additional Enhancements and a Self Study Opportunity

The task of adding households and persons to your database will undoubtedly reveal some tweaks you'd like to make to one or more of the forms you just created. We'll deal with some issues in the final chapter of this book. Others, I'll leave to you to work out on your own, if you want to.

I've always believed in the importance of learning by trial and trial. With the basic working forms in place, you should be able to accomplish the task of adding the data you need. But if you also want to take this opportunity to discover new things for yourself, here's your chance.

Backup, Backup, Backup

Before you start experimenting on your own, however, this would be another excellent time to make a backup copy of the database. You have invested a lot of time and effort in getting to this point. Protect that effort by creating a backup copy of your database.

Close your database, find it on your hard drive and make a copy in a safe place. Do that now.

Next, I want tell you how to get data back out of your database. I'll do that in the next chapter.

See you in a couple of hours.

11. Getting Data out of Your Database —Reports

Your database is now set up to accept and store names, addresses, phone numbers and email addresses. If you followed my suggestion to add all of your current contact information, you should have a lot of data in it now. To make that new data useful, you now need to set up reports and forms to print or display the contents of the tables in your database. This chapter discusses printed reports; the next chapter focuses on display-only forms.

Useful Reports and Forms

The most obvious use for a *personal* contacts database is to make it easier to create lists or labels so you can mail birthday cards, Christmas cards or letters to your family and friends.

For a small business, or for department within a larger organization, you might want a *business* contacts database to create mass mailings for your customers or suppliers. This would also provide customers and fellow employees with quick and easy access to phone and email address information.

To meet those needs you'll want at least the following reports:

> Mailing labels for cards, etc.

> Address list for letters, sorted and filtered

> Phone list for calls, sorted and filtered

> Email list for email, sorted and filtered

> Birthday list, sorted and filtered

As you use the database, you will most likely think of other reports you'd like to see. But the list above should be plenty for us to get a solid understanding of basic report writing in Access. In fact, I only have space in this book to show you how to create two of these reports in detail: mailing labels and a sorted birthday list. The rest you can create yourself, using these two as examples.

Let's start with one of the simplest reports, the mailing labels. They will have only three fields on them. Also, there is a report wizard specifically for labels. It will give us a hand as we get started with reports.

Mailing Labels Report Wizard

Select Reports in the database window. See Figure 11-1.

Figure 11-1 Create New Report Using Report Wizard

It shows the new report dialog that opens when you select New from the database window menu bar. It includes a wizard for creating mailing labels. That is the wizard we want. (If you used the shortcut, Create report by using wizard, in the database window, then that option isn't available. This is, in fact, one of the few times when one method for performing a task is preferable to another in Access.)

Select a Record Source

Select the Label Wizard option and then choose a table from the combo box. We're going to create labels for mailings, so the logical table to use is tblAddress. That won't be enough for the finished mailing label report because the address table only includes addresses and foreign keys from tblHousehold. To create labels with both household names and addresses, we'll need to modify the SQL statement that is the record source for this report. We'll have to do that later, after we complete the basic report with the wizard, because this wizard only lets us choose a single table.

The next step in the report wizard looks like Figure 11-2.

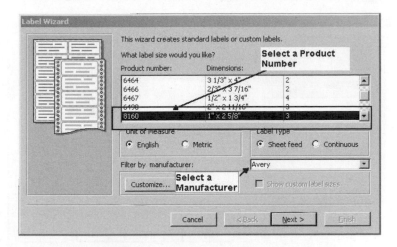

Figure 11-2 Select from The List of Manufacturers

Select a Label Format

Access offers a wide selection of labels from which to choose. I recently counted nearly 40 separate manufacturers in the list. The quantity of product numbers for each manufacturer ranges from two for Sigel up to almost 200 product numbers for Avery. With that much variety, it is quite likely that any labels you have in your home or office will be available to you in the wizard. If not, you can also customize your own!

I have a package of Avery labels, product number 8160. They come as single sheets of three columns. The size of each label on the page is 1" x 2 5/8", so that's the choice I selected for my labels. I'll base the rest of this example on that label size. If you have a different type of labels, you'll need to adjust the following instructions accordingly.

Select a Font

In the wizard, click Next to move to the next page of the wizard. Here you select fonts, font sizes, and font colors for your labels. Look at Figure 11-3.

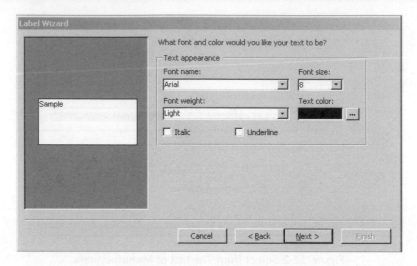

Figure 11-3 Select Font, Font Size and Font Color

I recommend that you leave the defaults as they are. Arial is a good, legible font. Although the font size offered—8 points—is relatively small, it's usually easier to increase the font size later if you have space on the label, rather than to try to squeeze text in a too large font onto a label. You may decide to increase font size when you're through creating labels. It depends on how much space is available and how readable the resulting labels are.

Add Fields to the Label

Click Next to move to the next page of the wizard and select the fields you want to appear on the label. The gray bar on the prototype label represents the current line. Select fields from the list on the left and click on the arrow button to add them to the label in the current line. With the cursor in the prototype label, press Enter to move to the next line on the label. Figure 11-4 shows the process in progress. Notice that I left a blank space above the address line in Figure 11-4. That's where the Household name will go when I add it to the record source for the label. Also notice in the third line where I've added the City field that I typed in the comma after it. That's the standard address format: City, ST ZIP for U.S. addresses. We can revise all of those fields later, if we want to do so; at this point we're really just creating a draft version of the label.

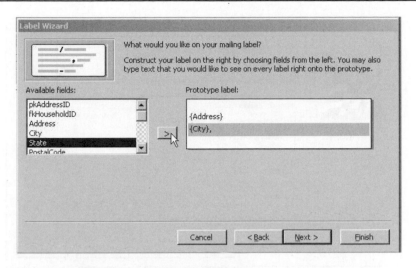

Figure 11-4 Adding Fields to the Address Label

Add the address, city, state, and postal code fields, making sure you leave a space between each value so they will lay out properly on the label. Click Next to go to the next page of the wizard. This page allows you to sort the labels onto the sheet. As a matter of fact, you'll probably want to sort alphabetically by household name in the completed labels, but that field isn't available in the record source yet. We will add it later. Just click Next to go on to the last page of the label wizard. Here you'll give your new report a name. See Figure 11-5.

The standard naming conventions for reports is like that for other Access objects. I prefer to prefix "lbl" rather than "rpt" for mailing labels, though. I called this one lblHouseholdAddress. Figure 11-6 is a preview of the way the labels will appear when printed.[14]

---

[14] When you complete the mailing labels and preview them for the first time, you may see an error message telling you that there is not enough space on the page for the number of columns and column spacing you specified. This is a known problem with Access 2002. Microsoft's website says this about the problem, "The label dimensions for certain Avery labels were modified in Access 2002 to be the Avery standard. In addition, certain labels may have a left margin that is smaller than what is allowed by many printer drivers. As a result, depending on the printer that you are using, the report may be created with a margin larger than the actual label."
They go on to suggest you ignore the error message and continue. Let's hope this gets fixed in future versions.

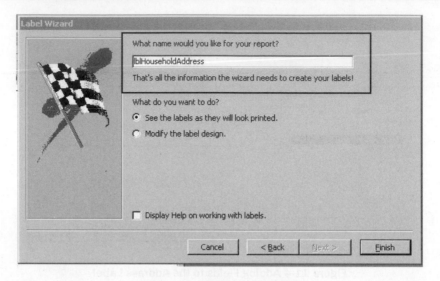

Figure 11-5 Name the Report

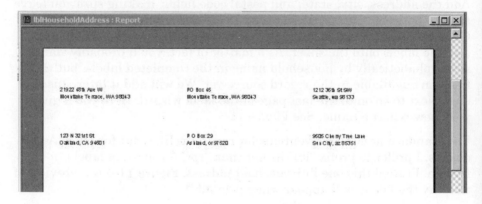

Figure 11-6 Preview of New Labels

Right now there is no household name because we haven't had a chance to add that yet. However, all of the addresses in my sample database appear in the spots where they'll print on the label sheet. Looks good so far. Let's switch the report to design view and take care of the remaining details. Design view should look like Figure 11-7.

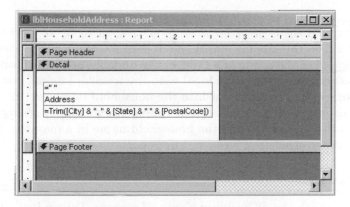

Figure 11-7 New Labels, Design View

The form wizard added a page header and footer by default. We don't
need them for a sheet of labels, so the first thing to do is click on
View-->Page Header/Footer and toggle them off to remove them.

Figure 11-8 Remove Header and Footer

Now take a look at the fields laid out on the report. There are three of
them, stacked one on top of the other. They are similar in some important
ways to the fields you saw when you were creating forms, but they do
have differences, don't they?

Empty Strings in Text Fields

The top field on the label is empty; it's record source is designated as (=" ") instead of the name of a field in the underlying table. Here's why. When you were designing this label with the wizard, I asked you to leave that top line empty to accommodate the household name, so Access did that by putting in an expression that represents an empty string. We'll come back to that field to add the household name in a moment. First, let's look at the other text boxes on the report.

Ordinary Text Field

Text fields are the basic building blocks of reports. Take a look at the second field, the one whose control source is Address. That field is as ordinary as it gets. The control source is one of the fields in the table that provides the report its record source. Most fields on your reports will be text fields, just like this one. They will be wider or narrower, taller or shorter than this one, depending on their contents and font sizes. You can give them borders, different background colors, different font colors and sizes, depending on whether you want to highlight them or de-emphasize them on the report. All in all, text fields are the workhorses of the report world. Most of them are just like this one.

You can see a difference in the way this control source is designated, though, from the way the empty string is designated for the first field. Let's take a closer look at that difference, so you can learn how to create custom expressions on your reports.

Expressions in Text Fields

Because the Address field is a field in the underlying record source, it doesn't need any special handling to be designated as the control source for a field on a report. However, the empty string, which is the control source for the first control on the label, isn't a field in the table, so Access must handle it differently.

Designating an Expression with the Equal Sign

The equal sign (=) in the field's control source tells Access to display an expression, i.e. something other than a field from the report's record source. The rest of the text in the control source for the field specifies what that expression is. In this case, it's the empty string, set off in parentheses. You'll see similar syntax in the last field on the label, where the city, state and postal code fields are concatenated into a single string.

You've seen concatenated fields in a query before. Here they are in the text box on a report. Same concept, different implementation.

Concatenated Fields as the Control Source for a Field

The expression in the last field on the label is built by concatenating the City, State, and Postal Codes into a single string. The syntax to do that, as you can see in the label, is:

```
=Trim([City] & ", " & [State] & " " & [PostalCode])
```

We need the "=" sign at the beginning of the line to tell Access this is an expression—something other than a field from the record source underlying the report.

Ignore for a second the keyword Trim at the beginning of the expression. Access added that for a reason, which I'll explain later. I want to explain the concatenation first.

This expression combines the city, state and postal code fields to create a single field. In the label wizard I told Access to add the comma and spaces (", " and " ") between the words so the concatenated string prints out correctly on the label.

Why, you might ask, do we go to the trouble of creating a concatenated field from these fields, instead of just laying the three fields end to end on a line, as shown in Figure 11-9?

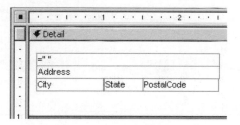

Figure 11-9 Non-Concatenated Fields

The answer is that the width of a text box on a report is fixed. In Figure 11-9, the text box displaying City will always occupy the same amount of horizontal space, whether it displays the name Afton, or the name Mountlake Terrace. This fixed width has two consequences.

First, you would have to draw the field wide enough to accommodate the longest name in the city field in your database. Otherwise it would either cut off some names when the label is printed, or it would wrap them to two lines, depending on what other properties you have set for the label.

Most of the time, having fields grow taller to accommodate their contents is not a good thing, although there are some cases where you can plan a layout to accommodate that. On a label, though, where space is tight and layout must be precise, letting fields grow taller is just not acceptable.

Second, the State field, which must be placed to the right of the City field, will print on the same position for every label, regardless of the length of the city name that goes with it. Drawing the City field wide enough to accommodate the longest possible city name means that there will be a gap of varying length between the end of the city name and the state.

In some reports—such as financial summaries displaying columns of numbers—having variable-width horizontal gaps between fields that make up the columns is acceptable as long as the items in each column line up vertically, like in a spreadsheet, for example.

However, with that label design the result would look something like Figure 11-10. See the gaps between City, State, and ZIP Codes? Also Mountlake Terrace wraps to a second line because the City text box is still not wide enough.

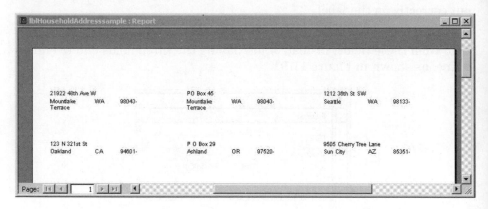

Figure 11-10 Preview of Non-Concatenated Fields

Users expect to see varying lengths of text and fixed gaps between fields on forms and some types of financial reports. On the majority of printed reports, however, gaps and fixed positions create an unprofessional appearance. The solution is to create concatenated strings for certain fields on printed reports.

String Concatenation in Reports

In many places on your reports, as in the case of city, state, and postal code for mailing labels, you can't predict ahead of time how well variable length strings will fit. Printed appearance is very important, as is consistent layout and spacing on printed forms. Being able to concatenate text strings, therefore, is a very valuable tool in creating good-looking reports.

Flip back to design view and look again at the second and third lines on the label. Address is on a line all by itself; it doesn't matter how long or short any given address is because there is nothing after it to worry about. Plus, if it is too long, it can be made to wrap to the next line, pushing the entire field for City, State, and ZIP Code down in the process. Address will always look right on the label because it doesn't need to share horizontal space with other fields.

Concatenating Fields and Static Text

You can simply combine fields to create strings as you need them, or, as you saw here, you can combine fields from the record source with static text you specify. For example, if you wanted to create a title for a report incorporating date information, you could create a text field and place the following text, or something like it, in that field's control source.

```
= "Installations completed prior to " & Date()
```

Date() is a standard function that returns the current date, so the report caption on this report would print out something like Figure 11-11, where this version was created on 11/26/2003.

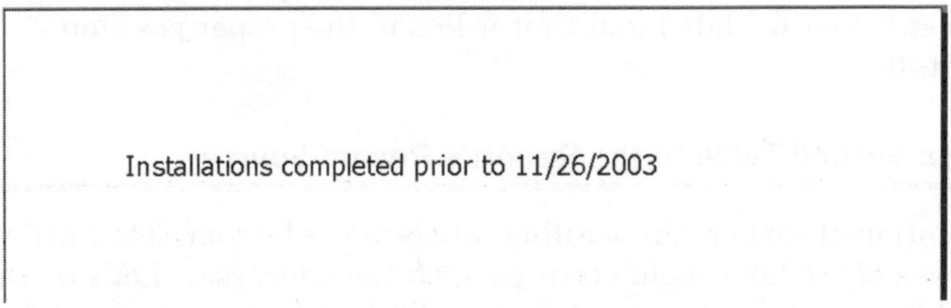

Installations completed prior to 11/26/2003

Figure 11-11 Report Caption with Variable Date

Each time this report prints, it will display the current date as part of the report title.

Data Display Versus Data Input

As you can see from these examples of concatenated display fields, one of the most important ways reports differ from forms lies in the fact that reporting usually calls for *combining* fields from underlying record sources in ways that are *meaningful to humans*—putting the city, state, and postal code into the expected format, for example. Data entry forms, on the other hand, are designed to *break down* information into the *smallest meaningful units* so that data can be inserted into the appropriate fields in the tables.

For that reason, your reports will tend to combine data from underlying fields. On the other hand, you'll create data entry forms with a number of discrete fields.

Hey, What Was that "Trim" Thing You Skipped Over?

I skipped over the Trim function in the third field on the label, but now that we've discussed concatenated fields and described the importance of spacing and layout on a report, let's go back and see what the Trim function does. You might even be able to guess its purpose from its name.

There are three related trim functions: LTrim, RTrim, and Trim. They remove, or trim, spaces from text strings, leading spaces (LTrim), trailing spaces (RTrim), or both leading and trailing spaces (Trim).

In this case,

```
= Trim([City] & ", " & [State] & " " & [PostalCode])
```
removes any *leading* or *trailing* spaces added to the text string when it is concatenated (but not the spaces you add between the words). You should be able to see how useful that would be in making sure the string fits the limited space on the label and that it lies in the proper position horizontally.

Adding a Second Table to the Report's Record Source

As I mentioned earlier, the mailing labels won't be complete until we add the names of the households that go with the addresses. Let's do that next. This process is very similar to modifying the record source for a form, which you learned how to do earlier. Switch to report design view and open the report's property sheet. Select Report and the Data tab. It should display tblAddress as the record source.

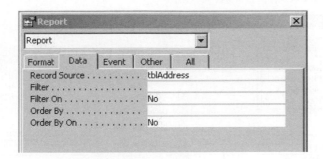

Figure 11-12 Record Source for the Mailing Label Report

Click to select the Record Source property and then use the builder button to open the query builder. Click Yes on the dialog box that appears. The query builder should look like Figure 11-13.

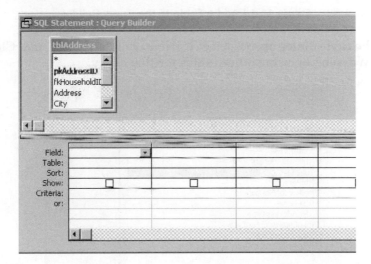

Figure 11-13 Query Window for Report's Record Source

The original record source, tblAddress, is already available, but not the household names table we need. Right mouse click on the table window portion of the query builder to open the short-cut menu. Select Show Table.

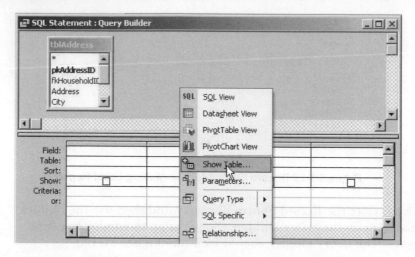

Figure 11-14 Add a Table to the Query Builder

When the table dialog opens, select tblHousehold and click Add. Close the dialog. We won't be using other tables for this query.

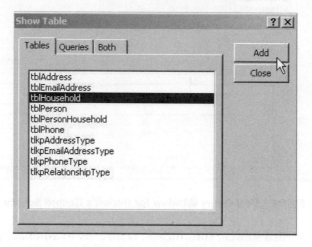

Figure 11-15 Add tblHousehold to the Query

Access adds tblHousehold to the query window. It knows about the relationship between tblHousehold and tblAddress, so it adds the join line between them in the query window as well.

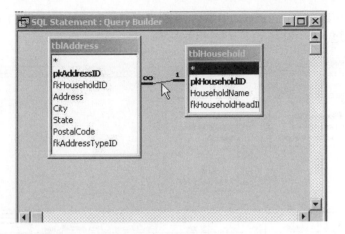

Figure 11-16 Automatic Joins

Now you are ready to add fields to the report's record source so they are available to create the mailing labels the way we want them. We do that by adding them to the query grid in the lower part of the query builder.

We will need the following fields in the query:

➢ tblAddress

- Address
- City
- State
- PostalCode

➢ tblHousehold

- HouseholdName

Primary and Foreign Keys

We don't need to include the primary and foreign keys in the fields that go into the record source. We're going to display these fields in a static, printed report. Access already knows about the relationships between the names and addresses to be printed; it's the query's job to handle that before the fields get to the report. This report itself doesn't need the primary and secondary key fields to sort and print properly. Finally, when we print the labels, we don't want to show the key fields.

It won't always be the case, but here at least we don't need the key fields in the report's record source. You'll see an example of a report with the opposite requirement later.

The result looks like Figure 11-17. The five fields displayed in the query grid will be available to the label report.

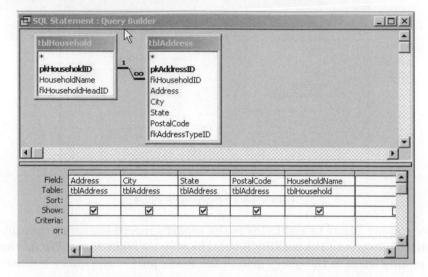

Figure 11-17 Query with Address and Household Tables

Save the query by clicking on the Save icon on the menu bar. When asked for a name, call it qryMailLabel. Close it and return to the report. Open the field list by clicking on the Field List icon on the menu bar.

Figure 11-18 Open the Field List

The field list now shows the HouseholdName field is available in the report, so we can add it to the mailing label.

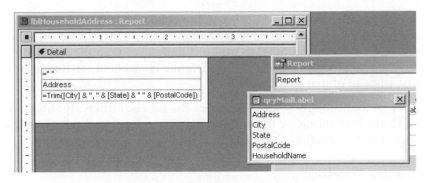

Figure 11-19 Field List Displayed

We're going to replace the empty string in the first field on the report with HouseholdName. Select the field, open the property sheet and select the Data tab. (You will notice when you select the field, the report wizard assigns it a default name, something like "text1". In a later step we'll convert default names of fields on the report to follow standard naming conventions. You can also take care of that yourself at any time.)

Click into the Control Source property for that text box control. Using the drop down arrow, open the list of fields and click on HouseholdName to select it as the control source. It will replace the previous empty string (=" "). If Access doesn't automatically remove the equal sign, do so manually. HouseholdName is a field name, not an expression.

Click the Save icon to save the revised report and switch to Print Preview to see the results. It should now like something like Figure 11-20.

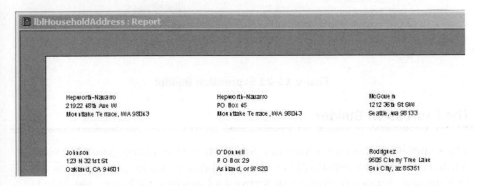

Figure 11-20 Print Preview, Labels with Household Names

If you look closely at Figure 11-20, you'll a couple of additional enhancements we can make. One is to add Family or Household to the household name for each label to make it more user friendly. In other words, you can have the labels say Rodriguez Household, or Rodriguez Family, instead of just Rodriguez.

The other enhancement would be to sort the labels, either alphabetically by the Household name, or by state or ZIP Code. Let's make both of these enhancements. Switch back to design view.

Create a New Expression

Select the household name field and open the property sheet to the Data tab. Click on the control source for this text box and use the builder button to open the expression builder. See Figure 11-21.

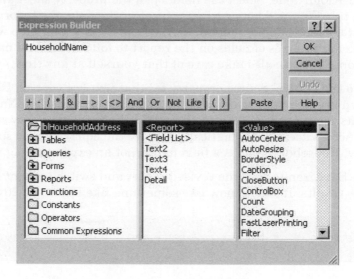

Figure 11-21 Expression Builder

The Expression Builder

The expression builder is another Access tool that makes your life easier while constructing reports. It is also available in many other places throughout Access, including in forms and queries, although we didn't have an opportunity to use it with the forms we created in Chapters 8, 9 and 10. Since this is the first time we've used it, let's take a few moments to see how it works, then we'll come back and use it to fix up this field on this report.

Creating Expressions

The expression builder offers shortcuts to various Access objects and functions along with all of the tables, queries, reports and forms in the database as well as the controls in them. *All* of it is right there to help you create new expressions for fields in forms, reports and queries.

Creating expressions in the expression builder is a multi-step process:

1. Click through lists and columns in the lower windows to find objects and functions in the database.
2. Click the Paste button to insert the selected objects and functions into the expression window at the top of the builder.
3. Edit the expression and add any additional text required to complete the expression.

The result is an *expression*, such as the one we need for the address label. In this case, the expression will be built from a field in the table and text strings you type in manually.

Click to Paste Expressions

The expression builder's *click to paste* technique has a couple of advantages to you as a developer.

Object Availability and Help

First, the builder keeps track of all of the objects and functions in your database, so you don't have to guess where and what they are. You can scroll through the components of the builder until you find the one you want and then select it to see its components and any associated events, where applicable.

All of the *built-in* objects and functions in the database are available in the expression builder along with the objects and functions *you create*.

In addition to making them available in searchable lists, the expression builder offers access to the help system for most objects and functions. Select it in the builder and click the help button.

Object Accuracy

Second, you don't have to remember names and spellings for all of the objects (tables, forms, reports, queries) in your database and the controls or fields in them. Simply click to select an object or element in the explorer list on the left hand side of the builder and double-click it to open its components in the center and right hand lists. Even if you are scrupulous about following naming conventions for your tables, forms, reports, and queries, having them here in the expression builder can be a big help.

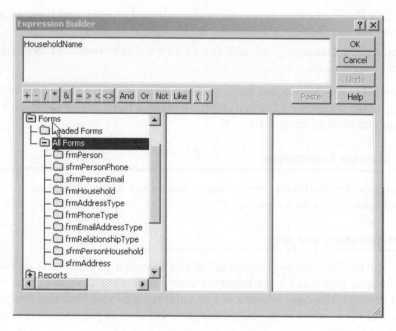

Figure 11-22 Forms List Opened

The left-hand list contains a tree view list all of the tables, forms, etc. in the database. Some of the folder icons in the tree view have a small plus sign (+) on them. That means there are other objects inside the folder. Double-clicking the folder opens it to display all of the objects in it. For example, double-clicking the forms folder expands it to show all of the forms in the database, grouped by whether they are currently loaded or not, see Figure 11-22.

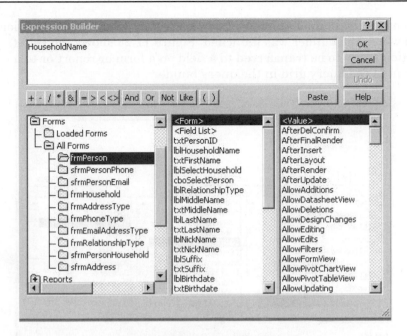

Figure 11-23 Field and Event List

Clicking on one of the forms in the expanded list of forms displays a list of the *controls* on that form in the center list. In the right hand list, the expression builder show the *events* available for the object or control selected in the center list. See Figure 11-23.

Scroll though the elements of the expression builder, double-clicking tables, forms, and reports to expand and review the list of objects in your database. The type of elements available in the center and right-hand lists change, depending on the object selected in the left-hand list.

Functions in the Expression Builder

Scroll to the bottom of the left-hand list and click on Functions to see the list of built-in Functions in the database. Access provides a number of built-in functions for handling things like dates and times, or performing mathematical or financial calculations.

For example, if you want to insert a function that will always return the current date, you can use the expression builder to find and insert the Date() function, as shown in Figure 11-24.

Select the function you want to use, then click on the Paste button to add it to the expression builder window. When you close the builder, the contents of the builder window will be transferred back to the location from which the builder was launched. Figure 11-24 shows the Date() function ready to be transferred to a field on a form or report or to a column in the query grid in the query builder.

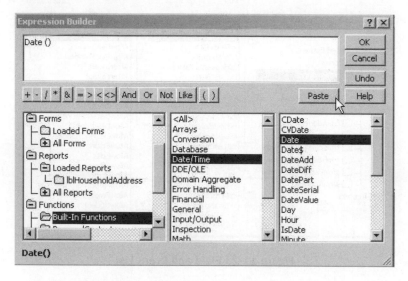

Figure 11-24 Insert the Date Function Example

Using the Expression Builder in our Labels

In this example, we want to use the expression builder to add some text to the existing field in the builder window, something like The Hepworth-Navarro Household. The string consists of a field from the report's record source and some static text we want to add to it each time it is printed on the report.

Adding Text to an Expression

When the expression builder opens from the household name field on the report, it looks like Figure 11-21. To add the text to it, move the cursor to the front of the expression and type in "The ". Make sure you include the quote marks and leave a space after the "e" in "the" so the space will appear in the completed text string on the report. Then, click on the ampersand (&) button to add it to the expression.

As you learned earlier, "&" is the operator you use to combine, or concatenate, elements in a text string. In this case you are concatenating a string with a field name.

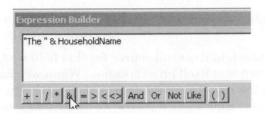

Figure 11-25 Syntax Buttons in the Expression Builder

Spaces and Parentheses

The elements of the expression in the expression builder must be separated by spaces so Access knows where one element ends and the next one begins. Make sure there is a space between the ampersand and the H in HouseholdName. That way Access knows that "&" is the concatenating operator, not part of the variable name that follows it. Move the cursor to the end of the expression and add a space. Add another ampersand and space and then type in " Household". The quote marks are there to tell Access that the characters inside them are a text string, not an object in the database like the name of a form or control.

"The " & HouseholdName & " Household"

Your completed expression will look like Figure 11-26 in the expression builder.

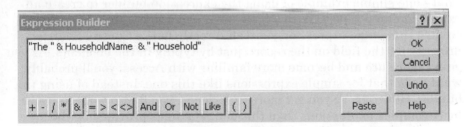

Figure 11-26 Completed Expression

When you click on OK, the expression builder transfers the newly created expression back to the field from which the builder was opened. In this case, it is the household name field on the label. (If you had opened the expression builder from a field in a form, or from a column in the query builder, this expression would be transferred back to that originating field in the form or query.)

When you close the expression builder, notice that Access *automatically* adds the initial equal sign in front of the expression. In this context, the equal sign is required; Access knows that, so it takes care of adding it for you.

As you recall, the original control source for this field was the empty string (=" "), which was itself an expression. When we changed that to a field name from the report's record source, the equal sign was no longer needed and Access removed it. But now we've created a new expression consisting of a text string concatenated with the field name, so the equal sign is back again.

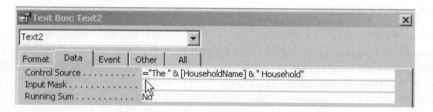

Figure 11-27 Inserted Expression as Control Source

Now, switch back to the print preview and see the result of the expression you just built. Looks better, doesn't it?

Using The Expression Builder

That's one simple example of using the expression builder to create an expression for a report. With a little more experience, you could have created that same expression yourself directly in the Control Source property for the field on the report, just by typing in the elements. As you gain experience and become more familiar with Access, you'll probably want to do that for simple expressions like this one, instead of using the builder. However, as you get more experience, you'll also want to create more complex expressions than this one. The tools provided by the expression builder will, no doubt, become increasingly useful to you, so it's still worthwhile to learn how to use it effectively.

Field Names

If you haven't already done so, let's fix the field names on the report before we go on to the final step in setting up this report to print labels. The wizard gave them default names like "text1", "text2", etc. Change them to the standard naming conventions you've learned before— txtHouseholdName, txtAddress, and txtCityStateZip, for example. With that out of the way we can concentrate on more advanced tasks like sorting the records.

Sorting Records

We need to set the *sort order* for records. By default, the sort order is the order in which the records were entered into the database originally. (That sort order would be reflected in the primary key for the household table.) In some cases, the primary key might provide the appropriate sort order for a report, but we want our mailing labels to come out sorted in a more user friendly fashion, say by family name or by state.

In fact, if this were a mailing list for a marketing letter to several hundred customers instead of a simple Christmas card list, the U.S. post office would probably require you to sort on ZIP Codes.

We can sort the report by any of the fields in its record source: ZIP Code, state, or household name. We could even have it sort by city or address, although neither of those options makes much sense to me. We will sort the records in the mailing labels by Household name.

Sorting Records in a Report.

Switch to design view and close the property sheet and field list. We need another tool for sorting. Find the Sorting and Grouping button on the report toolbar. That opens the Sorting and Grouping worksheet. It looks like Figure 11-28. Here's where you tell Access how to sort and group records for the report.

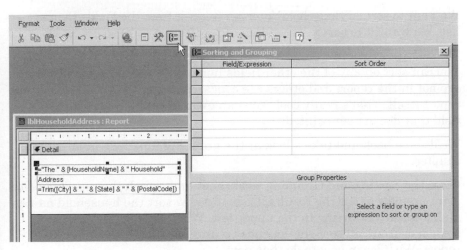

Figure 11-28 Sorting and Grouping Button and Work Sheet

We're only interested in the Sorting function at the moment. In the next example, when we create another report, I'll show you how to use the *grouping functions* of this worksheet to add groups to your reports. Put the cursor in the top row of the Sorting and Grouping worksheet and click on the drop down arrow to see the list of fields in the report.

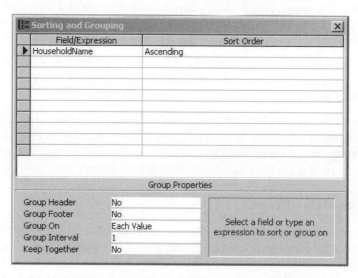

Figure 11-29 Sorting on Household Name

We want to sort on HouseholdName, so select it from the Fields/Expressions list. We want it to sort in ascending order (from A to Z) so accept the default.

You can sort on any of the other fields here, even though some of them are not in the report and others are concatenated with other fields on the report itself. That's really cool. You can even have the report sort on a field that doesn't get printed!

We'll come back and take a look at the grouping functions later in the chapter.

Close the Sorting and Grouping worksheet and switch the report back to print preview to see the results. It should now sort the household names alphabetically, starting in the upper left. Whether it sorts from top to bottom or from left to right depends on another property set for the report. We'll learn how to do that next.

Page Set Up

The last thing we need to do before we go on to a more complex report is look at the *page set up* for this report. The wizard created the default page set up for mailing labels.

You can set up a page format from either design view or print preview. Click File-->Page Set Up on the menu bar to open the page set up dialog.

The page set up dialog (Figure 11-30) lets you set a number of properties for this report, including paper size, whether the report displays in landscape or portrait view, page margins and, most importantly for our purposes at the moment, the number of columns to print.

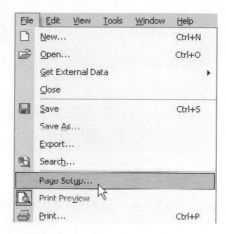

Figure 11-30 Page Set Up for Reports

Margins and Page Set Up

Access uses the same standard print dialog for margins and pages as other Windows applications, with which I assume you are familiar.

When the report wizard created the labels, it set the margins to those displayed in the dialog box. They are designed to fit the Avery 8160 label sheet, which is an 8 ½ x 11-inch page. Go ahead and click through the various options on the Margins tab of the page set up dialog. It should be self-explanatory.

Click on the Page tab and look over the options there. Again these options are quite self-explanatory, with one exception.

Specific Printer

Access allows you to decide whether the report will print to a default printer, or to a specific printer you designate.

Figure 11-31 Select a Specific Printer

You probably won't have much reason to use the specific printer option yet; I have only seen a few instances where it mattered. For example, you may have a report that includes color. You want to print that one report on a color printer instead of the local black-and-white only printer you have set as your default printer. You can designate the color printer here for that specific report and have all of your other reports go to the default.

Columns

Next, click the Columns tab to see how the columns for the label report work.

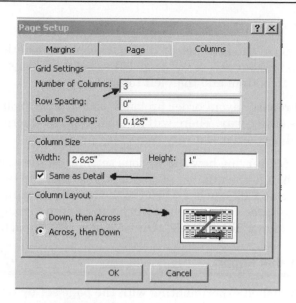

Figure 11-32 Column Set Up Dialog

The columns tab of the page set up dialog will look like Figure 11-32. The wizard that created the label report set the number of columns to three. That matches the number of columns of labels on the sheet I selected (Avery 8160).

With the number of columns set to three, the detail section of the report repeats three times horizontally across the page, i.e., it creates three columns from the detail section.

The wizard also matched the pre-defined row and column layout on the Avery labels I selected, setting the spacing between rows at zero inches and between columns at 0.125 inches.

Default Column Width

By default, the width of each column is the same as the width of the detail section of the report. Again, the wizard set this width from the definition of the Avery labels. You could adjust column width by un-checking the Same as Detail check box and setting your own width. Of course, that might mean your labels won't fit properly anymore for this particular report, so proceed cautiously.

Column Layout

The final section of the page set up dialog determines whether the records will be laid out across the page left to right and then top to bottom, or top to bottom and then left to right.

For this label report, layout order probably isn't crucial. You can use the mailing labels either way. There will be other reports where horizontal versus vertical sort order is a very important property.

For the sake of observing how the various settings in the page set up dialog work, change the number of columns from three to two, but leave the column size at 2.625 inches. Observe the results in print preview. Change back to three columns and switch the column layout from "across, then down" to "down, then across". Observe how this impacts the results.

Wrap up the Label Report

When you're finished experimenting with the page set up properties, return them their original settings, as in Figure 11-32, then save and close the report. The mailing label report is now set up to print sheets of mailing labels for all of the households in your contact database.

You're ready to mail your Christmas Cards!

Later in this chapter, I'll return to this report and show you one way to filter it so it only prints mailing labels for households you select.

Birth dates by Household Report

We're ready to create a slightly more complex report. This one will return a list of birth dates for each member of the households in our database. It will incorporate most of the features you just learned in the simple label report and add a couple of additional functions, specifically *grouping records* and displaying *subtotals for groups*.

Create a Query

In creating this report, I'm going to walk you though the report wizard again, but this time, instead of using tables, we're first going to create a query for the report's record source. Then, we'll use that query in the report wizard instead of the tables.

Up to this point, we've only created queries from within a form or report, so this will also be your first chance to design a query from scratch.

Report Requirement—Query Contents

The birthday report I have in mind will group people by household; in other words, we'll show the members of each household together under the household name. The report will display the first and last name of each household member and their birth dates.

Also, we'll create a field on the report to show the total number of people in each household and the total number of people in the birthday list. That's probably trivial information in this database, but it will serve as an example of a technique you can use to create subtotals in other situations where they are more useful.

The query we need for the birthday report will have to include fields from two tables: tblHousehold and tblPerson. From tblHousehold, we need HouseholdName. From tblPerson, we need FirstName, LastName, and Birthdate. We'll calculate the number of family members in each household on-the-fly, in the report itself.

Let's go to the database window and create the new query. Click New to open the query dialog box.

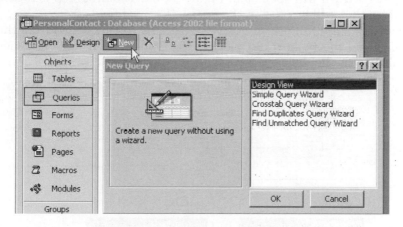

Figure 11-33 Query Dialog

The dialog offers you a choice of queries, including Design View and Simple Query Wizard. Let's use the query wizard. Select it from the list and click OK to start selecting tables and fields for the query.

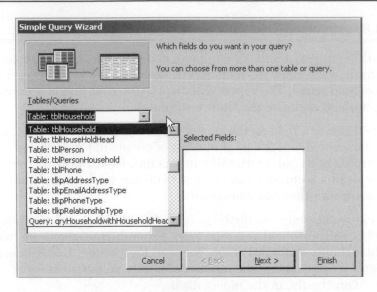

Figure 11-34 Select Tables for the Query

The query wizard will open as in Figure 11-34. The first step is to select the tables that will be used in the query. We need fields from tblHousehold and tblPerson. Start by selecting tblHousehold from the combo box on this page of the wizard. The fields in that table become available in the list below the combo box.

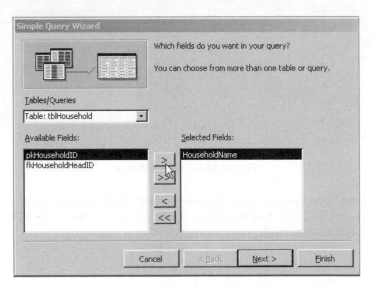

Figure 11-35 Select and Add Fields

From tblHousehold we need HouseholdName. Select it in the list and use the arrow button to move it to the list of selected fields.

Linking fields in a Query

The report will only display HouseholdName from tblHousehold, but is this the only field from tblHousehold we need to add to the query? Specifically, the relationship between tblHousehold and tblPerson depends on primary and foreign keys that join them in the junction table, tblPersonHousehold. Does the query we are creating need to include key fields to work properly as the record source for our report?

Based on our experience with the mailing labels we just created, it appears that the answer is "No, it doesn't". Relationships between these tables have already been defined and Access knows all about them. If this query were the record source for a form, it would need to include key fields so Access could place records in related tables properly. However, we decided that's not the case here, where we're only selecting fields to *display* in the report. Since we don't display key fields anyway, it doesn't look like we need to include them in the query, just as we didn't need them in the previous example.

You'll see the consequences of this decision when we have finished creating the query and can see the results in the query window.

Remaining Fields for the Query

Unlike the label wizard, the query wizard does give you the chance to add fields from other tables before moving on. So, instead of clicking OK, re-open the combo box displaying available tables and queries and select the second table you'll need for the record source for this report, tblPerson.

From tblPerson, add FirstName and LastName and Birthdate to the list of selected fields.

Now, select tblPersonHousehold in the combo box of tables. We need to include this table in the query because it is the junction table between tblPerson and tblHousehold. Without it we can't group people with other members of their household on the report. We really don't want to show any of its fields in the query; they're all primary or foreign keys. However, we do have to tell the wizard to include at least one field from the table to have it included in the query. Select the primary key from tblPersonHousehold. We'll change that later in the query window. The result looks like Figure 11-36.

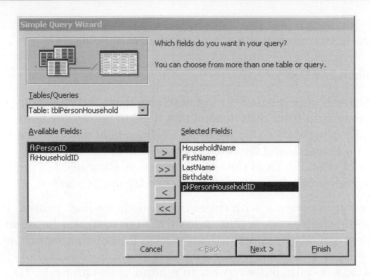

Figure 11-36 All Fields Selected for the Query

The result of the selections you've made will be a SQL statement with fields from the three related tables. Access will handle the relationships between these tables behind the scenes. Click Next to move to the next page of the wizard.

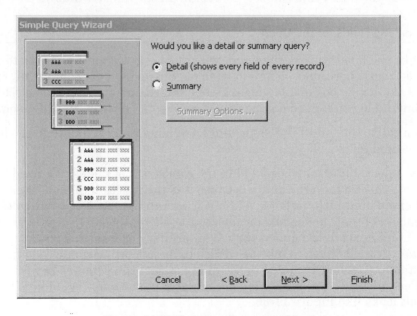

Figure 11-37 Detail or Summary Query

Detail or Summary Query

You can have the query wizard create summaries by counting records, adding up values in a field, or calculating an average value or a field. We're going to do that manually later to show you how to do it yourself, so select the Detail option. Click Next to go the last page of the query wizard and name the query.

Figure 11-38 Name the Query

The name should follow the standard naming convention, starting with the "qry" prefix. Add additional terms to describe the query. I called this one qryHouseholdBirthdayList; see Figure 11-38.

The query you just created will be the record source for the new report we are going to create next. Open it to see the fields in it. It will look something like Figure 11-39. Your query will have different names in it, of course, taken from your database.

Right now the query doesn't look exactly the way we want it to look. For example, some names appear two or three times. As is usually the case with Access wizards, the query wizard got us close to what we want, but some significant manual tweaks are still required.

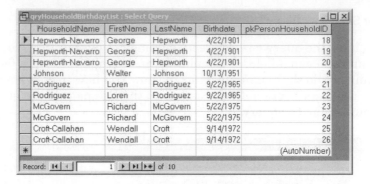

Figure 11-39 Query for the Birthday List

Switch to query design view, using the Query Design icon on the Query Datasheet toolbar.

Figure 11-40 Query Design Icon

The query design window will display as in Figure 11-41.

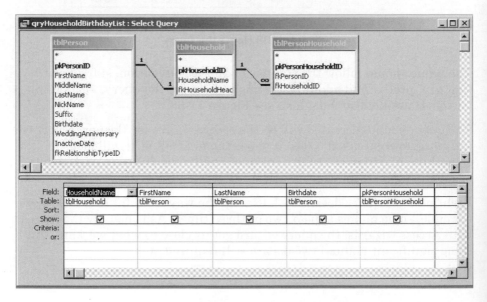

Figure 11-41 Query Design Window

The three tables we selected in the query wizard appear, along with relationships between them, in the window. The selected fields appear in the query grid below. Look at the field in Figure 11-42.

Figure 11-42 Query Field Causing Duplicate Records

This field is the reason we are seeing multiple instances of some names in the query and here's how it causes that to happen. To help you understand it, I need to tell you a little bit about *join types*. We'll start with the default type, inner joins.

Inner Joins

An inner join tells an Access query to match records in two tables on the join field between them. If there is a matching record in each table, the query *displays both records* in the query. If there is no matching record in both tables, the query *doesn't display a record from either table*.

For example, if the value 1 appears as the primary key for a record in tblPerson and as the foreign key in the join field for a record in tblPersonHousehold, the query displays the matching records from both tables. However, if the value 2 appears as a primary key for a record in tblPerson, but there is no matching 2 in the foreign key field in tblPersonHousehold, this query will not display the record from tblPerson with primary key 2.

The default for Access queries is to create inner joins like this.

Therefore, with an inner join between tblHousehold and tblPersonHousehold, this query matches records from tblPersonHousehold with records from tblHousehold on the join field between them: pkHouseholdID in tblHousehold, and fkHouseholdID in tblPersonHousehold.

In order for a record from tblHousehold to be displayed in the query results, there must be a matching record (that is, one with the same value in both key fields) in tblPersonHousehold. Because this is an inner join, each record in tblPersonHousehold is matched with a record in tblHousehold, one for one.

Displaying *All* Matching Records

Adding pkPersonHouseholdID to the query grid tells the query to include each occurrence of the primary key, pkPersonHouseholdID, in tblPersonHousehold in the results. There is one primary key for each person assigned to a household—in this example a total of 10 records.

The inner join requirement means that only records in tblPersonHousehold that match a record in tblHousehold will be displayed. It also means that the query *must* display any matching records from tblHousehold. The only field from tblHousehold currently displayed in the query is HouseholdName, which is why some of them appear multiple times in the query, once for each matching record, in tblPersonHousehold. We do want to see all ten records, because there are ten people in tblPersonHousehold, but we're only seeing some of those people—the ones with matching inner joins. And some of the people who are displayed appear multiple times.

We need to adjust the query to get the proper results. Let's start by removing pkPersonHouseholdID from the query grid.

Removing pkPersonHouseholdID from the query grid gives the results shown in Figure 11-43.

Figure 11-43 Query without pkPersonHouseholdID from tblPersonHousehold

That helped some; the duplicate records are no longer displayed, because we are not requiring the query to show one record from both tables for each record in tblHousehold. It now displays only those records that have matching values in the join field.

There is still another problem, though, requiring further modification to the wizard-generated query. All of the persons shown in Figure 11-43 are Heads of Households, because that is the join field in the query.

None of the other persons in tblPerson made it into the query. Switch back to design view to see why that's the case and what we have to do to fix it.

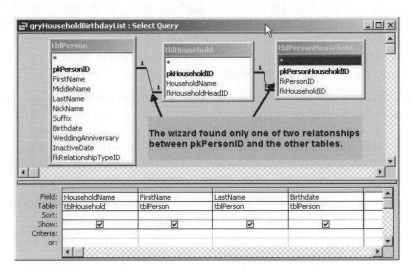

Figure 11-44 Query in Design View

Missing Join

You may have spotted the problem already. Figure 11-44 shows the wizard found, or recognized, only one of the relationships between pkPersonID and the corresponding foreign keys in the other two tables. Moreover, the one it did find isn't useful in this query. (And you ask me what I have against wizards of the Access kind?) The wizard recognized the one-to-one relationship between pkPersonID and fkHouseholdHeadID and created an inner join on that relationship. That's why we saw only those persons who are designated as household heads in the query results. The query only displays records if it can match values on both sides of the inner join. Not everyone is a Household head, so the people who aren't get left out of the query results.

Identifying a Missing Relationship

We want this query to show everyone in the person table, not just the household heads. We also want to relate people to the household to which they belong. Therefore, we need to make two adjustments to the query.

First, let's tell this query about the relationship between pkPersonID in tblPerson, and fkPersonID in tblPersonHousehold. To do that, put the cursor on pkPersonID, click and hold down the left mouse button (right button, of course, if you're left handed). Drag the cursor over to fkPersonID in tblPersonHousehold and release the mouse button. The inner join line will appear between the two fields.

Although we've already created that relationship elsewhere in the database, the wizard apparently didn't recognize it and didn't tell the query about it. However, if you save and close the query, then reopen it in design view, the appropriate one-to-many relationship will appear, meaning Access figured out what the relationship between tblPerson and tblPersonHousehold really is after we manually pointed it out.

The query can now match all people with the household to which they belong.

Deleting an Unnecessary Join In a Query

If you switch to datasheet view, you'll see that the query still doesn't show people who aren't designated as a household head. That's because of the *inner join* on the one-to-one relationship between tblPerson and tblHousehold. We need to change that now.

The way to accomplish our goal is simply to delete that join in this query. Doing so does not impact the underlying relationship between the two tables; it only affects the way they behave in this query.

Removing the inner join between pkPersonID in tblPerson and fkHouseholdHeadID allows the query to display all of the records from tblPerson—so long as they match a record in tblPersonHousehold, of course.

See Figure 11-45 and Figure 11-46.

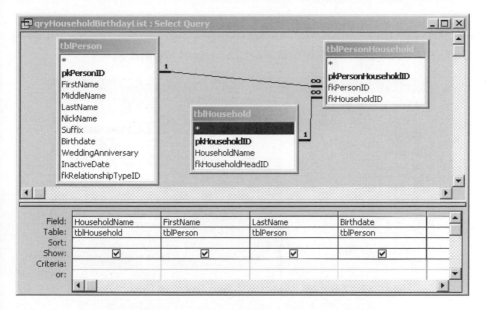

Figure 11-45 Inner Join between tblPerson and tblHousehold Removed

Figure 11-46 Resulting Query in Datasheet View

Finally, that's what we want to see.

You'll need to learn more about two other types of joins (called *left outer* and *right outer* joins) at some point in your career, but for now, knowing about inner joins is enough.

Let's move on to create the report from this query. Save and close it and let's start the report wizard.

Report Wizard—Birthday List

Go to the database window and start the report wizard.

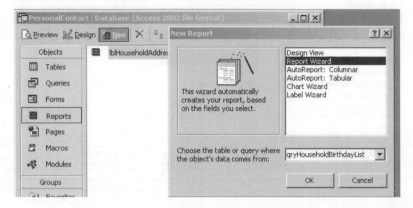

Figure 11-47 Report Wizard with New Query as Record Source

Select your newly created query as the record source for this new report. Click OK to move on to the next page of the wizard. We need all four of the available fields in this query, so click on the double arrow button to add them all.

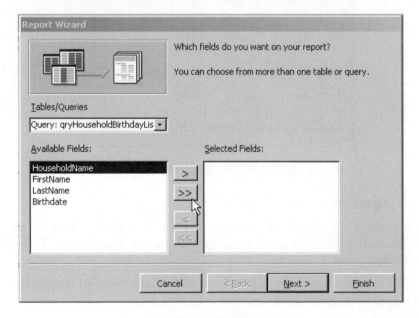

Figure 11-48 Add Fields to Report

Click Next to move to the next page of the wizard.

Report Wizard, Determine Top-Level Grouping and Sorting

This page of the report wizard allows you to decide how to group the records on the report. It won't give you the final layout (no wizard ever does), but will help. Sometimes, the report wizard offers suggestions for groups based on what it knows about the tables in the record source and the relationships between them.

In this case, it doesn't have any suggestions because the query we created doesn't include any primary or foreign keys, so we'll need to make our own choice. Since we want to group the records on the birthday report according to the family to which they belong, choose HouseholdName and click the arrow to move it to the preview pane on the right.

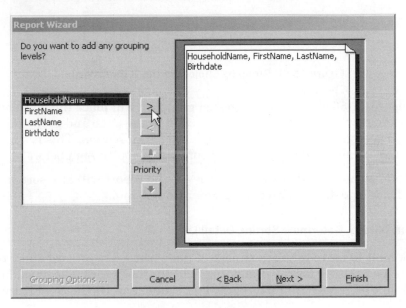

Figure 11-49 Grouping Choices

Figure 11-50 previews the grouping you just selected. Each Household will be grouped in a section of the report, with household members displayed for that group.

As you can also see in Figure 11-50, the wizard offers to show you more information to illustrate how grouping works. You may want to take a few moments and browse through that help screen before you continue.

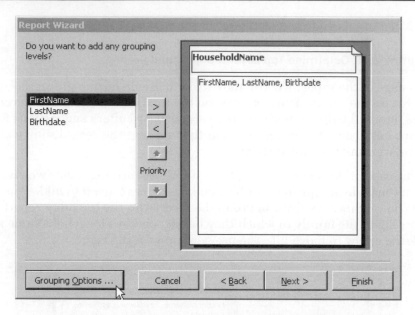

Figure 11-50 Grouping Choices in the Report Wizard

As Figure 11-50 shows, the suggested grouping will place the household head name at the top of the page or section of the page and group the related persons with that household in the detail section. This is similar to a form header and form detail layout, which you've seen before.

With Household head at the highest level, the report will also sort on that field, by default in ascending order from A to Z.

Report Wizard, Determine Sorting Detail Level

Click Next to move to the next page of the wizard. The wizard offers to create a sort order for the remaining fields in the report. The available fields in this report are FirstName, LastName, and Birthdate, Figure 11-51.

Since the records will be first sorted and grouped on HouseholdName, the sort at this level only applies to people *within* a household.

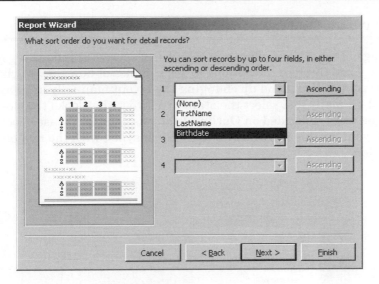

Figure 11-51 Sorting within Details

You can either sort by birth date (so the list shows the earliest birth date in each family first) or by name. Because the higher-level sort is Household Name, it makes more sense to be consistent and sort next by LastName and then by FirstName.

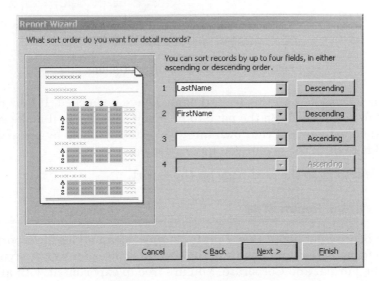

Figure 11-52 Sort Priorities Set

Click Next to move on to the next page of the wizard.

Report Wizard, Field Layout on the Report

This page of the wizard offers you a choice of several standard report layouts. Click through the options to see samples of how they might look on your report. You'll end up changing the layout manually anyway, so you will normally just select the standard layout that looks the closest to what you want. I decided on Outline 1 for this sample. Please choose the same layout for this report so we can stay in synch with the rest of the discussion.

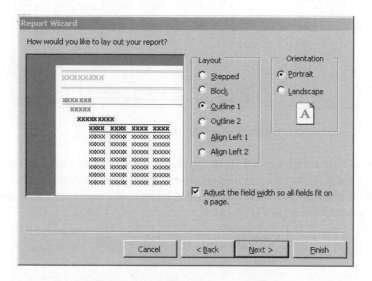

Figure 11-53 Standard Layout Options

There is a check box on this wizard page. Leave it checked. It tells the wizard to adjust fields on the page to fit. Even though you'll make some manual adjustments of your own later, this step can help by pre-sizing the fields to fit in the layout you have selected.

Click Next to go to the next page on the report.

Report Wizard, Report Style

Let me be up front about this. I prefer simple, clean styles for reports as well as forms. Therefore, my first and second choices for report style would be Formal and Corporate. You are free to experiment with all of these styles in your own reports. However, for now, please select the Formal style so we stay in synch with the discussion that follows. You can define your own preferred look for reports later on.

The Formal style will look like Figure 11-54 in the report wizard.

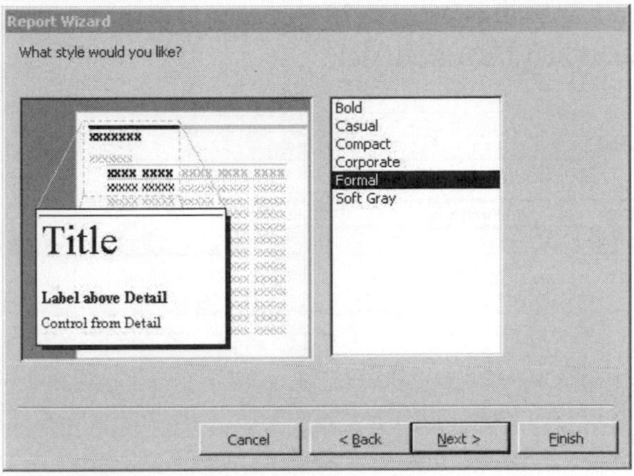

Figure 11-54 Report Style

We're almost done. Click Next to go the last page of the wizard where you'll name the new report. The wizard offers the name of the query as the default name for the report. Change it to reflect the purpose of the report, which is to create a printed birthday list. Don't forget to prefix "rpt", making it rptBirthdaysbyHousehold.

Click Finish to see the report you just created. It still needs a lot of work; so don't panic if it doesn't look quite right the way it is right now. Because we used the report wizard to create it, the results are not what you would have been able to produce manually. However, it does give us a lot of report features to look at and learn about and for that reason, it's a good place to start.

Let's sort all that out right now. Switch back to design view. It will look something like Figure 11-55.

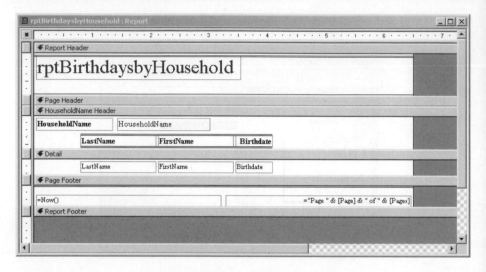

Figure 11-55 Report in Design View

Headers and Footers

By default, the report wizard creates the report with a report header and footer and with a page header and footer.

Report Header and Footer

The report header, which appears only on the *first* page of a multi-page report, displays information you want to have on the first page, but not on subsequent pages.

By default, the wizard puts the name of the report rptBirthdaysbyHousehold in a field on the report header. We'll change that, of course. You can do that now or later. The name I would put in that field would be Birthday List or something similar. Choose the title that makes sense to you. Since the control holding this title is a label, you can type over its contents in the label on the report, or open the report's property sheet and change the Caption property.

You can also change the name of the label while you're at it, or you can wait and change the its name later. Just don't forget to do it.

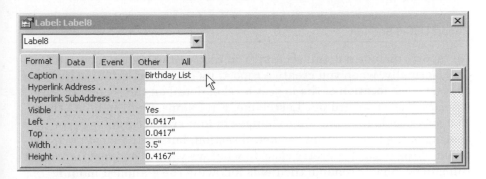

Figure 11-56 Label Caption

Since report headers and footers come in pairs, there is also a report footer on this report; it is empty and has a height of zero inches, because we don't have anything in it. If the report footer had any fields in it, those fields would appear at the end of the report.

Page Header and Footer

The report wizard also put a page header and footer on each page. Like report headers and footers, page headers and footers come in pairs, so there is a page header as well as a page footer, even though there is nothing in the header. The page footer contains fields that put the current date and page numbers on *each page* of the report. We'll leave them just as they are.

Dividing Lines

The style I chose for the report puts some horizontal lines on the report in the headers and footers. On reports, probably more than on forms, you can use lines and other graphic elements to enhance and highlight information. While they are very useful tools, they're not central to creating Access reports, so I won't discuss them in detail here. But don't overlook them as a way to enhance readability of your reports.

I'm going to skip over the group header for the time being. First, let's take a look at the report detail section.

Report Detail Section

All reports include a detail section. You really can't have a form without one. Normally, when you create a report, its detail section is, as its name suggests, the location of the lowest level of detail on the report. In this case, the report wizard put LastName, FirstName, and Birthdate there. You may decide to make some changes in font size, location, size, or spacing of the fields within the detail section, but for the most part, the result of the wizard is pretty close to what we want. The most important thing to be done is rename the fields following the standard naming conventions, i.e., txtFirstName, txtLastName, and txtBirthdate.

Grouping and Group Headers

Next, we need to step back and consider the report as a whole. In particular, we need to look at the *group header* immediately above the detail section and consider how it relates to the records displayed in the detail section. The report wizard placed the HouseholdName field in the group header; it placed the labels for the fields in the detail section in the group header, as well.

When we were walking through the report wizard we told the wizard to sort records and *create groups,* using the household name. The result is the group header on the report. By default, Access named it after the field on which groups are created: HouseholdName Header. Let's see how it works.

Sorting and Grouping Button and Worksheet

Find the Sorting and Grouping button on the toolbar and click it to open the Sorting and Grouping worksheet. You learned how to do that earlier (see Figure 11-28).

The Sorting and Grouping worksheet will open to show the properties set by the wizard. It should look like Figure 11-57.

The worksheet shows that the report is sorted *and grouped* on HousegoldName. It is also sorted on LastName and FirstName.

Figure 11-57 Sorting and Grouping Worksheet

Sort Order and Priorities

The Sorting and Grouping worksheet controls the sort order of records within the report. Sorting priorities are set from top to bottom, so in Figure 11-57, the sort order will be (1st) the HouseholdName field from tblHousehold, (2nd) last name from tblPerson, and (3rd) first name from tblPerson. That's exactly the order we want; so don't make any changes to that. I want to explain the other elements of the worksheet.

Grouping Symbol

Look at the first field in the Sorting and Grouping worksheet, the one with HouseholdName. The little symbol out there to the left of the field is the *Grouping* icon, which means the report creates groups on that field. Each time a new value appears in the HouseholdName field, a new group header is printed on the report, along with the details that go with the records in that group.

In Figure 11-57, the top field also has a small arrowhead visible, indicating it is the current field for which you are setting properties. The group properties to which this arrow refers are set in the lower portion of the worksheet, shown in Figure 11-57.

Group Properties

Look at the lower section of the Sorting and Grouping worksheet, outlined in Figure 11-57. This section defines the group properties for the field selected in the field list at the top of the worksheet. The Group Header property, obviously enough, determines whether or not there is a group header for that field.

Unlike report and page headers and footers, which come in pairs, you can separately designate whether a report group also has a footer. In this report, for example, the wizard set up a group header for the primary household key, but not a footer. We want a group footer. Change the value in that field from No to Yes. I'll show you what we want to put in this section of the report later.

Group On Properties

The Group On property tells Access how to identify groups. The choices here are Each Value or Prefix Characters. Each Value means grouping is based on the entire value of the primary key in the household table. Prefix Characters allows you to designate one or more characters at the beginning of a field as the group, rather than the entire value of the field.

When the Group On property is set to Each Value, the Group Interval property is set to 1. This means the *entire value* of that field is used for groups. It does not mean *only* the first character is considered for grouping.

However, when the Group On property is set to Prefix Characters, the Group Interval property does determine how many characters Access evaluates in creating groups. I, therefore, would group on the first letter or digit of the value in the field.

When might you use the Prefix Characters option instead of Each Value? One case might be if you wanted to create a phone list grouped on the first letter of each person's last name as you find in the telephone book published by the local phone company. You could use this option to group entries in that way, selecting Prefix Characters and a group interval of 1. This would result in groups based on A, B, C, etc.

Grouping by Dates

If the grouping field is a date field (such as the birth date field on this report), the Group Interval property determines whether grouping is done by year, month, day, etc. If we wanted a birthday list grouped by month, for example, we'd group on that field and set the group interval to month.

Fields in Group Headers and Footers

The report created by the wizard placed fields from the report's record source in the group header. It did so based on the choices we made in the wizard. The purpose of the report is to print a list of people and their birthdays, grouped *and sorted* by household. Therefore, the Household Name is in the group header, but other fields don't belong here. They are placed in the detail section. Each time the report comes to a new Household Name in its record source, it prints a new group header for that name and places the related people in the detail section for that group.

We're close now to a completed report. The report has a report header that shows a report title. It has a page footer with date and page numbers. We have only a few things left to accomplish. One is to change font sizes and font styles so the layout is more readable. Another is to change field names and report labels, making all of the field names consistent with standard naming conventions.

Adjustments to the Report Layout

The default font sizes for most of the fields are a bit too small for my tastes, 10-point Times New Roman. I believe they should be at least 11-point, probably 12-point. Of course, if the requirements of your report make space an issue, you might keep the current font size, or even use a smaller one.

Access offers an additional shortcut to creating good layouts. You can select multiple controls and make changes to them as a group. This can be a real time saver.

Selecting Multiple Controls

You can make changes like font size to a group of controls in a single step. To select all of the fields on the report, you can hold down the shift key while selecting them one at a time. Click on the fields, one at a time until you have selected the ones you want to changes as a group.

Another way to select them is to click and drag in the top or left margin of the report. Place the cursor in the left margin close to the top of the HouseholdName Group Header. Click and hold down the mouse button and drag it down to highlight all of the fields in the group header and detail section.

Figure 11-58 Multiple Selection

Adjusting and Sizing Multiple Controls

With all of the fields selected, you can make changes to them in one step. Find font size on the property sheet or in the formatting menu and change it to twelve.

Now, to accommodate the larger font size, you'll also need to adjust the size of the text fields and labels. Select Format-->Size-->To Fit on the menu bar and click it.

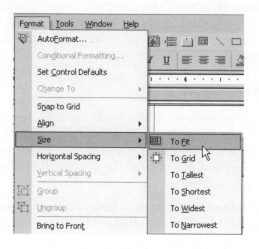

Figure 11-59 Size to Fit

Text boxes will grow vertically to fit the new font size. Labels will grow both vertically and horizontally to fit the new font size. However, you'll have to change the width of text boxes manually.

Experiment a little with the fields on your report to make them wide enough to fit their contents with a larger font size. You may also need to move fields to the left or right to make them fit.

Spacing and Aligning Multiple Controls

With multiple controls still selected, you can also have Access change the space between them, either vertically or horizontally. The result will be evenly spaced controls.

For example, select a group of controls, as in Figure 11-60 and click Format-->Horizontal Spacing-->Make Equal to space the selected controls evenly. You can also move them closer together or further apart until they fall in the desired location.

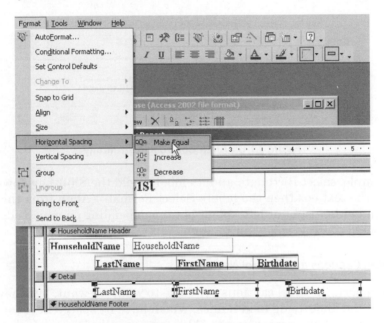

Figure 11-60 Space Controls Horizontally

Next, you can align text boxes with their labels.

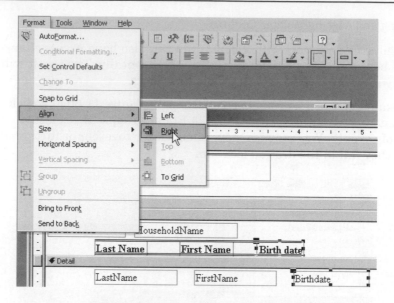

Figure 11-61 Align Controls Horizontally

For example, select Birthdate and its label. (Hold the Shift key down and click on the text box then the label). Select Format-->Align from the menu and either right or left, top or bottom depending on which edge of the selected controls you want to align.

Edit Label Captions and Control Names

In this report, the label captions are close to what we want, but they are based on the underlying field names, which have no spaces in them. Change them to the proper names. Also, rename all of the controls to follow the standard naming conventions. After making the adjustments discussed above, my report ended up looking like Figure 11-62. Yours should be similar, though not necessarily identical.

Birthday List

Household	Croft-Callahan		
Last Name	**First Name**	**Birth Date**	
Croft	Wendall	9/14/1972	
Callahan	Judy	9/14/1972	

Household	Hepworth-Navarro		
Last Name	**First Name**	**Birth Date**	
Hepworth	Yolanda	9/27/1922	
Hepworth	Lyndsey	2/17/1990	
Hepworth	George	4/22/1901	

Household	Johnson		
Last Name	**First Name**	**Birth Date**	
Johnson	Walter	10/13/1951	

Household	McGovern		
Last Name	**First Name**	**Birth Date**	
McGovern	Sally	9/22/1978	
McGovern	Richard	5/22/1975	

Household	Rodriguez		
Last Name	**First Name**	**Birth Date**	
Rodriguez	Loren	9/22/1965	

Tuesday, November 16, 2001   Page 1 of 1

Figure 11-62 Adjusted Report Layout

Creating a Calculated Field on a Report

You recall I had you add a group footer to the report, even though we didn't add any controls to it at the time. We're going to take care of that now. Although it is a trivial example, we're going add a field to show the number of family members in each household. I will show you how to add a calculated field to your reports.

Start by switching to design view.

Selecting a Field on which to Calculate

Open the field list by clicking on the Field List icon on the Report Format toolbar.

Figure 11-63 Field List Icon

We'll create the calculated field in the group footer by dragging one of the fields from the report's record source to the footer and creating an expression with it. The field list shows the four available fields in the report: HouseholdName, FirstName, LastName, and Birthdate. Which field should you use for the calculation? For this particular calculation, the answer is it doesn't matter.

The calculated expression is going to count the number of records in each group. Since each field in each record will appear the same number of times as every other field in each record, we can select any of them to count. It would be different, of course, if we were adding up values within a field, but we're not, we're only counting fields.

Let's pick HouseholdName for the counter. Drag it from the field list to the group footer in the report (Figure 11-64). Just drop it anywhere in the group footer. We'll fix the layout later.

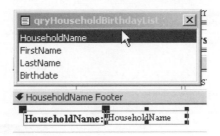

Figure 11-64 Field in Group Footer for Calculated Field

Build the Calculated Expression for the Group

Close the field list to get it out of the way and open the report's property sheet. You can do this either by clicking on the Property Sheet icon on the toolbar or double-clicking on the body of the report.

Select the field you just added, then select the Data tab on the property sheet, and then click on the field's control source. Use the builder button to open the expression builder.

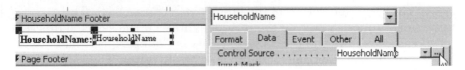

Figure 11-65 Open the Expression Builder

We're going to use a built-in function to create the calculated field. Specifically, the function we want is the SQL Count function.

Navigate through the builder, as shown in Figure 11-66. Select the Count function from the Built-in SQL Aggregate functions.

Count is only one of many functions available. As you can see in Figure 11-66, you can calculate an average (Avg), find the largest value (Max) in a range of values, or the smallest (Min). You can add a group of values (Sum), and so on. Other functions handle dates, strings of text, convert data from one type to another and so on. As you gain experience and expertise with Access, you will be using most of them in your databases. For now, we're going to use the Count function to calculate the number of household members in each household.

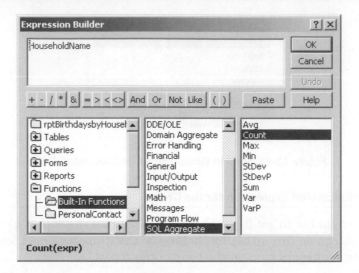

Figure 11-66 SQL Aggregate Function Count

Syntax Assistance

Look at the lower left corner of the builder in Figure 11-66. The expression builder shows you the correct syntax for the selected function. In this case, it shows you the correct syntax is Count(expr), where "expr" represents the object or control item you want to count. The value to be counted follows the function and is enclosed in parentheses.

Create the Expression

With *Count* selected in the expression builder function window, place the cursor in front of the value in the builder window at the top. As the syntax helper shows, the function comes before the value to be counted.

Click on the Paste button to paste the Count function into the builder window. The result will look like Figure 11-67. That might not be what you expected, and it most definitely isn't what we want, but it is normal behavior for the expression builder.

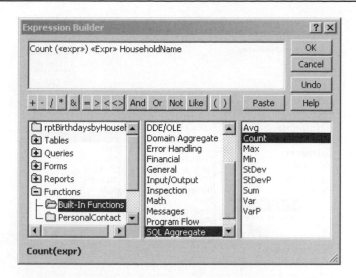

Figure 11-67 Function Pasted into Expression Window

The builder pasted the function into the expression window, using the proper syntax, with a prompt showing you where to insert the value to be counted. The expression builder has no way of knowing that what you wanted to count was the value was already in the window, so its default behavior is to assume you are adding an additional element, perhaps to be concatenated with the first. It provides a second prompt to let you know that you have to do something with it.

In this case, what we want to do is count the number of times HouseholdName appears in each group on the report, so we can just cut and paste it into the proper place in the expression, as in Figure 11-68. The expression is now ready to be transferred back to the field in the report. Click on OK to close the expression builder and transfer the expression.

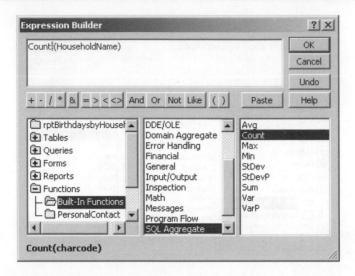

Figure 11-68 Completed Expression in the Expression Builder

The expression builder pastes the expression into the field's control source, adding the "=" sign, as you saw earlier.

Figure 11-69 Calculated Value for Control Source

Preview the report to see the result of the calculated field.

It should display the number of family members in each household on the report. Of course, the label is not appropriate—it's the default label Access created when you first dragged the field onto the report. Switch to design view, give the label an appropriate caption, such as Family Members or Count of Family Members, and rename the label and text box with appropriate names. You will also want to make the font size for this calculated field the same as other fields on the report and align it with other fields.

Add a Report Total

With the calculated field for each *group* in place in the Group Footer, you can easily add a second calculated field to the Report Footer to display the *total* number of people on the entire birth date list.

To do that, grab the lower edge of the report footer with the cursor and drag it down to create space for the field.

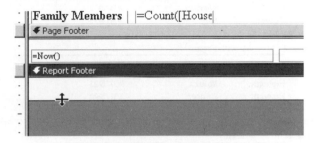

Figure 11-70 Expand Report Footer

Now, click on your new calculated field in the HouseholdName group footer and copy it. Move the cursor to the report footer and paste the field into it. Change the caption on its label to indicate its contents and move it into position, as in Figure 11-71.

Don't forget to rename the label and text box for this new control.

Figure 11-71 Report Total Calculated Field

Because the report footer is for the entire report, the Count function in it counts all occurrences of the selected field in the entire record source, giving you a total for all of the people in the birthday list. You know at a glance how many stamps you need to mail your birthday cards this year!

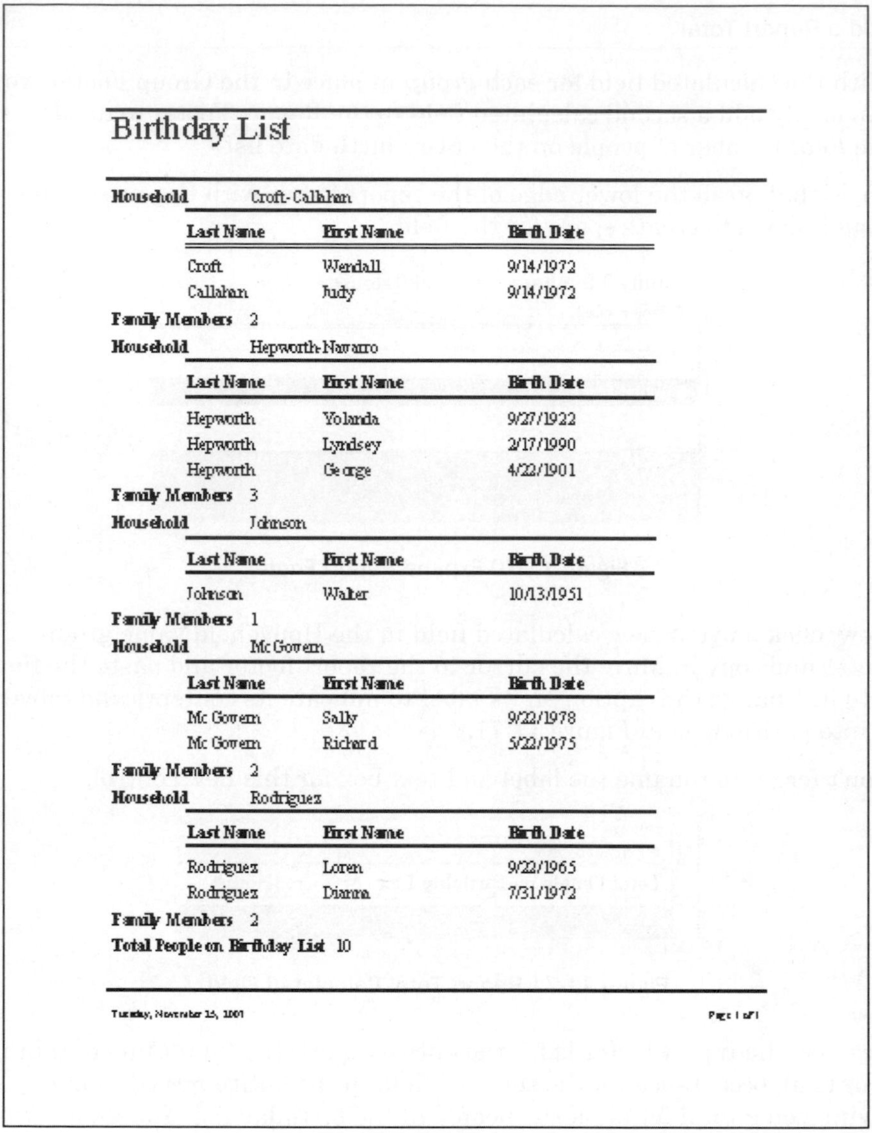

Birthday List

Household	Croft-Callahan		
	Last Name	**First Name**	**Birth Date**
	Croft	Wendall	9/14/1972
	Callahan	Judy	9/14/1972
Family Members 2			
Household	Hepworth-Navarro		
	Last Name	**First Name**	**Birth Date**
	Hepworth	Yolanda	9/27/1922
	Hepworth	Lyndsey	2/17/1990
	Hepworth	George	4/22/1901
Family Members 3			
Household	Johnson		
	Last Name	**First Name**	**Birth Date**
	Johnson	Walter	10/13/1951
Family Members 1			
Household	McGovern		
	Last Name	**First Name**	**Birth Date**
	McGovern	Sally	9/22/1978
	McGovern	Richard	5/22/1975
Family Members 2			
Household	Rodriguez		
	Last Name	**First Name**	**Birth Date**
	Rodriguez	Loren	9/22/1965
	Rodriguez	Diana	7/31/1972
Family Members 2			

Total People on Birthday List 10

Tuesday, November 15, 2001   Page 1 of 1

Figure 11-72 Report with Calculated Fields in Group Footer and Report Footer

I won't kid you; most of the calculated fields you create will be a bit more sophisticated than these two, but the technique is the same.

To count the number of times a field appears in a group, use the Count function with that field. To add up the total of the values for a numerical field in a group, use the Sum function in the group footer. To add a total for an entire report, put the same calculated field in the report footer.

Debugging an Existing Report

Up to this point, things have gone well, with few complications, in creating the birthday report. The result, illustrated in Figure 11-62, looks pretty good, but it hides a serious design flaw. That design flaw, which I deliberately left in the report so I'd have something to talk about in this section on debugging, won't show up until I add a few more records to the database. That's often the case with flaws in logic, which we usually refer to as *bugs*; they don't show up right away. This one isn't too serious, as bugs go, and it will be relatively easy to fix. However, it's worth going through the process to get a quick glimpse of what goes into finding bugs and fixing them.

The Root of the Problem

I have three brothers, all of whom share my last name. I have three sisters, two of whom have different married names. So far, I've only added my sisters under their married names, their spouses, and some friends to the database, as shown in Figure 11-62. But what will happen to the report when I add my brothers? Take a look at Figure 11-73 to see.

After adding two of my brothers and their wives to the database, I ran the report again. To my disappointment, all four of them were grouped as a single household, indicating I'd overlooked something in the report design. It isn't very difficult to spot this problem, or to figure out what caused it. (That won't always be the case, unfortunately.) Sometimes tracking down bugs is a lengthy, frustrating experience. In this case, it's pretty obvious I picked the wrong field to use as a group header. You may even have an idea why it was a bad choice.

HouseholdName is *not unique* to a household. We distinguish between households by their primary key. If you were concerned by the fact I didn't include any primary keys in the query that serves as the record source for this report, you were right to be annoyed. And this is the reason why. If you recall the discussion about including or not including key fields, you can see I made the wrong decision by leaving them out. We need at least one key field in this report after all.

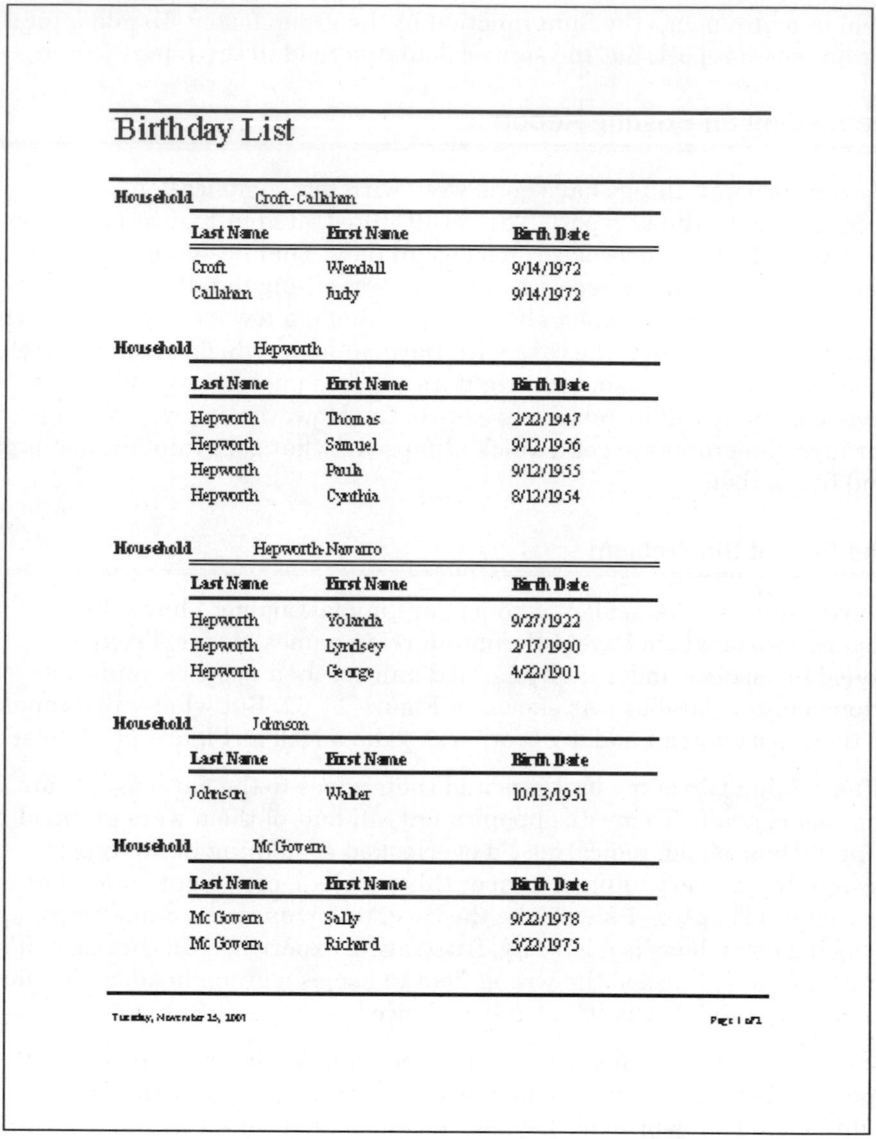

Birthday List

Household	Croft-Callahan		
Last Name	**First Name**		**Birth Date**
Croft	Wendall		9/14/1972
Callahan	Judy		9/14/1972

Household	Hepworth		
Last Name	**First Name**		**Birth Date**
Hepworth	Thomas		2/22/1947
Hepworth	Samuel		9/12/1956
Hepworth	Paula		9/12/1955
Hepworth	Cynthia		8/12/1954

Household	Hepworth-Navarro		
Last Name	**First Name**		**Birth Date**
Hepworth	Yolanda		9/27/1922
Hepworth	Lyndsey		2/17/1990
Hepworth	George		4/22/1901

Household	Johnson		
Last Name	**First Name**		**Birth Date**
Johnson	Walter		10/13/1951

Household	McGovern		
Last Name	**First Name**		**Birth Date**
Mc Govern	Sally		9/22/1978
Mc Govern	Richard		5/22/1975

Tuesday, November 15, 2001   Page 1 of 1

Figure 11-73 Flawed Report Design Appears

If you added people who share your last name to you database, you've already seen this bug yourself. If you haven't done so yet, now would be a good time to try it in your own database. If you don't have siblings with the same last name, make up a few people with the same name so you can follow the discussion in your own database.

Fixing the Bug

The first step in fixing our bug is to recognize that it exists by inspecting the output of the report. We've already done that. The next step is to figure out what caused the bug. We've done that, too, by realizing we need a unique identifier for each household, not just the household name, which is not unique.

The next step is to decide how to remedy the problem. We can do this by adding the primary key field from tblHousehold to the query.

Updating the Query

Open the query in design view. Click on pkHouseholdID in tblHousehold and drag it down to the query grid, as shown in Figure 11-74 and Figure 11-75.

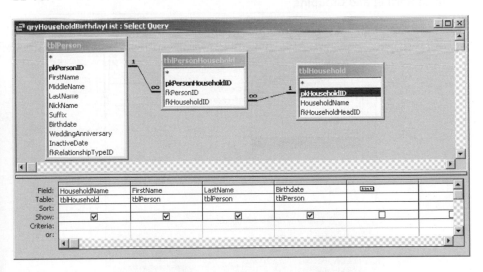

Figure 11-74 Add Primary Key to Query Grid

In Figure 11-74, you can see the little bar representing the field in the last field on the right in the query grid. When you release the mouse, the field will drop into the grid as in Figure 11-75.

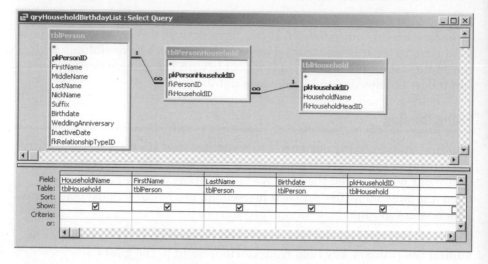

Figure 11-75 Primary Key Added to Query Grid

Now you have a unique key on which to group the households in the report. Save and close the query and open the report in design view.

Updating Sorting and Grouping

Open the Sorting and Grouping dialog, as shown in Figure 11-76.

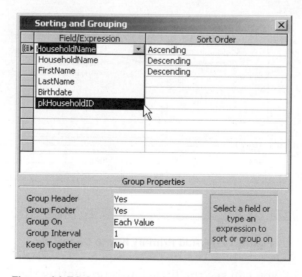

Figure 11-76 Select New Sorting and Grouping Field

You're going to change the value in the top-most field from HouseholdName to pkHouseholdID, as shown in Figure 11-76.

Select the Primary Key as the sorting and grouping field and save the report. Don't make any other changes yet. Preview the report to see the effect of the change. It is better; individual households sort together as groups. However, fixing one problem has caused another problem to appear. This one is predictable; in fact, we've already discussed it. The primary key field sorts in the order in which you add records to the database. That's seldom the way you want to see records in a report and is definitely not the sort order we want for this one. Although we want household *grouped* by their primary key, we want them *sorted* alphabetically, as they were in the original version of the report. Fortunately, the solution is simple.

Switch back to design view and open the Sorting and Grouping dialog.

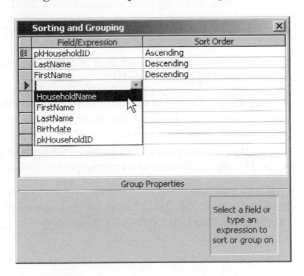

Figure 11-77 Add Household as A Sort Field

Click on an empty field at the bottom of the field list and select HouseholdName. As you know, the sort priority goes from the top to the bottom of this list. Therefore, to sort first in HouseholdName, you'll need to drag HouseholdName above pkHouseholdID.

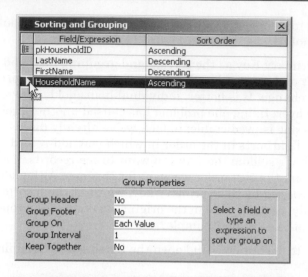

Figure 11-78 Move the Sort Field to the Top of the List

To move it, click on the selector at the left end of the field, click and drag the field up until it's above pkHouseholdID.

This next step is important. Leave grouping on for pkHouseholdID and leave it off for HouseholdName. Look at the group header in the report; you'll see it doesn't matter that grouping is based on the primary key while the text box in the header section is HouseholdName. The group header displays the HouseholdName that corresponds to the primary key.

Preview the report once more. It should now be sorted and grouped the way we want it to be. The bug is now fixed. I wish they were all that easy!

Report Filters

In the last chapter, when you learn about adding a user interface to your database, I'll show you how to apply *filters* to your reports, so you can select which records to print and which to leave out. Filters like the one I plan to show you how to use work best as part of a user interface designed for the purpose, so we'll tackle it along with other interface design considerations.

Wrap Up Report

In this chapter, you've learned a lot about creating, modifying and debugging reports by creating two basic reports using wizards.

You've also created a query from scratch with the query wizard and used it as the record source for a report. In one report you created multiple columns and used concatenated fields created with the expression builder. In the other report you created group headers and footers to create and sort groups and to calculate group and report totals.

Finally, you ran through a brief debugging exercise to correct an error in logic that occurred during creation of the report.

Take a short break while your printer kicks out a copy of the birthday list, or a set of mailing labels for your Christmas card list. Then come back and study Chapter 12.

Backup, Backup, Backup

Before you leave, though, this would be an excellent time to make a backup copy of the database. Close your database, find it on your hard drive and make a copy in a safe place. Do that now.

This page intentionally left blank.

12. Getting Data out of Your Database—Display-only Forms

In the previous chapter, you learned how to create reports so you can print information from your database. However, you don't always need or want to print a piece of paper for a simple piece of data, like finding out who has a birthday coming up in the next month.

Here's a way to create a form that provides display only access to information in your database.

Display-only Form

This form, a *display-only form*, is like an on-screen report in that its only purpose is to show the user data from the database. However, because it's a form, your users can dynamically filter the data it shows according to criteria they select.

Create an Unbound Form

Start by creating a new unbound form, one that doesn't have a record source. The records we view on this display-only form will be controlled through two list boxes on the form.

Create the List box to Select Months

Place a list box on the form, as in Figure 12-1. As you'll see in Figure 12-1, the label for the list box is a short statement instructing the user to select a month from the list to see all of the birthdays in that month. Leave space on the form for a second list box. This first one sets the filter criteria; the second one displays the results.

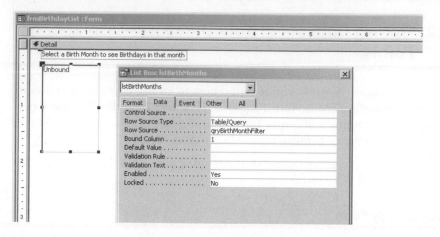

Figure 12-1 Birth Month List

Create the Selection Query

Click on the builder button for the list box' row source to create the query that will provide the list of months for the list box.

We need the birthdays from tblPerson so we can select and display the months. When the query builder opens, therefore, add tblPerson to the query window. Drag two copies of Birthdate to the query grid, as in Figure 12-2.

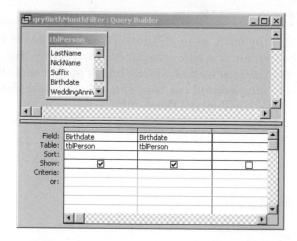

Figure 12-2 Query Grid for Birth Month Query

We're going to use the expression builder to create the values that will display in the list box. First, we want to create an integer value (1, 2, 3, etc.) for the months in Birthdate. For example, the birth month for 7/22/1955 is seven. Why do we need to do that, you might wonder? Two reasons: sorting and filtering.

First, we'll extract the birth months as digits and use those integer values to sort the list from one through twelve. If we sorted on the *names* of the months, July would sort before June, and August would sort before February. Second, we'll use the integer values to determine which birth dates to display. I'll show you that in a minute.

We set up the first column of the query for the benefit of Access (it uses integers to sort). We set up the second column for the benefit of the people who use it (it displays full month names from which to select). We want to show the user the names of the months, not their integer values, so we'll format the second birth date field to display month names.

Create the Expressions

Place the cursor in the first column and click on the expression builder.

Figure 12-3 Expression Builder

When it opens, place the cursor in front of the fieldname in the expression window. Navigate through the selection windows to find the built-in Date/Time function called Month, Figure 12-4.

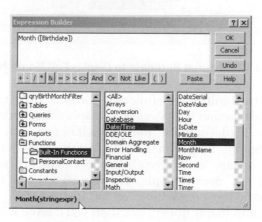

Figure 12-4 Paste the Month Function into the Expression

Paste it into the expression window and use the syntax example at the bottom of the expression as a guide in editing the expression. The expression Month([Birthdate]) will extract the integer value of the month from each birthday in the table.

Click OK to close the expression builder. Note that the query builder provides a default alias, something like Expr1, which you can accept or change to one that is more meaningful like BirthMonthDigit, as I decided to do.

Set the sort order for the first column, the one with BirthMonthDigit as its value, to Ascending, so the birth months will sort from one (January) to twelve (December).

Next, move the cursor to the second column in your query and open the expression builder again.

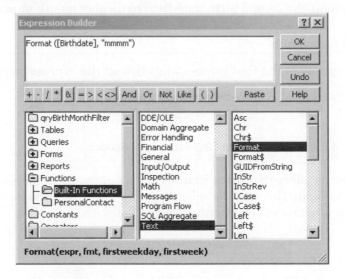

Figure 12-5 Format Birthdate to Display Full Month Name

This time select the built-in text function, *Format*. Edit it as shown in Figure 12-5. This function tells Access to display the birth date according to the format specified. "mmmm" means spell out the full name of the month, as in January. "mmm" means display the three letter abbreviation, as in Jan. "mm" means display the month as a two digit number, as in 01. "m" means display the integer value of the month, as in 1. (I suppose I could have used "mm" or "m" instead of the Month function for the other column in our query, but then you'd have missed the chance to see the Month function, too.)

Give this column a meaningful alias, BirthMonthText; save and close the query. Give the query a name, such as qryBirthMonthFilter, following standard naming conventions.

Unique Values vs. Unique Records

Now, switch to form view and observe the results. It should look something like Figure 12-6, depending on the birth dates in your database.

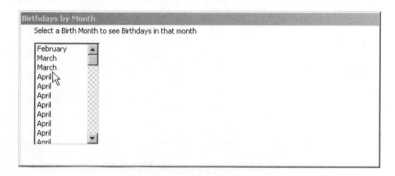

Figure 12-6 Month Names Repeated

Notice that some of the month names are repeated. That's because the query currently returns one row for each *unique record* in the table. So, if there are two birthdays in March and eight birthdays in April, the list displays March twice and April eight times.

That's not what we want for this particular list box. We want one row for each *unique value* of month in the table. So, let's switch back to design view, reopen the query, and change it.

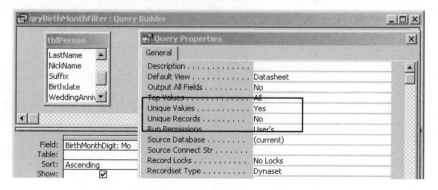

Figure 12-7 Set Unique Values Property to Yes

Open the query's property sheet and find the Unique Values property for the query. Change it to Yes.

By the way, Unique Values and Unique Records are mutually exclusive. Changing one to Yes automatically changes to the other to No. Try it out for yourself, but make sure to leave it with Unique Values set to Yes when you save and close the query. Now, the form should display more like Figure 12-8.

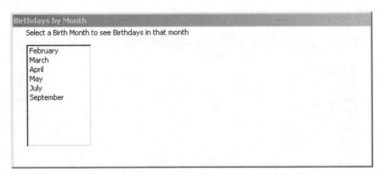

Figure 12-8 Unique Values for Month Names

That's what we want for the selection list, one entry for each birth month found in the field Birthdate in tblPerson. Note that it only displays month names if there is at least one birthday in that month in the table. That's why we used the query from tblPerson, rather than creating a list with all twelve months. Why show November if no one in the database as a birthday in that month? Now we need to add the control that will display the *full* birth dates for each selected month.

Create the Display List

Create a second list box on the form, as in Figure 12-9.

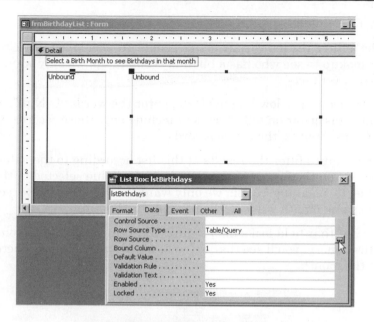

Figure 12-9 Display List Box

Name the list box according to standard naming conventions.

Click on the builder button for the list box' row source to open the query builder. Add tblPerson, which will provide us with the names and birth dates to display in the form.

Add the following five fields to the query grid: FirstName, LastName, BirthDate, InactiveDate, and a second copy of Birthdate.

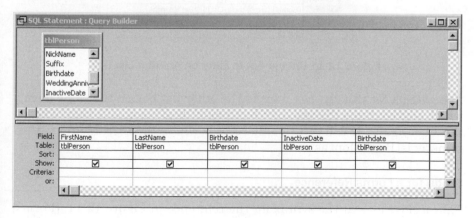

Figure 12-10 First Step in Display List Query

Creating Filter Criteria

First, let's filter the list so only *active* people are displayed. If we're doing a quick lookup to see who has a birthday coming up, we only want to see our current contacts.

In the criteria line below InactiveDate, enter the words "Is Null", exactly like that. This criterion tells Access to include only those records with no inactive date, that is, the active records.

Next, we want to filter the results of this list according to the value of the first list box on the form. In other words, if the value selected in the first list box is 03, meaning March, we only want this query to show records with the same month value in the person's birth date.

Here's what that field looks like, Figure 12-11. Actually, if you compare it to the first query, you'll see that we've used the same Month function to extract the month.

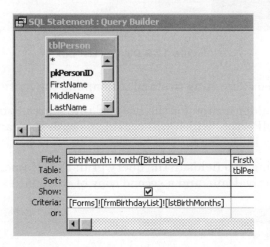

Figure 12-11 Criteria Set to Filter on Another List Box

The criteria for this list box refer to the other list box on the same form, which also contains the two digit birth months. This means that, when this query runs, it will return only records where the BirthMonth is the same as lstBirthMonths.

Syntax for a Forms Reference

Take a close look at the syntax for the reference in Figure 12-11. [Forms] refers to the collection of all forms in the database.

"!", sometimes called the "bang operator", means the next item is a member of that collection. In other words, it's a specific form. The specific form named here, of course, is frmBirthdayList.

You can't use Me in queries, even though, as in this case, the query is on the same form.

The last part of the reference is the name of the control on the form that contains the criteria value, [lstBirthMonths].

Updating a Query Result

With the selection criteria set in the query, the query returns a different set of records each time it is opened, or run, depending on the value of lstBirthMonths.

However—and this is an important point to remember—if this query is *already open* when lstBirthMonths is updated, *it won't update to reflect that change until you close and reopen it, or use VBA to requery it.*

In other words, changing the birth month selected in lstBirthMonths doesn't automatically cause lstBirthdays to show the new results. You have to force lstBirthdays to update itself. You'll see how we handle this issue in a moment.

Hiding Filter Criteria in a Query

Although we want to filter the records in this query by the two fields for which we've set criteria, we don't need to see those criteria fields themselves. Un-check the Show checkbox for those two columns. The query will still filter records on the criteria, but it will do so behind the scenes.

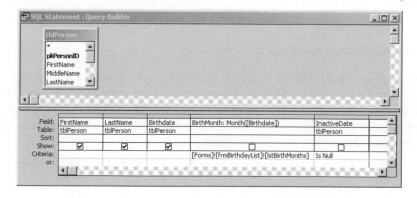

Figure 12-12 SQL Statement to Filter Records in a Query

This query will now return all records with the same month value as the value selected in the first list box on the form, excluding any records that have an inactive date.

Save and close the query, giving it a name like qryFilteredBirthdays.

Format the List Box

Select the Format tab of the property sheet.

As you can see in Figure 12-13, I've designated only three columns in the list box, even though there are five fields in the query. Why? Because two of the columns in the query are hidden. I set their Show property to No. There are only three columns to display.

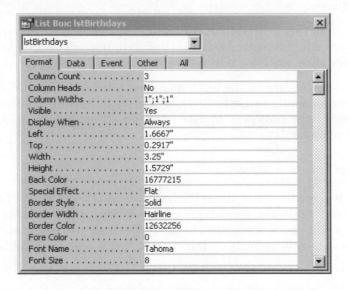

Figure 12-13 Format the List Box

Column Widths Plus Scroll Bar

I set them to equal widths to start, one-inch each. You can adjust the column widths in your list box to accommodate the names and birth dates in your database. Just make sure the total width of the list box is equal to, or greater than, the total of the column widths, plus ¼" to accommodate the vertical scroll bar, if it is required.

Lock the List Box

Select the Data tab and find the Locked property for the list box. Locking prevents the user from making changes to a control. We only want the user to see (and if necessary, scroll through) the list of birthdays. We don't want them to be able to select one. They can't do anything with the values in the list, but if the user can select one by clicking on it, they might think they *should* be able to do something, so we lock the list box to prevent confusion, Figure 12-14.

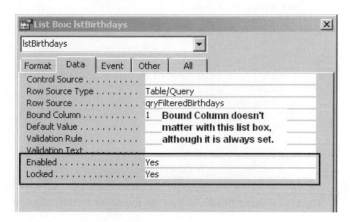

Figure 12-14 List Box Data Properties

Bound Column

Although list boxes always have a bound column, it doesn't make any difference in this one. The list box is unbound, as is the form, and we're not permitting the user to do anything with the names in the list.

However, if there were some action to perform, we would use the value of the bound column to do it, just as we do with the other list box on this form.

Well, that is just about it, one more step to go.

Creating an Event to Requery the Birthday List

As I mentioned earlier, the query in lstBirthdays is filtered so it displays birthdays where the birth month matches the month selected in lstBirthMonths. When the form first opens, there is nothing selected in lstBirthMonths, so there are no birthdays displayed in lstBirthdays.

Moreover, selecting a month in lstBirthMonths has no effect on the query in lstBirthDays, after the form is opened. So, what we need is an *event procedure* that will force lstBirthDays to requery its row source every time you select a new month in lstBirthMonths. You might have guessed already how we're going to do that. We're going to use the After Update event of lstBirthMonths.

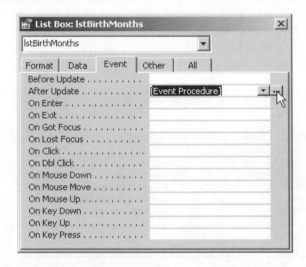

Figure 12-15 Open the After Update Event for lstBirthMonths

Open the form in design view and use the builder button to open the After Update event procedure for lstBirthMonths, Figure 12-15. We only need one line of code for this.

Figure 12-16 Requery After Update

Not much to say about that line of code. Each time you update lstBirthMonths by selecting a value in the lstBirthMonths list box, this code fires, causing the query in the lstBirthdays list box to requery the table and display the new set of matching birthdays, as in Figure 12-17.

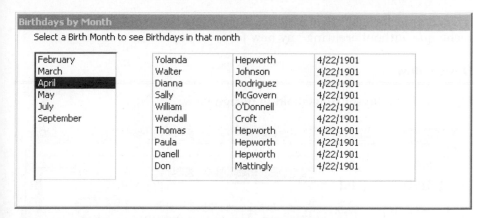

Figure 12-17 Birthday List Form Displaying Filtered List of
Birthdays

Other Filtered List Forms

You can use this same technique to create a number of different filtered
lists. For example, the filtering list could be based on states, with the
filtered list displaying all of the households in the selected state. Or you
could base the filtering list on area codes and have the filtered list
display phone numbers in that area code. The possibilities are endless,
although some of them, like filtering on area codes, might be a bit silly in
an application like this.

A more advanced technique usually referred to as cascading filters, uses
three or more list or combo boxes to create increasingly precise filters.
For example, the first list box filters on states, causing the second list box
to display cities in that state. Selecting a city from that list then causes a
third list box to display contacts in that city.

I'm afraid we don't have space in this book for more form examples, but
you can use what you just learned to try it on your own. However, I did
promise to show you how to use filtering techniques for reports, so I will
finish this chapter with an example of a filter for a report.

Filtering Records for a Report

The report we'll use for this example will be the birthday list by
household. We'll add a filter to it so it displays only the people whose
birthdays fall in the month selected on the form we just created. We'll
change the source of the filter later on, when we create a more user

friendly interface for our database. But for now, we can illustrate the technique without creating any new forms or reports.

Design View

Open rptBirthdaysbyHousehold in design view.

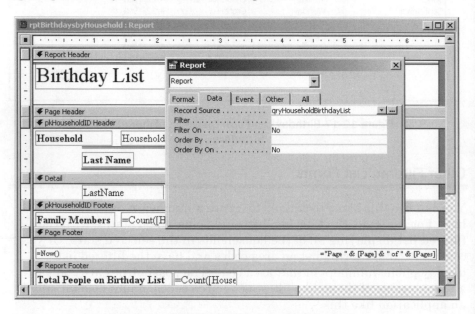

Figure 12-18 rptBirthdaysbyHousehold in Design View

I'm going to show you a shortcut you can use to save time when you need to create a new query or report, similar to one you already have.

Select the query you created as the row source for the filtered list box on frmBirthdayList. (I called mine qryHouseholdBirthdayList.) Open it in design view.

Place the cursor on the column head above the two criteria fields and click to select them both, as in Figure 12-19. The small dark arrow in the column head shows the selected columns. When they are highlighted, copy them.

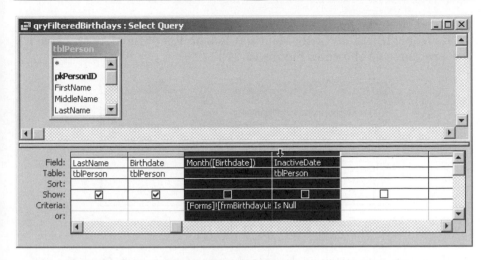

Figure 12-19 Select Fields to Copy from qryFilteredBirthdays

Close this query without saving changes. Now, open the query that is the record source for rptBirthdaysbyHousehold (qryHouseholdBirthdayList) in design view.

Place the cursor in the column head of any empty column in qryHouseholdBirthdayList and paste the two columns into the query. It will look like Figure 12-20.

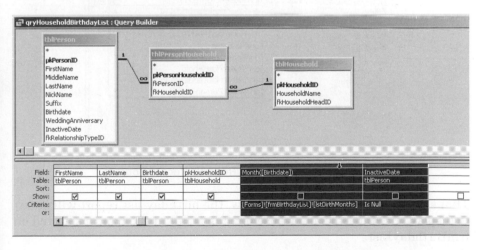

Figure 12-20 Past Selected Fields into qryHouseholdBirthdayList

Save and close the modified query under a new name, like qryHouseholdBirthdayListbyMonth. (Click on File-->Save As and give it the new name as shown in Figure 12-21.)

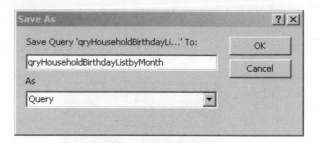

Figure 12-21 New Query

We'll use this new query as the record source for a report. Open the report in design view and select the Data tab of the report's property sheet. Change the report's record source in the record source drop down, as shown in Figure 12-22.

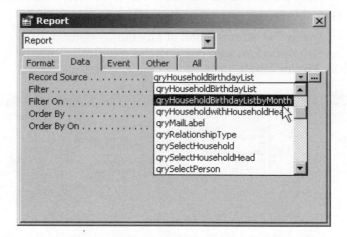

Figure 12-22 Change the Report's Record Source

That's just about all there is to it. Now, the birthday list report will open to display only those people whose birthdays fall in the month selected on frmBirthdayList.

Try it out yourself. Open frmBirthdayList and select a month. Then open rptBirthdaysbyHousehold. It should print or show a preview of only the people whose birthdays fall in the month selected on the form.

Save a New Version of the Report

Of course, the reason we developed rptBirthdaysbyHousehold was to show *everyone* according to which family they belong, not just a list of current birthdays. This filtered version of the report no longer meets that goal. Let's save it under a new name, one that reflects its purpose. Let's call it rptBirthdaysbyHouseholdbyMonth. Click on File-->Save As and save the report with the new name.

Figure 12-23 Save the Report Under a New Name

Now you can open either the report displaying everyone in our database, or the one that is filtered by the list box on the birthday list form.

Workflow with a Report Tied to Form

You may already have spotted a potential problem with this new report. It will only work if the birthday list form is open and a birth month selected in the birth month list. If you or another user tries to open the report first, it will generate an error. You'll learn how to deal with that in the next chapter, which will show you how to set up a user interface to control access to forms and reports.

In the last chapter in this book, we'll turn our attention from the individual components of an Access database to the overall interface through which your users will interact with the database.

Backup, Backup, Backup

Did it occur to you that this would be an excellent time to make a backup copy of your database? Close your database, find it on your hard drive and make a copy in a safe place. Do that now.

This page intentionally left blank.

13. Create a User Interface

At this point, you've seen and created most of the basic building blocks of an Access database: tables, forms, reports, queries, and even event procedures in VBA[15]. In this last chapter I'm going to show you how to put those bits and pieces together into an *application with a user interface*.

An application differs from a raw database in a couple of important ways.

Hands Off the DB Objects, Please

First, when your database is set up as an application with a well-designed and usable user interface, you and your users never (well, almost never) work directly with tables or queries. Adding new data, deleting obsolete or erroneous data, filtering data, and creating and printing reports are all accomplished by manipulating forms. Unless you put on your developer hat to perform maintenance on one of the pieces of the database itself, you shouldn't need to open a table directly, or look at the design view of a form, query or report.

One way to think of it is to compare it to driving a car. The user interface is like the driver's seat, where the steering wheel and other controls are located. That's the part of the machine you normally work with. Underneath and behind the driver's seat are the engine, drive train, exhaust system and all of those other dirty mechanical parts. You can turn the steering wheel and press on the accelerator or brakes just fine without knowing a whole lot about transmissions; the controls transmit your instructions accurately to the mechanical systems that do the real work.

---

[15] You may be asking yourself, "Hey, whatever happened to Macros? Doesn't Access have them?" The answer, of course, is "Yes, you can create Macros in Access." However, I've never been much of a fan of macros and I decided not to use valuable space in this book on them.

Almost everything you can do with a macro you can do with VBA, and usually do it better. Your databases will be much more polished, flexible and usable with VBA than they would be with macros. So, even though you might find macros to be a handy tool in the short run, I believe that in the long run you'll be much better off learning VBA and using it. For that reason, I think you might as well learn VBA now, rather than later, and save macros for your spare time.

You may have to fix a flat tire once in a while, but most of the time, you don't really want to touch that stuff. All you want to do is get in and drive to your destination. A well-designed user interface plays the driver's seat role in an application.

Ah, It *All* Makes Sense Now

Second, an application with a well-designed user interface presents a coherent, overall look and feel across all of its parts. Moving from data input to printing reports and back again should be a smooth process requiring your users to do a minimum of clicking or tabbing, opening and closing forms, etc. Your users should not have to hunt for the functions they need and they especially shouldn't have to click through layers of choices to get there.

Think again about the layout of the dashboard in your car. The controls you use most—steering wheel, accelerator and brakes are all within convenient reach for the average driver and, in most cars, you don't have to hunt around to find them because they're in familiar locations. Most of us would be appalled if car manufacturers required us to "close" the accelerator (perhaps by moving it manually to the Off position?) before "opening" the brake pedal and vice versa. (Actually, now that I think about it, if you've been around as long as I have and you grew up on a farm, you might remember a time when tractors often had accelerator controls just like that.)

A User Interface for Our Contacts Database

A user interface sounds good when you think about it that way, but creating a decent one can be a pretty tall order. In the rest of this chapter, I'm going to concentrate on putting together one interface design that I like. There are many other ways to go about designing an interface and some of them might be better. Still, we have to start somewhere and I like this design, so that's the one I'll show you.

Keep it Simple, Stupid

The first rule of design probably should be to keep things as simple as possible. We're lucky here because the tables, queries, reports and forms we've been building in this book aren't all that complex; therefore the interface for it need not be extremely complex. Even if we did have a lot more forms and reports to manage, however, we'd want a design that emphasizes simplicity over flash.

Navigation by Menus

Sticking with the automobile analogy for just a bit longer, a good user interface should be built around a "steering wheel", a central tool that allows the driver to navigate from place to place within the application while remaining firmly in control. That role is usually filled by a menu system of some type in an application.

Windows Menus

Every Windows application has menus. Users are familiar with them, know how to use them—at least in general terms—and usually don't need a lot of training in making them work.

Access has several built-in menus and toolbars. You've used many of them in creating the pieces of your sample database. They do generic things, things like sort or filter records in a table or form. Those are useful functions, to be sure, but none of them is specific to *your* application. Your interface also needs to give your users access to specific forms and reports as well.

And more importantly, your users can use built-in menus and toolbars to get to parts of the database you really want to protect from them, things like opening a table and changing or even deleting records or entire tables.

Our user interface, therefore, should de-emphasize the built-in menus and toolbars as much as possible in favor of a menu created specifically for that purpose. That's what our menu does.

Menus vs. Switchboards

Access allows you to create custom menus and tool bars. I will show you how to create a very simple one in this chapter. Creating an entire menu system for your application is probably a bit too advanced for us at this point in our experience, although you will certainly want to master them at some point. Instead, we'll use a special type of Access form—usually called a switchboard, but which I prefer to think of as a custom menu—that you can create with the level of expertise you already have.

What is a Switchboard

A switchboard is a form that is not bound to a record source and that has no input fields. Instead, it has command buttons, labels, or hyperlinks on it that, when clicked, open and close the working forms and reports in your application.

Access' Switchboard Wizard

Access has a Switchboard wizard that creates serviceable, if not really exciting, switchboards.

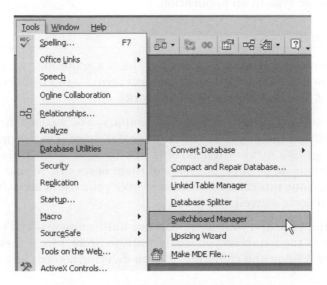

Figure 13-1 Access Switchboard Manager

You can find it on the menu, under Tools-->Database Utilities.

You already know I am not enthusiastic about most of the wizards in Access although they can be somewhat helpful in getting through the basic steps in creating a new table, query, form or report. My opinion of the switchboards created by the switchboard wizard isn't any better.

Unlike the objects created by other wizards, Access wizard switchboards aren't easy to modify tomake them work better or to conform to naming conventions for objects. So, other than the fact Access has a wizard to create them, you won't hear much more on the subject from me.

Instead, I'm going to show you how I created a switchboard, or custom menu, of my own design and walk you through the steps of creating one like it for yourself. One of the best features of this menu is that, after you've created it the first time, you can copy it from database to database and use it over and over with little or no modification each time.

A Menu-Based Switchboard

The idea behind this switchboard is that it is an Access form that mimics certain features of menus and tool bars. It isn't as sophisticated in some ways as a real menu, but it doesn't need to be. Here are a couple of its most important advantages.

Screen Location

First, this menu displays across the top of the screen, similar to the location of a real menu, and it remains visible as long as the application is open because other forms always open below it. In other words, the user never has to go hunting for it behind other open forms or reports.

Single Click to Navigate

Second, the menu handles all of the tasks of opening *and closing* other forms (a feature lacking in Access' wizard-generated switchboards). Forms in an application driven by this menu don't need their own Close or Done buttons; the menu takes care of that task. Not only does that cut down on the number of mouse clicks your users have to make, but also it cuts down on the number of times you have to create a Close button for a form. Moreover, not having to include the button saves a small amount of space on the form. Finally, it's just esthetically more pleasing, in my view.

It takes some coding to set up this switchboard the first time, but once it's done, it's done. And it's portable to any other application as well.

Possible Disadvantages

So far, I've not run into any serious disadvantages with this switchboard. It will even work in a compiled database, or MDE file[16]. Until you are advanced enough to be creating MDE files, of course, that won't be an

---

[16] The following is a quote from MS Access Help. "[S]aving your Microsoft Access database as an MDE file compiles all modules, removes all editable source code, and compacts the destination database. Your Visual Basic code will continue to run, but it cannot be viewed or edited. Saving your database as an MDE file secures you[r] forms and reports without requiring users to log on or requiring you to create and manage the user accounts and permissions that are needed for user-level security." Users can't make changes to the design of tables, forms, reports, etc. in an mde file. However, the VBA code that creates the menu does work in an mde.
Mde files are beyond the scope of this book.

issue for you. And when you do get to that point in your career, you'll be ready to create and manage your own menu systems.

The Grover Park Menu Switchboard

Enough sales talk; time to introduce you to my menu.

A Word of Warning

In the following discussion, you will encounter some serious Visual Basic for Applications (VBA) code. The menu relies on several VBA functions and it doesn't make much sense to read about it unless you are comfortable with, and prepared for, a more advanced look at certain aspects of VBA. If not, you might be better off stopping now and using the standard Access Switchboard Wizard to create a switchboard for your application. Come back and try this method when you have a little more experience under your belt.

Part One—The Form

Figure 13-2 is the menu switchboard form in the personal contacts application we've been creating.

Figure 13-2 Menu Switchboard from Personal Contacts

This version has seven menu items on it. Each menu item is a hyperlink with a label telling your user what it does. Because they are hyperlinks, clicking on one of them opens the appropriate form. Code in the form also closes any other open forms.

The text on each label is completely flexible. Changing it is as easy as making an entry in a table. You may recognize the names of some of the items on this menu—People and Households, for example. They refer to the two data entry forms you created earlier. Clicking on People opens frmPerson. Clicking on Households opens frmHousehold.

The Quit label is self-explanatory; you click it to quit and close the application. There are four additional hyperlinks on this menu. I'll explain what they do later. First, I want to show you what this form looks like in design view. Take a look at Figure 13-3.

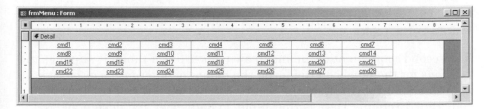

Figure 13-3 Menu in Design View

Surprised? I thought you might be. The form actually contains 28 identical controls, not just the seven you could see in form view. That means you can have up to *28 menu items* on this single switchboard. So far, I've not needed that many, but if you ever design an application with so many features you require additional menu items, you can add new rows of 7 very easily.

Each control on the menu switchboard is an ordinary label. The control names are an important part of making this switchboard completely portable. Each one is a combination of the prefix for standard command controls, "cmd", plus a number representing its relative position on the form. Control cmd1 is the first one on the left on the top row. It's followed by cmd2, and so on. I'll show you why the names and relative positions are important when I explain the VBA code that creates the captions for each label.

Control Properties

All of the labels on the form have the same properties. These properties are important for our purposes here.

> Name and Caption, as you've seen, must be "cmd" plus a number: 1, 2, 3, etc.

> Captions are <u>underlined</u>. This gives the controls the appearance of hyperlinks.

> The control's Visible property is set to No. When the form first opens, all of the labels are invisible. We only show the ones we need to show, as in Figure 13-2, by changing their Visible property to Yes.

> Each of the labels has the same On_Click event procedure, which I'll show you a bit later in the chapter.

Part Two—The Table

The second component of the menu switchboard is a table. It supplies the *captions* for the labels on the form, the names of *other forms or objects* called by the hyperlinks on the menu, screen tip text, and the type of hyperlink to create. Here is that table, in datasheet and design views (Figure 13-4) and (Figure 13-5).

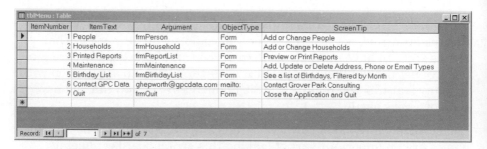

	ItemNumber	ItemText	Argument	ObjectType	ScreenTip
▶	1	People	frmPerson	Form	Add or Change People
	2	Households	frmHousehold	Form	Add or Change Households
	3	Printed Reports	frmReportList	Form	Preview or Print Reports
	4	Maintenance	frmMaintenance	Form	Add, Update or Delete Address, Phone or Email Types
	5	Birthday List	frmBirthdayList	Form	See a list of Birthdays, Filtered by Month
	6	Contact GPC Data	ghepworth@gpcdata.com	mailto:	Contact Grover Park Consulting
	7	Quit	frmQuit	Form	Close the Application and Quit

Record: ⏮ ◀ 1 ▶ ⏭ ▶* of 7

Figure 13-4 tblMenu in Datasheet View

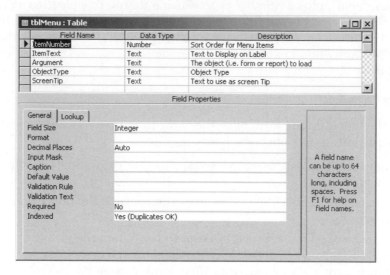

Figure 13-5 tblMenu in Design View

Fields in tblMenu

tblMenu has five fields. The first, ItemNumber, is a counter. It is not an autonumber because it is not a primary key and I like to be able to reuse the numbers in each application. The purpose of ItemNumber is to sort the records in the table into the order in which I want them to display on the menu form. ItemNumber 1, for example, will always be the first menu item on the top row on the left; Item 7 will be the last item in this menu.

The second field in tblMenu, ItemText, is the text that is displayed as the caption of the label on the menu. Changing the name for a menu item is, therefore, as simple as changing it here in the table. Keep in mind, though, this caption must fit on the label. If it's too long, you'll have trouble displaying it all.

The third field in tblMenu, Argument, is the name of a form, (such as frmPerson) or an action (such as mailto:). When your user clicks on a menu item in the switchboard, it calls up this *argument* and performs the designated action on it. For the most part, of course, that means opening another form.

The fourth field in tblMenu, ObjectType, tells Access whether the hyperlink is a form, a report, or an email address. This determines how the hyperlink is set up.

The fifth field in tblMenu, ScreenTip is the text for the screen tip displayed when the cursor moves over a hyperlink label.

The version of tblMenu in this application has only seven menu items in it. You can add other menu items as needed to handle all of the forms in your database. The only existing limit, at this point, is the maximum of 28 controls on the menu.

Part Three—The Code

Now let's look at the code that takes records from tblMenu and turns them into hyperlinks on the menu switchboard form. You saw code modules like this when you learned how to design and modify forms. You should recognize, for example, the *object* combo box on the upper left and the *event* combo box on the upper right.

Here's the code that runs each time frmMenu opens. It contains three lines of housekeeping code and one line that *calls a function* to create the menu.

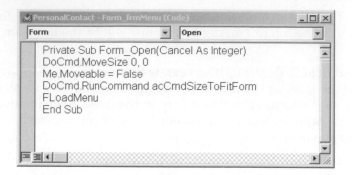

Figure 13-6 Code for the Form_Open Event of FrmMenu

Since the form should only be opened once—when the application first starts—this code should only run once during each session, recreating the menu items from the table.

The following discussion relies heavily on VBA, so take your time, refer to Access Help whenever you need more information and, above all, be patient. You will get it.

The code consists of four lines.

Line one,

```
DoCmd.MoveSize 0, 0
```

tells Access to move the form to a specific position on the screen, indicated by the two numbers "0, 0". That means it should be zero inches from the left side and zero inches from the top.

DoCmd Object

The DoCmd object is a very useful VBA tool. You can use the *methods* of the DoCmd *object* to run Microsoft Access actions—such as closing windows, opening forms, and setting the value of controls—from Visual Basic, just as if you'd clicked on an item on a menu or toolbar.

For example, DoCmd.MoveSize is similar to clicking on Window-->Size to Fit on the database menu bar, Figure 13-7.

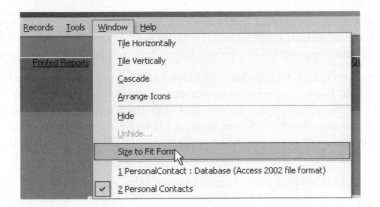

Figure 13-7 Menu Equivalent of DoCmd.MoveSize

Why We Use DoCmd Methods

One of the reasons for creating our own menu is to prevent users from getting to built-in menu bar options that might be harmful (such as deleting a table by accident). That has the unintended consequence of also preventing access to functions (such as resizing a form) that would be useful.

One option, as I've mentioned before, would be to create custom menu bars to provide functions we want the user to have. When you are more experienced with Access that will be a good option. But not yet.

So, we have to provide this function in code.

In this case, the MoveSize action of the DoCmd object moves the menu so its left edge is 0 inches from the left margin of the window and its top edge is 0 inches from the top margin of the window.

Line two,

```
Me.Moveable = False
```
tells Access not to let the user move the form from this position. In other words, once the form is placed at the top of the window, it is there to stay. (This property is not available in Access 97 or 2000, sorry).

As you learned earlier, Me refers to the object, in this case a form, on which the code is running.

Line three,

```
DoCmd.RunCommand acCmdSizeToFitForm
```
tells Access to resize the form to fit.

This instruction uses the RunCommand action of the DoCmd object. The RunCommand action runs a built-in Microsoft Access command. The command may appear on an Access menu bar, toolbar, or shortcut menu.

In other words, any action that could be called from one of the built-in Access menu bars, toolbars, or shortcut menus can be called from VBA code with this syntax. You can use DoCmd RunCommand to open and close a database, delete a record from a table, or even display Access Help. If it's available on any built-in menu or toolbar, you can call it in VBA.

That's a lot of power at your fingertips with the line of code,

```
Docmd.RunCommand "Command".
```

acCmdSizeToFitForm is an *intrinsic constant.* As you know, intrinsic constants are values defined in VBA to represent specific items, such as a menu or toolbar command. This one represents the menu command that causes a form to resize itself to its original size in case it was made larger or smaller by some action of the user or another event procedure.

Other intrinsic constants whose purpose you might recognize include *acCmdClose,* to close an object, or *acCmdSelectRecord, acCmdCut,* and *acCmdPaste,* to cut-and-paste a record from one table to another.

Line four,

```
FLoadMenu
```

calls another event procedure.

You can think of lines one to three as housekeeping commands. They are there just to make sure the menu stays where it is supposed to stay and looks the way it should look.

The fourth line, FLoadMenu, does the heavy lifting. It calls the event procedure to create the menu items on the form. Here's what it looks like, in Figure 13-8.

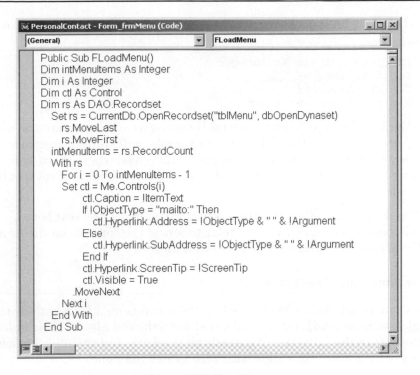

Figure 13-8 FLoadMenu

This is a full-fledged VBA event procedure and it's more complex than most of the ones I shown you so far. If you've stayed with me this far, I think you're up to the challenge of working your way through this one with me, aren't you? We'll go a step at a time.

First, notice that FLoadMenu is not attached to any control on the form; it's under the general section of the code module in the object combo box. It can be called from anywhere within the form, by any other event.

Also, notice that it doesn't refer to any specific control on a form by name. That's important because we need it to walk through any or all twenty-eight labels on the form and assign a value to each one, as appropriate. We don't know beforehand which controls, or how many of them, will be given a value, so we won't refer to them directly by name.

Finally, this code was written for DAO, rather than ADO. (Don't worry, those acronyms may not mean much to you right now, but they do to experienced database developers). The important point is DAO code is an older version, introduced in Access 2000; however, either should work for Access 97 as well as Access 2000, 2002, and 2003.

The first four lines declare several variables by giving them names and data types.

```
Dim intMenuItems As Integer
Dim i As Integer
Dim ctl As Control
Dim rs As DAO.Recordset
```

"intMenuItems" and "i" are integers. Integers, as you know, are the whole numbers, 1, 2, etc. intMenuItems, for example, will store the number of labels we need to display on the menu. In this case, where there are seven records in tblMenu, intMenuItems will have a value of seven when the code runs.

"ctl" is defined as a Control. You know what controls are: text boxes, labels, combo boxes, etc. We can refer to any of the controls on the form with this variable and the control's *index number*.

Okay, Smart Guy, What's an Index?

Glad you asked. Access keeps track of the controls on a form both by their names, such as cmd1, cmd2, cmd3, and so forth, and also by their index value within the collection of controls on the form. Index values are zero-based, which mean they start with zero rather than one.

In other words, if the there are twenty-eight controls on the form, the first one has an index value of zero, the second one has an index value of one, the third has an index value of two, etc.

So, no matter what the *name* of a control is, you can always reference it by its *index* within the Controls collection. We'll take advantage of that fact in the section of code that assigns captions to the labels, one at a time, based on their relative positions in the index, without having to worry about the real name of the label.

Recordsets and the Current Database Object

"rs" is a DAO *recordset*. Without going too far into the intricacies of DAO, I can tell you this much. You can use VBA to open a set of records without actually having to open the table or tables that contain the records or binding those records to a specific form. Usually a recordset includes records from a single table in the database.

Opening a recordset in VBA allows you to do things with the records without having to display them on a form, things like count how many there are or look for specific values in specific fields within the recordset.

In this procedure, we're going to open a recordset and use the values in it to create captions for the labels on the menu form. That's why we don't need to hard code those captions into the labels themselves and why the menu form can be copied into any other database and used without modification to the form itself.

The VBA Code Begins

The next line in the event procedure,

```
Set rs = CurrentDb.OpenRecordset("tblMenu",
dbOpenDynaset)
```

opens the recordset.

Set creates a reference to a specific recordset (records from tblMenu) in the database and assigns it to the rs variable. We've already created the variable rs as a recordset object, but it doesn't yet point to anything; it is empty until we use the Set command.

CurrentDb tells Access that the table is in the current database, the one in which the code is running. This implies you can open recordsets in other databases. And, in fact, you can. That's a bit too advanced for us here, but tuck that knowledge into your back pocket for later.

dbOpenDynaset is one of several modes in which you can open a recordset. The details aren't all that important right here. For now all you need to know about dynasets is you can move back and forth through the records in it, which is something we need to do.

The next two lines move to the end of the recordset and then back to the first record.

```
rs.MoveLast
rs.MoveFirst
```

Those moves allow Access to count the number of records in the recordset, to which we assign a variable in the next line.

```
intMenuItems = rs.RecordCount
```

intMenuItems is an integer variable and this line assigns it a value that is the RecordCount of the recordset rs. The record count will be equal to the number of records in tblMenu (seven in this case). We now know how many menu items to put on the menu form: seven, one for each record in the recordset.

The next block of code, everything between With Rs and End With, extracts the menu items from the recordset and assigns them as the names as the captions of the labels on the form, creates the hyperlinks, and defines the screen tips for each label.

The line,

```
For i = 0 To intMenuItems - 1
```

starts a loop. It tells Access to repeat the actions in the following lines over and over, from the lower limit until the upper limit is reached.

The loop starts with the value of variable is set to zero. Remember I told you control indexes are zero-based, which means the first one has an index value of zero. Therefore, we have to start the loop with zero to pick that first control. The upper limit is the number of records in the recordset, represented by intMenuItems. However, because the index starts with zero, not one, the last index value will be one less than the total number of records, i.e. intMenuItems − 1.

Because intMenuItems equals seven in this case, the loop will run seven times.

The next line assigns the value of the variable ctl to the controls collection of the form and selects the control with an index value of i.

```
Set ctl = Me.Controls(i)
```

At this point in the procedure, ctl refers to the first control on the form (designated by the keyword Me); it has an index value of zero.

The line,

```
ctl.Caption = !ItemText
```

assigns a value to the Caption property of this control.

The code gets the value for that caption from the ItemText field in the current record (which is the first record in the recordset when the loop starts). In this case, the value of ItemText in the first record of tblMenu is People, so the caption on the first control is now People.

The next line is a conditional. It's there because we need to handle email addresses differently from other types of objects (forms and reports). Forms and reports are *internal* objects, inside the database, whereas email is *external,* outside the database.

The line,

```
If !ObjectType = "mailto:" Then
```

checks the value of the field ObjectType in the current record.

The line,

```
ctl.Hyperlink.Address = !ObjectType & " " & !Argument
```

creates a *hyperlink* address (external to the database) if the object type is mailto:.

The line,
```
ctl.Hyperlink.SubAddress = !ObjectType & " " & !Argument
```
creates a *hyperlink subAddress* (internal to the database) if the object type is anything other than an email address.

The line,
```
ctl.Hyperlink.ScreenTip = !ScreenTip
```
creates a screen tip for the hyperlink from the value of the field ScreenTip in tblMenu. When the cursor moves over the hyperlink, this text displays.

The line,
```
ctl.Visible = True
```
changes the Visible property of the current control from False to True, meaning this control, with its new caption, is now visible on the form.

The line,
```
.MoveNext
```
moves to the next record in the recordset, ready to pull its values for the next label.

The line,
```
Next i
```
increases the value of i by one and starts the loop over again.

The loop continues until it has run through all of the records in the recordset, using the values in the ItemText, Argument, ObjectType and ScreenTip fields to create captions on the labels on the form, to create the hyperlinks, and to make those labels visible.

In order for this code to work correctly, three conditions have to be met.

1. The menu form can *only have labels* on it. The code doesn't check to see if the current control, identified by its index value—e.g. ctl(i)—is a label or not, or if it already has another caption. If, for example, you wanted to add a text box for the current date on this menu, this code would not check before trying to assign a value to that control's caption. Since text boxes don't have a Caption property, an error would occur.

2. The records in tblMenu must be sorted on the ItemNumber field so that the recordset is opened in the proper order to create labels on the menu.

3. The total number of records in the recordset can't exceed the number of labels on the menu form.

Try it Yourself

Go ahead and create a menu like this one in your database.

Create the Menu Table

Create a new table with the fields shown in Figure 13-5. Save it as tblMenu. Then open in it datasheet view and add seven records, as in Figure 13-4. There are some menu items in Figure 13-4 that don't yet exist in your database. We'll be creating them shortly.

Create the Menu Form

Create a new form. Put some labels on it. You don't have to create 28 of them—seven will do for now. You can add more later if you need them. Make each label the same width and height (1" wide by 0.1771" high, for example) and place them so there is no space between them. Use a font size appropriate for the size of the labels; say MS Sans Serif 8 point.

The menu form has no border, so set its Border Style property to None and set the Special Effect property of the form's detail section to Raised. Choose a background color you like.

Index Value and Order of Creation

The index value for each control is determined by the order in which you create them, so make sure you place the first label in the upper left corner, then the second label next to it and to its right, and so on.

If you shuffle the labels around after you create them, they will retain their index values and display labels in an order other than the one you want.

Create the Sub

1. Open the code module for the form and type in the event procedure in Figure 13-8 exactly as it appears there.
2. In the On_Open for the form, type in the event procedure in Figure 13-6. Save the form as frmMenu.
3. Switch to form view and see if the labels on your new menu display properly.
4. Click on the labels to see if they open forms properly. (You should get an error message when you click on labels for the forms you haven't created yet.)

Also, the forms will remain open until you close them manually. In the next section, we'll add some more code to the form to close one form when another one opens.

5. Click on Contact GPC Data. Send me an email message telling me you've made your first menu form and it works!

Using the Menu to Close Forms

Now, it's time to add the code that closes forms automatically when you click on a menu item to open a different form. I'm going to show you how to call a *function* directly from the Click event of a control. First, we need to create the function that closes forms.

Figure 13-9 shows the code for the event procedure, CloseAllForms.

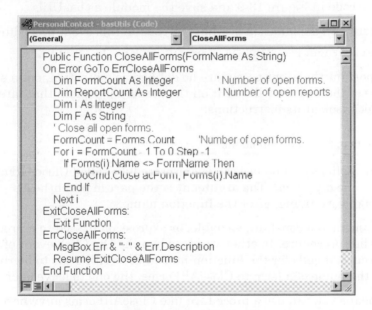

```
PersonalContact - basUtils (Code)
(General)                          CloseAllForms
Public Function CloseAllForms(FormName As String)
On Error GoTo ErrCloseAllForms
    Dim FormCount As Integer        ' Number of open forms.
    Dim ReportCount As Integer      ' Number of open reports
    Dim i As Integer
    Dim F As String
    ' Close all open forms.
    FormCount = Forms.Count         'Number of open forms.
    For i = FormCount - 1 To 0 Step -1
        If Forms(i).Name <> FormName Then
            DoCmd.Close acForm, Forms(i).Name
        End If
    Next i
ExitCloseAllForms:
    Exit Function
ErrCloseAllForms:
    MsgBox Err & ": " & Err.Description
    Resume ExitCloseAllForms
End Function
```

Figure 13-9 CloseAllForms Event Procedure

If you look closely at the title bar of the code window in Figure 13-9, you'll see is not part of a form. This event procedure is in a code module, which means that it's actually outside of any form. It is a *public* function. It is available to any object in the database. Any form can call it at any time.

To create it, select Modules in the database window and click New.

Figure 13-10 Create a VBA Module for the Function

Type the code in Figure 13-9 and save the module as basUtils.

Now, here's an explanation of what the code in this event procedure does.

```
Public Function CloseAllForms(FormName As String)
```

It's important the event procedure be defined as a function, not a sub because of the way we will use it on the menu. I'll explain that later. First, let's look at its instructions.

Arguments in Subs and Functions

This line defines and names the event procedure called CloseAllForms. It requires one *argument*. The argument is the part in parentheses (FormName as String) after the function name.

An argument is a constant, variable, or expression passed to a procedure by another procedure. In other words, when the On_Click event of the label occurs, it calls for the function named CloseAllForms to be run and passes the name of a form to CloseAllForms, the one to leave open.

That means you can use a procedure like CloseAllForms anywhere in a database to close all open forms, except for the form you want to keep open. Passing in the name of the form as an argument means you only have to create the event procedure once. After that you can call it anytime you need to close an open form or forms.

What if you want to close *all* open forms, without exceptions? Easy, just pass an empty argument to the event procedure.

```
CloseAllForms ("")
```

Since the function doesn't receive the name of a form to leave open, all open forms will be closed.

Now let's look at the rest of the code in Figure 13-9. (I'm going to skip over the error handling; you've seen that before.)

The first four lines define variables. Note the comments in the first two lines, indicated by the single quote in front of them. Comments are not part of the code. They help explain what is going on.

```
Dim FormCount As Integer     'Number of open forms.
Dim ReportCount As Integer   ' Number of open reports
Dim i As Integer
Dim F As String
```

This line,

```
FormCount = Forms.Count 'Number of open forms.
```

counts the number of forms currently open in the database. The *Forms* collection contains all of the currently *open* forms in a Microsoft Access database. (If you wanted to count all of the forms in the database, *open or closed*, you'd use the *AllForms* collection instead).

In the next line, the variable, FormCount, now has a value equal to the number of open forms. We have to close that many forms.

```
For i = FormCount - 1 To 0 Step -1
```

Here's the For loop again, but with a different logic. It counts *down to zero,* instead of up from zero. That's because we're closing forms, one at a time until there are none left to close, e.g. zero. We're going to leave one form open, though, so we want to run the For loop one fewer times than there are open forms. That's why the counter starts at *FormCount – 1*.

The next three lines form a conditional statement that closes forms that don't have the same name as the argument passed into the procedure.

```
If Forms(i).Name <> FormName Then
    DoCmd.Close acForm, Forms(i).Name
End If
```

Forms(i) refers to the index value of all open forms. Just like the collection of controls on a form, each form in the collection of open forms has an index value. We can use that index to refer to any open form without having to know its real name. Since the function doesn't know the names of open forms, we tell it to compare the names of each open form to the Name argument passed into the procedure to find the one we want.

First we check to see if the Name property of the form we are looking at matches the name we passed in as the exception to be left open. If they are not the same (<>), then we have Access close the form, using the Close method of the DoCmd object. The intrinsic constant acForm tells Access what type of object to close. The specific form is the one currently identified by its index value, `Forms(i).Name`.

If the name does match, of course, the next line of code is skipped over, leaving that form open.

The next line,

```
Next i
```

increments the value of the index by −1 and starts the "For" loop again, looking at the Name property of the next open form.

When the counter reaches zero, processing stops.

Coding Efficiency

The value of an event procedure like this is that you only need to write it once. Then, each time you need its functionality, you call its name, CloseAllForms, and tell it which form to leave open, if any. And, in this case, you'll need it twenty-eight times, once for each label on the menu form. That's a lot of coding you don't have to repeat.[17]

Assign the Function to the On_Click Event

Now I'm going to show you a neat trick. Remember I told you it is important to make CloseAllForms a function, not a sub? Well, the reason that's important is because we can use a function for the On_Click event for a control, but not a sub. Let me show you what I mean.

Select a Group of Controls

Open the menu form in design view. Open the property sheet and select the Events tab.

Now, select all of the labels on the menu. There are different ways to do this, of course. One is to hold down the Shift key while you click on each

---

[17] An alternative method of writing this procedure, to make it even more efficient in this application might be to *hard-code* the name of the menu form into the procedure so you don't have to pass it in as an argument. In other words, the procedure would not have an *argument*:

```
Sub CloseAllForms()
```

You would change the line to check for matching names in CloseAllForms to

```
If Forms(i).Name <> "frmMenu" Then
```

And the On click event for the labels could then be written:

```
CloseAllForms
```

However, this would restrict the usefulness of the procedure to this one purpose. It's a trade-off between wider usefulness (passing in different form names as argument) versus slightly less efficiency. I usually opt for the more generic, and hence more widely re-usable choice when it is available.

---

label. Another is to place the cursor in either the top or left ruler of the
form and click and drag to highlight and select all of the controls, as in
Figure 13-11.

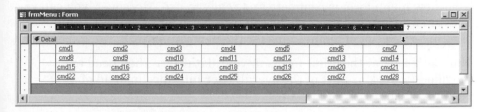

Figure 13-11 Click and Drag to Select Controls

With all of the labels selected, you can insert the CloseAllForms into the
On Click event of *all of them at once,* as shown in Figure 13-12.

Type the name of the event into the On Click property. Make sure you
include the equal sign in front of it and the form name in parentheses
after it. With all of the labels selected, this assigns the same function to
all of them simultaneously.

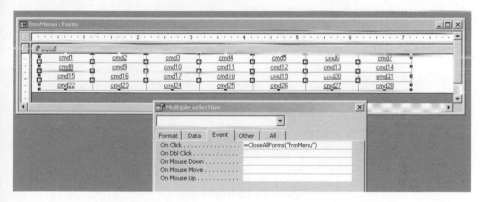

Figure 13-12 Enter the Function for Multiple Controls

That's quick and easy and doesn't require a lot of copy and paste or typing.

Final Housekeeping Step

There's one more piece of housekeeping code to add. In the On Activate
event of the menu form, add the line,

```
DoCmd.MoveSize 0, 0
```

This line assures that the menu always stays at the top of the window when it is active. We'll make some further changes later that make this piece of housekeeping redundant; but for now, it helps keep things tidy.

Your new menu form is complete and ready to use. Moreover, you can re-use it in any database, simply by importing the form and table and creating a new set of menu items for the new database!

Now, let's look at the other forms in your database. They need to be modified to work as part of the overall user interface instead of as separate forms.

Forms Consistency

Here's what frmPerson looked like when we finished creating it.

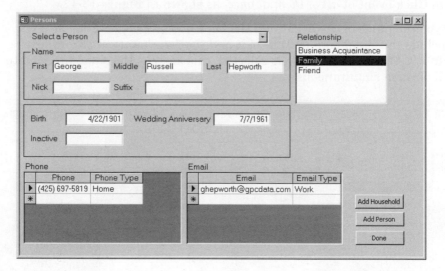

Figure 13-13 frmPerson

We had added three command buttons to the form. With the addition of a menu to our user interface, two of those three buttons are no longer needed: Add household and Done. Both functions are now handled by the menu, not by this form.

Switch frmPerson to design view; select the Add household and Done command buttons and delete them. Leave the Add Person button on the form.

Save and close the form. Open frmMenu. Now, click on <u>People</u> to open frmPerson. The result should look like Figure 13-14. Now, click on

Household. frmPerson should close and frmHousehold should open. Click back and forth between them a few times.

You can now open frmHousehold in design view and delete the Done button from it as well. Leave the other command button, the one for Add Household.

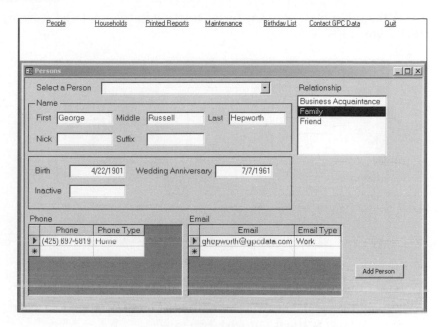

Figure 13-14 frmPerson Open with Menu

Now, let's add the other three forms identified on the menu, the ones we haven't created yet: Maintenance, Printed reports, and Birthday list.

Maintenance Forms

We have four small forms in the database for address types, phone types, email types, and relationship types. They are all in the database to make it easier to maintain lookup tables. I'm going to combine them into a single maintenance form, using a tab control.

You've seen and used tab controls many times in many windows applications. Here's how you go about making one of your own.

1. Create a new, unbound form. Save it as frmMaintenance.
2. On the toolbar, select the icon for the tab control.

Figure 13-15 Tab Control

3. Draw the tab control onto the form, starting in the upper left corner, as in Figure 13-16.

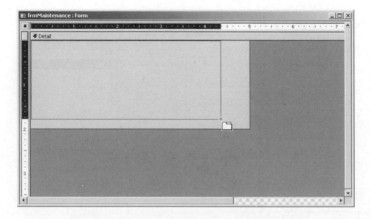

Figure 13-16 Draw a Tab Control on the Form

4. When you release the mouse, the tab control will be placed on the form. By default it starts out with two tabs.

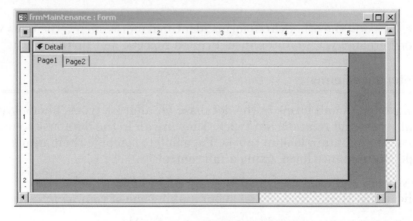

Figure 13-17 Default Tab Control

We're going to place one of the look up maintenance forms on each of the tabs, but since we have four forms, we need two more tabs.

5. You can add tabs in a couple of different ways, by using either the Insert menu (Figure 13-18) or the shortcut menu Figure 13-19.

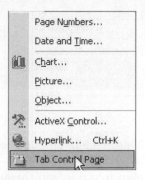

Figure 13-18 Insert a Tab Control Page-Insert Menu

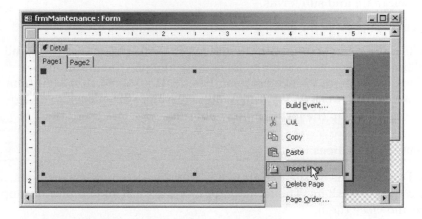

Figure 13-19 Insert a Tab Control Page-Shortcut Menu

6. You now have one tab page for each of the four maintenance forms. Draw a subform on the first tab page.

   Be careful! You want to be sure *to select the tab control page*, not the underlying detail section of the form. It's easy to get it wrong here. See Figure 13-20.

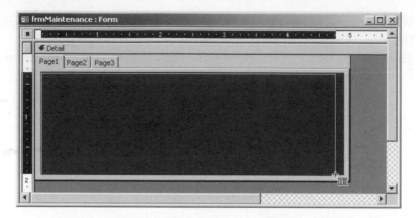

Figure 13-20 Insert a Subform On Each Tab Page

The subform wizard will open to guide you through the rest of the steps. Because this is an unbound form, there won't be any linking fields between main and sub forms.

Repeat this process for each of the tabs and subforms.

You'll make some additional refinements to the maintenance form and its subforms, but you can switch to form view and use the Maintenance option on the menu to click between People, Household, and Maintenance to see how they work. When you're done testing, switch back to design view and clean up the form and its subforms.

Remove Done Buttons

The Done buttons on the maintenance subforms are now superfluous, so you can remove them. The form footer on each form should now be empty; save and close them.

Remove Subform Labels

The subform wizard creates a label for each of the subforms. They have their own titles on them in their form headers, which makes the labels on the main maintenance form redundant. Remove them from the main maintenance form.

Consistent Size and Location

For a pleasing appearance, it's important that each of the subforms on the four tab pages are in the same location on their own tab and that they are all the same size. You'll have to experiment with this. Obviously, if they are to be the same size, you'll have to figure out which of the subforms is the largest and make the other two the same size. Mine ended up looking like this.

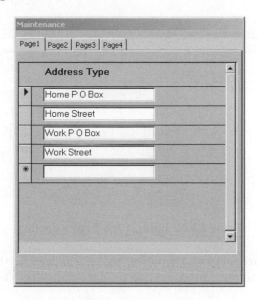

Figure 13-21 Tabbed Maintenance Form with Subforms

There are a few items still to clean up, but the form is definitely taking shape.

Form Clean Up

The maintenance form is not bound to an underlying recordset; therefore, both the record selector (that little black arrowhead in the left margin of the main form) and the navigation buttons are irrelevant. We'll turn them off. Also, we have tabs labeled Page1, Page2, and Page3. They need to be renamed. Finally, the form itself needs a caption. Maintenance would be good

Switch to design view, open the property sheet for the form and find the format properties for Record Selectors and Navigation Buttons. Set them to No. Give the form a caption.

Rename Tabs

Click on the first tab to select it. Find its Caption property. Name it to reflect the contents of the subform on that tab page, as in Figure 13-22.

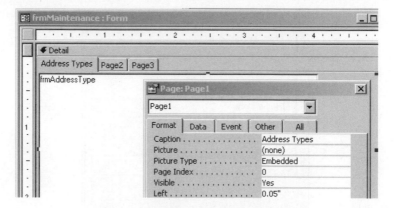

Figure 13-22 Giving a Tab Page a Caption

Find the Name property on the Other tab and name the tab page, following standard naming conventions, e.g. tabAddressType.

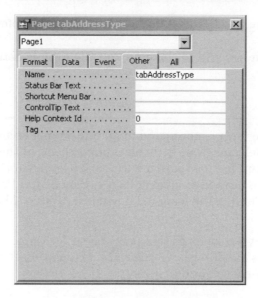

Figure 13-23 Name the Tab Page

Repeat these steps for the other two tab pages.

Other Considerations

The default for forms is to create a sizable border with a Control Box and Minimize, Maximize, and Close Buttons. The menu we just created handles form navigation, so I prefer to remove them as well.

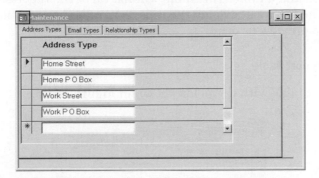

Figure 13-24 Form with Control Box and Minimize, Maximize, and Close Buttons

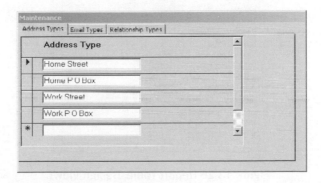

Figure 13-25 Form without Control Box and Minimize, Maximize and Close Buttons

You still need make some further adjustments to the layout of the maintenance form, but I'll leave that up to you. Right now, we need to create a form to control report printing.

Control Form for Printing Reports

You could use the menu system to print reports directly. In other words, you could add entries to the menu table for each report in your database and print them by clicking on the appropriate label. We have only two reports in our contacts database, for example, and plenty of empty hyperlink labels on the menu. However, just as I grouped all of the maintenance subforms onto a master maintenance form, I think printing all reports from a single *report control form* makes a more user friendly interface.

We'll need two components for this form, just as we did for the main menu: a form and a table. This table will list all of the reports in the database. The form will display the reports in a list box, so your users can select one to preview or print.

Create the Report Table

Create a new table with the fields shown in Figure 13-26.

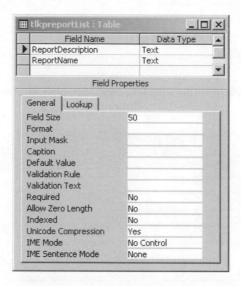

Figure 13-26 Report Table, Design View

Again, there isn't a primary key in this table. We will display the value in the field ReportDescription to the user and use the value in the field ReportName to open the requested report. Note that the field size for the report description is set to 50 characters. That limits the descriptions you can have for reports to that many characters. If you want to create longer descriptions, you can increase the field size.

Save the table, naming it tlkpReportList, conforming to standard naming conventions. Open it in datasheet view and add the names of the two reports in your database, along with a plain English description, as in Figure 13-27

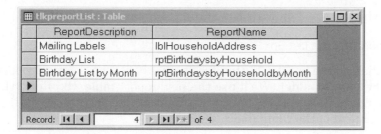

Figure 13-27 tlkpReportList with Reports

Create the Report Form

Now, let's create the report selection form. Create a new form in design view; don't give it a record source. It will be an unbound form. Save the blank form as frmReportList.

List Box

Draw a list box onto the form, as in Figure 13-28. The one in Figure 13-28 is taller than it really needs to be for only three reports, but I made it that size to accommodate growth in the number of reports I have in the database. Also, I made it wide enough to accommodate the widest report description in my report table. Of course, you'll need to do a little experimenting to get the height and width dimensions right for your list box.

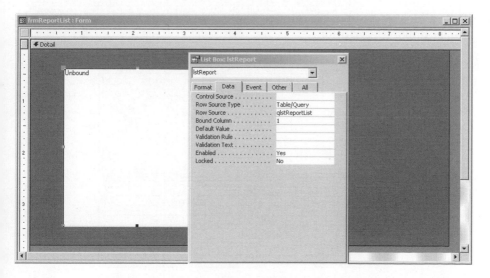

Figure 13-28 frmReportList with List Box Drawn

Name the list box, following the standard naming convention.

Row Source for the List Box

Now, click on the builder button for the list box' Row Source property to open the query builder. We'll use the new report table, tlkpReportList; however, I want to sort report descriptions alphabetically, so we'll use a query instead of the table itself.

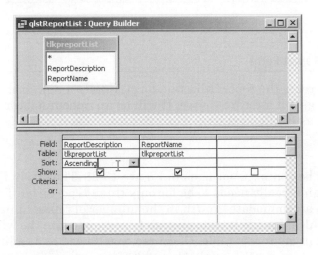

Figure 13-29 Step One in Query for lstReport

Take a look at column 1 in Figure 13-30. I've created an alias for the field name, ReportDescription.

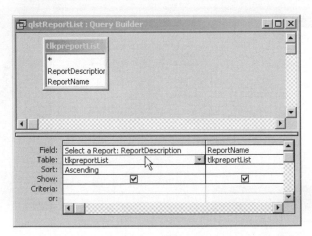

Figure 13-30 Create an Alias for a Query Column

I want to display Column Heads for the query in the List box. (That's a feature we've not seen in a list box yet). This alias will display the phrase "Select a Report" instead of the field name, ReportDescription, in the list box. Look at Figure 13-31.

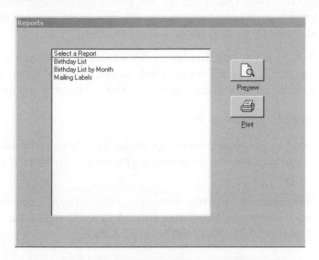

Figure 13-31 Report List, Column Header Displayed

If we hadn't created the alias, the list box would display the field name from the table here. I've seen that done in some databases, but it is so easy to create and use aliases, I don't see any reason not to do it for your users.

In the database window, find the query you just created and open it in design view again, as in Figure 13-30.

The alias, as you know, is the "Select a Report" string in front of the colon. The colon tells Access to use this alias as the column header for this query column instead of the field name after the colon. The alias can be anything you want as long as it fits the width on the list box that will display it.

List Box Bound Column and Column Widths

I set up this list box a little differently from those you've seen before in order to reinforce another point about the bound column in a list box. The list box has two columns: Select a Report: ReportDescription and ReportName.

The bound column is column 2, ReportName. When we look at the value of an item selected in the list box, it will be the value from this column, which is the name of a report.

We only want the user to see the report *description*, which is in column one, not the report *name*, so you should set the width of column 1 to one inch and width of column 2 to zero inches. The user will only see column 1 in the list box, although the value from column 2, the bound column, will be used.

We could have reversed the order for the columns, putting ReportName first. In that case, we would have made column 1 the bound column and set the column widths to zero inches and one inch.

Normally, when your list box displays values from a table with a primary key or a foreign key, its bound column will be set to one of those keys. That key will be in the first, or left-most column. That's the way we usually do it.

Command Buttons to Preview or Print

With the list box in place and working properly, it's time to add command buttons. You'll want two: one to preview the report on-screen and one to send it to a printer.

We can use the command button wizard to create them. And creating command buttons is one of the times I think the wizards do a decent job. Click on the Command Button icon on the toolbar

Figure 13-32 Command Button Tool

Draw the command button on the form. The Command Button Wizard will open. Select Report Operations and Preview Report. Then click Next.

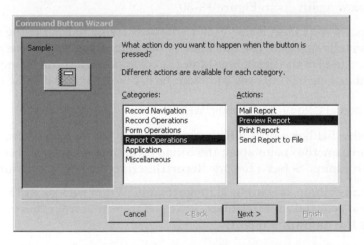

Figure 13-33 Command Button Wizard

Select one of the three reports from the list. We'll have to change this later, of course, because this command button will open the report selected in the list box, not a specific report. Click Next.

You can choose to display text or an image on the button. I usually prefer text captions on buttons, but for the sake of this example, I selected the image for Preview Document.

You can choose one of the choices offered, or click the check box to show all of the images available through the wizard, or even use the browse button to locate a custom-designed bitmap on your PC. Select an image and click Next. Name the button, following standard naming conventions, e.g., cmdPreview, or cmdPrintPreview.

Next, use the wizard to create a Print button for the same report.

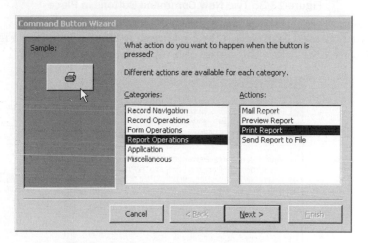

Figure 13-34 Create the Print Command Button

I selected the Printer icon for this button.

The result will be similar to Figure 13-35. Although the images are quite effective at indicating their purpose, I decided to enhance them by adding labels as you saw in Figure 13-31. You can add or omit the labels; whichever suits your taste.

Save the form. The next step will be to modify the On Click events for the two new command buttons so they will preview or print the report selected in the list box, instead of the report hard-coded into the event procedures by the wizard.

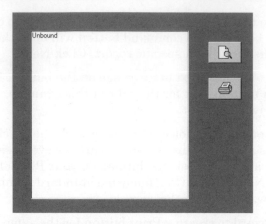

Figure 13-35 Two New Command Buttons in Place

The wizard-created expression for cmdPreview should look like Figure 13-36. Notice that it has the name of a report hard-coded into it.

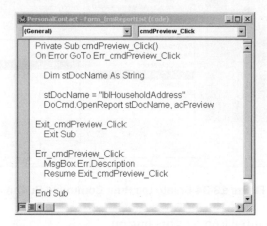

Figure 13-36 Event Procedure to Preview a Report

Most of the VBA code in this procedure should be familiar to you, so I'm going to concentrate on the three lines we need to change.

```
Dim stDocName As String

stDocName = "lblHouseholdAddress"
DoCmd.OpenReport stDocName, acPreview
```

The first line creates a variable called stDocName and defines it as a string. The second line assigns the name of the report selected in the Command Button Wizard to the variable. This is the standard Command

Button Wizard code; we're only going to modify that second line so it refers to the list box on the form instead of to a specific report.

The third line tells Access to open that report in Preview Mode using the OpenReport Method of the DoCmd object. acPreview is one of those intrinsic constants you learned about earlier. It represents the value two, which means to open the report in preview mode.

Edit the Code

Now, let's change that variable assignment line so it gives us the name of the report selected by the user in the list box instead of one hard-coded report name.

Delete everything after the equal sign and type in the following:

```
stDocName = Me.lstReport
```

Me, as you recall, refers to the form on which the code is running and lstReport is the name of the list box that displays all of the reports in tblReportList. Now, instead of referring to only one report, this code will refer to whichever report the user has selected in the list box, based on the value in the bound column of the list box.

Test and Debug the Form

Switch to form view and test the new command button for Preview. Any bugs? Actually, there is one, but you will only see it if you click on Preview before you select a report from the list.

To reveal the bug, close the form, reopen it and click on Preview *before* selecting a report. You should get a message like this:

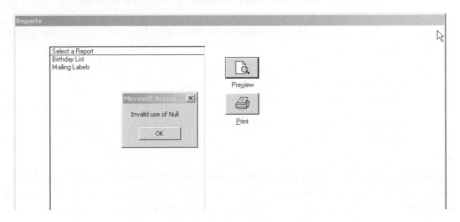

Figure 13-37 Invalid Use of Null

Invalid Use of Null pops up because there is nothing selected in the list box yet; it has a null value. When the code behind the Preview button tries to assign a null value to the variable stDocname, it fails with this error message.

There are two ways to handle this bug: trap it with the error handler, or revise the code to prevent it from attempting to assign a null value to the string variable in the first place.

There are arguments for both approaches, so I'm gong to take the somewhat arbitrary approach and revise the code to check for the existence of the Null value before trying to preview the report.

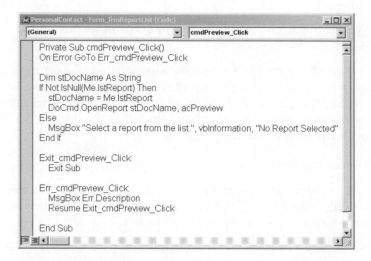

Figure 13-38 Event Procedure Revised to Check for Null Values

You've seen conditional statements before, so the logic in this one should be easy to figure out.

```
If Not IsNull(Me.lstReport) Then
    stDocName = Me.lstReport
    DoCmd.OpenReport stDocName, acPreview
Else
    MsgBox "Select a report from the list.", vbInformation,
"No Report Selected"
End If
```

When your user clicks on the Preview button, the code first checks the value of the list box, lstReport. If it is not null (meaning that it *does* have some value), then the next two lines of code are executed, assigning the value of the list box to the report name variable and opening the report in preview mode.

If it is null (which means the user hasn't yet selected a report from the list), the line after Else executes, showing the user a message informing them they need to select a report from the list.

vbInformation, by the way, is another intrinsic constant; it tells Access which type of button to display on the message box.

Edit the Other Command Button

Edit the event procedure for the Print button, as well. Make both event procedures test for null values and select the report name from the list box. The only difference you'll see in the other command button's event procedure will be the intrinsic constant *acNormal* instead of *acPreview*. acNormal tells Access to send the report to the printer; that's the normal print mode.

Your new report form is ready to use. Save and close it. Click on Printed Reports on the menu to open it and make sure it works.

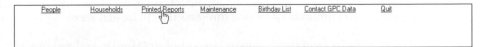

| People | Households | Printed Reports | Maintenance | Birthday List | Contact GPC Data | Quit |

Figure 13-39 Open Report Form from Menu

Filtering List box for the Printed Report

As you recall, when we created the display form to show the current month's birthdays, we also created a second version of the birthday list report, with a filtered record set so we could print a report filtered by birth month. One of the drawbacks of doing so was that the filtering had to be done on an open form. The form we used for that purpose, frmBirthdayList, is intended only for on-screen display. It made some sense to base the filtered report on it, but it did seem a bit awkward to have to open the form just to create the report.

However, we can address that issue easily now, because we have a report form, designed specifically to manage reports. All we need to do is copy the filtering list box from frmBirthdayList to frmReportList and modify the filter in rptBirthdaysbyHouseholdbyMonth to look at the report form, instead of the birthday list form.

Copy the Filtering List Box to frmReportList

Open both forms in design view. Click on the filtering list box, lstBirthMonths, on frmBirthdayList to select it.

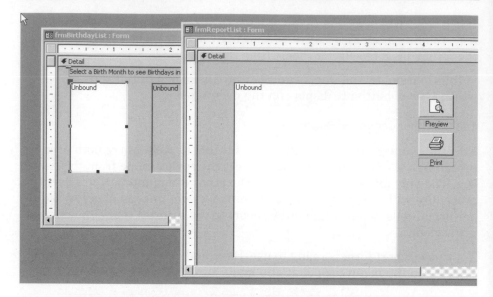

Figure 13-40 FrmBirthdayList and frmReportList in Design View

Copy the list box. Select rptBirthdaysbyHouseholdbyMonth and paste the list box onto it.

By default, the list box will go to the upper left corner of the detail section. That's what you'll see any time you paste a control onto a form or report.

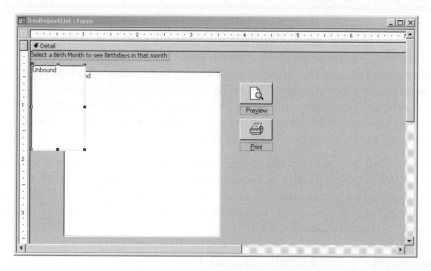

Figure 13-41 Paste the List Box onto the Form

Drag the filtering list box to a more appropriate position on the form.

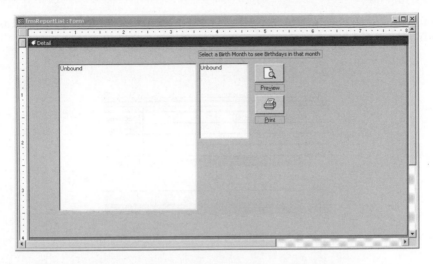

Figure 13-42 Locate Controls in a Functional Layout

As you can see in Figure 13-42, I decided to move the command buttons to the right and place the list boxes side by side. You can choose a different layout that suits your preferences.

Open the property sheet and make sure the pasted list box retained the name lstBirthMonths here on frmReportList. Save and close the form.

Now, open the filtered report, rptBirthdaysbyHouseholdbyMonth, in design view. Open its property sheet and select the Data tab.

Use the builder button to open qryHouseholdBirthdayListbyMonth, the query that is the record source for the report.

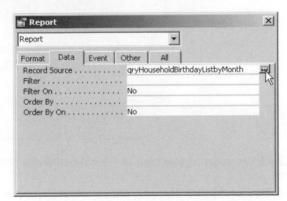

Figure 13-43 Open the Report's Record Source

You're going to change the criteria for BirthMonth from frmBirthdayList to frmReportList.

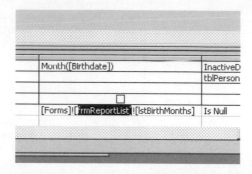

Figure 13-44 Edit the Criteria for Birth Month

As you can see in Figure 13-44, all you need to do is highlight the form name in the criteria and edit it. Save and close the query and then save and close the report.

This report will now filter against the selection in the filtering list box on the report control form instead of the one on the birthday list form.

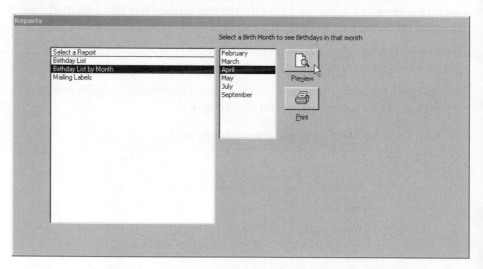

Figure 13-45 frmreportlist Modified to Filter the Birthday List Report

Select the Birth List by Month Report, select a birth list from the filter and click one of the print buttons to see the result.

Limited Function of the Filtering List Box

The filtering list box only affects that one report at this point. Other reports in the application can be modified to take advantage of it, if you choose. Or you may add other reports to the database that can be filtered by month.

In addition, there's plenty of room on the report control form to add other filters, "State" for address searches, for example. The only real limitation is your imagination.

Let's Get Outta Here

We need one more form, the little form called frmQuit that will pop up when you click on Quit. We could just let the application close when someone clicks on Quit, but that wouldn't be very user friendly. What if you click on it accidentally? Instead of just firing off a Quit command that will close everything down without any warning, we'll make a little message box form that will offer you a chance to confirm the close, or to change your mind. It looks like Figure 13-46.

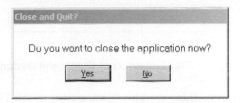

Figure 13-46 Quit Form

Although it looks a lot like one of Access' own message boxes, it is a form, one designed to closely resemble a message box, but which offers a couple of advantages.

First, we can give it a background color to match the other forms in the application. If we select a color scheme with blue backgrounds for all forms, for example, we can make this one match the rest of the forms. (The one in Figure 13-46 has a light background to make it more readable on the page.)

A more important reason for making our own form, however, is because we can load it into the menu along with the other forms in the application, so we don't have to write special code to handle closing in the menu itself. The form acts like all of the other forms except it has code behind the Yes button to close everything and quit Access.

Create the form in your database. Make it look like the one in Figure 13-46 and save it as frmQuit. Add a command button. Using the Command Button Wizard, you can create one that closes the application, Figure 13-47. Save it as cmdYes, making it look as much as you can like the Yes button on a standard Windows Message Box.

Then copy it and paste a second button on the form, naming it cmdNo.

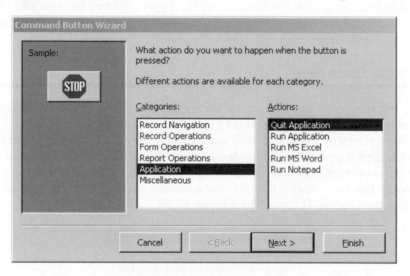

Figure 13-47 Default Quit Command Button

Using the expression builder for the Click event of cmdYes, look at the code generated by the Command Button Wizard.

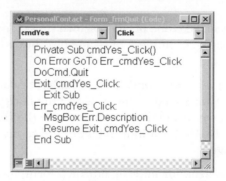

Figure 13-48 Event Procedure to Quit the Application

The Quit method of the DoCmd object closes Access when you click the Yes button. We can leave just like that.

Now, select the Click Event for the second command button, cmdNo.

Enter the following line in it. That's the same line of code you placed on each of the labels on the menu form. It closes all forms except the menu. If you click the No button, this line just closes the message box and does nothing else.

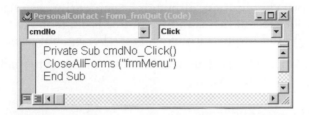

Figure 13-49 Close the Quit Form and Continue Working

Close and save frmQuit. Click Quit on the menu to open it. Try it out. Be forewarned: if you click Yes, your database will close.

Your menu and form system now has all of the parts it needs. Good work.

Consistency and Workflow

You have really accomplished a great deal. Your application now has a menu system to control workflow across all of the forms and reports, as well as a set of data input forms (frmPerson, frmHousehold, and frmMaintenance), a report control form (frmReportList), a data display form (frmBirthdayList), and a message box form to control how the user closes the application (frmQuit). That's a lot of work for your first application and you should be proud, but you're not quite finished.

The next phase in creating a user interface is to make sure all of the forms and reports in your database have a consistent appearance and that they all work the same way, as much as possible.

I'm going to leave that step largely up to you, although I will offer some guidelines.

Background and Foreground Colors

Obviously, because this is an application, as opposed to a random collect of objects in a database, you want all of your forms to have the same color, or if you're more artistically inclined, complementary colors, such as shades of blue or tan. In my applications, for example, I like to use either dark backgrounds, (royal blue) with white text, or very pale pastels (yellow) with black text.

Some color combinations are inexcusable; yellow text on orange backgrounds, dark blue text on black backgrounds. Don't go there, please.

I settled on blue (color number 12615680) for the backgrounds in my personal contacts application, although I temporarily used lighter colored backgrounds for most of the examples in this book, to make them easier for you to read. And I went with black text—boring, but safe.

In your application, choose combinations that are easy to read and don't draw attention to themselves.

Background Images and Icons

Some people like to put images on their forms, large background images, background patterns, and so on For example, you might put a small picture of your own family one of the forms in this database. Other people like to use small images like icons, as clues to functionality. For example, putting a mailbox or a telephone next to those subforms on frmPerson.

I have a strong preference for clean, simple forms without adornment. For one thing, images take up both screen real estate and storage space in the database file. For another, I believe graphic elements can be more distracting than useful if they're not done well.

Feel your own way in this area. Keeping in mind that your highest goal must be usability for the users of your application, it's not a bad idea to make it interesting to use as well.

Screen Resolution

I set my screen resolution to 1024x768, which is a very common choice; however, many people prefer 800x600. Higher resolutions are possible, but much less common. When you're designing a user interface, therefore, you need to take resolution into account.

A set of forms that works well at 1024x768 may be too large to display completely at 800x600. Forms that fill the screen completely at 800x600 will only take up a fraction of the screen at higher resolutions. Figure 13-50 is an extreme example.

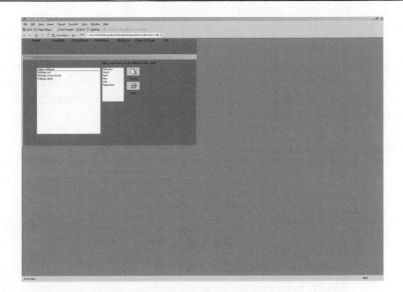

Figure 13-50 Screen Resolution 1600 x1200

Make sure you design forms that will work on your users' PCs. If you have no control over the screen resolution they use and have to design screens that will work for different resolutions, design them to fit the lowest resolution you'll encounter.

It is possible, with a good bit of effort, to adjust forms and controls on them to different sizes. Later, as you become an expert with VBA, you can visit www.utteraccess.com where you'll find code that allows you to determine the screen resolution on your user's PC and adjust your application accordingly.

Form Height and Width

Making your forms as uniform as possible may not seem so important when you're first designing them and you're mostly concerned about fitting all the necessary controls on them. However, in the final phases of design, where you're paying closer attention to the user interface you're presenting, you should take the time to calculate sizes that will work for all of the forms.

I think it makes sense to have all forms as tall as the tallest of the forms and as wide as the widest, if that is feasible. For example, in my personal contacts application, the menu form turned out to be the widest. It was eight inches wide. I made the other forms (except for the subforms in frmMaintenance) eight inches wide. However, because other forms have borders, while frmMenu doesn't, I had to adjust it to 8.05" to make them appear the same width on the screen.

frmPerson was the tallest form at four inches, so I adjusted the others (again, except for the subforms in frmMaintenance) to the same height. Of course, the menu form stays as short as possible, just large enough to accommodate the four rows of labels on it.

Form Open Event Procedures

To make sure each of the forms behaves the same, I also made sure they all have the same code in their Open and Activate Events.

This is just housekeeping code.

```
DoCmd.MoveSize 0, Forms!frmMenu.Detail.Height
Me.Moveable = False
DoCmd.RunCommand acCmdSizeToFitForm
```

It measures the height of the menu form and moves the top edge of the current form to that spot, so the top of each working form is always just below the menu.

It also makes the form unmovable. (This property is available in Access 2002 and 2003, not earlier versions). Your user can't slide the forms around the screen.

The last line just makes sure the form is returned to its original size, although this won't be necessary if you restrict users' access to form design menus so they can't change forms.

Menu and Tool Bars

MS Access comes with a full complement of built-in menu bars and toolbars—Form and Report Design toolbars, for example. Most of them, however, have functions that are only useful during development or maintenance. Some of them expose functions you really don't want users, especially inexperienced users, to get their hands on. You've spent a lot of time designing forms that look good and that work smoothly and efficiently; you don't want someone to be able to make arbitrary changes in them. And you especially don't want someone to start changing, or even deleting tables with valuable data in them.

Therefore, one of the things you'll want to do is hide the built-in menu and tool bars, as much as possible, from users. You can do that, to a certain extent, by setting *startup options* for the application.

On the menu bar, select Tools-->Startup.

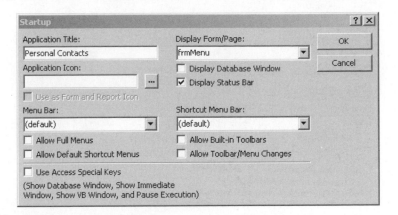

Figure 13-51 Start Up Options

In addition to controlling menus, this dialog lets you set several features of your application, including giving it a title that will display at the top of the database window when it opens.

You can designate a form to open when the application opens. Select your menu form for this purpose, as I did in Figure 13-51.

You can also hide the database window from your users (although knowledgeable users can reveal it again by pressing the F11 key). This is both a precaution against casual changing of objects and a housekeeping step that keeps your application screen cleaner.

Menu and Tool Bar Options

There are four checkboxes for menu and toolbars. Un-checking all of them prevents the user from getting to the Toolbox toolbar, Form and Report Design toolbars, etc.

You can use the What's This button on the startup dialog to see what each checkbox controls.

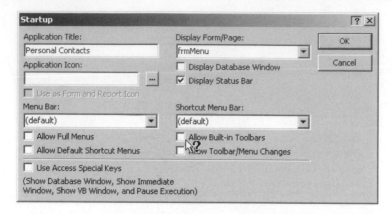

Figure 13-52 "What's This?"

With all of the menu and tool bar checkboxes un-checked, your user will only have access to the basic database menu bar, as in Figure 13-53.

Figure 13-53 Database Menu with Limited Options

As you can see, this menu offers limited options as opposed to the other menu and tool bars. Most importantly, it keeps your users away from uncontrolled access to objects in the database.

You can also create your own custom tool and menu bars to use in place of, or in addition to Access' built-in tool bars, as you can see on the startup dialog. I'll show you how to do that next.

A Custom Menu Bar

Although you do want to prevent users from getting unrestricted access to the built-in tool bars and menu bars, some of the functions of menu bars are very useful in any application. You can enhance your users' experience with a few functions, like checking spelling or sorting lists.

The solution is to create a custom menu bar. I'll show you how to create a simple one with a few basic functions on it.

Open the Toolbar Customization Dialog

To open the Toolbar Customization Dialog, right-mouse click on the menu bar. Depending on where you are at the time, one or more of the built-in menu and tool bars will be available on the short-cut menu.

Figure 13-54 Shortcut Menu for Toolbar Customization

For example, the shortcut menu in Figure 13-54 offers the Form View and Web menu bars. There is a check next to Web, indicating that it is currently visible; you can see part of it under the shortcut menu in Figure 13-54.

The last item on the shortcut menu, Customize..., is the one we want. It opens the Toolbar Customization Dialog. We'll use it to create a custom toolbar.

Figure 13-55 Toolbar Customization Dialog

As you can see, there are a number of built-in toolbars for all kinds of tasks. The basic one, Menu Bar, is checked here, meaning it is visible. You can turn it off by un-checking it. *Be careful about doing this*, because you can change settings in the Start menu so you not only can't see the menu bar, but you *can't get to this dialog to show it again*.

Create a New Toolbar

Click on New to create a new toolbar. When the dialog box opens asking for a name, call it tlbrGeneric, or something similar.

It will start out looking like the empty toolbar in Figure 13-56.

Figure 13-56 New Blank Toolbar

Click on the Commands tab. We're going to add a few functions that users might want to have available; specifically we'll add a couple of print-related functions: the spell checker and the sort function.

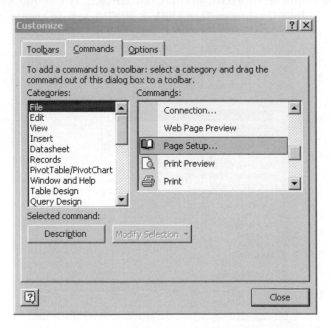

Figure 13-57 Add Commands to the Custom Toolbar

The list on the left shows all of the menu categories available and the list on the right shows the commands that are available in each category. The categories, as you can see in Figure 13-57, are those found on built-in toolbars, such as File, Edit, Query Design, etc. You can choose which ones you want to use for your custom toolbars.

For this generic toolbar I want to add the Page Setup, Print Preview, and Print functions. That will give users some control over the reports they print, but it won't let them change existing reports or create any new ones.

Adding commands to a toolbar is a simple drag and drop process. Grab the function you want, drag it to the toolbar, and release it there.

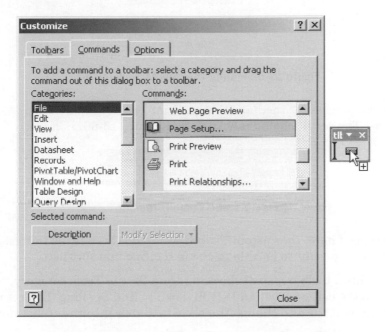

Figure 13-58 Drag and Drop Functions to the Toolbar.

Click on Modify Selection to change the style of the new command on the menu. The Default Style is checked. Change it to Text Only (Always) or Image and Text, whichever you prefer. I went with Image and Text for this example.

Figure 13-59 Modify The New Menu Function

Repeat the process for the Page Setup, Print Preview, and Print functions. The result should now look like Figure 13-60.

Figure 13-60 Custom Toolbar

If you stopped here, the custom toolbar would do these three things. But we said we also want to be able to check spelling and sort lists.

On the built-in toolbars, spell checking is under the Tools category, so select it in the category list and scroll down to find Spelling. Drag it to the custom tool bar and change the style to match the other functions.

Sorting is in the Records category. You'll need two functions here, one for ascending order and one for descending order.

Figure 13-61 Ascending and Descending Sort Functions

When you've added all of the functions to the toolbar, select the Toolbar tab again and click on the Properties button for the new custom toolbar.

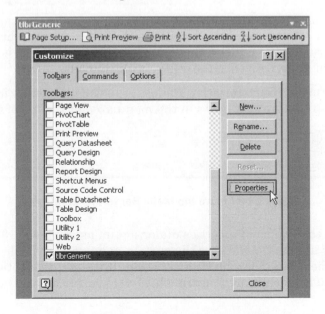

Figure 13-62 Change Toolbar Properties

You can make your custom tool bar into a menu bar, a tool bar, or a pop up. It might seem that there isn't a whole lot of practical difference between menu and tool bars. In fact, Access Help implies menu bars are a special class of tool bars.

However, menu bars do have one important characteristic toolbars don't. We can use a custom menu bar as the default menu for the entire application, instead of the built-in Access Menu bar. You can't do that with a toolbar. So, for this example, we'll make tlbrGeneric a menu bar.

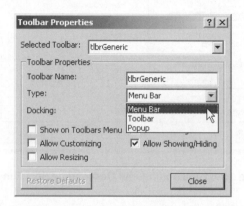

Figure 13-63 Make tblGeneric a Menu Bar

You can also set properties to allow your users to make changes to the menu bar. You're going to want to un-check those options to prevent that, but first, you want to position the menu bar where you want it to display: at the top of the screen with the other, built-in toolbars.

Close the Toolbar Customization Dialog, grab the title bar as in Figure 13-64 and drag it up so it *docks* in the menu area at the top of the screen.

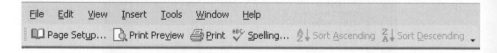

Figure 13-64 Move the Menu Bar to the Menu Area

Now, open the Toolbar Properties dialog again, as in Figure 13-65, to lock the toolbar in place. Make sure the custom menu bar is visible when you un-check the Allow Showing/Hiding option. If it's not, this option will prevent you from showing it again when you want to do so.

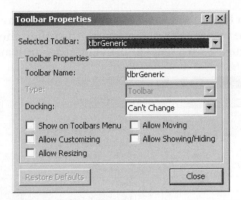

Figure 13-65 Un-check Toolbar Properties to Lock the Custom Menu Bar

Two more steps and we're done. First, we have to make this new generic Menu bar appear above the Menu form that controls navigation in the application; and second, we have to prevent the database' built-in menu bar from appearing.

Assign the Custom Menu Bar as the Default Menu

The next step is to make the new generic toolbar, tlbrGeneric, the *default menu bar* for the application. On the built in Menu bar, select Tools-->Startup. (This may turn out to be the last time you use the built-in Menu bar in this application.)

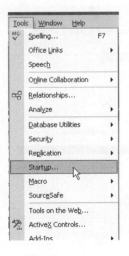

Figure 13-66 Select Tools-->Startup

When the Startup Dialog appears, change the Menu bar from Default to tlbrGeneric. While you're there, make sure the other check boxes are un-checked, as in Figure 13-67. They'll prevent other unwanted changes.

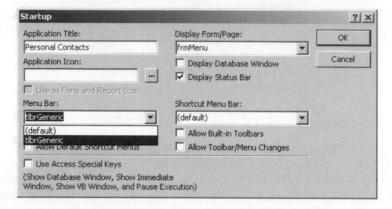

Figure 13-67 Change the Application Menu Bar

Hide and Lock the Menu Bar

In the Toolbar Customization Dialog, select the Menu bar from the list and un-check it, hiding it from view. See Figure 13-68. Again, you have to do this *before* changing the Allow Showing/Hiding property. With the Menu bar hidden, you can now un-check the properties that allow users to see it, move it, or change it.

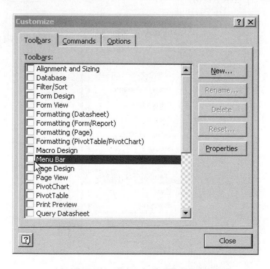

Figure 13-68 Hide the Menu Bar

In the Toolbar Properties dialog, select Menu bar and un-check all of its check boxes to lock it down.

Figure 13-69 Lock Down the Menu Bar

Close the application and reopen it. It should now look something like Figure 13-70.

Figure 13-70 Application with Custom Menu Bar

The custom menu bar has replaced Access' built-in Menu bar. It has only safe functions on it.

As you learn more about Access and become more proficient at creating complex user interfaces, you'll probably find other functions you'll want to add to a custom menu. You will even reach a point where you'll want to create custom menus for each of the forms and reports in your application. For now, though, this generic menu should be enough to get your first application ready for public display.

Bypassing Startup

At this point, some of you are probably sitting there looking at an application with a cool menu bar and navigation menu and no apparent way to get to the forms, reports, etc. in the database again. When you un-checked all of the built-in toolbars, menus, and so forth on the startup dialog, you effectively cut off access to those functions when the database opens normally. That's good if you don't want others to get to that stuff, but it's not so good if you need to do maintenance on the database, is it?

Well, I wouldn't lead you to this point if there weren't a way to bypass the startup options that lock things down.

It's really simple.

Press and hold down the Shift key while the database opens.

That's it. The database will open to the database window and you're ready to start killing bugs or adding enhancements and new features. Of course, if your users know this trick, they can do the same thing.

There are more advanced ways to secure your databases when you get ready to distribute them beyond your immediate work group, but that's a topic for another, more advanced book, I'm afraid.

An Application Ready to Test

At this point, you have completed all of the steps to create an Access application but one. Let's review what you've accomplished.

Identify Entities and Attributes

You started out with a goal: Create an application to track contact information (such as phone, address, and email) for family and friends.

To get things rolling, you identified each of the entities you needed to track: persons, households, addresses, phone numbers, and email addresses, along with the relevant details about them, which are called attributes in the world of database design. You created a set of tables designed to store information about the entities. The fields in the tables represent, for the most part, the attributes in which we are interested. The records in those tables are individual instances of the entities in which we are interested.

Normalization

With the tables in place, I led you through the process of normalization in which you sorted out the fields in each table so they satisfied the first Three Rules of Normalization.

First, you eliminated redundant data from each table and made sure each field in each table held the smallest meaningful values. You made sure you eliminated repeating groups from the tables.

Second, you analyzed and revised each table to make sure each non-key attribute in the table was functionally dependent upon the primary key.

Third, you analyzed and revised your tables to eliminate attributes not dependent upon the primary key by creating additional tables and moving those attributes to them.

Identify Relationships, Primary and Foreign Keys

Once you had identified all of the pieces of data you needed to collect and store, you turned your attention to the relationships between the entities.

You found the one-to-one, one-to-many, and many-to-many relationships between the entities and created primary and foreign keys in each table to establish those relationships in the tables in your database. The primary key in the table on the one side of a one-to-many relationship is linked to its corresponding foreign key in the table on the many side.

Get Data in, Creating Input Forms

After that, you turned your attention to getting data into the database. That was accomplished with a series of database objects called forms. You created several forms, including one for people (frmPerson) and one for households (frmHousehold). You also created subforms (such as sfrmPersonEmail) in order to facilitate the data entry between related tables where there is a one-to-many relationship.

Get Data Out, Creating Reports and Display Forms

With the data entry forms in place, you moved on to reports and display-only forms. These objects consolidate and present information from the tables in your database in either printed form, or in on-screen displays.

Manage Records and Forms

For both forms and reports, you used queries to create recordsets of data from one or more tables. These queries allowed you to take the raw data from tables and manipulate it in ways that served the purposes of reports or forms.

You also learned how to create and modify event procedures in Visual Basic for Applications, or VBA, so you could control events on your forms and reports.

Although you only learned a little bit about VBA in this book, you did learn how to use wizards to create command buttons that generate standard VBA expressions.

You learned how conditional statements work in VBA.

You also learned how to use the expression builder to create and modify expressions.

You learned how to concatenate strings in expressions and in text fields on reports.

Control the Application

Finally, in this last chapter, you learned about the importance of a good user interface. You used your new skills to create a menu system for your application. And, as a final task, you created a custom menu bar to control users' access to the internal parts of an application.

That's a lot of work. Congratulate yourself. You've actually created a complete, working application. I'm sure you've learned a lot along the way. There's still a lot left to learn, but you'll be building on a solid foundation as you go.

Where Do You Go From Here

I really hope you've enjoyed reading this book and using it to build an Access application. I had a great time writing it.

My goal was to help you get something of the big picture of all of the tasks that go into creating a working application, from conceiving the project through polishing it up for production.

Moreover, each of the examples in each chapter is intended to be a model, or template, from which you should be able to draw ideas, concepts and specific methods for accomplishing many of the most important aspects of creating the application.

Although I do think you've come a long way in getting this far, the truth is there is much, much more to learn, especially in the areas of interface design, security, and distribution. I encourage you to keep working on your skills.

Finally, there are a lot of small and large improvements that can be made, even to the simple forms, queries, and reports in this application. I just didn't have room to accommodate everything I would have liked to include in the space allocated for this book.

I urge you to spend some time finding those issues, especially in the workflow between the data input forms, figuring out ways to address them and, hopefully, continue to enhance your own skills as an Access Developer.

Download Personal Contacts

You'll find a copy of the completed database at www.gpcdata.com/downloads/personalcontact.zip (about 350KB).

You'll also find a more advanced menu technique at www.gpcdata.com/downloads/dynamicmenu.zip (about 1.5 MB).

This page intentionally left blank.

Appendix A

While I was looking for references on Normalization, I found very few good print discussions that are widely available. E. F. Codd did the seminal work. His text is listed here.

On the other hand, you'll find many good (and some not so good) discussions on normalization on the Internet. The references below are to websites that, in my opinion, do a good job of discussing the rules of normalization. Please let me know of any broken links, so I can update them in future editions.

E. F. Codd, *Further Normalization of the Database Relational Model.* R. Rustin, Ed. Prentice-Hall, Englewood Cliffs, NJ, 1972.

Chapple, Mike, http://databases.about.com/library/weekly/aa080501a.htm

McGegor, Mattie, http://www.ewebarchitecture.com/dbms.php.

Nicewarner, Mike, http://www.datamodel.org

I found literally dozens of other discussions, including many on websites at major universities (one at the University of Texas seemed particularly good). These can be helpful, but may be overly technical for our purposes at this point. Do a search for normalization and rules of normalization and check out the results. Some sites will be more useful than others, but you'll also get a variety of viewpoints, written in a variety of styles. You're sure to find something that suits you.

This page intentionally left blank.

Index

Coming March 2004 from Holy Macro! Books...

ISBN 0-9724258-6-1
380 Pages
Available March 2004

ALSO FROM HOLY MACRO! BOOKS

Shop for these titles at your local bookstore or order direct.
E-Mail: store@MrExcel.com **Mail**: 13386 Judy, Uniontown OH 44685
Online: http://www.MrExcel.com **Fax**: (707) 220-4510

Qty.	Title	Price	Total
	Your Access to the World (CD-ROM) ISBN 1-932802-03-7 (1450 Slides – 2004)	$99.00	
	Mr Excel ON EXCEL ISBN 0-9724258-3-7 (480 pages – 2003)	$35.95	
	Dreamboat ON WORD ISBN 0-9724258-4-5 (260 pages – 2003)	$19.95	
	Kathy Jacobs ON POWERPOINT ISBN 0-9724258-6-1 (400 pages – 2004)	$29.95	
	Holy Macro! It's 1,600 Excel VBA Examples (CD-ROM) ISBN 0-9724258-1-0 (1600 pages – 2002)	$89.00	
	Excel Knowledge Base (CD-ROM) ISBN 0-9724258-2-9 (12,700 pages – 2002)	$49.00	
	Slide Your Way Through Excel VBA (CD-ROM) ISBN 0-9724258-6-1 (734 Slides – 2003)	$99.00	
	Join the Excellers League (CD-ROM) ISBN 1-932802-00-2 (1477 Slides – 2004)	$99.00	
	Excel for Scientists (CD-ROM) ISBN 10-9724258-8-8 (589 Slides – 2004)	$75.00	
	Guerilla Data Analysis Using Microsoft Excel ISBN 0-9724258-0-2 (138 pages – 2002)	$19.95	

Check for new titles at www.HolyMacroBooks.com

Sales Tax: Ohio residents add 6.5% sales tax
U.S. Shipping included. International, add $5 per order.
Payment: Check to "MrExcel" or VISA/MC/American Express
Bulk Orders: Save 40% when you order 6 or more of any one title.

Name: _____

Address: _____

City, State, Zip: _____

E-Mail: _____

Card #:_____ Exp.:_____